"The essays in this initial volume in the set Research in Analytical Psychology expand importantly on the work of C.G. Jung, investigating the psyche from a variety of perspectives. The contributions are suggestive of directions to pursue toward approaching the ultimate goal of extending our consciousness and understanding of psychic reality." – **Murray Stein, Ph.D.**, author of *Jung's Treatment of Christianity*

"An outstanding collection in both breadth and depth that takes off from Jung's prescient attitudes to scientific and scholarly research. It will significantly enhance the presence of analytical psychology and Jungian studies in university environments. A welcome and distinguishing feature is that many of the chapters reflect contemporary clinical perspectives, grounding research in lived experience. Readers will note with approval the manifold ways in which Jung's colonial attitudes to culture and society are challenged and reframed for the contemporary reader. The book will greatly interest academics, scholars, students, and the clinical communities." – **Andrew Samuels**, Professor of Analytical Psychology, University of Essex, UK

"Here is a book that gives fresh impetus to ongoing research in analytical psychology, opening new pathways for its development. Its authors draw on clinical experience and theoretical practice to point them out, and integrate observations, methods, and investigations from other disciplines. As a result, interdisciplinary approaches and prospecting are at the very heart of the advancements suggested to us here." - **Christian Gaillard**, author of *The Soul of Art: Analysis and Creation* (Texas AM University Press, 2017); former professor at the National Academy of Fine Arts, Paris; former president, SFPA and IAAP

"This work is a welcome development in the field of analytical psychology. Expanding research beyond the clinical realm to include evocative interdisciplinary explorations of analytical psychology with such diverse disciplines as science, history and cultural studies will inevitably lead to an enriched and en-souled experience for both researcher and reader." – **Jeffrey T. Kiehl, Ph.D.**, Jungian Analyst, Santa Cruz, California, USA

RESEARCH IN ANALYTICAL PSYCHOLOGY

Research in Analytical Psychology: Applications from Scientific, Historical, and Cross-Cultural Research is a unique collection of chapters from an international selection of contributors, reflecting the contemporary field of research in Analytical Psychology with a focus on qualitative and mixed-methods research.

Presented in seven parts, this volume offers current qualitative research that highlights approaches to understanding the psyche and investigating its components, and offers a Jungian perspective on cultural forces affecting individual psychology. The book brings forward the connections between Analytical Psychology and other disciplines including neuroscience, psychotherapy research, developmental research, Freudian psychoanalysis, and cultural studies. Part I provides an introduction to the volume, establishes the nature of qualitative and interdisciplinary research and its applications for research in other fields, and outlines the presented work. Part II, Approaching Qualitative Research in Analytical Psychology, examines postmodernism and the value a Jungian perspective offers, and introduces Jung's correspondence as an emerging resource. Part III, Research on Symbolic Aspects of the Psyche, looks at archetypal theory and cultural complex theory. Part IV, Research on Consciousness and Emotion, presents chapters on meditation and the spectrums of emotion in mythologies, philosophy, Analytical Psychology, and the neurosciences. Part V, A Complex Systems Approach to the Psyche, addresses research on synchronicity, the geometry of individuation, and complexity, ecology, and symbolism. Part VI, Cross-Cultural Research, contains chapters concerning transcendence, psychosocial transformation, psychological infrastructure, and cultural complexes and cultural identity. Part VII concludes the volume by setting directions for potential areas of future study and collaboration. Each chapter provides an overview of research in a specific area and closes with potential directions for future investigation. The book will enable practitioners and researchers to evaluate the empirical status of their concepts and methods and, where possible, set new directions. It also presents the significance of contemporary Analytical Psychology and offers opportunities for cross-discipline collaboration and fertilization.

Research in Analytical Psychology: Applications from Scientific, Historical, and Cross-Cultural Research will be essential reading for analytical psychologists in practice and in training, academics and students of Analytical Psychology and post-Jungian ideas, and academics and students of other disciplines seeking to integrate methods from Analytical Psychology into their research. It is complemented by its companion volume, *Research in Analytical Psychology: Empirical Research*.

Joseph Cambray, PhD, is CEO-President of Pacifica Graduate Institute, USA. He is past president of the International Association for Analytical Psychology and has served as the US editor for *The Journal of Analytical Psychology*. He was a faculty member at Harvard Medical School in the Department of

Psychiatry at Massachusetts General Hospital, Center for Psychoanalytic Studies, and former president of the C. G. Jung Institute of Boston. He has published numerous books and articles, and he lectures internationally.

Leslie Sawin previously served as co-program director at the Jung Society of Washington, USA, and has designed programs, such as 'Jung and Aging' at the Library of Congress, to bring Jungian ideas to the community.

RESEARCH IN ANALYTICAL PSYCHOLOGY

Applications from Scientific, Historical, and Cross-Cultural Research

Edited by
Joseph Cambray and Leslie Sawin

LONDON AND NEW YORK

First published 2018
by Routledge
2 Park Square, Milton Park, Abingdon, Oxon OX14 4RN

and by Routledge
711 Third Avenue, New York, NY 10017

Routledge is an imprint of the Taylor & Francis Group, an informa business

© 2018 selection and editorial matter, Joseph Cambray and Leslie Sawin; individual chapters, the contributors

The right of Joseph Cambray and Leslie Sawin to be identified as the authors of the editorial material, and of the authors for their individual chapters, has been asserted in accordance with sections 77 and 78 of the Copyright, Designs and Patents Act 1988.

All rights reserved. No part of this book may be reprinted or reproduced or utilised in any form or by any electronic, mechanical, or other means, now known or hereafter invented, including photocopying and recording, or in any information storage or retrieval system, without permission in writing from the publishers

Trademark notice: Product or corporate names may be trademarks or registered trademarks, and are used only for identification and explanation without intent to infringe.

British Library Cataloguing-in-Publication Data
A catalogue record for this book is available from the British Library

Library of Congress Cataloging-in-Publication Data
Names: Cambray, Joseph, editor. | Sawin, Leslie.
Title: Research in analytical psychology : applications from scientific, historical, and cross-cultural research / [edited by] Joseph Cambray, Leslie Sawin.
Description: Abingdon, Oxon ; New York, NY : Routledge, 2018.
Identifiers: LCCN 2017059799 (print) | LCCN 2018002711 (ebook) | ISBN 9781315448602 (Master e-book) | ISBN 9781138213265 (hardback) | ISBN 9781138213272 (pbk.)
Subjects: LCSH: Jungian psychology—Research.
Classification: LCC BF173.J85 (ebook) | LCC BF173.J85 R47 2018 (print) | DDC 150.19/54072—dc23
LC record available at https://lccn.loc.gov/2017059799

ISBN: 978-1-138-21326-5 (hbk)
ISBN: 978-1-138-21327-2 (pbk)
ISBN: 978-1-315-44860-2 (ebk)

Typeset in Bembo
by Apex CoVantage, LLC

CONTENTS

Contributors x

PART I
Introduction 1

1 Qualitative research in Analytical Psychology: current
   perspectives and future opportunities 3
   Joseph Cambray and Leslie Sawin

PART II
Approaching qualitative research in Analytical Psychology 17

2 Jungian research and postmodernism: an antinomial approach 19
   Elizabeth Eowyn Nelson

3 The correspondences of C.G. Jung: a rich resource 35
   Thomas B. Kirsch

PART III
Research on symbolic aspects of the psyche 47

4 Some remarks concerning archetypal theory and its
   epistemology 49
   François Martin-Vallas

5 The cultural complex theory: scientific and mythopoetic
    ways of knowing   69
    Thomas Singer

PART IV
Research on consciousness and emotion   83

6 The spectrums of emotion: in mythologies, philosophies,
    Analytical Psychology, and the neurosciences   85
    Beverley Zabriskie

7 Jung and meditation: one path toward investigation   112
    Morgan Stebbins

PART V
A complex systems approach to the psyche   133

8 Research on synchronicity: status and prospects   135
    Roderick Main

9 Complexity, ecology, symbolism, and synchronicity   157
    Joseph Cambray

10 *The Tibetan Book of the Dead* needs work: a proposal for
    research into the geometry of individuation   172
    George B. Hogenson

PART VI
Cross-cultural research   195

11 The loss and recovery of transcendence: perspectives of
    Jungian psychology and the Hua-Yen School of Buddhism   197
    Toshio Kawai

12 Psychotherapy research in times of change   210
    Grazina Gudaitė

13 The loss of psychological infrastructure in the "ubiquitous"
    self-consciousness of our times   223
    Yasuhiro Tanaka

14 Cultural complexes and cultural identity in Brazil: the
development of an individual identity 238
Walter Boechat

PART VII
A glance towards the future **257**

15 Going forward 259
Joseph Cambray

Index *264*

CONTRIBUTORS

Walter Boechat, MD, PhD, is a psychiatrist and Jungian analyst in private practice. He was a member of the IAAP Executive Committee from 2007 to 2013. He is also a Founding Member of the Jungian Association of Brazil, and was part of the staff in charge of the Brazilian edition of the *Red Book*, editing the translation from the original German Edition into Portuguese. Dr. Boechat has published widely in Brazil and abroad. His publications include: *The Red Book of C.G. Jung: A Journey to Unknown Depths* (London: Karnac, 2016); a comprehensive study of myth: *Mythopoises of the Psyche: Myth and Individuation* (Rio de Janeiro: Vozes, 2009); and "Cordial Racism: Race as a Cultural Complex" in *Listening to Latin America* (Louisiana: Spring Journal Books, 2012). His main interests are: Brazilian cultural identity, race and inter-racial problems in Latin America, psychosomatics and body–mind totality, and the uses of myth in psychotherapy.

Joseph Cambray, PhD, is President/CEO and Provost at Pacifica Graduate Institute. He is past president of the International Association for Analytical Psychology, has served as the US editor for *The Journal of Analytical Psychology*, and is on various editorial boards. He was a faculty member at Harvard Medical School in the Department of Psychiatry at Massachusetts General Hospital, Center for Psychoanalytic Studies. Dr. Cambray is also a Jungian analyst now living in the Santa Barbara area of California. His numerous publications include the book based on his Fay Lectures: *Synchronicity: Nature and Psyche in an Interconnected Universe*, and a volume edited with Linda Carter, *Analytical Psychology: Contemporary Perspectives in Jungian Psychology*.

Grazina Gudaitė, PhD, is Professor of Psychology at Vilnius University and a Jungian psychoanalyst. Dr. Gudaitė is a member of the Lithuanian Association for Analytical Psychology. She is the author of several books and articles in analytical psychology, and co-editor with Murray Stein of *Confronting Cultural Trauma: Jungian Approaches to Understanding and Healing* (2014). Among her recently published books is *Relationship Towards Authority and Sense of Personal Strength* (2016). She has a private practice in Vilnius and teaches in the Analyst Training program in Lithuania.

George B. Hogenson is a senior training analyst at the C.G. Jung Institute of Chicago, and currently Vice President of the International Association for Analytical Psychology. He is also a member of the editorial board of the *Journal of Analytical Psychology*. He holds a PhD in philosophy from Yale University and an MA in clinical social work from the University of Chicago. Author of *Jung's Struggle With Freud*, he publishes regularly on the history of psychoanalysis and issues of theory in the work of C.G. Jung and analytical psychology more generally. He is in private practice in Chicago, Illinois, and lives in Oak Park, Illinois.

Toshio Kawai, PhD, is Director and Professor at the Kokoro Research Center, Kyoto University for Clinical Psychology. He is President-Elect of the IAAP. He is graduate of Kyoto University (1983), Zurich University (1987), and the C.G. Jung Institute of Zurich (1990). He has published articles, books, and book chapters in English, German, Italian, and Japanese. His papers "Postmodern Consciousness in Psychotherapy" (2006), "Union and Separation in the Therapy of Pervasive Developmental Disorders and ADHD" (2009), and "*The Red Book* from a Pre-modern Perspective" (2012) were published in the *Journal of Analytical Psychology*. He has published other papers and book chapters concerning psychological relief work after the earthquake disaster, interpretation of the novels of Haruki Murakami, and psychotherapy with psychosomatic patients and ASD patients.

Thomas B. Kirsch was President of the International Association of Analytical Psychology from 1989 to 1995, and President of the Jung Institute of San Francisco from 1976 to 1978. Dr. Kirsch's many publications include: *The Jungians*, *A Jungian Life*, and *Jungian Analysis, Depth Psychology, Soul*. He published many papers and was a popular lecturer internationally. He was also instrumental in having the correspondence between James Kirsch and C.G. Jung published. He worked in private practice in California, and was a lecturer in the Department of Psychiatry at Stanford University Medical School.

Roderick Main works at the University of Essex, UK, where he is Professor in the Department of Psychosocial and Psychoanalytic Studies and Director of the Centre for Myth Studies. He has a first degree in Classics from the University of Oxford and a PhD in Religious Studies from Lancaster University. He is the author of *The Rupture of Time: Synchronicity and Jung's Critique of Modern Western Culture* (Brunner-Routledge, 2004) and *Revelations of Chance: Synchronicity as Spiritual Experience* (SUNY, 2007), the editor of *Jung on Synchronicity and the Paranormal* (Princeton/Routledge, 1997), and the co-editor of *Myth, Literature, and the*

xii Contributors

Unconscious (Karnac, 2013). He has also published many articles and book chapters on the intersections of analytical psychology, religion, and society.

François Martin-Vallas, MD, PhD, is a psychiatrist, Jungian analyst, and supervising member of the French Society (SFPA). He received a PhD at Lyon 2 University in 2015 (*The Transferential Chimera*) and is an associated researcher at the university. He works with children in a public consulting centre, and with adults in a company offering jobs to persons with intellectual disabilities, most of them being former psychotic children and/or adults. He has written many papers, mostly in the *Cahiers Jungiens de Psychanalyse*, the *Revue de Psychologie Analytique*, and the *Journal of Analytical Psychology*. He is a former member of the IAAP Programme Committee and the chair of the Program Committee for the next European Congress of Analytical Psychology. He is also a former editor of the *Cahiers Jungiens de Psychoanalyse*, and editor-in-chief of the *Revue de Psychologie Analytique*. He won the National Association for the Advancement of Psychoanalysis honorary prize in 2003 and the Special Fordham Prize for the 50th anniversary of the JAP in 2006. His full bibliography can be found on: https://univ-lyon2.academia.edu/FrancoisMartinVallas

Elizabeth Eowyn Nelson, core faculty at Pacifica Graduate Institute, teaches a broad range of courses in research process, methodology, and dissertation development along with classes in dream, literature, and cultural studies. Her own research interests focus on shadow, gender, and power. Dr. Nelson's books include *Psyche's Knife: Archetypal Explorations of Love and Power* (Chiron, 2012) and *The Art of Inquiry: A Depth Psychological Perspective* (Spring Publications, 2017), co-authored with Joseph Coppin, which is now in its third edition. She has been a professional writer and editor for more than 30 years, coaching aspiring authors across a variety of genres and styles.

Leslie Sawin previously served as co-program director at the Jung Society of Washington, USA, and has designed programs, such as 'Jung and Aging' at the Library of Congress, to bring Jungian ideas to the community.

Thomas Singer, MD, is a psychiatrist and Jungian analyst in private practice in San Francisco. He is the editor of a series of books which explore cultural complexes in different parts of the world, including Australia (*Placing Psyche*), Latin America (*Listening to Latin America*), Europe (*Europe's Many Souls*), and North America (*The Cultural Complex*). He is currently working on a book about cultural complexes in Asia. In addition, he has edited *Psyche and the City*, *The Vision Thing*, co-edited the Ancient Greece, Modern Psyche series, and co-authored *A Fan's Guide to Baseball Fever*. Dr. Singer currently serves as the President of National ARAS, which explores symbolic imagery from around the world. His most recent chapters include "Trump and the American Selfie" in *A Clear and Present Danger* and "Trump and the American Collective Psyche" in *The Dangerous Case of Donald Trump*.

Contributors **xiii**

Morgan Stebbins, M.Div, LMSW, D.Min, LP, Certified Jungian Analyst, is a supervising analyst, faculty member, and former President and Director of Training at the Jungian Psychoanalytic Association in New York, where he also maintains a private practice. He has taught Religious Studies and Hermeneutics at the New York Theological Seminary in the Pastoral Care and Counseling program, and he developed a program in Contemplative Jungian Practice at the New York Zen Center for Contemplative Care, which includes contemplative Jung, Buddhism and Psychology, the history of Zen, and the psychology of the Zen sutras. He began his Zen training at the San Francisco Zen Center in 1979. He has written on symbol formation, dreams, the role of mindfulness in analysis, the meaning of compulsion, the archetypal relationship of Buddhism and psychology, and the structural parallels between the theories of Paul Ricour, Jacques Lacan, and C.G. Jung. His current project is to update the material and message of C.G. Jung to be more accessible to the general reader and more integrated with modern research and cultural developments including gender, relationship, and language. Recent and upcoming publications include a chapter on gender fluidity and psyche and a chapter on the relationship between mindfulness and alchemical discourse.

Yasuhiro Tanaka, PhD, is Associate Professor of Clinical Psychology at the Graduate School of Education, Kyoto University. He is also a senior analyst and honorary secretary of the Association of Jungian Analysts, Japan (AJAJ).

Beverley Zabriskie, L.C.S.W., is a Jungian analyst in New York City, and a founding faculty member and past President of the Jungian Psychoanalytic Association (JPA). Ms. Zabriskie is a past vice president of The Philemon Foundation, dedicated to publishing the unpublished works of C.G. Jung, and a past president of the National Association for the Advancement of Psychoanalysis. She is on the Executive Committee of the Helix Center for Interdisciplinary Investigation, and on the editorial boards of the *Journal of Analytical Psychology*, London, and the San Francisco *Jung Journal: Psyche and Culture*. She presented the 2007 Fay Lecturer "Transformation Through Emotion: From Myth to Neuroscience." Her many lectures and publications include "A Meeting of Rare Minds," the preface to *Atom and Archetype: The Pauli-Jung Correspondence* (2001); "When Psyche Meets Soma: The Question of Incarnation" in *About a Body* (2006); "Time and Tao in Synchronicity" in T*he Pauli-Jung Conjecture and Its Impact Today* (2014); "Energy and Emotion: C.G. Jung's Fordham Declaration" in *Jung in the Academy and Beyond: The Fordham lectures 100 Years Later*; and "Psychic Energy and Synchronicity," *Journal of Analytical Psychology* (2014).

PART I
Introduction

1
QUALITATIVE RESEARCH IN ANALYTICAL PSYCHOLOGY

Current perspectives and future opportunities

Joseph Cambray and Leslie Sawin

The genesis of this two-volume compendium of research in Analytical Psychology emerged from activities initiated by the international community of Jungian analysts. The mission of the International Association for Analytical Psychology (IAAP), the administrative body of the worldwide Jungian analytic community founded in 1955 (on the occasion of Jung's 80th birthday) encompasses the theory, practice, and research in Analytical Psychology. In particular, the Academic Sub-Committee of the IAAP's Executive Committee attends to links with academic institutions and supports the work of analysts who are involved in research. Commencing in the 1990s, this sub-committee began to foster and support some research efforts, initially focused on the efficacy of the Jungian methods for clinical benefit.

During the years of Joseph Cambray's presidency of the IAAP (2010–2013), there was a renewed and growing interest in recognizing and supporting the expanding fields of research on Jungian-related topics. These include:

- Historical research on the founders and sources for ideas incorporated into the classical canon of depth psychology, especially Analytical Psychology;
- Empirical studies (quantitative, qualitative, and mixed methods), including outcome studies;
- Cultural and cross-cultural research (spurred by the increasing diversification of interest in Analytical Psychology around the world, especially the numbers of people seeking training as analysts beyond the traditional Western European and North American groups);
- Studies on the employment of electronic media and telecommunication; efficacy of clinical methods and the training of candidates.

Others areas are referenced within the text. During this period there was an increasing need to develop effective and comprehensive systems to disseminate research project opportunities and findings, to coordinate interest in collaboration within the Jungian community of researchers, and also a growing sense that investigations in other disciplines were offering synergistic possibilities for collaboration with research efforts in common areas.

A set of meetings was held among interested parties involved in research within the Jungian community. The first meeting was the day after the Copenhagen Congress in 2013, followed by meetings in Basel and at Yale. It was agreed that there was a robust and productive Jungian research community with much to offer the scholarly world, including other disciplines as well as great opportunities for collaboration. One significant result of these meetings was the decision to put together two separate volumes based on the current work of members of the group as a first step in introducing this important body of research work and to begin the process of making it available for clinicians and other researchers.

This volume is oriented toward research from qualitative, historical, and cultural studies. Our companion volume provides a history of Analytical Psychology empirical research and a summary of current empirical research conducted by the authors therein. Both volumes also point toward directions for future investigation and collaboration. The two are seen as complementary and seek to provide a broad overview of the range of research being conducted in Analytical Psychology today.

Analytical Psychology: a new approach

Analytical Psychology is the name C.G. Jung gave to his approach to investigation of the psyche. He first coined the term in August 1913, framing it as an evolution out of Freud's psychoanalysis from which he was about to break. He also differentiated it from the idea of his psychiatric mentor, Eugen Bleuler of "depth psychology" fame, because he saw that as "concerned only with the unconscious" (Jung, 1961, para. 523). Jung sought an approach that encompassed the interplay of conscious and unconscious processes and the products which arose from those interactions – what he identified as symbols.

Jung strove to cultivate a symbolic attitude in himself and his followers, learning to observe and identify meaning in events beyond descriptions of surface behaviors. While people do not need to be made conscious of these meanings for there to be significant impact on their thoughts and actions, the trained observer can recognize patterns that implicitly carry such meanings. Inclusion of a symbolic approach to life tends to broaden consciousness and promote developments in the personality that lead to increased psychological maturity or individuation. Hence a focus on the symbol has been a staple of Jungian psychology and a part of its research interests and focus from early on.

In defining the symbol, Jung stressed the value of it being "alive" in the sense of containing a vibrant, contemporary inclusion of the unknown. Symbols have collective relevance, transcending the individual's psychology and reflecting the zeitgeist or time period in which they live: "Since, for a given epoch, it is the best possible expression for what is still unknown, it must be the product of the most complex and differentiated minds of that age" (Jung, 1971, para. 819). Jung began the development of his theories with his landmark association experiment. From this empirical research he developed his interest in the symbol as the central focus of his psychology, and through further self-exploration he articulated the concepts of the complex and the archetypes.

Analytical Psychology's research paradigms

As Jung moved away from classical psychoanalysis, which he saw as conflating signs with symbols, his attention increasingly turned to symbolism. As noted earlier, the symbol and its role in mediating between the unconscious and consciousness became a central tenet of his psychology. This also caused him to shift his focus from more traditional scientific, data-based research (his Association Experiments) toward phenomenological, hermeneutic, and narrative modes of inquiry. His own personal experimentation, brought on by a psychological crisis (as detailed in his *Red Book*; Jung, 2009), began with careful observation of his inner world which had been activated by personal traumatic loss.

This led him to a recognition of an objective dimension to the human psyche, however by this he did not mean an equivalency with the "objective world." Instead, as he explained in a letter to Jolande Jacobi dated April 15, 1948:

> I chose the term "objective psyche" in contradistinction to "subjective psyche" because the subjective psyche coincides with consciousness, whereas the objective psyche does not always do so by any means.
>
> *(Jung, 1973, p. 497)*

To explore and articulate this realm, he needed to do pioneering research on the nature and reality of symbols and the interface between objective and subjective aspects of experience using a qualitative approach. This involved research into the history and development of symbols and symbolic forms. He was able to demonstrate how some aspects of the dream life of individuals contain references to more universal aspects, often outside of their conscious awareness. The dreams series presented in *Psychology and Alchemy* (Jung, 1968) provides numerous examples.

Nevertheless, later in life Jung did return to a statistical approach when he first articulated the synchronicity hypothesis. With the help of Wolfgang Pauli he was able to let go of this attempt at scientism and opened up a pathway to allow the inclusion of affect as a part of the experimental process. The interplay of the subjective and objective aspects of reality, which Jung pioneered, is now making its way into some aspects of contemporary research and scholarship as can be seen implicitly throughout much of this volume.

In subsequent generations of analysts and scholars, the shift from traditional scientific research toward the symbolic has been embraced and amplified. For example, in addition to Jung's cases, detailed exploration of the evolution of symbolic themes over the course of long-term analyses has been published. Research on the unique clinical methods of Analytical Psychology, with their inflections through the personal idioms of practitioners, can be found in journal articles. There have also been studies of more general analytic approaches, such as on transference and countertransference, examining how these are employed within a Jungian context.

In one significant further development, James Hillman articulated Archetypal Psychology. While based on Jung's views on a deep universal layer of the psyche, Hillman revisioned the exploration from categories to qualities and processes underlying psychological phenomena. In this there was a shift from symbolic meaning to a more immediate "image-sense" with a penchant for attuning to the metaphoricity in and of experience rather than articulating essentialist structures, such as the hero archetype.

More recently there have been efforts to combine these strands, both in contemporary culture and in Jungian-based research. This has included studies examining the nature of consciousness, its origins, and its development. In particular, a group of researchers has been applying new concepts from the worlds of physics and neurobiology through the adaptation of neurobiological studies applied to corollary states of consciousness, which has led into the inclusion of the wider field of complexity studies. Ironically Jung almost titled his approach "Complex Psychology" (from the encouragements of Toni Wolff, a close confederate and early Jungian analyst), but ultimately felt it was too limited a view. With contemporary understandings derived from complexity studies, a reconsideration of this impulse may be warranted, as some of the chapters reflect.

A complex systems approach to the psyche does permit, even encourage, multiple research vertices to contribute to our fund of knowledge in ways that transgress traditional academic disciplinary lines. New perspectives demonstrating the interconnectedness of many facets of reality previously treated in isolation support the need for new theories and methods for describing these phenomena. The tools developed in studying systems of increasing complexity have begun to reveal a profound ecological basis for experience. The human psyche can no longer be taken in isolation, even in its collective dimension, but requires a new synthesis that includes nature as integral to consciousness. Many of Jung's methods were developed out of his personal struggles, such as the trial and error introspective research which forms much of his *Red Book*. These methods can be directly reconceived in terms of complexity with a quest for studying emergent phenomena.

An expanding community

The first generation of Jungians tended to stay close to the works of the master. Since Jung's death in 1961 there has been an expansion of the community of Jungians. Initially, interest in Jung's work was held by analysts trained in his approach and also by segments of the general public who were enchanted by what they could discover through his vision. The demographics of the community were primarily Western European and North American. The academic community was limited, as was the development of research efforts beyond affirmation of clinical efficacy of the treatment modality.

Gradually this community has been changing. Expansions beyond Western Europe and North America into Latin America, Africa, Asia, Eastern Europe, and Russia have brought scrutiny to implicit cultural assumptions and cultural relevancy of the theory and methods. The need for bidirectionality of influence has been highlighted through these cultural exchanges. The leap to archetypalizing theory without first articulating cultural contributions has led to confusion and a blurring of the incredible complexities involved at the many levels of psychological reality. Some of the chapters in this volume begin to address these and other related issues.

In recent years there has been a rise in the numbers of academically trained scholars and researchers in fields associated with and employing depth psychology. Many of the practitioners are non-analysts, without the same lines of filiation, and hence offer varying new perspectives. There are also increasing numbers of analysts who are pursuing scholarly work in parallel with their clinical practices. The contributions of these scholars will certainly broaden the interests and applications of Analytical Psychology. Much of this will involve careful critiques of all aspects of the various depth psychologies, including Jung's version. Already significant work is being done to de-colonize the theories, which were first articulated in the early 20th century amid cultural attitudes that are certainly not universal and can be seen through for their own unconscious political agendas.

While Jung valued the wisdom and traditions of many indigenous people, he also tended to see them as operating outside explicit conscious awareness and as forms of folk, proto-psychology. Careful historical analyses of the primary sources of the depth psychologists are helpful in this regard. Understanding the "provenance" of the ideas and how they are inflected within the various schools, as well as the evolution of the ideas through the lifetimes of the communities, are beginning to give us tools for a fuller historical and cultural analysis.

Applications from scientific, historical, and cross-cultural research

The focus of this volume is on research that draws upon and is conducted through qualitative and mixed methods, though some also borrow from the findings of quantitative studies while applying it to more subjective or complex phenomena. In this sense the works presented are congruent with the types of explorations Jung himself conducted from his *Red Book* period on.

Part II. Approaching qualitative research in Analytical Psychology

A central goal of this volume is to encourage interdisciplinary research among Jungian researchers and with researchers from other disciplines. To open this discussion, we examine two approaches: exploration of the potential for Analytical Psychology to contribute to postmodern thought, and for historical documents to enhance current research and point the way toward new approaches to developing research questions.

We begin our exploration with an insightful chapter by Elizabeth Eowyn Nelson, who examines the contexts of postmodern thought and Analytical Psychology and discusses how they might be related and work together. She outlines the horizontal principles and basic tenets of postmodern thought and the vertical perspective of Analytical Psychology. Through the analysis of four themes of postmodernism (the central importance of language, discourse and the social production of knowledge, researcher self-reflexivity, and theoretical pluralism) that have "particular relevance" for Jungian researchers, Nelson makes a strong case for an antinomial approach to research. She notes that the shared commitment to perspectivism and plurality might provide a rich and fertile common ground for conversation and collaboration. Raising a fundamental question, "How does the epistemological commitment to depth – with verticality as its primary metaphor – fertilize the horizontal breadth of social science research?," Nelson offers ways to collaborate and build upon this potential relationship.

Thomas B. Kirsch advances the idea that an examination of historical materials can serve as a fresh approach to the development of new directions for research and can identify historical areas that could promote collaboration between Jungian researchers and other social science investigators. He explores five recently published major correspondences that Jung conducted. The letters that Jung exchanged with the noted scientist Wolfgang Pauli, the theologian Victor White, his psychologist colleague Hans Schmid-Guisan, and analysts James Kirsch and Erich Neumann offer historical perspective on some of today's current concerns.

The correspondence between Jung and Pauli has led to the development and articulation of the concept of dual-aspect monism, which Atmanspacher notes in Volume 2 of this set, was not more than speculation at the time, and which may help us to clarify psychophysical phenomena beyond what our knowledge about the mental and the physical in separation are capable of achieving. Understanding the context of the conversation between Jung and his other correspondents could open new avenues for discussion and research today. From a historical perspective, these documents provide windows into the evolving thought of one of the most important psychologists of the 20th century. They contain a wide array of reflections not found in his published works which offer various possibilities for the future.

Part III. Research on symbolic aspects of the psyche

This part of the volume focuses on current research examining symbolic aspects of the psyche. One of the core concepts in Analytical Psychology is the collective unconscious with its resulting archetypal theory. Another singular concept from Analytical Psychology with broad relevance to today's social science research is the cultural complex theory. Research in both areas is examined.

François Martin-Vallas first explores the development of the concept of the collective unconscious and the theory of archetypes. Following a historical perspective, he traces the development of Jung's epistemology. He finds the ideas about archetypes and their function to be "a very diverse collection of ideas." He offers complex systems theory as a powerful analytic tool for understanding these core Jungian concepts. Describing key concepts from the vantage point of complexity science, such as emergence and its application and framework in physics, Martin-Vallas offers a new model of the psyche as itself a complex system. Using concepts from within this perspective, he describes the psyche as an example of an auto-organizing system and the archetypes as a related complex system with a fractal structure. He describes how this perspective can enhance both research and therapeutic work. Building on these insights, he then offers new ways of viewing the therapeutic relationship and understanding the structure of the psyche.

Thomas Singer introduces the concept of the cultural complex and summarizes the research that has been ongoing in this area. He argues that "cultural complex theory offers a rich avenue for cross-discipline research, for exploring cultural factors in the life of the group and individual psyche, and for bringing Jungian concepts, tools, and ideas to scientific inquiry outside of the Jungian community." He defines cultural complexes as "an autonomous, largely unconscious, emotionally charged aggregate of memories, affects, ideas, images, and behaviors that tend to cluster around an archetypal core and are shared by individuals within a group." He describes the forces that produce cultural concepts and how they operate in communities and civilizations. He notes that the cultural complex is part of the human condition.

Singer also discusses the research he has conducted from the definition of a working hypothesis through the development of an international research effort. He outlines possible approaches to working with cultural complexes and offers a discussion of different ways of knowing, the mythopoetic and the scientific. As part of this discussion, he describes his research framework for qualitative research and discusses the nature of qualitative evidence. An agenda for future research is offered.

Part IV. Research on consciousness and emotion

This part of the volume focuses on two universal experiences: emotion and individual consciousness. Both areas are rich in symbolic life and offer many opportunities to employ Jungian perspectives and tools.

Beverley Zabriskie explores the history of the experience of emotion and contemporary engagements with emotion. She reviews the mythologies and philosophies from the past surrounding emotion, traces some clinical observations from consulting rooms since the time of C.G. Jung, and then introduces the current neurosciences perspective on the framing of emotion. She examines various approaches and descriptions of emotional states and moments from and toward inter-disciplinary and cross-disciplinary discourse about the personal and social roles of emotion. Zabriskie then explores the neuroscientific perspective introduced earlier, its sources, and its similarities and differences with Carl Jung's seminal concepts about the purpose and dynamics of emotion in his clinical and theoretical framework. She suggests how Jungian concerns and concepts are at play in present emotion research and highlights the implicit and explicit convergence between Jung's theses and current neuroscientific research and philosophies of mind.

Meditation is a practice with a deep historical tradition and worldwide experience and application. Morgan Stebbins introduces us to the concept of meditation, its diverse forms of practice, research into its effectiveness, and understanding of its characteristics. He comments that one fruitful and important way of looking at meditation is through the lens of Jungian psychology. He introduces the relationship between Jungian psychology and meditation, summarizes the different forms of research in these areas to date, and offers avenues for collaborative research on meditation as both a personal and therapeutic practice using Analytical Psychology tools.

Stebbins notes: "From a Jungian point of view, meditation is attention to the psyche." He offers several distinct ways to view meditation:

> This can take the form of resisting instinctual urges (the level of control, described as the field of the psyche in Aion); playing with arising images (similar to guided meditations but without the guide); holding an emotion until it moves into an image; moving according to a kinesthetic image, noticing what arises (similar to meditations of steady awareness); allowing a psychic impregnation (like Tibetan dream yoga); hovering awareness with attention split between one's own process, the other's process, and the field, and attunement to what changes us (the numinous or devotional aspect).
>
> *(p. 129)*

He suggests that meditation *and* Analytical Psychology are about the connection of the daily and small to the eternal and cosmic, of the person to meaning, of the mortal to the image-of-god, and of one person to another – that is, to the enhancement of relationships.

Part V. A complex systems approach to the psyche

As briefly described earlier, complexity theory is becoming a major focus of research on the psyche. This part of the volume provides an in-depth review of current research in Analytical Psychology using complex systems theory. Three analysts conducting research using these concepts present their work and offer directions for the future and approaches for collaboration.

We open our discussion with a comprehensive review of the literature examining research on the concept of synchronicity by Roderick Main. Developed by Jung in correspondence with Wolfgang Pauli (see Chapter 3 for a discussion of the Pauli–Jung conjecture), Jung felt this idea would be relevant "not only for psychotherapy but also for the critique of modern science, religion and society." Main also notes that "in the years since Jung's death, there have been many varied attempts to elucidate, apply, and evaluate synchronicity, both within and beyond Analytical Psychology." He offers a detailed review of these multifaceted approaches to understanding and working with synchronicity and some promising areas for future research, including conceptual, empirical, historical, theoretical, clinical, and cultural engagement with the concept.

Main expands on his discussion of the varied approaches to working with synchronicity, saying that "these have recently burgeoned to the point where the need for orientation on the topic is pressing." His chapter therefore provides a detailed overview of existing research on synchronicity and highlights some promising directions for the future. He reviews his own research and notes that synchronicity is still rarely utilized in research by academics in other disciplines.

Joseph Cambray expands the discussion of the relevance of complexity theory for analytic approaches by focusing on holistic and non-local aspects of field research. As noted earlier, the heart of traditional Analytical Psychology is the idea that the *symbol* serves as the mediating factor between the interplay of conscious and unconscious dynamics. Symbols are seen as having collective relevance, transcending the individual's psychology and reflecting both a timeless component from the depth and more immediately the zeitgeist or time period in which they live. One way to re-evaluate and extend our view of the symbol is through the application of the principles of complexity theory.

The science of complexity emerged in the late 20th century and with technological advances in information processing has expanded to become one of the most important contemporary directions in scholarly studies. The application to Jungian and depth psychologies has developed in parallel, primarily through applications to theoretical understanding of core concepts. Cambray extends these studies in a way that indicates a revision of the sense in which concepts such as symbolism are viewed and applied against the backdrop of increased knowledge and understanding of our world. He notes, "Human beings' implicit separation from their environments, the planet and even the cosmos is no longer tenable, even within scientific formulations." He then urges a broad and thorough reconsideration of all of the basic assumptions about the symbol in light of evolving understandings offered through complexity studies, especially in its applications to ecological systems, of which psyche and symbols partake.

George Hogenson discusses the relevance of complexity theory to psychological life through an examination of Jung's analysis of the Tibetan *Book of the Dead*. His argument begins with the fascinating suggestion that Jung read the book "backwards," regarding the flow of libido in rebirth versus a Western, psychoanalytic developmental model. Hogenson goes on to compare the structure of elements in the *Book of the Dead* with Jung's *Red Book*. Central to Jung's conclusions about this Buddhist work is his idea that "the products of imagination are always in essence visual, their forms must, from the outset, have the character of images and moreover of typical images" (Jung, 1970, p. 845). This perspective is reinforced when examining the illustrations in *The Red Book*. Hogenson notes the relationship of the structures Jung used for his biomimetic forms and the work of Haeckel. They both have the emergent properties of fractal geometry.

Building on this observation of the similarities between the structure of the natural world and the depiction of internal symbolic life in Jung's *Red Book*, Hogenson reviews the history of the development of fractal geometry and coins the term "symbolic density" as a way of understanding the nature of archetypal images and other symbolic formations. He continues

> the symbol stands, in some degree, at the beginning of this process, and it would seem inconsistent with the degree to which fractal analysis of the natural world has progressed for those of us who traffic daily in the symbolic to overlook the insight that we can gain from reading back to the symbolic the larger insights provided by the geometry of fractals.
>
> (p. 190)

Hogenson describes the growing body of literature that lends additional insight into the relationship of the fractal structure of visual images and the deep structure of the psyche. He notes that research in Analytical Psychology needs to address the literature on fractal geometry in the context of an examination of Jung's focus on visual imagery as the fundamental expression of the deep psyche.

Part VI. Cross-cultural research

As noted earlier, an emerging focus of current research in Analytical Psychology is exploring individual development and treatment within a cultural setting and reframing Jungian concepts in light of cultural attitudes and experience.

Toshio Kawai begins our discussion by exploring the nature of the experience of the loss and recovery of transcendence from a Jungian perspective and from the perspective of the Hua-Yen School of Buddhism and offers some ways that this Buddhist perspective can be a useful therapeutic tool. He describes the development of the concept of transcendence in Jungian thought by citing the early experiences of C.G. Jung and how they helped to develop his concept of transcendence and its role in Jungian psychology.

He then discusses the loss and recovery of transcendence in Jungian psychology and in our present time. His focus is to demonstrate how lost transcendence can be found immanently in reference to the Hua-Yen School of Buddhism. Summarizing the Hua-Yen perspective, he notes that "God or transcendence is neither dead nor lost, but has been absent from the beginning. This absence is, however, at the same time fullness which flows into reality as energy and light." Interdependence and emergence are ontological events according to the Hua-Yen School, individuation is not a goal or process, but rather an event. The Hua-Yen School has a unique position in presuming this enlightened standpoint. Even if one never consciously reached the undifferentiated, eliminated state of *li* or emptiness it describes, Kawai feels that one can presuppose this position to be taken by the therapist. So the therapist can be present in the therapy as *li* or emptiness or, in Jungian terms, pleroma which would enhance the patient's capacity for verbalization, imagination, and transformation.

Grazina Gudaitė advances our first look at the role of culture on individual development. She explores the effect of living under an authoritarian regime on the individual's perception of authority. As she notes,

> Analytical Psychology offers a unique perspective on and a valuable tool for psychological research into personal transformation. Because of its basic definition of the unconscious as including multiple levels internally and having a collective nature, Jungian principles can be used to investigate both cultural and individual transformations.
>
> (p. 210)

Gudaitė examines how Analytical Psychology tools can parse the relationship between culture and change to help understand the process of an individual's transformation experience.

She presents two studies: the first explores the individual experience of psychotherapy; the second probes the relationship of an individual to authority as part of the therapeutic process. Gudaitė identifies three important elements for effective psychotherapy: (1) measurement of objective parameters, (2) understanding the subjective experience of the individual, and (3) "that force which stands beyond behavior and beyond subjective experience," such as cultural complexes and cultural identity. In the second study, the representation of authority in the initial stage and later stages of psychotherapy was examined in light of the effects of living under an authoritative regime given the task of developing an internal authority. The role of cultural trauma is discussed. In both studies, deeper understanding of the emergence of hope and inspiration is also an important theme for further research in psychotherapy effectiveness as well as in exploring the multidimensional picture of a sense of identity. Further studies of cultural identity and the individual's relatedness to culture can be an important focus of future research on healing sources for the individual and for a culture.

Speaking from a different perspective, Yasuhiro Tanaka discusses the relationship between postmodern culture and psychotherapy. He begins with a review of the development of psychology. Developed in the late 19th century as an essential way of understanding the human experience and psychopathology based on the then new perspective of "modernism," psychology was created using the idea of observation of the self. In particular, self-observation became a central tenet of Analytical Psychology and its vision of the self as its psychological infrastructure. He examines this central tenet from the standpoint of postmodern culture and applies Jungian principles to cultural and personal issues in Japan.

With the advent of the internet and global communication, the focus has shifted from an internal perception to an externally driven experience of self. The role of psychological infrastructure in the age of the "ubiquitous" self-consciousness or today's internet is the central focus of this discussion. Tanaka notes that "Analytical Psychology, which was also born in modern times, is based on the premise or 'base structure' of self-relation, i.e., 'psychological infrastructure.'" He describes how this premise of an internally developed self has already been broken down in the information age and through the rise of the internet. He calls this the "the 'ubiquitous' self-consciousness of our times." It is important to learn that even our sense of "oneself," or construction of our "self-consciousness," may vary with the tide of the times. As discussed earlier, the "'ubiquitous' self-consciousness" developed as part of the information age may be the dominant manner of experiencing self in our current culture. Tanaka finds that it might be inevitable that psychotherapists must open themselves to such a *new* modality of "oneself," to be *clinical* in its truest sense. He presents clinical experiences of psychotherapy with patients whose sandplays or dreams reflect a new "psychological infrastructure."

Walter Boechat explores the relationship between culture and individual growth from a different perspective. The interaction between the individual and the culture in which he/she lives is a core question when discussing the development of personal identity. Boechat examines this interplay between individuals and their culture in terms of the effect that culture can have on that quest to develop and experience individual identity. As a case in point, he analyzes Brazil and the symbols and culture complexes that belong to the country's history. Boechat notes that

> in fact, Latin American culture has a unique structure. In some ways its history may resemble that of North America, which also suffered the trauma of slavery and had waves of immigration. But the multi-colored social tissue of Brazil and Latin America as a whole is a very peculiar one. One fact deserves special attention: the strong racial blending in Brazil.
>
> (p. 238)

Building on this perspective, he closely examines the racial history of this culture and the myths that support current cultural life. He discusses working with the cultural complex in psychotherapy and presents case studies that illustrate the complex issues of culture in Brazil.

Part VII. A glance towards the future

The final chapter, "Going Forward" by Joseph Cambray, offers directions for future investigation and suggests new trajectories for ongoing collaboration. Building on the idea of "adjacent possibles," these directions start from the work presented here in the areas of historical methods, studies in archetype, culture and consciousness, cross-cultural collaboration and research, and the paradigm shifts in our understanding of the world resulting from the application of complexity theory. In this last section, we will attempt a few tentative suggestions for nearby possible topics.

References

Jung, C.G. (1961). *Collected works IV, Freud and psychoanalysis*. Princeton: Princeton University Press.

Jung, C.G. (1968). *Collected works XII, psychology and alchemy*. Princeton: Princeton University Press.

Jung, C.G. (1970). *Collected works XI, psychology and religion*. Princeton: Princeton University Press.
Jung, C.G. (1971). *Psychological types, collected works 6*. Princeton: Princeton University Press.
Jung, C.G. (1973). *C.G. Jung letters, 1906–1950* (G. Adler in collaboration with A. Jaffee, Eds.). Princeton: Princeton University Press.
Jung, C.G. (2009). *The Red Book* (S. Shamdasani, Ed.). New York: W.W. Norton.

PART II
Approaching qualitative research in Analytical Psychology

2

JUNGIAN RESEARCH AND POSTMODERNISM

An antinomial approach

Elizabeth Eowyn Nelson

This chapter begins with an active imagination or, for those unfamiliar with Jungian practices, a thought experiment. What would happen if a postmodernist struck up a conversation with a Jungian? A more colorful variation might be: *A Jungian walks into a postmodern bar* . . .

I like to imagine that something meaningful would ensue, that the two scholars would step boldly beyond their intellectual domains and engage in a wide-ranging conversation that clarifies their disciplinary commitments and stimulates new interdisciplinary thinking. I like to imagine that the pair would agree to disagree on some fundamentals, but not let their disagreement get in the way of collaboration. That may be optimistic, since postmodernists reject the idea of a psyche, a central ontological commitment of depth psychology, and instead view subjectivity as socially produced (Jones, 2007, p. 4). Moreover, "postmodern thought focuses on the surface, with a refined sensibility to what appears" (Kvale, 1992, p. 37), in contrast to a Jungian depth sensibility, which Jung personified in *The Red Book* (2009) as the Spirit of the Depths. Nevertheless, the commitment to perspectivism and plurality that Jungians and postmodernists share just might prompt the two scholars to continue the conversation with curiosity rather than animosity, and discover how their approaches to research complement and enhance one another even if they do not agree. So let us imagine they close down that bar in the wee hours of the morning – oh, and remember a few things the next day.

Introduction

Postmodernism has a fluid history that begins around the middle of the 20th century and slowly permeates the arts, culture, and scholarship. Charles Jencks, speaking as an architect and philosopher, offers a sweeping view when he asserts that "an intense commitment to pluralism is perhaps the only thing that unites every post-modern movement" (1996, p. 29). Raya Jones, social scientist and Jungian, describes postmodernism as "a form of social study that prompts the evaluative – and primarily qualitative – description of the particular, historical, local and discursive aspects of human life" (2007, p. 4). Phenomenologist Steiner Kvale describes postmodernism as "a departure from the belief in one true reality – subjectively copied in our heads by perception or objectively represented in scientific models" (1992, p. 32), and thus it is explicitly decentering and destabilizing. Literary theorist Steven Connor describes it more as "an effort of renewal and transformation" in which "the questions raised by postmodernism were always questions of value" (2006, p. 5). There is also a good deal of debate now about the dissolution of postmodernism, an argument from different quarters (see, for instance, Turner [1995]) that we are, in fact, in a "post-postmodernist moment." No one has quite agreed on what to call it, a conundrum drawing attention to the problem of naming a movement with the literally interminable prefix "post." Connor (2017) notes the same naming difficulty, but argues that this "post-post" moment is a return to modernism. Whether or not this is wholly true, postmodernism introduced ways of thinking about knowledge, in particular the rejection of grand narratives in favor of local, partial knowing, that have and will continue to have durable consequences for the conduct of research.

Connor (2006) names four distinct phases of postmodernism, asserting that "by the beginning of the 1990s, the concept of the 'postmodern' was ceasing to be used principally in the analysis of particular objects or cultural areas and had become a general horizon or hypothesis" (p. 2). Accordingly, one might say that all scholarly researchers now live, think, and work "in a postmodernist climate, a time when a multitude of approaches to knowing and telling exist side by side" (Richardson & Adams St. Pierre, 2005, p. 961). Though many would agree with Richardson and Adams St. Pierre that postmodernism is a fortunate intellectual moment, Jungians find the postmodern climate only partly habitable because we are committed to precise and robust ideas about the psyche without which Jungian psychology would be unrecognizable. They include structural ideas such as the unconscious, complexes, instincts, and archetypes; philosophical concepts (that are also lived experiences) such as the Self, fate, the soul, and synchronicity; processes such as individuation; and the meaningfulness of myth, symptoms, dreams, and visionary experience. Nonetheless, there is value in placing postmodernism and Jungian research in dialogue because the premises of depth psychology, a product of and a response to high modernism, are also postmodern in some respects. Equally, the value derives from the ways depth psychology is *not* postmodern and, therefore, calls into question some of postmodernism's cherished ideas and values.

For instance, what distinguishes depth psychology as a discipline and practice is commitment to a foundational premise, the unconscious, which Jung describes as "the very source of the creative impulse" (1931/1969c, p. 157 [para. 339]) and "the matrix of a mythopoetic imagination which has vanished from our rational age" (1961, p. 188). The unconscious, or unconsciousness as *not knowing*, completely encompasses consciousness and is continuously creative. Consciousness is "an island surrounded by the sea; and, like the sea itself, the unconscious yields an endless and self-replenishing abundance of living creatures, a wealth beyond our fathoming" (1946/1966, p. 178 [para. 366]). Thus, as Jungians, our commitment to a stable idea, the unconscious, means that we each live within the tensions of two ways of knowing or experiencing that coexist. This has particular importance for those engaged in Jungian research, since the fact of unconsciousness destabilizes all knowledge claims. Adopting a Jungian approach offers the humbling reminder that no one will ever have the last word because the substance of knowledge continually dissolves into unknowing.

Although postmodernists would not agree to the stable idea of the psyche or the fact of unconsciousness, there is much that ensues that they would recognize in the Jungian approach. That is, if the two scholars were able to remain in dialog past the fundamental disagreement over these important initial ideas, they would likely find common ground in their experience of the instability of knowledge, the appreciation of partial and local truths, and the humility demanded in the practice and outcomes of scholarly research.

A second commitment in Jungian psychology, to meaningfulness (1932/1969b, p. 331 [para. 498]), also appears to be at odds with postmodernism. The desire to find meaning, an expression of the religious instinct, radically connects humanity with the more-than-human world of nature and spirit. We seek to understand our place in the cosmos and may be unique among species in our ability to feel awe at its mystery and grandeur. The healing experience of the numinosum, the wholly Other, "is a key part of [Jung's] theoretical system," says Corbett, which returns "the care of the psyche to the province of spiritual practice, as was the case in antiquity" (1996, p. 13). The religious instinct is described in many different ways, but consistently points toward foundational ideas such as fate, necessity, and the soul. Such ideas are suspect if not actually antithetical to postmodernism and *its* large ideas. (The irony, I hope, is apparent.) *Foundational*, like *fundamental*, is an "F word," a postmodern profanity. Yet, once again, we can see that if postmodern researchers are truly committed to discovering local and particular truths and to representing the deep subjectivity of the participants in the study or their own subjective response to texts in a hermeneutic project, then the experience of meaningfulness, fate, necessity, and the soul may enter the frame.

Since we cannot abandon the unconscious or ignore the religious instinct and still call ourselves Jungian, some may say the conversation ends there and walk right out of the bar. As should be apparent from the two preceding examples, I disagree. My stance is antinomial (Saban, 2012), a both/and approach that sets Jungian and postmodern research alongside one another. Like Jung, I value the sparks that fly when incompatible opposites meet, because generative conversation often includes friction. As Jones (2007) put it, "we should acknowledge the existence of misalignment, the failures of agreement, which renders any integration of Jungian and postmodern psychologies a dubious enterprise. And why 'integrate'? Each psychology is thriving without apparent need for the other" (p. 5). Why integrate, indeed.

The aim of this chapter is not integration but exploration of four themes within postmodernism that have particular relevance for Jungians engaged in research: first, the central importance of language; second, discourse and the social production of knowledge; third, researcher self-reflexivity; and fourth, theoretical pluralism. Familiarity with postmodernism may facilitate generative interdisciplinary inquiry by demonstrating how a Jungian approach enriches the pursuit of knowledge. The central question at the heart of this chapter is deceptively simple: how does the epistemological commitment to depth – with verticality as its primary metaphor – fertilize the horizontal breadth of social science research?

First, a confession: I have been in lively dialogue with this topic for months now without inscribing one word on the page. I keep returning to the beginning, again and again, trying to find the question at the heart of it. This is what I ask my dissertation students to do: spend a great deal of time finding the central question. Finding implies that it exists somewhere, that articulating the central question – which crucially shapes the path one takes – is a discovery process like detecting or archaeology or astronomy. We follow the evidence. Postmodernism urges skepticism toward these metaphors because they imply the instrumental stance characteristic of modernism. Instead, postmodernism views knowledge as socially constructed in which the categories of "researcher" and "participant" break down. It is a participatory epistemology that *appears* congenial with a depth approach. As a depth psychologist, I would (and have) said it this way: knowledge is not just what we seek, *it is what seeks us* (Coppin & Nelson, 2017, p. 11). When we do Jungian research, we are developing a relationship with the psyche, which frequently responds to respectful, sustained attention by emerging in one of many forms: image, idea, mood, emotion, mental intuition (with its airy quality), felt sense (an earthy, somatic intuition), and symptom.

The last sentence may have dissuaded some readers from continuing. I named the unconscious the *psyche* and implied that it is a responsive participant in the research process. Doing so reveals an entire world of experience and an epistemology that grows out of that experience. Jungian research, at its most radical, follows Jung's proposition of "allowing the soul to get a word in" (1954/1969d, p. 159 [para. 343]) to counteract the assumption that the soul is already completely familiar and known. We can begin by paying attention to meandering language, from "unconscious" to "soul" to "psyche" (which also hints at the mythic Psyche, a rather complex young woman), to consider Jung's unnerving suggestion that Psyche speaks. However, scholars in other disciplines, as well as other Jungians, may find this proposition too animated, too "enchanted," preferring to conceptualize the unconscious and note unconscious mental processes, for instance. For them, it is enough to say that there is a strong affective relationship between researcher and topic, and that is fine. Both approaches align with postmodernism's emphasis on subjectivity and the participatory nature of research.

The remainder of this chapter adopts an antinomial stance to explore the four themes previously mentioned: language, discourse, self-reflexivity, and theoretical pluralism. The purpose is to describe areas of difference as well as agreement between Jungian and postmodern approaches to research and to articulate areas for fruitful discussion and collaboration in the future.

The central importance of language

As noted earlier, Jungian and postmodern approaches to research necessitate multiple layers of awareness at every stage of the process. Both approaches concern themselves with how unconsciousness is a persistent aspect of any inquiry and the ways in which unacknowledged biases and assumptions are ultimately inscribed in the language of the finished thesis, dissertation, essay, or book. Whereas Jungian researchers tends to emphasize the activation of unconscious psychological complexes while designing a study, conducting it, analyzing the data, and writing it up, postmodernist researchers emphasize the social and political nature of knowledge construction and the hidden power relations that inhere in language. "A central concern of postmodernism," says Hauke, is that "the relationship between things, ideas, and words may no longer be taken for granted in an uncritical fashion" (2000, p. 24). Rather, language, used thoughtlessly, can be coercive. Accordingly, a hermeneutics of suspicion is no longer optional; it is obligatory, commensurate with "loss of belief in an objective world and an incredulity towards meta-narratives of legitimation" (Kvale, 1992, p. 32).

Jung's understanding of the coercive potential of language was presciently postmodern. In his essay *Two Kinds of Thinking*, he defines "directed thinking" as "thinking in words" which is "manifestly an instrument of culture" (1912/1967, p. 16 [para. 16]). Thus, not only are researchers obligated to be aware of the rich and complex history of words, they equally are obligated to ruminate on the cultural horizon within which their word choices live. How does language conceal as well as reveal? For postmodern and Jungian scholars, these are not idle questions. "Language is clearly a repository of cultural experience; we exist in and through this medium; we see through its eyes" (Palmer, 1969, p. 27).

Some may wonder what is in a name such as "the unconscious," but Jungians and postmodernists agree: a great deal. Calling attention to small moves in language with big implications demonstrates the central importance of language in depth psychological research and postmodernism. When we pause and speculate about "a 'concept,' its 'word,' and its 'meanings' – what it refers to in 'reality' – we are already living within what the postmodern draws our attention to," says Hauke (2000, p. 24). The relationship among them, "the baseline of both scientific and social 'truth,' is not a 'given,' and yet to put it another way, it has been given to us" (p. 24).

The Jungian tradition has a long history of paying close attention to language, for a reason implied by Hauke's statement. Language has been given to us. Words have stories, some of them more intricate and paradoxical than others, which can explain the depth psychological predilection for etymology. We go back through a word's history, listening to its varying usage and meaning over the centuries, particularly fascinated by its remote, alien, or mythic allusions, a process that "takes on added meaning when it is discovered that *etymos* means truth. That makes etymology 'truth speaking, the truth of a word speaking through itself'" (Lockhart, 1983, p. 72). Postmodernists would likely cringe at the idea of "the truth of a word." A central assertion, particularly in Derrida, Foucault, and Lacan, is that scholars cannot trust language systems to convey truth since there is no stable relationship between signified and signifier. Because certainties and frameworks have broken down, the very idea of seeking truth is absurd. All is play or, to use Derrida's term *jeu libre* ("free play"; 1981). Yet when etymology is considered as a practice, it becomes eminently postmodern because truth *seeking* – regardless of whether there is a truth to be found (there is not; only many truths) – reveals a word's polyvalent history. In fact, we can imagine etymologists entering into *conversation* with a word, a congenial idea to discourse-loving postmodernism. The life of the word over time illuminates the multiple legitimate claims to truthfulness that have arisen and subsided, been remembered and forgotten, then recalled once again. We may agree with Galileo, himself an inventor of no small consequence, who describes writing as "surpassing all stupendous inventions" (quoted in Calvin, 2004, p. 137).

Finding language to express oneself, along with the desire to be understood, fuels research. It also is crushingly difficult since researchers who want their work to have impact must aim for evocative, detailed speech that "leads to participation, in the Platonic sense, in and with the thing spoken of, of stories and insights which would evoke, in the other who listens, new stories and new insights" (Hillman, 1975, p. 206). Even the driest, most factual quantitative study seeks to tell a story. Researchers cannot evade the challenge of the blank page because writing "is intended to recall 'research' to its epistemological condition: whatever it seeks, it must not forget its nature as language – and it is this which ultimately makes an encounter with writing inevitable" (Barthes, 1986, p. 316).

One aspect of the encounter is awareness of the "constant danger of objectifying vocabularies of understanding, and thereby closing off options and potentials" (Gergen, 1992, p. 26). Without a sense of this danger, researchers may become blind to how their discipline or tradition has become a self-limiting culture, a "preferred discourse" (p. 24) that imposes fixed patterns of thinking. The question for researchers is how to keep one's eyes fresh. Frequently, Jungians fall into speaking of the unconscious as a thing that exists, which is easy to do even for Jung, and a fine example of the danger of "objectifying vocabularies." Elsewhere, though, Jung sounds far more radical: "The concept of the unconscious *posits nothing*, it designates only my *unknowing*" (1975, p. 60). This Jung, says Miller, "was postmodern before the times. He knew unknowing before Derrida's version of Heidegger's insight that the most crucial moment is the deconstructive one" (1990, p. 326). This Jung invites us "to forget our Jungian concepts and categories . . . listening not to Jung but to the soul" (p. 326). Unknowing is a very useful starting point for the researcher because it reminds us of the importance of epistemic humility in the journey toward knowing. The tension between unknowing and knowing can restrain the researcher's confidence in any settled or certain ideas. If unknowing is a constant companion in research, then regardless how expertise expands during the progress of the study, fluidity, novelty, chaos, and structure are of equal value.

Discourse and the social production of knowledge

Critical attention to language leads to a second key feature of postmodernism: emphasis on discourse, "the linguistic and social construction of reality" and the "interpretation and negotiation of the meaning of the lived world" (Kvale, 1992, p. 35). In research, "knowing the self and knowing about the subject are intertwined, partial, historical, local knowledges" (Richardson & Adams St. Pierre, 2005, p. 962). Since knowledge emerges in dialogue and, therefore, is fluid and contextual, research is collaboration; the human *subject* is crucially reframed as *participant*. Knowledge is not extracted but rather arises between those engaged in the study in that moment. They are conjoined in an effort at truthfulness, which is "a credible account of a cultural, social, individual, or communal sense of the 'real'" (p. 964).

The discursive turn in research reveals a point of friction between postmodernists and Jungians: the postmodern ear for language, in its effort to critically differentiate many current meanings of concepts and their relation to "reality," is more horizontal than vertical, more broad than deep. "Postmodern psychology, which means locating human consciousness in the materiality of discursive practices, eschews the very assumption of a psyche" and "views subjectivity as an emergent property of discourse" (Jones, 2007, pp. 4–5). And not only subjectivity, but the subject herself. "From the social or dialogical view, the social context is the surrounding by virtue of which the surrounded can exist at all" (p. 100). This may explain my frustration with much sociological and postmodern research: it is flat, aiming toward horizontal extension without the verticality that intrigues the depth psychologist. It also claims so much for social discourse that one can easily forget the silent communion with the ineffable soul that grounds subjectivity. In fact, the social, discursive idea of subjectivity contrasts sharply with Jung's notion of "the development of personality," which is "the supreme realization of the innate idiosyncrasy of a living being" (1934/1954, p. 171 [para. 289]). The jarring word for postmodern ears is "innate," an idea that Jung repeats and deepens throughout the essay in his use of organic imagery, including "ripeness," "seed," "germs," "germ-state," "fruit," and "undiscovered vein" (pp. 171, 172, 173, 186 [paras. 288, 290, 293, 323]).

Whether the setting is an analysis or a research project, Jungians are not and cannot be postmodern to the extent that our language aims at care of the soul or psyche through the pursuit of meaning. For Jungians, the assumption that the people and things of the world have profound interiority and depth is an ontological commitment of great value. We follow Jung, who revives the classical idea of a unique guiding spirit that acts like a law of god. The person, whether analyst, patient, or researcher, "must obey his own law, as if it were a daemon whispering to him of new and wonderful paths. Anyone with a vocation hears the voice of the inner man: he is called" (1934/1954, p. 176 [para. 300]). The idea of the *daimon*, which implies an inner law, an inner spirit, and interiority itself – all antithetical to postmodernism – encourages patient, careful attention and the capacity to listen into the space between words for the poetics of silence. Elsewhere my co-author Joseph Coppin and I have described this as the "yin of inquiry" (Coppin & Nelson, 2017, p. 11). It is the active willingness to receive, a posture that is familiar to those engaged in deep creativity, including composers, authors, artists, and researchers in depth psychology. At such moments of reverie, psyche's own language, image (Jung, 1931/1967b, p. 50), becomes more apparent.

For the researcher, images that arrive in moments of reverie carry the obligation to write. "The march, from image to thought to language, is treacherous. Casualties occur: the rich, fleecy texture of image, its extraordinary plasticity and flexibility, its private nostalgic emotional hues – all are lost when image is crammed into language" (Yalom, 1995, p. 180). I don't agree that *all* is lost, though Yalom's warning is apt. So long as researchers remain flexible, developing a fine tactile sense for images and a nose for where they want to lead, writing precise and evocative prose makes it possible for author and reader to follow the image. In fact, such following is a form of love. Then, one image can be set alongside another, and another, ultimately producing a multi-hued portrait of the present moment. To translate into postmodern language, distinct images are like distinct strands in discourse – valuable for their own sake and valuable when woven together.

Researcher self-reflexivity

Postmodernism eschews grand narratives in favor of limited and partial knowledge in which the subjectivity of the researcher is valued. "Our selves are always present no matter how hard we try to suppress them" (Richardson & Adams St. Pierre, 2005, p. 962). The pure, rational objectivity prized by modernists is not possible. No matter how coldly mechanical the instruments we use to inspect nature or human nature, no matter how reductive the outcome (especially in quantitative research), there is always a warm, fleshy human being who gathers and interprets the data, trying to understand the story it tells. "How we write is a reflection of our own interpretation based on the cultural, social, gender, class, and personal politics that we bring to research. All writing is 'positioned' and within a stance" (Creswell, 2013, p. 215). For social science research, the question "who is the researcher?" can be answered without recourse to the unconscious, soul, or psyche.

Though there appears to be agreement between Jungians and postmodernists, since both value subjectivity in research, depth psychology pushes subjectivity much further than a sociological-discursive understanding. "Inner experience is complex and many-sided and it is this fact, this truth that requires us to be objective about our subjectivity" (Hewison, 2010, p. 590). For Jungian researchers, self-reflexivity is an especially arduous undertaking because it involves the unfathomable psyche of the whole person and the nuanced ways in which body, mind, spirit, and soul underlie and inform the research process. Yet these are dimensions of experience many researchers, regardless of whether they are self-consciously postmodern, would deny or ignore. Jungian self-reflexivity also includes imaginative consideration of the forces that worked to bring the researcher here, now, to this topic, wherein he or she can say "my life and the world's life are deeply intertwined" (Abram, 1997, p. 33). We begin with the premise that our interest is not disinterested. It may be that our wounds have drawn us into the work, as Romanyshyn (2007) asserts. Or researchers may feel the presence of the daimon, mentioned earlier, that Hillman describes as "a spark of consciousness" which "has our interest at heart because it chose us for its reasons" (1996, p. 12). We might speak of Ananke, the goddess of necessity, or other fateful influences from our classical past. I have consistently found that my students are drawn to the topic through an activated archetypal image, and "the researcher's voice and the archetypal image work in tandem, each engendering the other. What emerges as the finished work is a collaboration of psyche and scholar that molds the text in deep and sometimes unnamable ways" (Nelson, 2013, p. 333).

These irrational ideas may be difficult to accept for the committed rationalist. Likewise, the deep interiority they affirm may be equally difficult for postmodernists to accept, because as pointed out earlier, postmodernism views subjectivity as socially produced and discursive, arising between persons. Regardless of how the experience is named by the researcher, acknowledging the wound, daimon, necessity, fate, or activated image transforms social science research into depth research. All of these names point toward and posit an enigmatic but ultimately creative Other in the process, a *psychopompos* "pregnant with significance and intention, a necessary angel as it appears here and now and which teaches the hand to represent it, the ear to hear, and the heart how to respond" (Hillman, 1983, p. 62).

The Jungian approach, which accounts for the nuanced relationship between researcher and topic, additionally offers valuable insights for working with participants in the study. When we turn the same complex eye and ear toward them, we listen differently. Of course, highly skilled interviewers in many social science disciplines note alterations in tone, cadence, or volume in the participants' speech, hesitations in response or complete silence, and expressive body language such as shifts in posture, surprising gestures, and changes in breathing, eye focus, or complexion. Jungian researchers wonder about them differently, which is a kind of wandering in a specific direction first suggested by Heraclitus: downward, into the depths, and back through the layers of culture sedimented in the psyche. There we recognize the shape of recurring human concerns: death, meaning the gods. Working with participants as well as with texts, Jungian researchers value "the imaginative possibilities in our natures, the experiencing through reflective speculation, dream, image, and fantasy – that mode which recognizes all realities as primarily symbolic or metaphorical" (Hillman, 1975, p. xvi). Our wondering, too, always rests on the first ontological commitment, to the unconscious or not-knowing. Depth psychological researchers must remain humble, not only because the production of any knowledge is always partial in a social-historical sense, but also because each human soul is fathomless, unknown to the person and unknown to another.

When research takes Jungians into the field, they have the opportunity to bring eye, ear, and nose for depth to the land and its inhabitants. Sensitivity to woundedness, so necessary in analytic work, can open the Jungian researcher to neglected wounds and the wound of neglect that are hiding in plain sight in our local communities. Here the heuristic value of the unconscious as not-knowing recurs. Researchers can ask, "What is the not-known, the not-seen, the not-felt in my own backyard?" Sensitivity to neglect can also lead researchers to the more-than-human world and its wounds. My students are frequently drawn toward ecology as a subject, and also as a perspective that "strives to enter, ever more deeply, into the sensorial present . . . to become ever more awake to the other lives, the other forms of sentience and sensibility that surround us in the open field of the present moment" (Abram, 1997, p. 272).

The open field is increasingly toxic. Many researchers are working to address the ecological crisis, aware of the urgency of the question posed by Rachel Carson in her chilling book *Silent Spring* more than 50 years ago (1962, p. 99): Can any civilization "wage relentless war on life without destroying itself, and without losing the right to be called civilized?" Twenty years later, Hillman argued that the breakdown of the world is the world seeking our attention. It appears as "pollution and street crime, the loss of literacy and the growth of junk, deceit and show. We now encounter pathology in the psyche of politics and medicine, in language and design, in the food we eat" (1982, p. 74). As I write this more than three decades after that, it is far worse, and I fully agree with Hillman that ignoring the sickness of the world is its own kind of pathology. In fact, David Tacey argues for holism in research because of the world's dire need:

> An ecological emergency is upon us and this has placed the function of knowledge in a different light. Knowledge which continues to fragment the world, to separate humanity from nature, to split spirit from earth and mind from body, is being viewed with a new kind of suspicion, the like of which we have not seen before.
>
> *(2012, p. 18)*

Tacey calls for "large theories" to comprehend the profound interrelatedness of the world (2012, p. 18). On the one hand, this may sound anything but postmodern – too like the grand narratives that postmodernism rejects. On the other hand, research that can begin to grasp the complexity of the world's wounds must foster discourse among disciplines to overcome the fragmentation and splitting Tacey describes. Isn't this what postmodernism values?

Theoretical pluralism

There is a world of difference between fragmentation and differentiation. The discourse so prized among postmodernists requires differentiation among theories so that each strand of the conversation is clearly perceived. Discourse is purposeful when each strand and the local, particular, subjective knowledge it represents is placed alongside the others, with an eye toward their intertextuality. More important, the multiplicity or plurality of discourse strands can only be produced by scholars committed to the truthfulness of their research process and faith in the value of its particular, local outcome. I agree with Hewison (2010) that "the lumping together of 'multiplicity' and 'pluralism' with 'the abandonment of a conception of truthfulness'" is a misreading of postmodernism. Postmodernists and Jungians, guided by the desire for truthfulness, value the "fragments of understanding" (Polkinghorne, 1992, p. 160) that emerge in the research process as building blocks – not scattered shards. Because they are united by the desire for holistic understanding, the best of them respect the fragments produced by good-willed researchers across diverse disciplines. "The ragged untidy process of groping for and sometimes grasping something of how the world is is not a male thing or a white thing, but a Human thing" (Haack quoted in Bell, 2009, p. 344).

Fostering multi-, inter-, and trans-disciplinary discourse is partly a matter of translation. Although many languages are spoken, researchers can seek common meanings and common values, which also implies holding substantial ideas a little loosely. For instance, David Bohm sounds quite postmodern when he asserts that "all theories are insights, which are neither true nor false but, rather, clear in certain domains, and unclear when extended beyond these domains" (1983, p. 3). The question remains if scholars are willing and able to articulate their own theories, as well as psychologize or "see through" them as Hillman (1975) advocates. A helpful approach is suggested by the etymology of the word *theory*, which is a cognate of *theater*, as Bohm, who was both a theoretical physicist and a philosopher, observes:

> In scientific research, a great deal of our thinking is in terms of theories. The word "theory" derives from the Greek "theoria," which has the same root as "theatre," in a word meaning "to view" or "to make a spectacle." Thus it might be said that theory is primarily a form of insight, i.e. a way of looking at the world, and not a form of knowledge of how the world is.
>
> *(1983, pp. 3–4)*

A theory presents something to us, gives us a view, and it is always a view from somewhere (Bell, 2009, p. 333). Thus, research demands a paradoxical combination of rootedness and flexibility. Can researchers remain sufficiently grounded in their knowledge, sufficiently self-reflexive about themselves and their theoretical position, to be fluid contributors to the larger discourse?

To become such a contributor, researchers must be willing to examine the health of their theories. When a theory is no longer one presentation but *the* presentation, it becomes tyrannical, like a king without his jester to point out the folly of a single position. Just as a king declines and grows decrepit, isolating himself to protect his frailty, so, too, do theories. This analogy is reminiscent of Hillman's point about ideas. He recalls the Greek word *eidos*, which "means originally that which one sees and that by which one sees" (1983, p. 36), then elsewhere says:

> Ideas decline for many reasons. They too grow old and hollow, become private and precious; or they may detach from life, no longer able to save its

phenomena. Or they may become monomaniac, one particular idea crediting itself with more value than all others, and in opposition to them.

(1975, p. 115)

Monomania is a continued temptation for the researcher, understandable when considering the sheer amount of time spent acquiring expertise. Then, the danger of erecting theory as a barricade against not knowing, against doubt, and against others who disagree is quite real. But as the Grail myth tells us, the possibility of rejuvenation is found by recognizing the deep relatedness of all things and the necessity of death in the full cycle of rebirth. "This has to happen for the eternally self-renewing psychic life to flow up from the depths and for its ungraspable, eternally fresh and unexpected aspects to be retained" (Jung & von Franz, 1970, p. 197). Luke describes the Grail itself as "the cup from which each individual life receives its essential food and drink," without which "all the 'ten thousand things' must exist in a state of unrelatedness to each other – a chaos without meaning" (1992, p. 73). Perhaps postmodern discourse might be reimagined as a vessel, one strong and capacious enough to overcome the unrelatedness of knowledge silos, since "without a vessel no transformation on any level can take place – no cooking of ingredients in a kitchen, no chemical experiments or alchemical search for 'gold,' no metanoia in a human soul" (p. 73). Moreover, in a world that is clearly ailing, the researcher may need to be a modern-day Parsifal who finally learns to ask the right question.

In conclusion: listening to psyche's own language

Jungian research can enhance postmodernist discourse by expanding the notion of what should be included in that discourse: the psyche. But this is only possible if social scientists are open to the discomforting co-existence of the rational with the irrational that includes the unfathomable, soulful interiority of all things. A recent trend in scholarship, the antinomial approach, may be very helpful. It "tends to erode the sedimented categories and oppositions" and instead reveals "the tensions and contradictions that have been hitherto unseen or, at best, perceived as marginal" (Saban, 2012, p. 24). Jung's psychology "insists upon the critical importance of precisely these antinomies" (p. 24). So does Jungian research. Noting the movements and manifestations of the psyche radically deepens our epistemology. It also shapes methodology primarily by prompting a number of key moves that researchers can adopt (Coppin & Nelson, 2017). In other words, if postmodernism rests on the idea that reality is constructed through language, let us bring in the spirit of the fathomless depths by adding soul to the conversation.

The psyche's own language, says Jung, is image (1931/1967b, p. 50 [para. 73]). Elsewhere he asserts that "the psyche consists essentially of images" (1928/1969b, p. 325, [para. 618]) that have far more vitality and autonomy than reified concepts: "Concepts are coined and negotiable values; but images are life" (1970, p. 180 [para. 226]). Vivid images have particular power, something like vivid characters in fiction.

Their effect is forceful, precise, and unmistakable. They possess self-coherence and integrity, which dissuade sloppy comprehension. The forcefulness is like that of a magnet, attracting to it only those associations that belong and repelling those which do not. Thus the image has the effect of focusing the mind.

In this context, it is helpful to remember that the Latin word for hearth means "focus," and that the deity of the hearth in the classical tradition is the goddess Hestia. In fact, she is not so much the one who presides over the hearth as she *is* the hearth, the focus, "the center that sustains the place of return" (Demetrakopoulos, 1979, p. 61). The influence of Hestia is the felt sense of quietness, no matter how noisy the environment. Some researchers, in fact, seek the ambient noise of a crowded café in part because they can better hear and feel the quiet of Hestian focus descend. (Yes, it is a cliché to say that quietness *descends*. The direction is meaningful.) It is as though Hestian focus comes more easily in an environment full of potential distractions. We could say that the journey of the researcher is guided by a search for the Hestian hearth, one's focus which becomes one's intellectual, spiritual, and soulful home for the duration of the project. Finding the central focus of the work is arduous, particularly in a world rich with distraction and all the "mod cons" (a phrase suggesting both convenience and trickery) that makes focusing on one thing at a time a commendable feat.

To conclude, I return to Jung: psyche is image and image is iconoclast, self-coherent yet always exceeding, on every side and in every way, anything we might say about it. Because the unconscious, the psyche, Psyche presents itself through the image, I offer an image of Jungian research in a postmodern milieu: the maypole dance.

Scholars disagree over the origins and meaning of the traditional maypole dance, although in northern Europe it seems a vestige of pre-Christian ritual practices and beliefs that may be associated to the world tree Yggdrasil from the Norse tradition and, more generally, the concept of the *axis mundi*. As a child, I did not know this. I only knew that sometime in the spring our schoolteachers would attempt to organize a group of 20 or so children around a tall, sturdy pole in the playground to enact the dance. The pole, about a foot thick and 12 feet tall, was capped with ribbons of every color, one for each child. With our assigned ribbon in hand, which tethered us to the pole, we walked as far from the base as the length of the ribbon-tether allowed until we formed a large circle. Every other child would face clockwise, her nearest neighbor facing counterclockwise. When the music began, we would move in "our" direction around the maypole, dancing around the children who moved toward us, in and out, in and out. As we circumambulated the pole, our ribbons created a beautiful multicolored wrapping from the top toward the base. The ribbons would slowly grow shorter, drawing us near each other until we stopped, grinning, clustered near the base of the pole in awe of its magical transformation.

The maypole is a fecund image of Jungian postmodern research, a way to imagine the dance of scholarship. If asked, *What is Jungian research like?* I can say, *It is like a maypole dance*. Here is what I mean. The maypole is like the central focus of the project, our "stake in the ground" around which scholars who share our interest organize themselves. It can become, for a period of time or an entire life, the *axis mundi*, a living entity that inexorably roots itself in the soul of the researcher. The maypole is like the research topic or question, standing in a particular place and time. It is not the only maypole. Others exist, and have existed, throughout centuries, and will exist in the future. The ribbons sprouting from the top of the maypole are like the variegated perspectives through which the topic can be approached – a notably apt image of postmodernism's discourse strands. Each dancer in the circle has a partial view of the pole, which is like the partial perspective of the researcher toward the topic. For maypole dancers, the ribbon is a tether. Thus, the way the dancer is tethered to the maypole is like the way the researcher is tethered to the topic. Holding the end of the ribbon-tether is like holding onto one's perspective, one's strand. Unless researchers do this, they cannot fulfill their unique portion of the work or realize its truthfulness. The distinctive color of the ribbon is like the distinctive view they bring to the topic. It is not accidental that we often describe our view of a situation, object, or question as "colored." Ultimately, the maypole dance is like Jungian research in a postmodern milieu because the weave of the differently colored perspectives around the topic makes the whole more complete and more beautiful. At the end of the dance, the physical proximity of the children is a hopeful image of the distance researchers have overcome between one another while circling around their topic. In the end, it is what may be possible when researchers from different disciplines dance together.

I arrive at the end of this essay and get up to pour a cup of coffee. Ruminating, it occurs to me that a wealth of images has appeared in the last few pages: ailing king and Grail legend, the quiet warmth of Hestia, and finally the maypole dance with its association to fertility rites, Yggdrasil, and the *axis mundi*. In deep discourse with this topic, and with Psyche, the images poured forth. I did not create them. I never do.

References

Abram, D. (1997). *The spell of the sensuous*. New York: Vintage.
Barthes, R. (1986). *The rustle of language* (R. Howard, Trans.). New York: Hill and Wang.
Bell, D. (2009). Is truth an illusion? Psychoanalysis and postmodernism. *International Journal of Psychoanalysis, 90*, 331–345. doi:10.1111/j.1745-8315.2009.00136.x
Bohm, D. (1983). *Wholeness and the implicate order*. London: Ark Paperbacks.
Calvin, W. (2004). *A brief history of the mind*. Oxford: Oxford University Press.
Carson, R. (1962). *Silent spring*. Boston: Houghton Mifflin.
Connor, S. (2006). Introduction. In *The Cambridge companion to postmodernism* (pp. 1–19). Cambridge: Cambridge University Press.
Connor, S. (2017). Epilogue: Modernism after postmodernism. In V. Sherry (Ed.), *The Cambridge history of modernism* (pp. 820–834). Cambridge: Cambridge University Press. doi:10.1017/9781139540902.050
Coppin, J., & Nelson, E. (2017). *The art of inquiry: A depth psychological perspective* (3rd expanded ed.). Woodstock, CT: Spring Publications.
Corbett, L. (1996). *The religious function of the psyche*. London: Routledge.

Creswell, J. (2013). *Qualitative inquiry and research design: Choosing among five approaches* (3rd ed.). Los Angeles, CA: Sage Publications.
Demetrakopoulos, S. (1979). Hestia, goddess of the hearth. *Spring Journal, 39*, 55–75.
Derrida, J. (1981). *Dissemination* (B. Johnson, Trans.). Chicago: University of Chicago Press.
Gergen, K. (1992). Toward a postmodern psychology. In S. Kvale (Ed.), *Psychology and postmodernism* (pp. 17–30). London: Sage Publications.
Hauke, C. (2000). *Jung and the postmodern: The interpretation of realities*. London: Routledge.
Hewison, D. (2010). Review of 'Is truth an illusion? Psychoanalysis and postmodernism'. *Journal of Analytical Psychology, 55*, 587–610.
Hillman, J. (1975). *Revisioning psychology*. New York: Harper Perennial.
Hillman, J. (1982). Anima mundi: The return of the soul to the world. *Spring*, 71–93.
Hillman, J. (1983). *Healing fiction*. Woodstock, CT: Spring Publications.
Jencks, C. (1996). *What is post-modernism?* (4th ed.). New York: St Martin's Press.
Jones, R. (2007). *Jung, psychology, postmodernity*. London: Routledge.
Jung, C.G. (1954). The development of personality. In R.F.C. Hull (Trans.), *The development of personality, the collected works of C.G. Jung* (2nd ed., Volume 17, pp. 167–186). Princeton, NJ: Princeton University Press. (Original work published 1934)
Jung, C.G. (1961). *Memories, dreams, reflections* (A. Jaffe, Ed.). New York: Pantheon.
Jung, C.G. (1966). The psychology of the transference. In R.F.C. Hull (Trans.), *The practice of psychotherapy, the collected works of C.G. Jung* (2nd ed., Volume 16, pp. 163–323). Princeton, NJ: Princeton University Press. (Original work published 1946)
Jung, C.G. (1967a). Two kinds of thinking. In R.F.C. Hull (Trans.), *The collected works of C.G. Jung* (2nd ed., Volume 17, pp. 7–33). Princeton, NJ: Princeton University Press. (Original work published 1912)
Jung, C.G. (1967b). Commentary on 'The secret of the golden flower'. In R.F.C. Hull (Trans.), *Alchemical studies, the collected works of C.G. Jung* (Volume 13, pp. 1–56). Princeton, NJ: Princeton University Press. (Original work published 1931)
Jung, C.G. (1969a). Psychotherapists or the clergy. In R.F.C. Hull (Trans.), *Psychology and religion: West and east, the collected works of C.G. Jung* (2nd ed., Volume 11, pp. 327–347). Princeton, NJ: Princeton University Press. (Original work published 1932)
Jung, C.G. (1969b). Spirit and life. In R.F.C. Hull (Trans.), *The structure and dynamics of the psyche, the collected works of C.G. Jung* (2nd ed., Volume 8, pp. 319–337). Princeton, NJ: Princeton University Press. (Original work published 1928)
Jung, C.G. (1969c). The structure of the psyche. In R.F.C. Hull (Trans.), *The structure and dynamics of the psyche, the collected works of C.G. Jung* (2nd ed., Volume 8, pp. 139–158). Princeton, NJ: Princeton University Press. (Original work published 1931)
Jung, C.G. (1969d). On the nature of the psyche. In R.F.C. Hull (Trans.), *The structure and dynamics of the psyche, the collected works of C.G. Jung* (2nd ed., Volume 8, pp. 159–234). Princeton, NJ: Princeton University Press. (Original work published 1954)
Jung, C.G. (1970). Mysterium coniunctionis. In R.F.C. Hull (Trans.), *The collected works of C.G. Jung* (2nd ed., Volume 14). Princeton, NJ: Princeton University Press.
Jung, C.G. (1975). *C.G. Jung: Letters, Volume 1* (G. Adler and A. Jaffe, Eds. and R.F.C. Hull, Trans.). Princeton, NJ: Princeton University Press.
Jung, C.G. (2009). *The red book* (S. Shamdasani, Ed.). New York: W.W. Norton and Co.
Jung, E., & von Franz, M.-L. (1970). *The Grail legend* (2nd ed., A. Dykes, Ed.). Princeton: Princeton University Press.
Kvale, S. (1992). Postmodern psychology: A contradiction in terms? In S. Kvale (Ed.), *Psychology and postmodernism* (pp. 31–37). London: Sage Publications.
Lockhart, R. (1983). *Words as eggs: Psyche in language and clinic*. Dallas: Spring Publications.

Luke, H. (1992). Dindrane. In *Kaleidoscope: 'The way of woman' and other essays* (pp. 73–89). New York: Parabola.

Miller, D. (1990). An other Jung and an other ... In K. Barnaby and P. D'Acierno (Eds.), *C. G. Jung and the humanities* (pp. 325–330). Princeton: Princeton University Press.

Nelson, E. (2013). Writing as method: Depth psychological research and archetypal voice. *International Journal of Multiple Research Approaches, 7, 3*, 330–342.

Palmer, R. (1969). *Hermeneutics*. Evanston, IL: Northwestern University Press.

Polkinghorne, D. (1992). Postmodern epistemology of practice. In S. Kvale (Ed.), *Psychology and postmodernism* (pp. 146–165). London: Sage Publications.

Richardson, L., & Adams St. Pierre, E. (2005). Writing: A method of inquiry. In N. Denzin and Y. Lincoln (Eds.), *Handbook of qualitative research* (3rd ed., pp. 959–978). Thousand Oaks, CA: Sage Publications.

Romanyshyn, R. (2007). *The wounded researcher: Doing research with soul in mind*. New Orleans, LA: Spring Journal Publications.

Saban, M. (2012). The dis/enchantment of C.G. Jung. *International Journal of Jungian Studies*, 4(1), 21–33, doi:10.1080/19409052.2012.642480

Tacey, D. (2012). *The Jung reader*. London: Routledge.

Turner, T. (1995). *City as landscape: A post post-modern view of design and planning*. London: Taylor and Francis.

Yalom, I. (1995). *Love's executioner and other tales of psychotherapy*. New York: Basic Books.

3

THE CORRESPONDENCES OF C. G. JUNG

A rich resource

Thomas B. Kirsch

C.G. Jung was born on July 26, 1875, and died on June 6, 1961. He lived at a time when letter writing was an important way of expressing one's most profound thoughts. It has been pointed out by Sonu Shamdasani that Jung's literary deposit includes many thousands of letters, most still unpublished. According to Aniela Jaffe, who served as Jung's secretary at the end of his life and who edited the German edition of his collected correspondence, the preservation of his letters began in earnest in the 1930s. By the late 1950s it was clear that Jung had a huge repository of this material. This chapter will highlight a selection of the immensely rich and intellectually valuable correspondence of C.G. Jung that is currently available in print and comment on its importance for future research in Analytical Psychology.

The Freud–Jung letters (1974) were the first of Jung's correspondences to be published, and this important exchange has been widely discussed and will not be a part of this chapter. In the late 1970s, a collection of Jung's letters to a number of correspondents was published both in German and English edited by Aniela Jaffe and Gerhard Adler in two volumes: *Volume 1, 1906–1950,* (Jung, 1973) *and Volume 2, 1950–1961* (Jung, 1975). However, in reading the collected letters one does not know the exact content to which Jung was responding as the correspondents' side of the exchanges was not included.

In recent years several correspondences of Jung's have been published, including those with Erich Neumann and James Kirsch, two Jewish students of his; Victor White, a Catholic priest; Wolfgang Pauli, a Nobel Prize-winning scientist; and Hans Schmid-Guisan, a colleague interested in psychological type theory. There will be more to come. These recent correspondences have both sides of the conversation which more clearly reveal Jung in a more personal light and at greater ease than in his previously published professional writing. We will now examine several correspondences that may be of particular interest to researchers within the Jungian community and others from different disciplines.

The Jung–Pauli correspondence: a dialogue between physics and Analytical Psychology

The first of these correspondences was between Jung and Wolfgang Pauli (Pauli Jung correspondence, 2001), who was not officially a patient but who sought out Jung for consultation. Jung and Pauli met in 1930 and their letters began at the end of 1932. At the time, Pauli was already a professor at the Eidgenossische Technische Hochschule (ETH), the Swiss equivalent of the great engineering schools in the United States like Massachusetts Institute of Technology (MIT) and California Institute of Technology (Caltech). He was a leading scientist in the emerging field of quantum mechanics for which he was to receive a Nobel Prize in 1946. He had already done the work that led to the Nobel Prize when he was appointed chair of theoretical physics at the ETH. Jung was also a professor at the ETH, so it was natural that Pauli would have known about him, though he was referred to Jung by his father. However, Jung did an unusual thing. Instead of seeing Pauli himself, he referred the physicist to Erna Rosenbaum – at the time a relative newcomer to Analytical Psychology. Jung wanted to reduce his own influence on the psychological process that was to follow. Pauli was a prolific dreamer and Erna Rosenbaum showed many of the dreams to Jung. This process continued for three months, at which time Jung himself took over the analysis, and for another two months Pauli and Jung worked together on Pauli's dreams.

Meanwhile, they began a correspondence comparing the results of quantum theory with Jung's psychology. On the surface one would not have thought there was much connection between the two subjects, but as the two men continued to explore topics in their correspondence, they found many areas of mutual interest. Of note is the following quote from Jung's essay "On the Nature of Psyche" in 1948:

> As the phenomenal world is an aggregate of the processes of atomic magnitude, it is naturally of the greatest importance to find out whether, and if so how, the photons (shall we say) enable us to gain a definite knowledge of the reality underlying the mediative energy processes . . . Light and matter both behave like separate particles and also like waves. This . . . obliged us to abandon, on the plane of atomic magnitudes a causal description of nature in the ordinary space-time system, and in its place to set up invisible fields of probability in multidimensional spaces.
>
> *(Jung, 1947, para. 438)*

This quote sounds very much like a theoretical physicist speaking, but it is Jung in his most mature essay on the nature of psychological experience in 1947.

Pauli gave Jung permission for Jung to use his dreams in demonstrating alchemical symbolism. This began with "Dream Symbolism in the Individuation Process" in 1936, and it culminated in the first volume of the collected works in English, *Psychology and Alchemy* in 1953 (Jung, 1953). There was not written documentation that these were Pauli's dreams, but it has become common knowledge over the years that they were in fact his.

One of the central areas of interest between the two men was that of synchronicity. Pauli was pursuing Jung's synchronicity thesis while Jung was fostering Pauli's understanding of archetypal and collective factors in the psyche. Both were interested in the notion of complementarity introduced by Niels Bohr, whose studies provided an understanding of the paradoxical relationship between waves and particles. It could also be applied to the relationship between the conscious and unconscious in psychology, and Pauli was most interested in that connection.

Their common interest in synchronistic phenomena led to the publication in 1952 of their joint volume, *The Interpretation of Nature and the Psyche*. Pauli's article was on "The Influence of Archetypal Ideas on the Scientific Theories of Johannes Kepler," a famous astronomer and philosopher of the 17th century. Jung's article "Synchronicity: An Acausal Connecting Principle" described in depth his notion of synchronicity. Jung had first publicly mentioned the concept of synchronicity in his memorial speech for Richard Wilhelm in 1930 and again in 1950 with his introduction to the *I Ching* (Jung, 1950/1969).

When the C.G. Jung Institute in Zürich was opened in 1948, Pauli was made a patron of the institute and became its scientific advisor. Pauli was not entirely pleased with the focus of the institute on training analysts, as he had hoped that a more scientific and academic approach to the psychology of the unconscious would ensue. He voiced his concerns to Professor C.A. Meier, the first president of the Jung Institute in Zürich, but it does not appear that Pauli's criticisms were taken seriously.

Pauli died at the relatively young age of 58 from cancer in 1958, and so we can only surmise what might have been the future relationship of Pauli to the Jung Institute. We are left with this correspondence between two of the greatest minds of the 20th century, attempting to form a unitary theory of both the psyche and physics. Most of the correspondence is quite abstract, and as a psychologist and medical person I find the terms from physics not easy to understand (a useful exploration of both the physics and psychology can be found in the volume by historian of science and psychotherapist Suzanne Geiser, *The Innermost Kernel* [2005]). With the original work of Jung and Pauli in the background, contemporary readers may be interested in the collaborative efforts between analytical psychologists and physicists evident in the recent research of Harald Atmanspacher published in the *Journal of Analytical Psychology* (see for example Atmanspacher, 2014).

The Jung–White correspondence: a dialogue on the psychology of religion

Another important correspondence was with Father Victor White, a Dominican priest and theologian who became Jung's most important theological conversation partner and friend near the end of both of their lives. Throughout his long career, Jung had carefully studied and written about the psychology of religion. Given this history, it is not surprising that Jung, even at age 70, was interested in engaging in a relationship with Father White of Oxford; their back-and-forth continued until Father White's death in 1960, a year before Jung's own. This correspondence had a special meaning for Jung, and the letters between the two were kept in a separate place to be watched over by Franz, Jung's only son. Although ambivalent about publishing the letters in their entirety or just those with general professional, scientific, and religious content, Franz Jung chose to include all, as they conveyed a riveting and meaningful human story and relationship.

Their communication actually began many years earlier, when White first wrote to Jung in August 1945 at the time international mail service was resumed after World War II. He enclosed four journal articles he had authored about a proposed synthesis of Jung's psychological work and his own reflections on Roman Catholicism. In these essays White explored key writings by Jung and criticized the work of fellow theologians who tried with mixed success to discuss the psychologies of Freud and Jung from varying standpoints. With different educational backgrounds and methodologies for approaching knowledge and belief, Jung and White struggled from the outset to find a common language to adequately represent their complex and individual viewpoints.

Jung was firmly committed to a theory of knowledge that arose from a neo-Kantian philosophy and viewed the soul (psyche) as the primary source of knowing. Jung always started from and returned to a conviction that the psyche is the only available lens through which images of reality are experienced and interpreted. In this theory, everything – even such unfathomable realities as the soul, nature, and God – is known subjectively, experientially, or as Jung liked to say, empirically. By contrast, White's theological method began with the Church's three classic sources of authority – revelation, tradition, and reason – to which White added "experience," an important fourth source of knowledge. "Experience" did not occupy the same place of importance for many of White's Dominican contemporaries, but it was a very important part of White's theology and the part which made him genuinely open to Jung's thought.

The beginnings of the Jung–White correspondence should be squarely placed within the post-war context, a time when they were struggling to come to terms with the impact of extreme suffering and the meaning of collective evil. They hoped to build a solid bridge between their divergent modes of thought but, unfortunately, that was not to be. Father White believed throughout that evil was the *privatio boni*, the absence of good. For Jung, evil was a reality unto itself and was not just an absence of good. The two men argued about their relative interpretations of evil and were never able to find a middle ground upon which they could both agree. In 1955, after Jung's publication of *Answer to Job* (1952) and *Aion* (1951), Father White wrote a blistering attack on *Answer to Job* (Lammers & Cunningham, 2007, appendix 6). That could well have been the end of the correspondence between them; however, after a period of silence Jung and White resumed their conversation, but the intensity never reached what it had been prior to the confrontational dialogue on the meaning of evil. To their credit, these two older sparring partners from divergent backgrounds and traditions found some degree of reparation, perhaps more than Jung ever found with his father or Yahweh.

With this historical relationship in mind and from Jung's own theories about the tension of opposites and the emergent transcendent third, we might remember the value of attempting to understand and empathize with perspectives of other professionals researching and writing about common topics. It can be all too easy to split from the "otherness" of the "other" and lose opportunities for expanding knowledge across disciplines, cultures, languages, and so forth. Jung's amazing capacity to engage in dialogue with Father White along with many divergent individuals and collectives may serve as a model for remaining open not only to influencing but to being influenced; it is out of such intense involvement and availability that new and creative possibilities come into being. Symmetry is essential for stability and asymmetry is necessary for change and growth.

Jung–Kirsch correspondence: the Jewish question?

In this next section, I will reflect on my father James Kirsch's correspondence with Jung. This correspondence includes 44 letters that for many years were stowed in Jung's closet. In 2005, I learned that these same letters were being housed by the Jung archive in Zurich. Some had been translated into English and were published in *Jung's Collected Letters* (1973) and in *Psychological Perspectives*. The letters were eventually translated from their original German into English and published as the *Jung–Kirsch Letters: The Correspondence of C.G. Jung and James Kirsch* in 2011, edited by Ann Lammers; a second edition with added material was published in 2016. I refer the reader to either edition for the details of my father's biography, and will here focus on the relevance of their correspondence in relation to the others described in this chapter. (Hereinafter I will refer to my father as Kirsch.)

Raised as an Orthodox Jew, Kirsch was a psychiatrist living in Weimar Germany during the 1920s, a time of great economic and social change. In the fall of 1928, he wrote a letter of inquiry to Jung and proceeded to Zurich in May of 1929, where he spent two months in analysis with Jung and Toni Wolff. Not long after, in 1930, Kirsch was invited by the Analytical Psychology Club in Zurich to offer a lecture on the dreams of his Jewish patients. This began a correspondence which lasted for 33 years, with some interruptions, particularly during the war, until Jung's death in 1961. Clearly, Kirsch was drawn to Jung's methods and thought, and while still in Berlin he was part of a German Jewish intellectual group including Erich Neumann, Heinz Westmann, Werner Engel, and Gerhard Adler – all future Jungian analysts who were forced to leave before the Nazis assumed power in 1933.

In the Jung–Kirsch correspondence, readers can find numerous discussions regarding the differences between Judaism and Christianity, including elaborations on the "Christ complex" along with Kirsch's explication of his own Jewish perspectives and beliefs. (Resonances can be found in the Jung–Neumann letters, which will be described later in this chapter.) I underscore the Jewish–Christian dialogue as a way to clarify Jung's actual opinions regarding "Jewish psychology" with the hope that readers can assess for themselves accusations of anti-Semitism that have persisted for decades – I think unfairly so. It is this ongoing controversy that motivated the publication of the book.

Some of the allegations revolve around Jung's decision to accept the presidency of the General Medical Psychotherapy Association in 1933. Unfortunately, what may not be well known is that Jung moved forward with this position with a great deal of reflection and two stipulations: first, that the organization become international and include a number of national groups; second, that German Jewish members could remain as individual members of the international organization. By this time, the national German organization had become completely Nazified and was under the direction of Dr. Matthius Goering, a distant cousin of the future air marshal Hermann Goering; Jewish members were no longer eligible as members of the national association. Matthius Goering was a psychiatrist and became the head of the Goering Institute, the primary center for psychotherapy training during the Nazi regime. Jung's position as president of the International General Medical Psychotherapy Association has had long-term damaging effects on his reputation, even though this move was an attempt to keep the door open for Jews to maintain some kind of membership.

In a lecture entitled "The State of Psychotherapy Today" delivered in 1934, Jung described the differences between Aryan, Jewish, and Chinese psychologies (Jung, 1970). Unfortunately, some of the language that he used was similar to the language of Nazi propaganda which espoused that Jews were parasites of host cultures, not capable of producing one of their own. Jung's ideas about the dependent nature of the Jewish people in some ways resonated with what the Nazis were putting forward and consequently resulted in strong reactions from James Kirsch and Erich Neumann. Kirsch, who was by then living in Palestine, took it upon himself to write to Jung about his mentor's opinions about Jews and Judaism that were entering public and private conversations. Jung completely denied any anti-Semitism and explained that his views were grounded in the ongoing relationships with and observations of his many Jewish patients and colleagues. The reader can find a detailed, nuanced dialogue between Jung and Kirsch about this controversial area in the published correspondence. It should be emphasized that these letters, in particular, motivated me to push forward with putting this material into the public domain. *One hears directly from Jung speaking to a Jewish colleague in Palestine about his assessment of the Jewish psyche in 1934.* By today's standards, Jung's comments would be seen as racist, even though Jung himself believed that he was not at all anti-Semitic. Certainly, many of the things that Jung has been accused of such as meetings with Hitler, going to Hitler parades, and supporting Nazism are false; there is just no evidence for any of these defamatory rumors. The letters written to Kirsch document Jung's actual words and ideas and provide primary source material for those interested – whether they be researchers, analysts, or historians – to formulate their own judgements based on *what he actually said* during this tumultuous period in history.

When the horrors of the Nazi regime ended, Jung apparently had come to regret what he had written about the Jewish situation in the 1930s, as evidenced by his immediate apology to Kirsch upon his first post-war visit to Zurich. The reader will see that the letters in the first half of the book revolve around questions of Jews and Judaism, Christianity, and the culture of the time. Following the war, Jung and Kirsch continued their complex relationship through mail and trips to Switzerland from Los Angeles, where Kirsch and his family now lived. The thread of their abiding shared interests in theology and religion runs through the second half of the book, but over the years they opened new territory with exploration of other areas such as clinical supervision, personal analysis, the opening of Jungian training programs, theoretical questions, and synchronicity.

The correspondence first came out in 2011, then in German in 2014, followed by an updated English edition in 2016. Added to the 2016 volume is the lecture that James presented to the Analytical Psychology Club in 1930 (described earlier), along with an additional letter from Aniela Jaffe on May 27, 1961, just ten days before Jung's death. She informs my parents that Jung had suffered a stroke and had spoken in several languages but was no longer coherent. Not much is known about Jung's final illness, so this letter is an interesting document historically. The second edition is in paperback and hopefully it will spark additional interest in Jung's life.

This book is, in essence, a firsthand account of Jung's complex and, at times, conflicted thoughts about Jews, Judaism, and collective cultures as they evolved over time within the context of a long-term relationship with a worthy intellectual companion and sometimes challenger. Intellectual and cultural historians mine unpublished memoirs, correspondences, and diaries rather than focusing only on well-known chronological, linear documentation of wars, battles, and elections as a method of comprehending the past and how it relates to the present and future. (See Andrew Samuels's *The Political Psyche* [1993] for a critical review of Jung's attempts to develop a collective, cultural psychology.) The Jung–Kirsch letters would be a good fit for those interested in psychoanalytic history to find firm ground in what Jung actually said and believed prior to and following World War II, rather than relying on hearsay from those who did not know Jung, have not read his work, and have only been exposed to extreme reactive positions.

The reader has the opportunity to formulate his/her own assessment of Jung's possible racism and anti-Semitism. Finally, there can be a move from accepted, biased, collective belief to the opportunity for a differentiated, individual evaluation. By reading the letters, perhaps contemporary practitioners can see beyond long-standing and often inaccurate accusations and open up to his prescient clinical and theoretical writings. For example, Jung's experiences within himself and with patients led to profoundly important discoveries regarding the mutual influence between doctor and patient and the dissociability of the psyche evident in complex theory (something that he encouraged students and researchers to pursue) along with his concept of the transcendent function, all of which resonate with now popular notions from the relational/intersubjective psychoanalysts who do not cite

Jung but believe that they have discovered a two-person psychology, the multiplicity of selves and the co-created third. Unfortunately, these remarkable correlations are not evident in the current psychoanalytic literature largely due to the stain on Jung's reputation dating back to the 1930s. This book gives hard evidence of Jung's vulnerability, mistakes, and biases, and of most importance, his willingness to engage at a deep level with a German Jewish man who fled from and survived the Holocaust.

Jung–Neumann correspondence: interpretation or orthodoxy

Erich Neumann was a member of the same Berlin Jewish intellectual circle that included James Kirsch in the 1930s, and like Kirsch, he fled the Nazis, immigrating to Palestine where he lived until his early death in 1960. Neumann and Kirsch had, what seems to have been, an ongoing conflicted relationship that revolved around competition for Jung's favor. Their 120 exchanges of letters began in 1933 and went through 1959.

As is evident in Neumann's letters to Jung, issues about orthodoxy were of great concern. Was there only one true interpretation of Jung's psychology, and one authorized group of interpreters? This was the essence of Neumann's question to Jung. In his reply, on August 12, 1934, Jung gave him the answer: "above all, be assured that there is no secret society of Jungian disciples – the Word has been freely given to all" (Jung & Neumann, 2015). In another letter dated February 19, 1935, the theme of orthodoxy again emerged seemingly stimulated by the rivalry between Neumann and Kirsch, the only Jungian analysts practicing in Tel Aviv at the time (Jung & Neumann, 2015).

In the early years of correspondence, Neumann attempted to involve Jung in conversation about interpretations of the Old Testament and various other Jewish texts. Neumann wrote long letters to Jung vigorously explaining his understanding of Jewish theology and psychology. However, the responses indicate that although Jung read the material respectfully, he did not engage at the deep level that Neumann might have hoped to have received. Neumann was also extremely disappointed in Jung following *Kristallnacht* in 1938; Jung made no comment on the event, and instead in a much later letter wrote to Neumann about his fascination with the spiritual exercises of Saint Ignatius of Loyola.

As with Kirsch, there was no correspondence between Jung and Neumann during World War II. It resumed immediately after the war, and a great deal of the renewed communication had to do with Jung's attempts to help Neumann find an appropriate publisher for his writing. An avenue for publication opened for Neumann through the Eranos conferences as Neumann became a regular, major speaker. As part of his yearly trips to the conferences each summer, Neumann would visit Zurich in order to meet with Jung and others in the inner circle, with whom he was not particularly popular. Even though the other followers were not so welcoming,

Jung always promoted Neumann and his work. Perhaps due to the gap caused by the war or to his own personal, religious, and cultural background, Neumann was developing theoretical ideas that were diverging from Jung's, unlike those of the inner circle in Zurich who were amplifying the master's original work. It was unclear to the Zurich analysts why Jung was spending so much time with Neumann but, in retrospect, it is possible that Jung was attracted to the brilliance of another individual capable of carrying Analytical Psychology forward in his own creative way.

Jung's relationship to Neumann was an extremely important one in the history of Analytical Psychology. Jung himself considered Neumann to be his intellectual and spiritual son, not unlike the Freud/Jung relationship. In the foreword to Neumann's *Origins and History of Consciousness* (1949/1954), Jung writes, "he arrives at conclusions that are among the most important ever to be reached in this field" (p. xiv). Jung also implies that if he were younger he would have taken the direction that Neumann has done in this major work. However, in the following statement to Kurt Eissler (1953), Jung reveals his ambivalence:

> I have a very talented student, Neumann, in ... Tel Aviv. He is truly a significant person! And, he took hold of some of my material and did something with it. You know, when one is overtaken in this manner, it is not easy for someone who has been in front.
>
> *(1953 interview in the Library of Congress; see http://freudarchives.org/jungintro.htm)*

One of Neumann's central theoretical concepts, centroversion, that is the coming together of introversion and extraversion, is not part of general Jungian theory today except in Israel where Neumann is studied intensely. However, another of his notions, the ego-self axis, which was also picked up by Edward Edinger, is more well-known as an intrapsychic amplification of Jung's model of the psyche (Edinger, 1972).

Neumann was a prolific writer and his books cover a number of areas in psychology and culture. Many of his works have remained unpublished but are now in the process of being published. There have been several recent conferences coming out of the Jung–Neumann correspondence, as well a book of essays about the importance of this exchange, *Turbulent Times, Creative Minds: Erich Neumann and C.G. Jung in Relationship (1933–1960)*, edited by Erel Shalit and Murray Stein. Hopefully there will be a renewal of interest in Neumann's work, because as Jung said, Neumann's work closely follows his own and deepens it.

Jung–Schmid-Guisan correspondence: psychological types

The final correspondence that I will discuss is that between Hans Schmid-Guisan and Jung. This short correspondence focuses on psychological type theory popularized during the last half century through the Myers-Briggs Type Indicator (MBTI), a questionnaire with widespread use in psychology, business, and organizations. The terms *extraversion* and *introversion* originating in type theory are part of common language around the world but are often not attributed to Jung.

Hans Schmid-Guisan was a Swiss doctor who became interested in Jung's psychology in 1912. He moved to Zürich, where he underwent a period of analysis and they developed a collegial relationship. Schmid-Guisan was an extravert and Jung was an introvert, and Jung thought it would be an important exercise to have a dialogue between the two of them. At the time, extraversion was connected with feeling and introversion was connected with thinking; the other two functions, sensation and intuition, had not yet been differentiated by Jung. The particulars of their articulated thoughts about extraversion and introversion make it difficult for the reader to follow their explorations. Originally, the editors of the Jung's *Collected Works* debated about whether or not to include the Jung–Schmid-Guisan documents within an appendix to *Psychological Types* (Jung, 1971), but ultimately Sir Herbert Read decided that the correspondence was too detailed and proceeded to publication without them.

The letters did not enter the public domain until 2013 under the co-editorship of John Beebe and Ernst Falzaeder, who translated them from German into English (Beebe & Falzaeder, 2013). Jung terminated the correspondence in 1916 and never resumed, as he seems to have lost interest. Jung and Schmid-Guisan continued their friendship until Schmid-Guisan's untimely death in 1932 from sepsis following a wound infection. Jung was deeply moved by the death of Schmid-Guisan and wrote a touching obituary of his friend.

Jung went on to use intuition and sensation as one axis for conceptualizing psychological types and thinking and feeling as a second axis once he separated these last two from introversion and extraversion. Jung lays out his understanding on psychological types in *CW 6* and that text has been used as a basic standard ever since. Others have worked on variations of Jung's original theory, including John Beebe, the co-editor of this correspondence. For those interested in the development of Jung's psychological type theory, this correspondence adds valuable details. For a rich complex reading and application of Jungian typology see the recently published text by Beebe: *Energies and Patterns in Psychological Type: The Reservoir of Consciousness* (2016).

Conclusion

This chapter attempts to briefly summarize recent publications of letters between Jung and a variety of intellectual partners, including a physicist, a Roman Catholic theologian, two German Jewish psychiatrists/analysts, and a Swiss doctor. Their conversations were wide-ranging and involved topics like quantum mechanics, theology, the nature of evil, typology, cultural issues, and psychological theory. Interested readers may also wish to consider a 1998 book by William Schoenl called *C. G. Jung: His Friendships with Mary Mellon and J.B. Priestley*, not summarized here. All of the books described offer portals of entry into Jung's personal and professional relationships in his own words. The letters are not formal papers; rather they convey Jung's thoughts and impressions as they were evolving in very human ways. His capacity to meet such extraordinary people of such divergent backgrounds and interests and engage with them in depth is quite remarkable. Intellectual and cultural historians will find a treasure trove of primary sources in these pages that will open the door to looking at the influences of personal interactions on theory making and the influences of theory on personal and professional interactions.

References

Atmanspacher, H. (2014). Psychophysical correlations, synchronicity and meaning. *Journal of Analytical Psychology, 59, 2,* 181–188.

Beebe, J. (2016). *Energies and patterns in psychological type: The reservoir of consciousness.* London and New York: Routledge.

Beebe, J., & Falzaeder, E. (Eds.). (2013). *The question of psychological types: The correspondence of C. G. Jung and Hans Schmid-Guisan, 1915–1916.* Princeton: Princeton University Press.

Edinger, E. (1972). *Ego and archetype: Individuation and the religious function of the psyche.* New York: Putnam for the C.G. Jung Foundation for Analytical Psychology.

Eissler, K. (1953). Retrieved from http://freudarchives.org/jungintro.htm

Freud, S., & Jung, C.G. (1974). *The Freud/Jung letters: The correspondence between Sigmund Freud and C. G. Jung* (William McGuire, Ed.). Princeton, NJ: Princeton University Press.

Geiser, S. (2005). *The innermost kernel.* Berlin, Heidelberg and New York: Springer.

Jung, C.G. (1934/1966). The state of psychotherapy today. In *The practice of psychotherapy, collected works 16.* Princeton: Princeton University Press.

Jung, C.G. (1947/1954/1969). On the nature of the psyche. In *The structure and dynamics of the psyche, collected works 8.* Princeton: Princeton University Press.

Jung, C.G. (1950/1969). Foreword to the 'I Ching'. In *Psychology and religion: West and east, collected works 11.* Princeton: Princeton University Press.

Jung, C.G. (1951/1959). *Aion: Researches into the phenomenology of the self, collected works 9ii.* Princeton: Princeton University Press.

Jung, C.G. (1952/1969). Answer to Job. In *Psychology and religion: West and east, collected works 11.* Princeton: Princeton University Press.

Jung, C.G. (1953/1968). *Psychology and alchemy, collected works 12.* Princeton: Princeton University Press.

Jung, C.G. (1966). Richard Wilhelm: In memoriam. In *The spirit in man, art, and literature, collected works 15.* Princeton: Princeton University Press.

Jung, C.G. (1970). *Civilization in transition, collected works 10* (2nd ed.). Princeton: Princeton University Press.

Jung, C.G. (1971). *Psychological types, collected works 6.* Princeton: Princeton University Press.

Jung, C.G. (1973). *Letters, Volume I. 1906–1950* (G. Adler in collaboration with A. Jaffé, Eds. and R.F.C. Hull, Trans.). Bolingen Series XCV. Princeton, NJ: Princeton University Press.

Jung, C.G. (1975). *Letters, Volume 2: 1951–1961* (G. Adler in collaboration with A. Jaffé, Eds. and R.F.C. Hull, Trans.). Bolingen Series XCV. Princeton, NJ: Princeton University Press.

Jung, C.G., & Kirsch, J. (2011). *Letters.* (2nd ed., 2016, A. C. Lammers, Ed.).

Jung, C.G., & Neumann, E. (2015). *Analytical psychology in exile* (M. Liebscher, Ed. and Trans.). Princeton: Princeton University Press.

Jung, C.G., & Pauli, W. (1955). *The interpretation of nature and the psyche.* New York: Pantheon Books.

Jung, C.G., & Pauli, W. (2001). *Atom and archetype: The Pauli/Jung letters, 1932–1958* (C.A. Meier and C. Paul Enz, Eds.). Princeton: Princeton University Press.

Lammers, A., & Cunningham, A. (Eds.). (2007). *The Jung – White letters*. London and New York: Routledge.

Neumann, E. (1954). *The origins and history of consciousness*. Princeton: Princeton University Press.

Samuels, A. (1993). *The political psyche*. London and New York: Routledge.

Schoenl, W. (1998). *C.G. Jung: His friendships with Mary Mellon and J.B. Priestley*. Asheville, NC: Chiron Publications.

Shalit, E., & Stein, M. (Eds.). (2016). *Turbulent times, creative minds: Erich Neumann and C.G. Jung in relationship (1933–1960)*. Asheville, NC: Chiron Publications.

PART III
Research on symbolic aspects of the psyche

# 4

SOME REMARKS CONCERNING ARCHETYPAL THEORY AND ITS EPISTEMOLOGY[1]

François Martin-Vallas

Translated from French by Ann Kutek

The concept of the collective unconscious and its resultant archetypal theory is a core tenet in Analytical Psychology. It has become widely embedded in Western culture and the concept of "archetypes" is extensively used throughout the culture, in the social sciences, in art history and interpretation, and cultural analyses, as well as in literature and philosophy. This chapter will first examine the development of the concept of the collective unconscious and archetypal theory from its intellectual origins, and then explore the underpinnings of these concepts from the perspective of complex systems theory. We begin by examining the intellectual and philosophical underpinnings that led to the formation of the notion of the collective unconscious and the ongoing development of archetypal theory to support it.

Ever since Jung formulated his notion of a psychic structure common to all of mankind, it has been met with trenchant attacks from many quarters, and the more he tried to describe what he had in mind, the more such frankly frenzied criticism intensified and persists to this day (e.g., Le Quellec [2013]).[2] Some of our contemporary colleagues have returned to this basic aspect of Analytical Psychology, especially Jean Knox (2003) in the United Kingdom and George Hogenson (2004, 2009) in the United States, followed more recently by Christian Roesler (2012) in Germany and my own contributions (Martin-Vallas, 2005a, 2005b, 2009a, 2013, 2015) in France.

The response to various criticisms and the need to reformulate the archetypal hypothesis is a challenging undertaking and, not surprisingly, rather more complicated than it may at first appear, since in setting out to redefine the archetype in terms of complexity theory one is immediately confronted by the whole edifice of Analytical Psychology, and in particular by the model of epistemology upon which the theory is predicated. For this reason, the task of the present chapter is to revisit the principal aspects of Jung's epistemological reflections and to have such a reading informed by recent developments in complex epistemology along with observations from chaos theory. The update I am proposing here is enabled by the work of the French thinker Edgar Morin (1990) and has been previously applied in the fields of social science and psychology by a number of other authors (Butz, 1997; Kiel & Elliott, 1997; Blackerby, 1998; Chamberlain & Butz, 1998; Stern & Garene, 2003; Gottman, Murray, Swanson, Tyson, & Swanson, 2003; Leffert, 2010).

Epistemological basis of the ideas forming archetypal theory

The British analytical psychologist Ann Addison (2009) has noted that even before embarking on his psychiatric training, Jung had been markedly influenced by the vitalist movement, which presupposes there is only one source of energy that animates the body and the soul, that is a belief that opposes Cartesian dualism with its sharp distinction between matter and psyche. Against this background and thus influenced, Jung went on to adopt Driesch's concept of the *psychoid*[3] and applied it to his burgeoning theory in a modified form (linked to his theory of complexes). I can easily embrace Jung's idea of the psychoid; moreover, it appears to me that from the standpoint of his use of epistemology Jung very quickly parted from classic vitalism. This occurred in two steps, first by introducing a theory of complexes, then by developing from this his theory of archetypes. He did not return to the psychoid till much later, and then from a quite different angle, in the context of his idea of synchronicity (Jung, 1952) with a significantly altered definition of the psychoid than had been assumed until then.

When the newly qualified Jung arrived at the Burgholzli Hospital, the medical superintendent Eugen Bleuler set him to work on his Word Association Test and encouraged him to conduct research into its applications. The test as conceived by Francis Galton (1883) and practiced by Bleuler relied simply on thought associations arising from trigger words. However, Jung, encouraged by his cousin Franz Riklin, had an idea which was to give the test a new dimension: he introduced the measurement of potential physiological changes, mainly the respiration rate and the galvanic skin response. This allowed him to demonstrate that some trigger words could give rise to neuro-vegetative effects in given subjects, which he interpreted as evidence of heightened affect.[4] Thus he became arguably a precursor of modern experimental cognitive science. In fact, the clinical world of his time did not demur, and he rapidly acquired a far-reaching international reputation.

This was only the beginning of his research, no less his theoretical explorations. Thus, it must have been that he constructed his concept of the psycho-affective complex while still in the wake of the vitalist movement, but with the difference that he brought in a new, more nuanced vision of the connections between body and spirit. It was also from this same platform that he sought out Freud, particularly the Freud whose concept of the libido was also firmly anchored in the biological sphere. Even though Jung was a psychiatrist while Freud was a neurologist, neither was fundamentally going to be easily satisfied with a simplistic or even hierarchical vision of the relationship between body and soul, such that the body was merely the housing for the spirit any more than that the psyche was conversely but a secretion of the brain. Their research led each, on his own account and in his own way, to put forward an innovative vision of that relationship, to draw up a narrow formulation of both spheres, body and psyche, where neither aspect would lose its heterogeneity. As will be shown in this chapter, the aim for each of these two men was to discern a basis for an unconscious formulated in terms of complex theory in the current sense of the term.

Those word association experiments, backed up by physiological measurements, led Jung to hypothesize the existence of complexes not merely confined to the individual. In fact, he published an article on family complexes (Jung, 1909), which might easily have led him to speak of a familial or group unconscious had that become the object of his research. Indeed, in a rare gesture from the psychoanalytic side, one of the pioneers of Family Therapy recognizes the debt they owe C.G. Jung as their precursor in the field (Skynner, 1976). What preoccupied him, however, is the nature of the libido and the origin of the incest taboo, questions which filled his discussions with Freud and which ultimately caused the two men to go their separate ways.

The nature of the libido: a reframed definition of psychic energy and the incest taboo

In light of the profound bearing the question of the nature of psychic energy had on the historic development of psychoanalysis on the one hand and of Analytical Psychology on the other, it is essential to dwell on it here. Given that the postulates put forward by Jung were quite different from those proposed by Freud, their theoretical constructs represent quite divergent epistemologies.

At the time of his exchanges with Jung, Freud's assumptions concerning the psychic structuration were as follows: by imposing the incest taboo, the father declares his intention of reserving for himself exclusive sexual rights to his partner, the mother. An incest anxiety ensues: it is the result of a fear/threat of punishment by the father (castration and/or killing of the son). This position is necessarily connected with the idea of sexual libido, since the son must at some level have experienced a prior sexual desire toward his mother for his father to have imposed upon it a prohibition in his attempt to set the boundaries of the child's psychic organization. Freud therefore appears to have had in mind an apparently linear chain of causality, such that:

- The son has sexual desires toward his mother
- The father prohibits the son from having sexual access to his wife
- The son fears his father's wrath
- The fear imposes a horror of incest.

For Jung, primacy has to be given to the horror of incest (Chatillon, 2010), while incestuous desire – at that developmental stage – as expressed on the eve of the break with Freud, can be seen as the desire for "*a deep personal longing for quiet and for the profound peace of non-existence*" (Jung, 1912, p. 390, 1956, para. 253), in other words, experienced as a desire for death.[5] In Jung's terms, therefore, the libido has no need to be exclusively sexual in nature, and thus his method of reasoning becomes radically different from Freud's, since what the latter deems to be a consequence ranks as the beginning for Jung. One concludes thus that what counts most for Freud are internalized environmental factors, in this instance the father, while for Jung the determinants are primarily of an intra-psychic order. Moreover, it is striking that in Freud's conception the libido is oriented from the start toward an external object – a drive to life. This is in marked contrast to Jung's idea of an initial orientation toward disappearance, a death contrary impulse: a fear of death which speaks of a desire for life, an urge compatible with dying,[6] as depicted in a multitude of resurrection myths to which Jung refers.

One could be forgiven for thinking that two positions so radically opposed from the very beginning would result in two radically different proposals for a potential psychic structure. In fact, this is not the case. A Jungian perspective indicates that, on account of the fear projected onto the father, one would be led rapidly to a causal chain, exactly as that described by Freud. In both instances the presence of the father gives rise to a triangular relationship, and his absence leaves the child to face alone the experience of a terrorizing mother. However, the fundamental difference between the two conceptions is on one hand Jung's intra-psychic, or on the other Freud's[7] environmental origin to the structuring of the psychic apparatus as well as of the family itself. I would venture that here lie – long before he clarified them – the premises for a concept of the archetype as an intra-psychic organizer of the human soul. Here also Jung's theory becomes complex in the sense of complexity theory we will develop further on.

This fundamental divergence between Freud and Jung about the origin of the horror of incest would seem to consist of a divergence of epistemological premises. From a classical viewpoint, this would imply a necessary incompatibility between two theories so constructed. Yet this was not how Jung saw it. Instead, throughout his professional life he never ceased to assert that Freud's contribution should not be ignored.

Some elements of Jung's epistemology

On numerous occasions Jung, who specifically did not consider himself a philosopher, refers explicitly to Immanuel Kant and his notion of the principle of *a priori*, which is one of the tenets in the organization of his theory of knowledge. It is anyway a pillar of his concept of the archetype and underscores his use of the term "transcendental,"[8] which for him as it does for Kant denotes that which cannot be represented in the mind.[9]

Yet when it comes to the archetype, Jung was not confined by the Kantian notion of *a priori*. As shown by Jean Knox (2003, p. 29), he developed different models of the archetype, more or less (in)compatible with each other. To borrow Knox's fourfold classification, here are her principal models of the archetype:

- Biological entities in the form of information which is hardwired in the genes, providing a set of instructions to the mind as well as the body;
- Organizing mental frameworks of an abstract nature, a set of rules or instructions but with no symbolic or representational content, so that they are never directly experienced;
- Core meanings which do contain representational content and which therefore provide a central symbolic significance to our experience;
- Metaphysical entities which are eternal and therefore independent of the body.

It might likely be deduced from these four models that Jung is inconsistent in his theorizing, since only the first two models of the archetype are compatible with the Kantian idea of *a priori*, whereas the third one excludes it, while the fourth would vitiate any assertions by Jung concerning metaphysics, in that it has no place in his research.

Furthermore, Knox's third definition frequently appears in Jung's work. The fourth is debatable. In fact, Knox relies on Jung's elaboration of his ideas about synchronicity and, more particularly, the notion of the psychoid which he develops in 1952. In this regard, I would suggest Jung is quite clear: he postulates the psychoid as a logical concept and certainly not as a metaphysical reality. Moreover, following Jung's train of thought, the psychoid organizes matter as it does the psyche, and I do not share Knox's assertion that it would be independent of biology, hence of the body.[10] I am minded therefore to reformulate Knox's fourth model of the archetype thus:

- A concept in logic necessary to facilitate thinking about the relations between psyche and soma.

However, the reformulation I am proposing of Knox's model still does not answer the difficulty posed by the contradictions that exist between the different uses of the archetype that Jung makes. Indeed, Knox's approach becomes even more complicated when one considers that Jung often contrasts instinct with the archetype, while at the same time with comparable frequency using instinct as one of the poles of the archetypal continuum, with spirituality as its polar opposite. Finally, another contradiction emerges in Jung's approach to the idea of archetypal creativity, which he counterbalances with archetypal destructiveness, such that the polarization of creativity and destructiveness becomes itself an inherent part of archetypal dynamism, while in other passages this dynamism is either linked to the self or to attributes predicated in the operation of the transcendent function.

Gathered together, these formulations amount to a very diverse collection of ideas that might seem either alien to one another or just simply contradictory. On that basis, one is tempted to discard entirely the notion of archetype or to try to redefine it as Knox has done. And yet, without in the least disparaging Knox's initiative – specifically her remarkable work in linking archetypal theory with contemporary findings in developmental psychology – it strikes me that a third way might be possible. This involves not yet another redefinition of the archetype as a concept, but inquiring into its potential epistemological roots.

What I shall endeavor to do is to show that this incoherence can be seen as inherent in the elusive object of Jung's research and is not necessarily an insufficiency in his thought. In other words, the object of research, "the human psyche," could be in its ontological reality heterogeneous in nature, not fully recognizable as itself according to the part of it being examined or according to the method used in the study. What would seem pertinent here is a property of complex systems: the break in symmetry. An idea now accepted by many researchers, Edgar Morin (1990) among them, is that the human mind is itself a complex system. To help understand what I am suggesting, it is appropriate to develop here certain aspects of complex systems. The hypothesis I am developing also complements the work of Hogenson (2001) on the theme of Darwinian theory as reformulated by Baldwin – that is, taking into account cultural factors so intimately linked with adaptation in evolutionary selection. Thus in the case of Baldwin, Darwin's natural selection has become a cultural as much as a natural selection, operating conjointly and interactively according to the behavior of a complex system. Therefore, the transmission of acquired characteristics (Lamarck, 1809) would take place within Darwinian theory, according to a simultaneous cultural transmission.

The idea of emergence and complex systems: inklings of a new epistemology

The idea of emergence[11]

Emergence refers to the appearance of new properties in a system as a result of its evolution, such that these properties could not have been deduced from the previous properties of the system. One example of emergence is carbon crystal (the diamond), a pertinent example since Jung refers to it as a metaphor to talk about the archetype. What is captivating in this example is the extreme dependence on environmental conditions during the formation of the diamond out of carbon.

It is worth noting that the idea of emergence in no way contains any magical idea of a creation *ex nihilo*, even when the emergent properties of a system were neither present nor predictable prior to their appearance. Obviously, the idea of emergence is by definition different from the idea of structure: the emergence of a new structure is triggered by the inherent organization of the system; the structure is not itself a condition of the emergence, but its result.

Complex systems in physics[12]

A complex system is a physical system whose dynamic is, in certain states, non-linear. Take the flow of a river through a city, where it is banked on either side.

When properly dredged, its flow is generally tranquil, so that an object floating on its surface advances more or less at an even and predictable rate with the flow. When the flow encounters the pillar of a bridge, then the trajectory of floating objects becomes problematic, with some on the right bank finally taking a leftward route while others spin on themselves before going off again in a different direction before passing the obstacle, and so on. So whereas before the bridge the direction of the flow was largely linear, when approaching the obstacle presented by the pillar, the flow becomes turbulent and non-linear.

This set of behaviors signifies the appearance of specific attributes common to complex systems:

- *The sensitivity to initial conditions* makes these systems unpredictable; the margin of error inherent in all physical measurement prevents any long-term predictions. Its unpredictability is a function of the state of the system and is called a horizon: right up to the horizon, the system is predictable; beyond it, it no longer is. This horizon and its vagaries, according to the state of the system, impacts on our daily lives through weather forecasts, at times incredibly precise over a few days, and at times utterly wrong within hours. There is an obvious analogy to be made with the human psyche, each one of us being to an extent predictable or not according to our psychological state.
- *The break in symmetry* characteristic of these systems means that to study a part of the system tells us nothing about it globally. To know a person in one set of circumstances only rarely allows one to get to know them, as they may reveal themselves to be quite different in changed circumstances.

Other essential characteristics are also deducible:

- *Complex systems are self-organizing,* as a result of the many interactions and retroactions of its constituents. Each level of self-organization calls forth a higher level of emergence, and thereby a collection of new attributes emerges. The same applies to interactions between complex systems, which implies:
- *The boundaries of a complex system are hazy and indefinable in a very precise way.* Just as a complex system is most often made up of sub-systems, either simple or complex, so two or more complex systems interacting with one another create a new emergent complex system, whose attributes may be quite different from the two original constituents. The haziness of the boundaries is one of the reasons I was motivated to develop the idea of a transferential chimera (Martin-Vallas, 1998, 2006, 2008, 2009b, 2015). I was struck by the extent in the analytic situation to which it is often impossible to tell whether what arises in the consciousness of one or other of the protagonists really belongs to one or the other or is the product of the analytic constellation itself. The transference in the sense that Jung (1946) developed it suggests it is the outcome of a partial erasure of the boundaries between analysand and analyst. The French psychoanalyst Michel de M'Uzan (1976) has also developed the idea of a chimera in the analytic situation. Among analytical psychologists, George Bright

(1997) with his use of the notion of synchronicity, Joseph Cambray (2006) with his idea of co-construction developed by the Boston Change Process Study Group (2004), Jan Wiener (2009) with her concept of the transference matrix, and recently Richard Carvalho (2014) noting unexpected physiological phenomena occurring synchronistically in the analyst and the patient, have all arrived at similar conclusions.

- *A complex system is by nature robust*, regardless of its initial conditions and the haziness of its boundaries. The quantity of interactions and retrospective effects at its center make it improbable that it would dissolve under the effects of its interactions with its environment. Clinically speaking, it is known that the risk of psychological breakdown is greater among rigid personalities, which seems to have a kind of linear dynamic than among those deemed to be apparently less stable, who seem to have a chaotic dynamic.

The psyche as a complex system

From the foregoing arguments, it would seem the human psyche can and should be considered as a complex system. Besides its unpredictability and non-replicability, it manifests all the attributes characteristic of such systems. When it comes to the notion of archetype, what is of obvious interest is the quality of auto-organization, as well as the phenomena of emergence which are likely to appear at different levels of its processes.

The idea of the strange attractor

What we call attractor in the field of dynamic systems are portions of phase space[13] or sometimes real space,[14] such that it is a set of numerical values toward which a system tends to evolve for a wide variety of starting conditions of the system (and, if system values get close enough to the attractor values, they remain close even when slightly disturbed, hence the notion of attractor). The attractor will be termed "strange" if the determined space is other than a point, a circle, a sphere, and so forth – that is, a figure of whole dimension (which suggests a periodic movement). In contrast, strange attractors are fractal figures, otherwise figures that appear as identical to one another on different observational scales and which are not of whole dimension.[15]

The strange attractor and auto-organization

From the fact that the strange attractor attracts the dynamic of the complex system into a certain portion of phase space, it is intimately linked to the auto-organizing capacities of the systems. Where a system responds to the laws of chance, it is liable to have all possible destinations, a complex system is greatly limited as to its evolution, by the alternatives open to the strange attractors which govern its dynamic. This is how it becomes capable of auto-organization, and therefore to become complex. The auto-organization is also the basis of the emergence of new attributes.

The auto-organizing property of complex systems can thus be expressed in the numerical values of the strange attractors, and in the biological sphere it is analogous to the idea of autopoiesis (Colman, 2012), as already defined in 1972 by Maturana and Varela (1980). They postulated that in biology, the ability of biological systems to auto-reproduce internally allows them to maintain themselves by constant reproduction. We can say that life itself is a property that will have emerged from a certain level of complexity, which in turn gives rise to the emergence of that newly discovered attribute of autopoiesis.

One of the principal properties that Jung associated with his notion of the archetype is precisely this: an auto-organized psychic life, which is self-sustaining and remains related to its environment while constantly adapting to it.

The archetype: a complex system with a fractal structure?

It is therefore arguable that Jung proposes thinking of the archetype by means of a system complex in itself – that is, thought. Butz (1998), who examined the idea of energy in Jung's work, seems to have arrived at a similar conclusion. It strikes me that in this respect, Jung is very close to the idea of complex thinking such as that developed by Edgar Morin (1990). Moreover, Jung asserts this complex thought in response to Freud, who in 1910 was still talking about a way of thinking steeped in simple causality, or that he still sought to make simple. Subsequently, Freud himself proceeded to a different form of complex thought, first with his death instinct (1920), then with his second topic (id, ego, superego; 1923), and especially with his *Moses and Monotheism* (1939), followed by the post-war Freudians and eventually taken up by the entire psychoanalytic movement. I would say that Freud has chosen different Poincare sections, no more and no less valid than those of Jung (Atmanspacher, 2014, developed a similar position). From my perspective, this is where clinical practice alone can discern the pertinence of one or another approach.

Taken together, all these considerations help us to understand more clearly what Jung was getting at with the notion of archetype, its constants, its variations, and all its contradictions. If one returns to the classification suggested by Knox (as I have reformulated it above), it becomes possible to distinguish different ranges of meaning for the concept, such that:

1 The archetype as a logical concept necessary to thinking about the relationship between matter and psyche.
2 The archetype as an innate biological organizing principle.
3 The archetype as an abstract mental structure not capable of representation *per se*.
4 The archetype as a nucleus of representation of highly symbolic value.

Each of these ranges corresponds to a scale of observation, or more accurately, since it is only possible to observe the last of these ranges, on a scale of abstraction from the most general to the most particular. Thus, if it is accepted that the archetype might be structured in the manner of all other complex systems which are characteristic of the world, it is no longer surprising that Jung's applications of the term should be different and indeed at times divergent. According to the application, there are different emergent properties, and the relevant description in each case must therefore also be different, when all the while the reference remains the same.[16]

It then becomes possible to think of the different archetypes described by Jung as each corresponding to a strange attractor, as might have been revealed to him as part of a mental activity equivalent to a section of Poincare, of the global psychic system. Thinking along those lines enables one to grasp the Jungian idea of activating an archetype, an idea easily confused with magical thinking, as if every archetype were some dormant spirit liable to wake up at any time. However, the epistemology of complex systems requires a very different formulation, on the premise that there is a global psychic system, animated by a more or less chaotic dynamic diversity, such that when changes occur in the dynamics, not necessarily at all levels of the system, there is either an emergence or an erasure of strange attractors around which those dynamics arrange themselves.

This line of reasoning also serves to answer the objections of Knox and Roesler as to the allegedly inherent biological origin of archetypes. In fact, it would seem important to invalidate the Jungian idea of an innate origin of the archetype in order to replace it with its developmental emergence.[17] However, in a complex approach, this is redundant since the emergence of its properties in a system are quite as dependent on its nature as on its interactions with its environment. The basis of Knox's arguments no longer needs to postulate the existence of archetypes *per se*, but can rely on the properties of the system, which through its interaction with its environment gives rise to the type of dynamics that Jung described as archetypal – in fact, this is the realm of epigenesis. It therefore is no longer necessary to oppose their various alleged origins, whether biological, genetic, environmental, intra-psychic, and so forth.

Carl Gustav Jung: a theoretician of subjectivity?

At the start of this chapter, I briefly discussed Freud's and Jung's differing concepts of energy (libido) and the nature of the human psyche. Much of the work that led to Jung's development of the concept of the collective unconscious and the archetypes that allow it to be experienced within the psyche was done during the period between 1914 and 1920 when Jung entered a period of intense emotional turbulence and scientifically studied his experiences. This examination of his process became *The Red Book*. There has been much discussion in the literature about the nature of Jung's experiences during this period and what his process meant for him as an individual and for the development of the theory of the archetypes and its application to clinical practice. I will now examine these in terms of understanding archetypes as complex systems.

Following the publication of *The Red Book* (Jung, 2009), a number of Jungians advocated a strategy to defend against a potential temptation to describe the work as psychotic outpourings, as if this word was an anathema (Gaillard, 2011). The difficulty is that it is unclear what each of those authors understands by the term psychosis: could it be a reference to the functioning of some layers of the mind? Alternatively, could it be a commentary on the function or dysfunction of the ego? In other words, is it necessarily about pathology, or rather is it about a type of mental dynamic which, like neurosis, has its own pathological presentations?

I shall only skim over the debate, which deserves a far longer exposition than is possible here, but I can assert that for me there is no anathema in speaking about psychosis. Anyway, Jung himself writing to Patricia Hutchins on the subject of James Joyce (Shamdasani, 2012, p. 147) states:

> His "psychological style" is definitely schizophrenic, with the difference, however, that the ordinary patient cannot help himself talking and thinking in such a way, while Joyce willed it and moreover developed it with his creative forces, which incidentally explains why he himself did not go over the border.
>
> *(quoted by Ellmann, 1984)*

Which is why I share Schwartz-Salant's (2010) position, when reviewing *The Red Book*, he writes:

> To think of Jung as mad, or as having been schizophrenic, and somehow creatively curing himself, is surely wrong. But to recognize that Jung, like everyone, to one degree or another, had mad parts in his otherwise sane personality, and that this madness had a tormenting, and eventually both a limiting and a transforming effect, is a very reasonable hypothesis.
>
> *(p. 13)*

In any event, it would seem that the idea of Jung's "madness" stems from the book review Winnicott (1964) wrote about *Memories, Dreams, Reflections*. Besides, Winnicott never put forward any hypothesis about schizophrenia or any other psychosis concerning the adult Jung: he talked of childhood psychosis, which is another matter altogether. Suggesting the hypothesis that Jung was able to cure himself of childhood psychosis seems to speak of the great importance of the work. All who have experience of working with psychotic children, and more so with adults who suffer the consequences of such childhood disturbance, will need little convincing that the working through in such cases is lengthy, painful, and indeed uncertain.[18] What seems at play here is an attempt to activate the alpha function (Bion, 1963) with the aim of transforming the remaining beta elements into imaginable and thinkable alpha elements.

It seems to me possible to assert that what Jung was confronting during his "immersion in the unconscious" (Jung, 1961, pp. 198–232) was an excursion, which was not capable of representation, or at the very least not yet represented. As Sonu Shamdasani (2012, p. 107) observes, "He felt the need to represent his innermost thoughts in stone and to build a completely primitive dwelling";[19] and "words and paper in my eyes were an insufficient reality; something else was needed" (Jung, 1961, p. 260); and later (2012, p. 130), "*Liber Novus* has emerged out of a crisis of language and out of a parallel quest to find fitting expression for speaking to and about the soul." Is there, I ask, a better definition of the alpha function than this: "to find fitting expression for speaking to and about the soul"?

Initially, he sought to hang onto reality with the aid of breathing and yoga exercises, evincing on the contrary how his narcissism[20] attempted to shore up his physical being against the assaults emanating from his explosive affects. He accepted a formal regression by yielding to childish construction games, showing the imperious need to give shape to his emotions. I rate this as an excellent clinical example of confrontation with beta elements and of the mental disturbance it involves. Yet at this stage, unlike in the case of the childhood episodes Winnicott may have been referring to, Jung resisted the temptation to yield to psychotic defenses. Just as when, as a pre-adolescent, he decided by an effort of will to visualize the phantasy that was oppressing him (God who dropped a turd on Basel Cathedral), similarly, at almost forty years of age, he decided to give full rein to any phantasies that he experienced or came to him. According to him, this was a matter of brute force.

And strength he needed not only to retain his relationship to external reality, but also to oblige his experiences to become imaginable, and then to find in himself the capacity to put them into a concrete and graspable form. This is what led him to building games and drawings like most children. But he had to maintain his position as an adult, for his own sake, not only as an adult married male, but also as a doctor, a psychiatrist, and a researcher in a new science. This is how I make sense of his need to give a completed form to his fantastical productions, a form whose craftsmanship and artistic quality can be appreciated in *The Red Book*. It was, I believe, a process of reactivating the alpha function which Jung thus invented (a process he was to formalize by the term active imagination), a process through which emotional experience in its raw aspects, beta elements, can be made subject to and therefore integrated into conscious life. The challenge for him was to facilitate the personal incarnation of energies emanating from what he quickly came to call the impersonal unconscious.

Such an incarnation needed to point to his true being, and not by some sleight of hand, which could easily have slipped into that of an artist,[21] of a philosopher, of a prophet, or whoever else I might name. This, of course, is not to say that such a process is not possible for an artist, a philosopher, or a prophet, but just that Jung was none of them – at least this is what he always said. Jung was, however, a doctor, psychiatrist, and scientific researcher. The paintings, drawings, and prophetic texts one finds in *The Red Book* could only have been a stage in the lengthy process of subjective representation of his impersonal energies, an indispensable stage in his self-analysis, having nonetheless to give expression to a scientific representation in the field of his social incarnation. After the construction of a bridge between the impersonal and the subjective, he had to build another bridge between the subjective and the collective of his social appurtenance, to medicine and science. It was the task of the *Gesammelte Werke*, a work which precedes, accompanies and follows *The Red Book*.

So after having wrenched from the impersonal those representations that could be integrated into his subjective being, he had to retrace his steps in the opposite direction, toward a different form of the impersonal, that is, the conceptual formulation of theory destined for the human collective, the community of mankind. This is where the complexity of his thought appears in its fullness. It is a complexity necessary to give an account of the different levels of lived experience in the course of his self-analysis, then of his analytical work and that of his successors.

In Figure 4.1 I have summarized schematically this evolution, grouping the various levels of the two complementary processes, one of subjectivization and the other of theorization, the latter being organized in a dual movement of objectivization and of abstraction. It is important to keep in mind the sustained interactions and retroactions of the different processes between themselves; moreover, each elaboration made possible in this way produces a non-elaborated residue (the broken arrows) which feeds a previous and/or subjective level. Here the object of

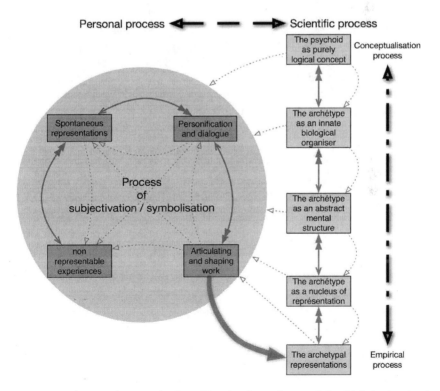

FIGURE 4.1   The complex organization of Jung's epistemology: each level is in interaction/feedback with the others

research is complex and the epistemology of the research is itself complex, just as is the resultant theory.

The second period of Jung's work should be added to this formulation. His work on *The Red Book* broke off in 1928, at the point when he came across the Chinese alchemical treatise, *The Mystery of the Golden Flower* (Jung, 1929). From then on he immersed himself in his studies of alchemy, and one may suppose he found a type of coherence between his subjective process and his scientific work. He thus proposes to his readers a unified, complex way of thinking, although in being unified it is not homogenous thought. It is a way of thinking which intricately accommodates the subjective dimension alongside a certain scientific objectivity. This does not require the reader to confound their subjectivity with that of Jung (he is not a prophet); rather it means to build, each in their own way, a personal and complex way of thinking, with their own interweaving of personal subjectivity and scientific objectivity.

The question of teleology and synchronicity

Before concluding this chapter, it behooves us to consider the task at hand from a teleological angle, since according to Jung it is central to archetypal dynamics. Furthermore, it is an important point from a historical point of view, since it was part of the fundamental discord that arose between Freud and Jung. It is also important today, since it lies at the heart of the debate raging between the scientific fraternity on behalf of Darwinism and the extremists of diverse stripe who are pushing for a return to creationism. This debate is not so pronounced in France, but it is gathering pace in the United States and in Muslim countries (Hameed, 2012): it cannot be ignored.

The question is whether Jung's teleological stance can be confused with the notion of final causes, the "finality" of the ancients, one that presupposes a creator, and a divine strategy as an outcome of the act of creation (Le Ru, 2012).

Jung is probably at his most explicit on this topic in his article on synchronicity. There he introduces synchronicity as an acausal principle: there cannot be a creator of meaning, or a strategy that would give rise to phenomena whose meaning was waiting to be discovered. The teleological approach is quite different from creationism or some ultimate design of Nature. Then, Jung (1952, para. 948) goes far beyond the paranormal in his article:

> If that is so, then we must ask ourselves whether the relation of soul and body can be considered from this angle, that is to say whether the coordination of psychic and physical processes in a living organism can be understood as a synchronistic phenomenon rather than as a causal relation.

So with the introduction of the notion of the psychoid, envisaged by him quite differently from its previous usage (Addison, 2009), he is quite adamant it is a formal concept, a logical necessity. Yet, it must be said that a doubt persists in what he means, for instance, when he introduces the notion of absolute knowledge, of a meaning existing of itself. This hesitation, which lingers throughout his oeuvre, seems to me to have brought about numerous alternative interpretations of his thought, or rather of his intuition based on the various expressions of his thinking.

It seems possible to surmise that Jung had a clear intuition of emergent phenomena, but not having at his disposal an adequate conceptualization, he sought, for better or for worse, to formulate one. That is why I think I am able to say that his notion of synchronicity, a formidable intuition about the relational acausal principle, is one that itself possesses emergent properties. However, he was unable to represent to himself such a principle without falling back on earlier concepts, that is, by reverting to a type of causality: if meaning emerges out of a fortuitous (non-causal) encounter between an external event and a psychological event, it would be a logical necessity for there to be some pre-existing meaning in the universe. It is precisely what the current idea of emergence enables one to avoid. So before there was ever water in the universe, it might perhaps have been set down that two hydrogen atoms and one oxygen atom were likely to join quite strongly to form a stable molecule, but nothing could have decreed that it would be liquid only between 0 and 100 degrees Celsius, nor that its density in its solid state would be less than that of its liquid state. It is a property that existed nowhere, not even in a possible *a priori* state, until its eventual emergence. Thus it has been throughout the universe we know and which in the course of its evolution since the Big Bang does not cease from exemplifying its organization with, at each stage, the emergence of not only new properties, but also new laws of physics (Laughlin, 2012).

This is an important nexus from the metaphysical standpoint, since it avoids the predicate of a pre-existing or even potential structure of laws, properties, and/or form said to emerge with each level of complexity: the avoidance of metaphysical hypotheses is one of the foundations of the scientific method. Hence the work, for example of Conforti (1999) – one of the first researchers to have examined the archetypal concept in light of emergence theory – and of Vezina (2001), does not appear to account fully for the theory since they deduce from it, as Jung did before them, that emergence nevertheless contains a pre-existing potential for archetypal structures.

In psychology, especially in the study of occult phenomena, emergence opens the way to an approach that is not driven by magical causality, nor by hermeneutics, nor by final causes in the sense of creationism, which then allows the Jungian model of synchronicity, as an acausal principle, to become an example of the emergence of meaning arising simply from what occurs, that is, "ordinary" coincidence. Carrying on this line of thought, Bright (1997), followed by my own work (Martin-Vallas, 2011, 2015), has applied the principle of synchronicity to understanding the emergence of meaning in the field of psychoanalysis, specifically as a property of the transference. This, I believe, is how we can now talk about teleology without abandoning scientific discourse in the psychological field, in the sense that Paul Ricoeur had it (1967, p. 125): "Teleology is not the same as final causes: the nodal points in dialectical teleology are not final causes, but the significance that develops into meaning out of the process of encompassing that overtakes them."

Conclusion

What Jung is specifically able to offer analysts is an opening into a way of thinking that can take place in clinical practice, so that the analysand has the freedom to live out his subjective experience, while by his side the analyst is able to pick up that subjective experience through the prism of and interwoven with his theoretical thought processes. So if one follows the Jungian train of thought as I have tried to make it explicit, there cannot be just one unique way for the analyst to make sense to himself of what might be going on in the treatment. On the contrary, one of the major advantages of this approach is to oblige us, on the grounds of complexity, to choose (or to be chosen by) a direction of travel in assessing a clinical situation in the knowledge that there are always other possible routes with the result of a differential assessment. This very choice – we recognize it in our practice – is often only "conscious" in retrospect, even if it has emerged in us in the "here and now" of the transference situation: it is an expression of what I have termed the transferential chimera (Martin-Vallas, 2006, 2008, 2009b, 2015).

Not only should this prevent us from falling asleep with pre-packaged thoughts about our patients, but it demands that we interrogate our countertransference precisely on the manner of our theoretical thought process, and not just remain stuck on our affects, fantasies, and/or bodily occurrences (cf. Carvalho [2014] as a synchronicity). Only when approached in this way can we appreciate that the transference is present not only in the space between the analysand and his analyst, but it also encompasses and therefore affects the subjective as well as the theoretical thinking of the analyst.[22] This type of thinking is not confined by a defensive mode – to shelter the self from emotional experiences that are inadequately imagined or integrated – quite the reverse: it is a mode open to the interweaving of affect, imagination, bodily sensation, and conceptualization. It is truly the work of a weaver that Jung exhorts the analyst to undertake in his clinical practice as much as in his efforts to understand; for it demands intricate connections, in the manner of a Borromean knot[23] consisting of the many and various connected aspects of the self.

Notes

1 This chapter is based on an earlier article published in the *Revue de Psychologie Analytique* (Martin-Vallas, 2013) and on an extended discussion as part of a doctoral thesis for the Lumière University of Lyons 2 (Martin-Vallas, 2015).
2 Translator's note: Le Quellec's "Jung et les archétypes – un mythe contemporain" is written by a French anthropologist, a specialist in African cave art. His richly annotated 450-page volume is an attempt to dismantle Jung's archetypal theory as "scientifically" vacuous. While he makes valid criticisms of Jung's sometimes perfunctory or ill-conceived references to other disciplines, the book contains numerous misreadings and misrepresentations of Jung's work.
3 [Driesch] defined his psychoid as an intra-psychic factor providing the unconscious ultimate foundation of the conscious ego and linking the conscious ego and the body-in-action. It is important to understand that overall Driesch saw his psychoid as neither body nor mind but as something occupying a third position in between and relating to both. [. . .] Further, this psychoid is teleological and purposive in the sense that it

Archetypal theory and its epistemology 65

constitutes an ordering principle urging behaviour along paths of adaptation to the environment based on intentionality of the ego and on historical experience.
(Addison, 2009, p. 128)

4 The idea has been replicated in recent neurophysiological experiments, notably by Antonio Damasio (1995).
5 But in difference with Freud's later development, this desire for death is not, for Jung, in opposition with Eros. It is part of it, longing for non-existence with the aim of rebirth.
6 Obviously this is a reference to death as it can only be thought about in the mind of a living person. Of itself, "death" belongs in the sphere of metaphysics and is not a concern for psychology.
7 I am talking about the time when relations between the two men were active, in the knowledge that the idea of primary phantasies did not appear in Freud's writings until 1915.
8 Translator's note: In the *Critique of Pure Reason*, Kant contrasted his usage of "transcendent" and "transcendental." The former means "going beyond" any possible knowledge of a human being, whereas the latter refers to the conditions for acquiring knowledge. He states: "I call all knowledge *transcendental* if it is occupied, not with objects, but with the way we can possibly know objects even before we experience them" (Kant, 1781, A12).
9 Certain Jungian authors quite frequently talk of transcendence in its metaphysical sense, as if that was Jung's position. This is regrettable since he was very clear on the matter, and the divergence is perhaps due to some of his pupils who did not share his clarity.
10 It is a concept especially pertinent in the theory of psychosomatics (Ramos, 2004), and a view which is found in Jung (1952, para. 123).
11 George Hogenson (2004, 2009) and Joe Cambray (2004, 2006, 2010) have specifically focused on the phenomenon of emergence.
12 The interested reader can consult the very accessible book by James Gleick (1988).
13 Phase space is a mathematical construct that enables every state of the dynamic system to be represented as a unique point of the space.
14 The organization of atmospheric humidity into cloud formation, say a cumulus cloud in the sky, is an everyday example.
15 The idea of a dimension that is not whole, which may seem impossible to imagine, is not so complicated. If one takes a line segment, and one doubles its size, the segment will be twice as long. If one takes a square and doubles its dimensions, the surface will be four times larger. If one does the same operation on a cube, its volume will be eight times greater. The relationship between enlargement (A) of the figure and its dimensions (d) can be expressed as $A = 2^d$ when one doubles the dimensions. A property of a fractal is that its size is superior that of the space in which it is located.
16 Translator's note: Here Rom Harré's groundbreaking work on use of social rules including language into the formation of the self comes to mind.
17 This has been a debate between Stevens (2003) and Hogenson (2004) at the Cambridge Congress of IAAP (2001).
18 I think that most of the people who get labeled as "borderline" in fact present the consequences of childhood psychosis, which usually becomes traceable during analytic treatment, with the revisiting of childhood and infancy.
19 Translator's note: Cf. also Kutek's *A Jungian Spoke in the Planning Wheel* (in press), which goes beyond Jung's need to represent mere thoughts in stone but to actually project himself in stone. Hence he dispensed with architects and became the builder, an expansion of the manikin of his childhood.
20 By narcissism I refer here to that property that guarantees the permanence of the ego as the center of consciousness of the inner and outer world, an ego capable of toiling on the simultaneous adaptation to the exigencies of both orders of reality.
21 See for instance his dialogue with the anima (Jung, 1961, p. 213).
22 Which seems to chime with Michel de M'Uzan's idea of paradoxical thinking (1976).
23 The knot is named after the Borromeo family coat of arms. It contains a figure of three rings interlinked in such a way that if only one is cut, all three become separated.

References

Addison, A. (2009). Jung, vitalism and 'the psychoid': An historical reconstruction. *Journal of Analytical Psychology, 54*, 1.
Atmanspacher, H. (2014). Le monisme à double aspect. *Revue de Psychologie Analytique, 3*, 105–133.
Bion, W. (1963). *Elements of psychoanalysis.* London: Karnac Books, 1984.
Blackerby, R. F. (1998). *Applications of chaos theory to psychological models.* Austin: Performance Strategies.
Boston Change Process Study Group. (2004). The something more than interpretation: Sloppiness and co-construction in the psychoanalytic encounter. *International Journal of Psychoanalysis*, 85.
Bright, G. (1997). Synchronicity as a basis of analytic attitude. *Journal of Analytical Psychology, 42*(4), 613–635.
Butz, M. R. (1997). *Chaos and complexity: Implications for psychological theory and practice.* London: Taylor.
Butz, M.R. (1998). Chaos, energy, and analytical psychology. In L.L. Chamberlain and M.R. Butz (Eds.), *Clinical chaos: A therapist's guide to nonlinear dynamics and therapeutic change* (pp. 41–53). Levittown: Brunner-Mazel.
Cambray, J. (2006). Towards the feeling of emergence. *Journal of Analytical Psychology, 51*, 1e.
Cambray, J. (2010). Emergence and the self. In S. Murray (Ed.), *Jungian psychoanalysis: Working in the spirit of C. G. Jung* (pp. 53–66). Chicago: Open Court.
Cambray, J., & Carter, L. (2004). *Analytical psychology: Contemporary perspectives in Jungian analysis.* New York: Brunner-Routledge.
Carvalho, R. (2013). A vindication of Jung's unconscious and its archetypal expression: Jung, Bion and Matte Blanco. In A. Cavalli, L. Hawkins and M. Stevens (Eds.), *Transformation: Jung's legacy and clinical work today.* London: Karnac Books [can be read on Google Books].
Carvalho, R. (2014). Synchronicity, the infinite unrepressed, dissociation and the interpersonal. *Journal of Analytical Psychology, 59*, 366–384.
Chamberlain, L.L., & Butz, M.R. (1998). *Clinical chaos: A therapist's guide to nonlinear dynamics and therapeutic change.* Levittown: Brunner-Mazel.
Chatillon, N. (2010). *Penser depuis l'inconscient.* Paris: Grego.
Colman, W. (2012). *Bounded in a nutshell and a king of infinite space: The embodied self and its intentional world.* Second European Conference on Analytical Psychology, St Petersburg, unpublished.
Conforti, M. (1999). *Field, form and fate: Patterns in mind, nature, and psyche.* New Orleans, LA: Spring Journal, 2006.
Damasio, A. (1995). *Descartes' error: Emotion, reason, and the human brain.* New York: Penguin Books, 2005.
Ellmann, R. (1920). Beyond the pleasure principle. *SE XVII*, 7–64.
Ellmann, R. (1923). The ego and the id. *SE XIX*, 12–59.
Ellmann, R. (1939). Moses and monotheism. *SE XXIII*, 7–137.
Ellmann, R. (1984). *James Joyce.* Oxford: Oxford Paperbacks.
Gaillard, C. (2011). Transcendance et croyance en psychanalyse jungienne à la lumière du Livre Rouge. *Cah. Jung. Psychanalysis, n° 134.*
Galton, F. (1883). *Inquiries into human faculty and its development.* London: Macmillan.
Gleick, J. (1988). *Chaos: The making of a new science.* New York: Penguin Books.
Gottman, J. M., Murray, J. D., Swanson, C., Tyson, R., & Swanson, K. R. (2003). *The mathematics of marriage: Dynamic nonlinear models.* Cambridge: Massachusetts Institute of Technology Press.

Hameed, S. (2012). La contagion gagne les pays musulmans. *La recherche, HS n°48.*
Hogenson, G. (2001). The Baldwin effect: A neglected influence on C.G. Jung's evolutionary thinking. *Journal of Analytical Psychology, 46*, 591–611.
Hogenson, G. (2004). Archetypes: Emergence and the psyche's deep structure. In J. Cambray and L. Carter (Eds.), *Analytical psychology: Contemporary perspectives in Jungian analysis* (pp. 32–55). New York: Brunner-Routledge.
Hogenson, G. (2009). Archetypes as action patterns. *Journal of Analytical Psycholysis, 54,* 3.
Jung, C. G. (1909). The family constellation. In *C.W. 2*. London: Routledge.
Jung, C.G. (1912). *Psychology of the unconscious: A study of the transformation and symbolism of the libido*. A contribution to the history of the evolution of thought. Princeton: Princeton University Press, 1992. Retrieved from www.questia.com/library/7351122/psychology-of-the-unconscious-a-study-of-the-transformations
Jung, C.G. (1929). Commentary on 'The secret of the golden flower'. In *CW 13*. London: Routledge.
Jung, C.G. (1946). The psychology of the transference. In *The Practice of Psychotherapy, CW 16*, London: Routledge.
Jung, C.G. (1952). Synchronicity: An acausal connecting principle. In *The structure and dynamics of the psyche, CW 8*. London: Routledge.
Jung, C.G. (1961). *Memories, dreams and reflections*. London: Collins.
Jung, C.G. (2009). *Liber novus, the red book*. London: W.W. Norton.
Kant, E. (1781/1999). *Critique of pure reason*. Cambridge: Cambridge University Press.
Kiel, D. L., & Elliott, E.W. (1997). *Chaos theory in the social sciences: Foundations and applications*. Ann Arbor: University of Michigan Press.
Knox, J. (2003). *Archetype, attachment, analysis – Jungian psychology and the emergent mind*. New York: Brunner-Routledge.
Lamarck, J.-B. (1809). *Philosophie zoologique*. Paris: Dentu. Retrieved from https://fr.wikisource.org/wiki/Philosophie_zoologique_(1809)
Laughlin, R. (2012). L'émergence inattendue de lois physiques. *La recherche, Les dossiers de la recherche n°48.*
Le Quellec. (2013). *Jung et les archétypes: Un mythe contemporain*. Paris: Editions Sciences humaines.
Le Ru, V. (2012). Le réveil de l'obscurantisme. *La recherche, HS n°48.*
Leffert, M. (2010). *Contemporary psychoanalytic foundations: Postmodernism, complexity, end neurosciences*. London: Routledge.
Martin-Vallas, F. (1998). *La chimère transférentielle*. Mémoire d'admission à la Société française de Psychologie Analytique, non publié.
Martin-Vallas, F. (2005a). Towards a theory of the integration of the other in representation. *Journal of Analytical Psychoanalysis, 50*(3), 285–293.
Martin-Vallas, F. (2005b). Vers une théorie de l'en-deçà de la représentation. *Cah. Jung. Psychanalysis, 116*, Paris.
Martin-Vallas, F. (2006). The transferential chimera: A clinical approach. *Journal of Analytical Psychology, 51*(5), 627–641, London.
Martin-Vallas, F. (2008). The transferential chimera II: Some theoretical considerations. *Journal of Analytical Psychology, 53*(1), 37–59.
Martin-Vallas, F. (2009a). From the end time to the time of the end: Some reflections about the emergence of subjectivity. *Journal of Analytical Psychology, 54*(4), 441–460.
Martin-Vallas, F. (2009b). Y-aurait-il des bases neurophysiologiques au transfert? *Cah. Jung. Psychanalysis,* 130, Paris.
Martin-Vallas, F. (2011). Бессмысленность инцеста, проверенная анализом [The meaninglessness of incest in the analytic context]. *Jungian Analysis,* 2.

Martin-Vallas, F. (2013). Quelques remarques à propos de la théorie des archétypes et de son épistémologie. *Revue de Psychologie Analytique, 1,* 99–134.

Martin-Vallas, F. (2015). *La chimère transférentielle: Proposition épistémologique, neuroscientifique et clinico-théorique du transfert psychanalytique comme système complexe.* Thèse de Doctorat en Psychologie, Université Lumière Lyon 2. Lyon: Université Lumière Lyon 2. Retrieved from http://chimere.martin-vallas.fr (English version in translation).

Maturana, H., & Varela, F. (1980). *Autopoiesis and cognition.* Dordrecht: Kluwer Academic Publishers.

Morin, E. (1990). *Introduction à la pensée complexe.* Paris: Le Seuil, Nouvelle édition, coll. Points, 2005.

M'uzan de, M. (1976). Contre-transfert et système paradoxal. In *De L'art à la mort.* Paris: Gallimard, 1977.

Ramos, D. (2004). *The psyche of the body: A Jungian approach to psychosomatics.* London: Routledge.

Ricoeur, P. (1967). Une interprétation philosophique de Freud. *La Nef, 31,* 125.

Roesler, C. (2012). Are archetypes transmitted more by culture than biology? Questions arising from conceptualizations of the archetype. *Journal of Analytical Psychology, 57,* 2.

Schwartz-Salant, N. (2010). The mark of one who has seen chaos: A review of C.G. Jung's Red book. *Quadrant, 40*(2), 13.

Shamdasani, S. (2012). *C.G. JUNG: A biography in books.* London: W.W. Norton.

Skynner, R. (1976). *One flesh, separate persons: Principles of family and marital psychotherapy.* London: Constable.

Stern, D., & Garene, M. (2003). *Le moment présent en psychothérapie: Un monde dans un grain de sable.* Paris: Odile Jacob.

Stevens, A. (2003). *Archetype revisited: An updated natural history of the self.* Toronto: Inner City Books.

Vesina, J.-F. (2001). *Les hasards nécessaires: Le rôle des coïncidences dans les rencontres qui nous transforment.* Paris: Éditions de l'homme.

Wiener, J. (2009). *The therapeutic relationship: Transference countertransference and the making of meaning, Tamu.* College Station: Texas A&M University Press.

Winnicott, D.W. (1964). Memories, dreams and reflections by C.G. Jung. *International Journal of Psychoanalysis, 45,* 450–455.

5

THE CULTURAL COMPLEX THEORY

Scientific and mythopoetic ways of knowing

Thomas Singer

Introduction

The cultural complex theory offers a rich avenue for cross-discipline research, for exploring cultural factors in the life of the group and individual psyche, and for bringing Jungian concepts, tools, and ideas to scientific inquiry outside of the Jungian community. In this chapter, we examine the cultural complex theory, the current status of research studying the theory, an agenda for future research efforts, and offer some investigative questions that would support collaboration in the future.

A cultural complex is defined as an autonomous, largely unconscious, emotionally charged aggregate of memories, affects, ideas, images, and behaviors that tend to cluster around an archetypal core and are shared by individuals within a group. A more detailed definition and attributes for a cultural complex will be discussed later in the chapter.

A Jungian approach to the scientific method and research might sound like an oxymoron to some scientists. The Jungian tradition does not lend itself easily to scientific investigation because of the subjective and inner experience of both patient and analyst, and an individual's inner life is often our primary focus. In that sense, it is much easier for us to describe our work in poetic rather than scientific language, and few in our tradition have tried to find ways of measuring outcomes and other meaningful measures of our therapeutic technique.

Indeed, even speaking of therapeutic technique is somewhat foreign ground to many who call themselves Jungian. But the fact that the language of science and of Jungian analysis are a bit like oil and water should not serve as a rationalization for an unwillingness to consider how we might engage effectively in scientific research. Bringing the scientific and mythopoetic ways of knowing together – without reducing the value of either – represents a great challenge and investigative opportunity for the Jungian tradition. The split between science and religion is deeply embedded in the Western psyche, symbolized most dramatically in Galileo's struggle with the Catholic Church when his heliocentric theory based on scientific observation came into conflict with the churches geocentrism based on scripture. Today that same split is alive and well between the biblical creationists and those who embrace Darwin's theory of evolution. It reached absurdist proportions when the American politician Sarah Palin stated that dinosaurs and humans were roaming the earth together some 5,000 years ago at the dawn of creation, or in the increasingly senseless debate between those who affirm or deny climate change. The danger for Jungians is to inadvertently align themselves with those who are unwilling or unable to embrace the scientific method as an approach to understanding the human psyche. One of our tasks as Jungians is to help bridge the age-old split between science and religion. Rather than reinforce the split, we should seek to find creative links and layerings between the language of the soul that is frequently used to talk about the psyche and the language of neuroscience that is used to describe the functions of the brain.

When I was invited to contribute to this volume and thought about the scientific methodology I have used to explore the cultural complex theory over the past decade, I realized that I had not given much conscious thought to the question of scientific methodology and had simply started asking questions and asking colleagues to share in that process of asking questions. The fact is that I had not set about defining a precise methodology for inquiring about the cultural complex notion when I began to explore it in my own intuitive way – which, of course, is a more common way for Jungians to proceed. However, I did not turn my back on scientific methodology when I begin to formulate the theory of cultural complexes. In fact, when I first began to put together a formulation of the basic concept of cultural complexes I quite consciously had in mind my early studies about the scientific method. I wanted to create a valid theoretical model. It was not so much in the formulation of the theory itself that I was not attentive to the scientific method. Rather it was in the methodology for researching the theory that I found myself falling back on a more intuitive rather than scientific approach.

Nevertheless, in later thinking about the scientific method and my research methodology I have been pleasantly surprised to discover that some of my methods are actually grounded in legitimate scientific research techniques. With regard to what constitutes the gathering of valid qualitative evidence, I have been more in the ballpark of accepted social science research methods than I thought. Finally, I hope that this chapter's discussion of the cultural complex theory and its research honors both the scientific and mythopoetic ways of knowing

The cultural complex theory

Jung often wrote about the collective psyche in such volumes as *Civilization in Transition* and *Man and His Symbols* with essays that explored the rise of Nazism, differences in national character, thoughts about Europe "after the catastrophe," and the differences between cultures. Most often his thoughts were framed in terms of how contents of the collective unconscious would make themselves known at different stages or critical periods in a culture's life. Over the years, the topic of the collective psyche and how it lives both in the individual and group psyche has become a central concern of my own thinking, particularly as non-rational and frequently virulent destructive forces get activated in competing ethnic, economic, and religious groups within nations, between nations, and sometimes flooding over into regional and global conflicts. These conflicts do not erupt in a vacuum; they are the result of potent forces within the psyches of individuals and groups becoming activated by economic and other social upheavals.

Jung's early theory of complexes addressed such forces in the individual psyche – mostly originating in parental, familial, and cultural patterning. But, his theory of complexes did not explore how cultural factors – originating in unique geography, economy, sociology, mythology, economics, and religion – formed their own cultural complexes which often become central in the psyche of groups and individuals living within these groups. Cultural complexes are not the same as individual complexes, although each deeply influences the other. It is the memory, history, economics, and all the other factors that contribute to the life of a group and its complexes and over generations create the living matrix in which an individual psyche takes shape. It is the group or cultural psyche and its complexes that is at the heart of this research. It relies on Joseph Henderson's contribution to Jung's original formulation of the psyche by including a level of the "cultural unconscious" between the "personal unconscious" and "the collective unconscious."

Research on the idea of cultural complexes

The main goal of the research into cultural complexes is to explore that part of the individual and group psyche which swims in the history, memory, affect, images, thought patterns, and behavior of past generations of peoples in a particular region. How is psyche shaped by landscape, language, and the various groups that have intermingled with one another over centuries in a specific locale? What does the Jungian focus on psychic life as expressed in the mythopoetic language of the cultural complex theory have to contribute to such well-established disciplines as history, anthropology, sociology, economics? One can easily wonder why would we need a separate theory of cultural complexes to understand what happens in the psyche of a specific group of people. One reason is that none of these specific disciplines addresses the question of how these various forces take shape and live in the psyche of contemporary individuals and groups. A Jungian point of view can bring a different perspective to these important and interconnected disciplines.

In order to answer questions about where economic and other cultural forces live inside of people, we need to take into account the reality of the psyche. The kinds of opinions and emotional reactions that people have to events both close to and far away from home usually have bits and pieces of history, economics, sociology, and so on in them – but their life in the psyche of the individual or the collective is not organized according to these disciplines. In fact, what order these ideas and feelings have in the psyche can be inchoate, rapidly shifting and yet paradoxically long-standing, and often quite immune and impermeable to the reason that traditional disciplines of thought would impose on them.

Our central thesis is that all of these various forces take shape in what we are calling *cultural complexes*. This is how they live in the psyche. I believe a theory of cultural complexes helps us understand how people think and feel about many of the major events and forces that shape their lives. In that sense, this is not sociology, which is descriptive of how these things look from the outside – not how they live inside. The study of cultural complexes is more like an inner sociology with a bit of history, psychology, anthropology, economics, mythology, sociology, and even poetry thrown into the stew.

To the question of "why a cultural complex theory," the simple answer is that these disciplines do not adequately describe what actually lives in the psyche of groups and individuals. The shape that our inner history, our inner anthropology, our inner sociology, and economics take frequently has nothing in common with how these disciplines appear in books or rational discourse. In the psyche of a group, the inner, more subjective representations of these disciplines live as cultural complexes. And often the inner representations of history, memory, economics, sociology, and anthropology bear little resemblance to what the more traditional disciplines posit. I view cultural complexes as naturally occurring structures of the psyche, and I also believe that in time we will be able to demonstrate their existence in the human brain as pathways that link group memory, affect, image, thought, and behavior. I believe that we will soon begin to develop a social neuroscience that will take into account how the life of the group and its complexes are "housed" both in the brains of individuals and in the interactive "field" between the brains of individuals living in groups. Combined with the methodologies and language of the other social sciences, the resultant tools might be very powerful.

Defining basic characteristics of the cultural complexes hypothesis

For some time, I have been interested in the interface of mythology, politics, and psyche – an interface that obviously is as much about the collective psyche as it is about the individual psyche. One bridge to linking those concerns is the cultural complex theory which takes into account the unique history, economics, psychology, and sociology of place – with the idea that all these forces are fuel and fodder for the psyche's constant urge to construct a narrative of identity in a particular time and place. But to give the theory legs, I was also aware of the need to define basic characteristics common to the structure of cultural complexes anywhere and anytime.

When I first began to discuss the basic formulations of the cultural complex theory with Sam Kimbles in the collaboration that led to our book, *The Cultural Complex*, I quite consciously had in mind my early studies about the scientific method as an undergraduate at Princeton University and as a medical student at Yale Medical School. In my freshman year at Princeton, I enrolled in Eric M.

Rogers's physics course for pre-medical students. He had just published *Physics for the Inquiring Mind: The Methods, Nature and Philosophy of Physical Science*. A showman lecturer, early in the course Rogers addressed the students in the lecture hall with the question, "How do you know for sure that friction is not caused by gremlins?," and he showed a picture of little creatures lined up on the surfaces of two objects and the gremlins of one surface were wrestling with those of the other surface. I can't remember the answer to Rogers's question, but I do remember the question. Rogers's book is still in print and is described in the following way:

> For lasting benefits the intelligent non-scientist needs a course of study that enables him to learn genuine science carefully and then encourages him to think about it and use it. He needs a carefully selected framework of topics – not so many that learning becomes superficial and hurried; not so few that he misses the connected nature of scientific work and thinking. He must see how scientific knowledge is built up by building some scientific knowledge of his own, by reading and discussing and if possible by doing experiments himself. He must think his own way through some scientific arguments. He must form his own opinion, with guidance, concerning the parts played by experiment and theory; and he must be shown how to develop a taste for good theory. He must see several varieties of scientific method at work. And above all, he must think about science for himself and enjoy that. These are the things that this book encourages readers to gain, by their own study and thinking."
>
> (*Physics for the Inquiring Mind*, http://press.princeton.edu/titles/1818.html)

In pursuing the scientific method, Rogers emphasized the role of a working hypothesis that one could test and that would lead to new questions. The process of exploring a theory should continue until it becomes clear that it is either not true or no longer generates additional inquiry. So the building and exploring of a theory requires that one establish a hypothesis and then test it in the world, and that is what I have tried to do.

The cultural complex hypothesis states that there is a part of the psyche, generated in the cultural unconscious, that takes the form of complexes. As noted earlier, a cultural complex is defined as an autonomous, largely unconscious, emotionally charged aggregate of memories, affects, ideas, images, and behaviors that tend to cluster around an archetypal core and are shared by individuals within a group. Cultural complexes are active both in the psyche of the group as a whole and in the individual at what we can think of as the group level of the individual's psyche.

Cultural complexes have the following characteristics, based on a model that Chauncey Irvine, MD, and I developed about personal complexes when we taught psychiatric residents at the Langley Porter Institute of the University of California, San Francisco (UCSF) Medical School for over a decade:

- *Cultural complexes are autonomous.* They have a life of their own in the psyche that is separate from the everyday ego of an individual or group. Sometimes

they are dormant. Sometimes they become active in the psyche and take hold of one's thoughts, feelings, memories, images, and behavior.
- *Cultural complexes are repetitive.* The ongoing life of a cultural complex continues uninterrupted in the psyche of an individual or group, sometimes for generations and even millennia. When they are activated, they are surprisingly unchanged, in the sense that they are recurring, repetitive, and expressive of the same emotional and ideological content over and over again.
- *Cultural complexes collect experiences and memories that validate their own point of view.* Once a cultural complex has established itself, it has a remarkable capacity – like a virus replicating – not only to repeat itself but also to make sure that whatever happens in the world fits into its pre-existing point of view. Cultural complexes are extremely resistant to facts. Everything that happens in the world is understood through their point of view. Cultural complexes collect experiences and self-affirming memories.
- *The thoughts of cultural complexes tend to be simplistic and black and white.* Although they form the core cognitive content of a cultural complex, the thoughts themselves are not complex. They are unchanging and without subtlety. They are rigid and impervious to modification. Indeed, they seem to be impermeable to any outside influence.
- *Cultural complexes have strong affects or emotions by which one can recognize their presence.* Knee-jerk affectivity or emotional reactivity is a sure sign that one has stepped on a cultural complex.
- *Not all cultural complexes are destructive; not all cultural complexes are ego-dystonic to the cultural identity of a group or individual.* Indeed, some cultural complexes can form the core of a healthy cultural identity.

Another parallel set of criteria that I have developed as a way of identifying a cultural complex involves a series of questions about the various types of mental activity that are recruited when a cultural complex is triggered. A good way to think about a particular cultural complex is to ask the following questions:

- What feelings go along with this complex?
- What images tend to appear with this complex?
- What memories come to mind when this complex is activated?
- What behaviors are triggered by a particular complex?
- What stereotypical thoughts recur with a particular complex?

Taking the hypothesis into the world: developing a methodology

The study of the history of science teaches us that a working hypothesis is only as valuable as the research that it spawns. In fact, that is the purpose of good theory: to stimulate further study, not to stop the speculative mind from wondering about man, nature, and the cosmos. Good theory does not explain away the object of its inquiry, but opens doors to the curious mind to ask more questions, including challenging the validity of the theory itself. In time, the research that is generated by a theory either gives it legs to stand on or it doesn't. With these purposes in mind, I have been conducting a global research project by engaging colleagues around the world in the study of the cultural complex theory.

Universality and specificity

I did not set out with a fixed research methodology to test the cultural complex theory when I first began work on *The Cultural Complex* with Sam Kimbles. However, I was keenly aware of wanting to craft an addition to Jungian theory in general and Jung's theory of complexes in particular by articulating basic principles that may in time lend themselves to additional scientific research. When I sought to broaden the area of inquiry into cultural complexes in the Spring Journal Books Cultural Complex Series that I have edited, I did not create a questionnaire or survey and I did not try to design a clear scientific protocol for studying the hypothesis. Rather, a methodology evolved over time as each of the various book projects began to come into focus and bear fruit. I did, however, set out to explore the theory in both as broad and as specific a way as possible. By "broad," I mean that I wanted to get material from as many parts of the world as possible, and by "specific," I wanted the material to be as unique to each region and topic as possible. On the one hand, I thought that the theory would prove to be universal in that it states that cultural complexes are actually innate forms or structures of the human psyche and brain. On the other hand, I also thought that the content of each cultural complex would be unique to a specific place, history, and people. Just as Jung envisioned the archetype as an innate potential of the human psyche, the specific content of which would be filled in by unique cultural expressions, I envisioned the cultural complex as an innate potential of the human psyche, the specific content of which would be filled in by unique cultural expressions. Universality rules to the extent that a cultural complex is a basic structure of the psyche that applies to all groupings of humans around the world, and specificity rules in terms of the uniqueness of content that belongs to each cultural complex arising from a particular group of people of a particular place and time. Central to the theory, then, is the principle that cultural complexes are both universal and specific.

Contributors

Following the principle of universality and specificity, I sought to involve colleagues from around the world in the research project with the idea of establishing that cultural complexes as a structure of the psyche are a worldwide phenomenon and that cultural complexes are unique to a specific group of people, time, and place. As a result, the Spring Journal Books Cultural Complex Series includes volumes from Australia (*Placing Psyche*), Latin America (*Listening to Latin America*), and Europe (*Europe's Many Souls*), and we are currently in the early stages of developing a book about Asian cultural complexes. Including the original book, *The Cultural Complex* from Routledge, the four books published to date contain research articles from 60 different contributors from 23 countries and five continents.

For each volume, I started by networking with colleagues at our triennial Jungian International Congress to identify people with expertise in different regions of the world who might be interested in contributing to the project. Eventually I enlisted a group of regional editors for each book to lead the project in their region and to help in identifying additional potential contributors. I then sent out a letter to all regional editors and individuals they had identified as possible contributors to the study. In the letter, I outlined the cultural complex theory and its characteristics and the call for proposals to write chapters exploring the cultural complex idea. I was quite clear that each author should find their own way into working with the theory and that their contribution should reflect a personal and professional connection to the topic. I encouraged each author to reflect on those cultural issues that most deeply affected how they think and feel. I asked them to give consideration to their personal experience of how cultural or group psychological issues, influenced by history, geography, economics, religion, gender, and race, most deeply affected them and those around them. I asked them to look at their own experience and to look at the experiences of others around them who do not necessarily share their own perspective.

In short, I asked each of the contributors to look at a cultural complex that seemed most real and formative to their own development and their culture's development. Several authors have noted how difficult it is to be objective about one's own culture and experience. They liken it to trying to describe a fog from the outside while actually living inside the fog. I used the same process to develop each of the Spring Journal Books.

Mythopoetic and scientific ways of knowing

As Jungians exploring our theories, we face the challenge of not only creating a scientific model that we can investigate in the mode of "physics for the inquiring mind" but of also being able to bridge the language of science and the language of the soul – which most often seem and feel like polar opposites. There is, in fact, a big difference between how one knows something through scientific inquiry and how one knows something through the language of the soul. And the fact is that both ways of knowing are real and valid, although not easily reconciled. Ever since science and religion split at the end of the Middle Ages with the rise of the scientific method, these two ways of knowing have seemed irreconcilable. In the latter part of the 20th century and into the early 21st century, there has been a beginning rapprochement – even reconciling – of these two ways of knowing, perhaps most visible in how traditional Western medicine has begun to open up to alternative, non-Western healing traditions. Still, we need to constantly keep in mind the question: is there a way to bridge the language of science and the language of soul, the way science knows something and the way the soul knows something?

I think the cultural complex research project incorporates both ways of knowing: we started with a hypothesis and set of characteristics which reflect the scientific way of investigating; we have collected qualitative evidence by using key informants about which I will have more to say shortly (the social science way of knowing); and our authors/investigators/key informants have been encouraged to let their own soulful or mythopoetic way of knowing mingle with their informed observations as social scientists, or at least as keen social observers. I would suggest that the result is a research project that has used both the scientific and mythopoetic ways of knowing as reflected in the way each contributor has gone about exploring his or her specific cultural complex of interest. In a sense, each contributor was encouraged to be a soulful, mythopoetic, social scientist. In the next section, I will outline how we went about creating the right cultural context in which to explore the cultural complex.

Key informants and the nature of qualitative evidence

When I was thinking about the cultural complex research project in terms of its methodology, I had the good fortune to consult with Linda Mitteness, a former chair of the Department of Medical Anthropology at the UCSF Medical School. She is intimately familiar with social science research methodology and with both qualitative and quantitative research techniques. She steered me to the most highly regarded articles on two essential aspects of qualitative research in the social sciences with regard to:

1   What qualifies our authors as valid researchers of the cultural complex theory?
2   What qualifies their "data" as valid evidence for the theory of cultural complexes?

Before suggesting a response to these two questions, I want to make it clear that I do not want to argue that this research meets the high standards of empirical scientific research, but I do want to argue that we have used methodology that at least puts us in the ballpark with regard to conducting legitimate social science research.

What qualifies our authors as valid researchers of the cultural complex theory?

We have used our authors as "key informants" from different cultures to inform us about the nature of cultural complexes in their country or region. "Key informants" are defined by the University of California, Los Angeles (UCLA) Center for Health Policy Research in the following way:

> Key informants must have first-hand knowledge about (their) community, its residents and issues or problems one is trying to investigate. Key informants can be a wide range of people, including agency representatives, community residents, community leaders, etc.
> *(http://healthpolicy.ucla.edu/programs/health-data/trainings/ Documents/tw_cba23.pdf)*

What qualifies our key informants' "data" as valid evidence for the theory of cultural complexes?

This is a most challenging issue, and what I learned by researching this question surprised me greatly. My comments are based on the paper "On the Nature of Qualitative Evidence," a superlative summary of contemporary thought on the subject by Yvonna S. Lincoln.

I will summarize a few of her most important points, but I strongly recommend reading the paper in its entirety to understand its rather unexpected conclusions which incorporate but are not limited by a postmodernist perspective. Lincoln begins by stating:

> Many of the arguments over what we consider validity are themselves questions regarding the nature of evidence and what constitutes knowledge. I have begun to see that, in fact, much of what we call "data" is itself phenomenological – that is, socially constructed and "there" only because we are attuned to looking for it. Not only socially constructed but in fact, little more than social construction, an artifact of social and communitarian processes among disciplinary members who agree among themselves about how they will talk, and what the rules of talking will be.
>
> *(Lincoln, 2002, p. 3)*

Lincoln goes on to make what might be her most relevant statement in terms of how we have gone about conducting research on the cultural complex project. She writes:

> First and foremost, no "evidence" is evidence until we see it from some theoretical paradigmatic or metaphysical framework (Fisher, 1977). Berger (1994) echoes this by saying: "No evidence without explicit theory." Thus, what constitutes evidence and therefore, what justifies it, is the result of not only what questions are posed, but of the framework in which they are posed.
>
> *(Lincoln, 2002, p. 4)*

She continues:

> The metaphysical paradigm with which one begins implies a pre ordinate sense of what "evidence" is, of where that might be obtained, of how it might be collected, and a set of implicit and explicit rules for judging how good (rigorous, thorough, "grounded") those evidences might be (Fisher 1977).... The paradigm, or metaphysical position of the researcher also has embedded in it the regulations for condensing, re-arraying and making plausible the arguments which are made, the implications teased out, and the conclusions drawn. As a result before qualitative evidence is judged, we have to know the metaphysical framework – the paradigm – within which is was originally collected, analyzed and presented.
>
> *(Lincoln, 2002, p. 4)*

In other words, the question of the validity of qualitative evidence must begin not with the evidence itself but with the theory or metaphysical framework in whose name the evidence is being collected. Just as in the existentialist formulation that "existence precedes essence," in conducting qualitative social science research, "theory precedes evidence" and even determines what evidence is. This is precisely how we began this project: with the cultural complex theory. Then we set out to find evidence that may lend credibility and reality to the theory. In a very real sense, I began with the theory and then set out to find out if there is evidence to validate the theory.

About the nature of evidence, Lincoln goes on to say:

> Qualitative data is any form of empirical materials, observable "traces" (film, TV, etc.) or observation which is largely non-quantitative. Into the category of empirical materials would fall, for instance, letters, memoranda, requests for proposals, interview notes, tape transcripts, formal records, films, photographs, official records, material "traces."
>
> *(Lincoln, 2002, p. 5)*

And Lincoln concludes her discussion of the nature of evidence/data with the following:

> Evidence is data brought to bear on specific questions, theories or experiences. Evidence is data with a purpose. The purpose may be historical, theoretical, evaluative or descriptive, but it is arrayed to some larger end, and it is arrayed in a specific kind of order. Evidence represents data to which have been added a layer – or multiple layers – of interpretation and rhetorical strategy. . . . All of these things – empirical materials, material traces, and observations – fall into the category of "data." That is, they can be collected, subjected to analysis, aggregated and disaggregated, rearranged, compressed and rearranged in order to advance arguments and insights regarding the nature of social life. Data, however, is not evidence until two things happen: first someone recognizes it as data and second, an inquirer subjects it to some form of systematic analysis, which turns it into evidence directed to some question or argument.
>
> *(Lincoln, 2002, pp. 5-6)*

To summarize, our research methodology from a social science perspective has been to use key informants from a variety of cultures to collect qualitative evidence in support of the cultural complex theory. Our contributors have functioned as key informants and have collected evidence from several sources suggested by the theory of cultural complexes as a way of grounding the theory in the world of specific group, time, place, and history. This qualitative evidence takes into account contributions from fields as varied as psychology, theology, anthropology, geography, economics, and history. It seeks to establish a solid foundation on which to generate additional questions about the cultural complex theory.

It is my hope that the scientific foundations for the study of the cultural complex will be strengthened by research in the neuroscience laboratory, in which cultural complex trigger words will be shown to light up those areas of the brain that are recruited when a cultural complex is stimulated or triggered. I imagine those areas to include centers associated with cognition, memory, image, affect, and behavior. And most importantly, it is my hope that the cultural complex research project stimulates lively inquiry and conversations about how the culture of diverse groups, often in conflict with one another, lives in the psyche of the group itself and its individual members.

Conclusion

I have come to think that what Jung said of personal complexes is equally true of cultural complexes. Cultural complexes are the hand that fate has dealt us as individuals and groups in our specific cultural climates. The fact that cultural complexes exist is no rarity or special circumstance of one particular group or place. Cultural complexes seem to be a naturally occurring part of the human condition. What makes them interesting is not that they exist but what human beings choose to do or not to do about them.

The easiest, perhaps most natural, thing to do about them is nothing and allow them to pass unchallenged and unconscious from generation to generation. They can give a deep sense of belonging to a particular group, clan, tribe, or nation, even as they occasionally wreak destructive havoc in the social order.

Another possible course of action with a cultural complex is to try to bring it into individual and group consciousness so that something new may happen. I view this way as having the potential for soul-making at the group level of the psyche. I believe that soul-making occurs in a culture when the painful tensions between different groups or within one group are endured and struggled with long enough to open up the possibility for transformation in the sense of leading to new feelings, new behaviors, new attitudes, and new possibilities. This may be rare, but it is possible. More usually, the tensions generated by cultural complexes tend to pit groups against one another and often end in prolonged stalemates or dangerous regressions.

Acknowledgments

This chapter would never have seen the light of day without the ongoing support of Nancy Cater, publisher of Spring Journal Books. Her belief in this project has been the sustaining force in its development. All of the authors and regional editors who have contributed to the Cultural Complex Series have brought the theory into the laboratory of the real world, where it has been able to take on the flesh and bones without which it would not be alive.

References

Lincoln, Y. S. (2002). *On the nature of qualitative evidence.* A paper for the annual meeting of the Association for the Study of Higher Education, Sacramento, CA, November 21–24, 2002.

Roger, E. (1960). *Physics for the inquiring mind: The methods, nature, and philosophy of physical science*. Princeton: Princeton University Press.

Singer, T., & Kimbles, S. (Eds.). (2004). *The cultural complex: Contemporary Jungian perspectives on psyche and society*. London and New York: Routledge.

Books and articles related to the cultural complex

Books

Amezaga, P., Barcellos, G., Capriles, A., Gerson, J., & Ramos, D. (2012). *Listening to Latin America*. New Orleans, LA: Spring Journal Books.

Europe's Many Souls: Exploring Cultural Complexes and Identities, edited by Thomas Singer and Joerg Rasche Spring Journal Books. January 25, 2016.

Kirsch, T. (Ed.). (2007). *Initiation: The living reality of an archetype*. London and New York: Routledge.

San, R., Dowd, A., & Tacey, D. (Eds.). (2011). *Placing psyche: Cultural complexes in Australia*. New Orleans, LA: Spring Journal Books.

Singer, T. (2000). *The vision thing: Myth, politics and psyche in the world*. London and New York: Routledge Press.

Singer, T. (2004). *The cultural complex: Contemporary Jungian perspectives on psyche and society*. London: Routledge.

Singer, T. (2010). *Psyche and the city: A soul's guide to the modern metropolis*. New Orleans, LA: Spring Journal Books.

Articles and chapters

Singer, T. (2002). The cultural complex and archetypal defenses of the collective spirit: Baby Zeus, Elian Gonzales, Constantine's sword, and other holy wars. *The San Francisco Library Journal, 20*(4), 4–28.

Singer, T. (2003). Cultural complexes and archetypal defenses of the group spirit. In J. Beebe (Ed.), *Terror, violence and the impulse to destroy* (pp. 191–209). Zurich: Daimon Verlag.

Singer, T. (2004). In the footsteps: The story of an initiatory drawing by Dr. Joseph Henderson. In Kirsch, T., Rutter, V.B. and Singer, T. (Eds.), *Initiation: The living reality of an archetype*. London: Routledge, 2007.

Singer, T. (2006a). The cultural complex: A statement of the theory and its application. In *Psychotherapy and politics international*. San Francisco, CA: Wiley.

Singer, T. (2006b). Unconscious forces shaping international conflicts: Archetypal defense of the group spirit from revolutionary America to conflict in the Middle East. *The San Francisco Jung Institute Library Journal, 25*(4), 6–28.

Singer, T. (2007a). A personal meditation on politics and the American soul. *Spring Journal, 78*, 121–147.

Singer, T. (2007b, September). ARAS: Archetypal symbolism and images. *Visual Resources, 23*(3), 245–267.

Singer, T. (2009a). A Jungian approach to 'us vs. them' dynamics. *Psychoanalysis, Culture and Society, 14*(1), 32–40.

Singer, T., with Kaplinsky, C. (2009b). The cultural complex. In M. Stein (Ed.), *Jungian psychoanalysis: Working in the spirit of C. G. Jung*. Chicago: Open Court.

Singer, T. (2010a). Playing the race card. In G. Heuer (Ed.), *Sacral revolutions: Reflecting on the work of Andrew Samuels*. London: Routledge.

Singer, T. (2010b). The transcendent function in society. *Journal of Analytical Psychology, 55*, 229–254.

Singer, T. (2010c). Afterword: St. Louis. In *Psyche and the city* (pp. 403–411). New Orleans, LA: Spring Journal Books.
Singer, T. (2012). The meshugana complex: Notes from a big galoot. *Jung Journal: Culture and Psyche*, 6(1), 72–84.
Singer, T. (2013). Amplification: A personal narrative. In E. Shalit and N. Furlotti (Eds.), *The dream and its amplification*. Sheridan, WY: Fisher King Press.

PART IV
Research on consciousness and emotion

6

THE SPECTRUMS OF EMOTION

In mythologies, philosophies, Analytical Psychology, and the neurosciences

Beverley Zabriskie

This chapter is concerned with historical and contemporary engagements with emotion in the history of *Homo sapiens*. It reviews the mythologies and philosophies of the past, traces some clinical observations from consulting rooms since the time of C.G. Jung (1875–1961), and presents the framing of emotion from current neurosciences. It pursues various approaches and descriptions of emotional states and moments from and toward interdisciplinary and cross-disciplinary discourse regarding personal and social roles of emotion.

As our inherited stories and rituals allow glimpses into the human experience of the generations, while our philosophies reveal the reflections of thinkers and musers, we will address how emotions have been depicted and unpacked from the earliest societies and parsed in our philosophical and more esoteric pursuits. For a time, emotion was neglected in 20th-century research and then revived as a subject for serious study in the neurosciences. We will amplify its sources, similarities, and differences with Carl Jung's seminal concepts about the purpose and dynamics of emotion in his clinical and theoretical framework.

We will suggest how Jungian concerns and concepts are at play in present emotion research. We will highlight implicit and explicit convergence between Jung's theses and the hypotheses of current neuroscientific research and philosophies of mind, noting how their commentaries weigh and value certain issues. These include:

- The emergence of emotion from a physiological basis transmittable via our mammalian origins and common ground of being;
- Psychological development on an arc from what Jung termed the infrared of instinct to affect to emotion to feeling to the ultraviolet of archetypal imagery;
- The arenas of inherent survival emotions around basic and significant life issues vis-à-vis the expression and images with contextual valence of cultural and social emotions;

- The affective basis for the disassociability and multiplicity of psychological states;
- The mandate for affective regulation and equilibrium for an intentional life;
- The connections between emotion and imagination, emotion and communication, emotion and cognition – that is, emotion and psychic energy *per se*.

The basic difference in the goals of the many traditions which embrace emotion will be mentioned. The why of emotion in depth psychology and the what of emotion in neuroscience will be a hovering background for this discussion.

The heart in humanity's histories

Across the known millennia, emotion has been at the heart of most matters. Spectrums of affect, emotion, and feeling have been at play in species-wide encounters as well as personal and group engagements. Human history has been shaped and reshaped, colored, and gauged by the appraisals, use, and misuse of emotion. Cultural, intellectual, religious, and scientific stances on emotion have impacted turns of mind and pivots in history. Indeed, it could be said that emotion is the source of all we perceive as process.

Mythopoetic cosmologies anthropomorphized the external world by projecting emotion as the dynamic source of the universe. Emotionally laden origin stories; the cosmogonies of our cultures and creation stories of our tribes; the rites of birth, death, and rebirth; the imagined first seconds of the universe; and the embodied first moments of life have been linked by our emotive associations.

Ritual has aimed to transform emotion. Our visual, kinetic, and musical arts have sought to evoke, express, and educate our species about dreaded and desired emotion. Indeed, thought and language, thesis and conceit, dogma and opinion, experiment and result have emerged from the matrix of emotion, a fundamental source of psychic energy.

The ancient Egyptians supported the "thought of the heart" and the "tongue that speaks the hearts' words." The poetry of the Sumerians intoned romantic and existential longing. The Song of Songs expressed passion through stunning imagistic portrayals of the beloved.

In many civilizations, speculations about and definitions of emotions have historically been a purview of philosophy, from the symposia of ancient Greece, the schools of Greco-Roman discourse, and the ponderings of Church Fathers.

Ecclesiastical figures such as Augustine and Aquinas bore down with a devotional sobriety and suspicion of emotions as Eden-like vectors toward lust and concupiscence. The personal pleasures and ravages of the instinctual/emotional spectrum were matters for sublimation, abstinence, deserving of penance for oneself or punishment by others. In the Roman Catholic tradition in which I was raised, the motto was "Nothing is so good that the giving up of it isn't better."

In the Christian dispensation, paradoxically subjective emotion was suspect as inferior and heretically individualistic, while collective religious emotionality was evoked as an antidote to unseemly or destructive affect, a stimulant for moving through the righteous life into a redeemed beyond. It was also the glue and gloss which bound and congealed congregations through evocative and symbolic liturgies and sensual aesthetics of images, scents, and embracing architecture.

From the 17th century onward, the purveyors of an Age of Enlightenment framed the individual as a dualistic entity of body and mind, or body and soul, or body and spirit. Personhood, in this proto-psychological philosophy, was a binary of cool cognition emanating from the brain, while suspect affects, emotions, and feelings emanated from the body to heat and cloud the mind.

Meanwhile, religious and philosophical Western traditions often overlapped. In *Soul Machine: The Invention of the Modern Mind*, George Makari traces how Descartes's 1637 *Meditations* were countered by Spinoza's 1667 *Ethics*, with its assertions of both a natural soul and soul in Nature, of a thought as material, of affects as "inadequately known ideas . . . and passions as dim ideas that required control" (Makari, 2015, pp. 111–112).

The Cartesian "thing that thinks" aimed to quell and distance emotions lest they confuse, complicate, or undo certain rational thought on which identity rested. Descartes opined that if one could think of a self as in "I am," one could be held apart from body and a "passive, mechanical Nature" (Makari, 2015, pp. 27–29). Thus liberated from the sweat of emotions, the thinker would be linked to divine mind.

Descartes's near contemporary Spinoza, meanwhile, fostered the notion of parallelism rather than dualism. For him, mind is constituted via its idea of the body, which we notice through its changes, active affects, and confused passions which impact the mind. In his view, achieving balance through an economy of affect would allow for freedom from bondage for the Mind as a finite part of the whole substance of the universe. In Spinoza's scheme, God was accessible through perceptions and experiences of nature, not only via the rational. No surprise then that the neuroscientist Antonio Damasio found himself *Looking for Spinoza* as his research delved into emotion, and into the core and extended consciousness he perceived as dependent on the mapping of the body in the mind.

For both these theorists, as well as Hobbes, Leibniz, Newton, and Kepler, the mathematics of mind and world would be revealed through mechanistic constructs of formulas and number. This is relevant background in the current discussions of mathematical psychology and computational behavioral theory, as emotions as theorems extend into behavioral economics, artificial intelligence, and robotics.

Equators and margins of experience

The view of humans as special emanations of divine mind, entirely apart from other beings, was dealt an existential blow when the naturalist explorer Charles Darwin crossed hemispheres and the equator and transgressed establishment boundaries and philosophical limits. When he gathered his courage to publish his findings, Darwin challenged the intellectual and religious establishments by positing a common ground of species-crossing emotions.

The question of who we are remained within the domain of the human until Darwin extended not only instinctive but also emotional links between the human species and animals. His work impacted Jung at an early age. Jung wrote:

> I grew up in a house two hundred years old ... mentally my greatest adventure had been the study of Kant and Schopenhauer. The great news of the day was the work of Charles Darwin.
>
> (Jung, 1977, para. 485)

In his 1872 *The Expression of the Emotions in Man and Animals*, Darwin traced emotion in facial and bodily expressions, reactions, and responses, not only from the human heart and brain, but also from animal behaviors. This initiated a new phase of scientific inquiry that widened the language and deepened the observations of ranges and registers of emotion. In our current era, researchers trace emotion active on the spectrum from the reptilian to the human. The affective neuroscientist Jaak Panksepp, for instance, urges that we learn about play and laughter among rats (Panksepp, 1998, p. 282).

Jung was also interested in the effect of those personalities whose work dominated the 19th century, albeit from contrasting backgrounds, temperaments, and positions. Goethe's dramatic elaborations of humankind's Faustian bargains engaged Jung from adolescence throughout his life.

Jung's most ambivalent tussle was with Friedrich Nietzsche, whose passion he admired while the unrealized aspects of his life and values evoked a negative fascination.

In 1883, the restless, individualistic Nietzsche, a philosopher, who deemed himself a psychologist, brought his hermit idealist Zarathustra down from his mountain top for direct and grounded, messy encounters with skeptical earthbound crowds. His entanglements with the common and ordinary relativized the projections of superiority on the only spiritual quest. Emotion was inserted as a matter for layered real-life experience to complement the metaphysical reaches of much philosophy. In *Thus Spake Zarathustra*, Nietzsche pronounced "Joy – deeper still than grief can be" (Hollingdale, 1960, p. 103).

Nietzsche hovers in Jung's psychic background, emerges in the topic of Jung's seminars, and informs Jung's seminal *Red Book*, where Jung plunges into and confronts his own "dread emotions."

Meanwhile, across the Atlantic, William James was inserting the topic of emotion into Harvard's Philosophy and Psychology Department, publishing *What Is an Emotion?* in 1884. James differentiated Darwinian generalized evolutionary theory in the context of physiological psychology which suggested individual differences in consciousness, to be studied as a laboratory science.

His insistence that emotion emerged from a "bottom-up" primacy, placed emotion on body to mind register of physically induced emotional experience, both preceding and leading to understanding.

Unlike his ongoing ambivalence toward Nietzsche, Jung often noted his debt to James with expressions of gratitude. Following James's claim on religious experience and occult experiment as margins of the psychological, the young Jung had visited séances in Switzerland (Jung, 1968, paras. 527–530). He often cited James's work:

> You will invariably find that you apply the word "emotional" when it concerns a condition that is characterized by physiological innervations. Therefore, you can measure emotions to a certain extent, not their psychic part but the physiological part. You know the James–Lange theory of affect. I take emotion as affect, it is the same as "something affects you." It does something to you – it interferes with you. Emotion is the thing that carries you away. You are thrown out of yourself; you are beside yourself as if an explosion had moved you out of yourself and put you beside yourself. There is a quite tangible physiological condition which can be observed at the same time. So the difference would be this: feeling has no physical or tangible physiological manifestations, while emotion is characterized by an altered physiological condition.
>
> *(Jung, 1977, para. 46)*

Just as James individualized Darwin's contribution to species categorizations of emotion, so Jung later noted his difference from James as he attempted to differentiate instinct, emotion and feeling, and devotion. Jung perceives that William James's description of the idealist as religious and the empiricist as irreligious depends on his definition of religiousness. If religious is taken to mean an attitude in which religious ideas (rather than feelings) are dominant, then James's empiricist type can be called irreligious. However, a religious attitude can also represent feeling; moreover, psychological (uncritical) devotion to either the idea of God or the idea of matter can exist, although this attitude can be called "religious" only when it is absolute. Thus the empiricist can be religious. Jung concluded that, in developing these terms, James was led astray: "we must once again assume that he was thrown off the rails by his emotions, as can happen all too easily" (Jung, 1968, para. 530).

A Britannica Encyclopedia entry on emotion reads:

> From the very beginning of scientific psychology, there were voices that spoke of the significance of emotions for human life. James believed that "individuality is founded in feeling" and that only through feeling is it possible "directly to perceive how events happen, and how work is actually done." The Swiss psychiatrist Carl Gustav Jung recognized emotion as the primal force in life.
>
> *(www.britannica.com)*

In *The Nature of Emotion, Fundamental Questions* (editors Ekman and Davidson), James Averill's chapter title, "I Feel, Therefore I Am, I Think," indicates a current vector in mainstream emotions theory. He notes:

> Two types of emotion theories can be distinguished, corresponding roughly to the distinction between feelings of and feelings about. The well-known theory of William James is a good example of the former. According to James, emotions are basically feelings of bodily changes as they occur. Carl Jung

provides an equally good illustration of the second view. According to Jung (1921) emotional feelings are essentially value judgments – feelings about. From a Jungian standpoint, if I am asked to describe my emotional feelings, I would not describe bodily sensations: instead, I would indicate how I evaluate the situation. Most contemporary theories of emotion tend to combine feelings of and feelings about.

(Ekman & Davidson, 1994, p. 381)

Another Jamesian notion, of several part selves, stimulated Jung's perception of complexes which functioned as "splinter psyches," and of the psyche itself as a 'multiplicity within a unity.' Depth psychology and analytic practice delved into the enigmas of these multiple layers of a self, especially in its intense identifications with emotional states.

From philosophy to psychiatry to depth psychology

In 1903 Jung had written "If there is any field of experience that teaches the dependence of action upon emotions, that field is certainly psychiatry" (Jung, CW I, 1970, para. 220).

As a young psychiatrist, Jung traveled to Paris, became familiar with Charcot, and attended Janet's grand rounds. While a 29-year-old psychiatrist under Bleuler at Zurich's Burgholzli clinic, Jung further developed the word association experiment, tracing those autonomous psycho-physical markers such as delayed timing, frozen or fraught reactions, akin to emotional tics he termed "complexes." (His experiments later became misused in lie detector tests for suspects, as if a complexed reaction was an implicit admission of guilt rather than a marker of any unresolved issues.) These non-ego knots, bundles, or quantums of energy, like James's part selves and Janet's splinter psyches, impressed Jung with the disassociability of the personality and influenced his frequent description of the psyche as a multiplicity within a unity.

Jung had read Freud. He sent the older Viennese neurologist the word association data as proof of the existence of the unconscious. Their discourse began. The analyst and theorist James Hillman notes the context:

> Jung like Freud, had been writing about emotional phenomena for many years, and like Freud, has no single explicit theory of emotion. Both consider it of first importance and both understand it through that system of operations called the unconscious. But where Freud was influenced in his explanation by a neurological and biological background, Jung's first views on emotion takes rise in psychiatry and his association with Bleuler. "The essential basis of our personality is affectivity. Thought and action are only, as it were, symptoms of affectivity." (DP) But where Bleuler treated emotion or affectivity as a kind of molar, quantitative, and generalized event, Jung showed an interest in the differentiation of this general affectivity.

(Hillman, 1972, p. 59)

Jung saw the complexes as unconscious phenomena; he sent his results to Freud. Their connection and correspondence lasted from 1902 to 1912, to be severed by Jung's divergence from Freud's thesis that all psychic energy is sexual in essence. As we shall see, influenced by the physicists of his day, Jung came to his theory that psychic energy is a matter of intensities, neutral in content, rather than a carrier of sexual libido per se.

From the late 19th century onward, depth psychology and analytic practice delved into the enigmas of these multiple components of a self, especially in its intense identifications with and disassociations from emotional states. Meanwhile psychiatry moved away from emotions toward the treatment of moods through medication.

We will explore how the current research of the neuropsychiatrist and neurobiologist Rodolfo Llinas on the distinct agendas of different cells, and the developmental psychobiologist and psychiatrist Myron Hofer's work on embodied emergent phenomena, are contemporary extensions of this interior multiverse sensibility.

In a parallel process, to use James's terms, "tough-minded" 20th-century neuroscience perceived emotions as too "tender-minded" to warrant serious research. Then, in the 1990s, the predispositions of instinct, emotion, and feelings became a more robust topic in our neurosciences. As we shall discuss, simultaneous conversation about emotional transmission, which Jung had described in his texts on transference, was highlighted by the discovery of mirror neuron systems of communication.

While there is little agreement on what constitutes which emotion, there are traditions and schools of emotions studies which extend past traditions. Jung could be called a neo-Jamesian neo-Darwinian. Contemporary researchers such as Jaak Panksepp of the Affective Neuroscience School, and Paul Ekman, who studies micro and macro cross-cultural emotional expressions, posit both universal survival enhancing emotion, and secondary social emotions affected by surround and context. This jibes with Jung's model of a patterning psyche, as a process with a predisposition to create images and themes around significant experience, described as archetypal when discussing basic survival emotions, while the cultural and personal iterations of social emotions were adaptive to the environment of families, groups, and communities.

Multiple domains of emotional experience

James's intuition and observation claimed several domains and disciplines – philosophy, religion, and science – as margins of the psychological. He also embraced the scientist Maxwell's idea of "fields" and hence pursued varieties of psychic experience in the range Jung came to term the ultraviolet experience of archetypal concepts presented as the revelations and inspirations of religious experience.

On the other end of his spectrum, James also astutely saw correspondence between Niels Bohr's notions of complementarities in physics with depth psychology's framing of the subconscious in a complementary axis with consciousness.

Jung conversed with Albert Einstein and later, with the quantum physicist Wolfgang Pauli, coined the notion of synchronicity for those surprising episodes of convergence between interior ideas and outer events, felt as links of mind with matter through the interface of the human brain with the surrounding world.

In 1932, Jung wrote of his belief that as psychological events are bound up with the organic nervous system: it

> is simply impossible to imagine any experimental set-up which could prove that the psyche exists independently of living matter. This is not to say that it could not exist without matter, since we also take it for granted that matter exists without psyche, doubtful as this appears in the light of the latest finding of quantum physics.
>
> *(Jung, 1973a,* Collected Letters V *1, pp. 87–88)*

Jung's embrace of a parallel perspective opened his thinking both to the psychophysical vectors of psychic energy and a mind–matter continuum. His recognition of this relevance to personal process is traceable in his perceptions of liminal "psychoid" phenomena inevitable in the incarnated consciousness of a personal self.

Jung and Einstein taught at Zurich's Polytechnic Institute (ETH). In a January 1911 letter to Freud, Jung recounts a home dinner with Bleuler and another invited guest, a young physicist: "we spent the whole evening talking with a physicist about . . . the electrical theory of light" (The Freud/Jung Letters, 1974, p. 171). Conversations with Einstein about energy per se stimulated Jung's unease with Freud's notion of all psychic energy as sexual. In his September 1912 lectures at Fordham University, Jung's assertion of non-sexual libido finally alienated him from Freud. Jung later wrote:

> the sexual instinct enters into combination with many different feelings, emotions, affects . . . to such a degree that the attempt has even been made to trace the whole of culture to these combinations.
>
> *(Jung, 1970, para. 238)*

Jung referred instead to

> various manifestations of energic processes and thus as forces analogous to heat, light, etc. Just as it would not occur to the modern physicist to derive all forces from, shall we say, heat alone, so the psychologist should beware of lumping all instincts under the concept of sexuality.
>
> *(Jung, 1965, pp. 208–209)*

In his later biographical interviews in *Memories, Dreams, and Reflections*, Jung remembers reformulating drive-based libido into

> a psychic analogue of physical energy, . . . a more or less quantitative concept, which . . . should not be defined in qualitative terms. . . . to escape from the

then prevailing concretism of the libido theory – ... in other words, I wished no longer to speak of the instincts of hunger, aggression, and sex, but to regard all these phenomena as expressions of psychic energy.

(Jung, 1965, p. 208)

Jung's model of emotion

Jung's model of an affective psyche infused with neutral psychic energy as intensities rather than specific qualities is a key concept in his formulations of both energy and emotion. It allows transformation, as distinct from sublimation, in that a neutral energy transcends any qualitative content and form. Thus various complexes formed around unresolved emotions forge the "royal road" to the unconscious through the operations of dreams.

Psyche's essence and task, Jung believed, was to regulate the discharges of reflexive primal instinct, to calibrate and channel expressions of primary emotions. Thus the unresolved emotions knotted in complexes informed the teleological intentionality toward resolution woven in the fabric of dreams. The capacity to carry the tension of affective opposites and emotional ambivalence became a treatment goal, the integration or *coniunctio* necessary for individuation.

> Fluctuations of emotion are, of course, the constant concomitants of all psychic opposites, and hence of all conflicts of ideas, whether moral or otherwise. We know from experience that the emotions thus aroused increase in proportion as the exciting factor affects the individual as a whole.
>
> (Jung, 1971, para. 329)

Emotional ordering through affect regulation is the sought path to value-laden feeling discernment and appraisal. Otherwise,

> We see how the psychic energy applies itself wholly to the complex at the expense of the other psychic material, which in consequence remains unused. All stimuli that do not suit the complex undergo partial apperceptive degeneration with emotional impoverishment. Even the feeling-tone becomes inappropriate: trifles such as ribbons, pressed flowers, snapshots, *billets doux*, a lock of hair, etc. are cherished with the greatest care, while vital questions are often dismissed.
>
> (Jung, 1960, paras. 102–103)

The word association experiment revealed emotional disruption and dissociation, which Jung addressed throughout his work. He saw that "what is 'primarily characterological' is, in the wider sense, the feeling-tone, whether it be too little or too much."

> The flow of objective thought is constantly interrupted by invasions from the complex, there are long gaps in one's thought filled out with erotic episodes.

> This well-known paradigm shows clearly the effect of a strong complex on a normal psyche, with a smile or with complete indifference.
>
> *(Jung, 1960, pp. 102–103)*

Jung anticipated subsequent brain research would confirm his observations. Indeed the word association test Jung conducted more than a century ago is still a valid precursor of current neuroscience probings.

At the 2014 Congress of Neuro-psychoanalysis, researchers from Bonn's German Center for Neurodegenerative Diseases reported the results of their fMRIs in "Two Studies on the Neurobiology of Repression." They noted that "Carl Gustave Jung developed an experimental design based on free association to empirically detect a person's complex (similar to the Freudian conflict)." While a Jungian would describe this as guided association and perceive disassociation rather than repression, the results confirm Jung's work in physiological terminology.

In the first study,

> Associations to conflict-related sentences were more likely to be forgotten than associations to not-conflict-related sentences, and were accompanied by increases in skin conductor responses (SCR) and reaction times (RTs). We observed enhanced activation of the anterior cingulate cortex and deactivation of hippocampus and para-hippocampal cortex during association to conflict related sentences.

In the second study,

> Associations to individualized conflict-related sentences were more likely to be forgotten than associations to not-conflict-related negative sentences, and were accompanied by increases in SCRs and RTs.

The neurobiological conclusions:

> These two experiments demonstrate that high autonomic arousal (measured via SCR) during free association predicts subsequent memory failure. These results were furthermore accompanied by increased activation of conflict-related and deactivation of memory related brain regions. The results are consistent with the hypothesis that during repression, explicit memory systems are down-regulated by the anterior cingulate cortex.
>
> *(Schmidt, 2014)*

Personal complexes and dread emotions

After his 1913 break from Freud, and amidst premonitions of an impending World War I, Jung began a personal record of transformation, *The Red Book*. When he closed this journal, Jung focused his scholarship on alchemical texts and the alchemists' attempts to diagram humanity's place in the cycles of the planet and its moving galaxies. From 1928, Jung studied the psycho-physical valences of philosophical and experimental alchemy as mind–matter projective engagement seeking combinations and extractions, integrations, and separations.

Alchemical texts seem a strange detour for a hands-on clinician. However, Jung traced the al-chemistry of affective psychic energy, a Rorschach-like model of interaction between results in retorts and introjected analogies of emotional dynamics.

In the anthropic view of philosophical alchemy, humankind was framed as an integral entity of both mind and matter, and human figures drawn by artists such as Robert Fludd were superimposed as micro figures on the macro reality of a created universe.

Jung had been powerfully impacted by the alchemist/physician Gerald Dorn, who extended the crucial question of "who" to "what" we are, a question pursued today as "dual aspect monism" (Atmanspacher, 2012). Indeed, in the analytic consulting room, as well as casual self-descriptions of emotional states, we evoke the images and terms of physics, and the dynamics of the elements – earth and fire, water and air – active in Western alchemical operations. The dual-function terms of Gestalt Psychology also recognized that self-state expressions emerge from physics – we are cool and fluid, grounded and embedded, volatile and dynamic, hot and enflamed.

Jung's river analogy in his seminal 1928 "On Psychic Energy," his emphasis on an alchemical *solutio* as an essential start for process seems to flow from this nearly alchemical passage from James:

> The traditional psychology talks like one who should say a river consists of nothing but pailful, spoonful, quartpotsful, barrelsful, and other moulded forms of water. Even where the pails and the pots are actually standing in the stream, still between them the free water would continue to flow. It is just this free water of consciousness that psychologists resolutely overlook. Every definite image in the mind is steeped and dyed in the free water that flows around it. With it goes the sense of its relations, near and remote, the dying echo of whence it came to us, the dawning sense of whither it is to lead. The significance, the value, of the image is all in this halo or penumbra that surrounds and escorts it, or rather that is fused into one with it and has become bone of its bone and flesh of its flesh.
>
> *(James, 1890, p. 255)*

One hears alchemical echoes when Jung writes of emotional psychic energy as fiery:

> [T]he fire of affects and emotions, and like every other fire it has two aspects, that of combustion and that of creating light. On the one hand emotion is the alchemical fire whose warmth brings everything into existence and whose heat burns all superfluities to ashes (*omnes superfluitates comburit*). But on the other hand, emotion is the moment when steel meets flint and a spark

is struck forth, for emotion is the chief source of consciousness. There is no change from darkness to light or from inertia to movement without emotion.
(Jung, 1969, para. 179)

Evoking air, Hillman writes:

> Psychologically we could say, every affect tends to become an autonomous complex, to break away from the hierarchy of consciousness, and, if possible, to drag the ego after it.... Spirit in this case is the image of an independent affect, and therefore the ancients appropriately called spirits also *imagines*, images.
> (Hillman, 1972, p. 61)

The alchemists introspection about their internal and surrounding physical world seemed to Jung a proto-science – a proto-chemistry, proto-physics, and proto-psychology. The probing of those philosophical alchemists pursued the correspondences among their subjective opus, their micro experiments in their retorts, and the macro operations of the perceived universe.

Affect and emotion in the consulting room

Analysts ask not what is an emotion but rather what is the source and purpose of emotion. Jung grasped the personal and familial complexes of the personal unconscious, the impacts of the cultural unconscious, and the impersonal, universal dominants of the collective unconscious. These hint of both Darwinian notions of natural selection and descent in evolution, and the currently revived neo-Lamarckian attention to epigenetics.

Psychic equilibrium among degrees of intensity in the conscious, the complexes, and the unconscious is the aim of Jungian treatment. Discerning reflection allows affect regulation, options for expression, and emotional integration to achieve value-laden feeling appraisal and a stable stance based on understanding. Internal engagement with both the conjoined conscious and unconscious, and a calibrated receptivity to one's external context, balances affect, attention, focus, memory, and relationship. This produces a consciousness akin to what the neuroscientist Gerald Edelman has termed the "remembered present" (Edelman, 1992).

In Jung's analytic psychology, emotional development of the individual as a mind–body continuum is a multi-aspected process emerging from a spectrum of instinct, affect, emotion, feeling – and embedded mood. While conscious and unconscious are in a compensatory or complementary dynamic with each other, they are both the "kissing cousins" of psyche in interactive conjunctions on a fluid threshold of different kinds of knowing.

In this sense Jung is a monist, perceiving the unity that contains the multiplicity. While he posited the conscious–unconscious dialectic, he is not a dualist nor a theorist of the binary. Rather psyche is "an equilibration of all kinds of opposites."

From the bundles or "quantums" of different intensities, energy may be released to flow along internally interactive axes or knotted in unresolved internal biases and conflicts, given the "splinter psyches" of emotionally toned complexes. Jung perceived the human personality as a process among various instinctive, emotional, and archetypal tendencies, each with its own agenda. Equilibrium is attained via internal discourse among interactive and disparate agendas. As mentioned, the modern notions of part-selves on a monistic spectrum is akin to the today's Mind-Brain Continuum theorist Rodolfo Llinas, whose experiments find different agendas in each cell.

Jung's 1948 address at the founding of the Zurich Jung Institute reveals his abiding concern with complex phenomena:

> The manifold possibilities for the further development of complex psychology correspond to the various developmental stages it has already passed through. So far as the experimental aspect is concerned, there are still numerous questions which need to be worked out by experimental and statistical methods. I have had to leave many beginnings unfinished . . . the potentialities of the association experiment are by no means exhausted yet. For instance, the periodical renewal of the emotional tone of complex-stimulators is still unanswered, the problem of familial patterns of association has remained stuck in its beginnings . . . and so has the investigation of the physiological concomitants of the complex.
> *(Jung, 1977, para. 1137)*

Decades of later research about the multiple agendas of human parts and layers, organs and cells, confirm his model.

Today, Myron Hofer writes of "component processes underlying the psychological constructs we use to understand attachment to convey the idea that these biological processed 'embody' the psychological constructs" (Hofer, 2014, pp. 16–17). Hofer perceives "the mental life of humans and the observed events and inferred processes of the psychoanalytic situation as having 'emerged' in both evolution and development from the biological level." He explains:

> I have used the words "emerge" and "embody" here because they seem to me to be the best and simplest ways to refer to the still mysterious processes through which the unconscious and conscious processes of humans derive from their bodies and brains. Both words are used . . . in the sense of "emergent" properties of complex dynamic systems and embodied cognition.
> *(Hofer, 2014, pp. 16–17)*

From the Jungian tradition, Hillman summarizes and encompasses the sources, directions, ends, contexts, and locales of emotion.

> Having the four hypotheses of the four causes of emotion, the integration asked for takes places as follows: Emotion is symbol, energy, psyche,

transformation. Each emotion has: its own pattern of behaviour and quality of experience which is always a total attitude of the whole psyche (*causa formalis*); its own distribution and intensity of energy in the field of the human body situation (*cause materialis*); its own consciousness; its own achieved transformation which has some survival value and is some improvement compared with non-emotional states (*causa finalis*).

(Hillman, 1972, p. 286)

Emotions as images in psyche and neuroscience

In Jung's 1955 introduction to his final opus, he noted that the structure and function of the bodily organs including the brain are the same everywhere, hence "the psyche is to a large extent dependent on this organ" (Jung, 1955, p. xix). Hence our images and narratives for our significant experience have common foundations, although valued differently in diverse cultures.

In current research and philosophy of mind, Rodolfo Llinas describes his theory of "endogenous" images, as he posits that "the brain consists of intrinsic images, which exist before and apart from sensory perception" (Llinas, 1997, p. 4). His laboratory suggests a neurological basis for an internal, image-creating process. They speak of "endogenesis," wherein sensory experience is created not via incoming signals from the world, but by intrinsic, continuing processes of the brain. They see the central nervous system as a closed system whose basic organization is oriented toward generating intrinsic images. Brains are self-activating and capable of generating cognitive representations in the absence of sensory input. Sensory inputs specify internal states and modify activity in this closed system. The role of sensory input is to "trellis, shape, and otherwise sculpt" (Llinas, 1997, p. 4) intrinsic neural activity to produce survival-enhancing representations.

Llinas posits dreams as key evidence, even suggesting that "dreaming and wakefulness are similar from electro-physiological and neurological points of view." Turning our biases upside down, he posits wakefulness as a dreamlike state modulated by sense perceptions. Such images emerge when pressed by what Ekman categorizes as basic survival emotions, instigating Jung's most fundamental tendencies toward expression via word and images:

> *Emotions* have a typical "pattern" (fear, anger, sorrow, hatred, etc.); that is they follow an inborn archetype which is universally human and arouses the same ideas and feeling in everyone. These "patterns" appear as archetypal motifs chiefly in dreams.
>
> *(Jung, 1975, Letters, volume 2, p. 537)*

Emotion studies have crossed and connected the depth psychological engagements of our psychotherapies and the psychiatry of mood disorders, sharing borders with contemporary neuroscience to confirm our knowledge of emotional process. Jung's theory of the universal emotional dominants of the archetypes per se and cultural iterations of the archetypal is aligned with some current notions of basic survival-enhancing emotions and secondary adaptive cultural and social emotions. From affective neuroscience, Jaak Panksepp notes "the evolutionary layering of the brain, the raw affective substrates of mind have a more ancient evolutionary history than our sense of cognitive awareness (Panksepp, 1998).

From V.S. Ramachandran's perspective, "although emotions are phylogenetically ancient and regarded as more primitive, in humans they are probably just as sophisticated as reason" (Ramachandran, 2004, p. 7). The researcher of emotions, Joseph LeDoux, notes that "feelings come about when the activity of specialized emotion systems get represented in the system that gives rise to consciousness, and I'm using working memory as a fairly widely accepted version of how the latter might come about" (LeDoux, 1998, p. 283).

For him, "the central revelation of the scientific study of emotion is that our brain is as much if not more an emotional organ as it is a cognitive one." He asserts "emotional experience derives from emotional schemas not just from cognitive interpretations or physiological arousal." He writes:

> The concept of basic emotions accounts for the similarity of basic emotional expression across individuals and cultures and display rules take care of many differences.... Many emotions are products of evolutionary wisdom, which probably has more intelligence than all human minds together.
> *(LeDoux, 1998, pp. 36, 118)*

LeDoux also links emotion to memory in his thesis that prior emotional learning and emotional memory is stronger than our cognitive learning or emotional process.

In his chapter, "Sleep, Arousal, and Mythmaking in the Brain," the affective neuroscientist Jaak Panksepp concurs:

> Each day our lives cycle through the master routines of sleeping, dreaming and waking. All our activities are guided by the age old rhythms of nature, and many neural mechanisms assure that we remain in tune with the cycling of days and nights across the seasons. Our brains contain endogenous daily rhythm generators, and also, perhaps calendar mechanisms that respond to monthly lunar cycles, as well as the transit of the seasons.
> *(Panksepp, 1998, p. 125)*

As to our species interactions amidst these attunements, Paul Ekman's Facial Action Coding System of the innate emotions – anger, disgust, fear, joy, sorrow, and surprise – demonstrates emotions expressed and recognized across cultures. While other researchers have objections to his system, it has had a neo-Darwinian impact on current affective studies and is an implicit basis for transmissions of mood and emotional states across cultural borders.

The discovery in the 1990s of the mirror neuron system in emotional transmissions and learning through imitation added another dimension to our understanding of how emotions are transmitted between persons and groups.

Jung's clinical remarks are prescient regarding the discovery of mirror neurons. Our physiological sense perceptions and our nervous system's "neuronal coupling" play a leading role in mirror neurons transmissions in learning and communication.

For Jung, emotions are the mercurial messengers between psyche and soma, in the psycho–physical or "psychoid" life, and between seemingly separate species and individuals. He modeled a face-to face clinical engagement between analyst and analysand as a means for fuller affective engagement.

In the analytic process and life's interactions, experience emerges from embodied presence. Jung remarks:

> Not for nothing did alchemy style itself an "art," feeling, and rightly so – that it was concerned with creative processes that can be truly grasped only by experience, though intellect may give them a name. . . . Experience . . . is what leads to understanding.
>
> In psychotherapy, even if the doctor is entirely detached from the emotional contents of the patient, the very fact that the patient has emotions has an effect upon him. . . . It is even his duty to accept the emotions of the patient and to mirror them.
>
> (Jung, 1977, para. 319)

The psychotherapist may become

> psychically infected and poisoned by the projections. . . . it may even disturb his sympathetic system . . . as the peculiar emotional condition of the patient does have a contagious effect. . . (and) arouses similar vibrations in the nervous system of the analyst.
>
> (Jung, 1977, para. 356)

Jung's terms and language may belong to earlier eras, but his observations on emotion are echoed when neuroscientists write of "theories of other minds," of attunement, mirror neurons, strange-loop exchange, the conjunctions of emergence from complexity, the transmitting of moods and emotions, and neural coupling among individuals. Since the mid-nineties discovery of "mirror neurons" by Gallese and Rizzoleti in Parma, we are more alert to human and animal, person to person imitation learning. Group family and generational transmission are being traced via the genetic pre-dispositions, epigenetic influences, and cultural norms affecting individuals and aligned kinship circles. The functions of mirror neuronal imagination, when reading literature or watching sports or pornography is well documented.

Psycho–psychic energy

The neutrality of psychic energy impelled Jung and Jungian theorists toward ecumenical explorations from various disciplines. Without apology, Jung borrowed analogies and amplifications from many fields. He perceived aspects of psyche in human constructs, experiments, and invention. Indeed the human mind-body being can see and project itself as part of the cosmos, an odd amalgamation of random gases described by alchemists as personality traits and reactions. In the current shift from the anthropic to Anthropocene age, the emotion-laden motivations and intentions of our species will have a far more profound effect on our planetary environment than a choleric alchemist had on the sulfurs and substances in his retorts.

Arising first from physical awareness, emotions secrete our al-chemistry, and form the hues, temperatures, weights, and measures in the wiring of our brains and the biology of body, and Hillman notes:

> an essential fact of emotion is that it terminates in the subject's own body. Whether one likes it or not, the fact remains as psychosomatic symptoms demonstrate. Therefore, the very first step in the development of emotions is going with the downward discharge.
>
> *(Hillman, 1972, p. 28)*

Early on, James and Jung announced emotions' effect on the sympathetic nervous system, the heart, the vagus nerve, and gut. The peptide theory of Candace Pert, and the Polyvagal Theory of Steven Porges, continue these lines of investigation. Pert speaks of her research on peptides and "emotional resonance" as the way emotions change every cell in the human body and also literally change the frequencies of nonverbal communication:

> If we accept the idea that peptides and other informational substances are the bio-chemicals of emotion, their distribution throughout the body's nerves has all kinds of significance. Sigmund Freud would be delighted, because the idea that the body, in its totality, is also the unconscious mind, would be the molecular confirmation of his theories. Body and mind are simultaneous. I like to speculate that the mind is the flow of information as it moves among the cells, organs, and systems of the body. The mind, as we experience it, is immaterial, yet it has a physical substrate that is both the body and the brain.
>
> *(www.lowenfoundation.org/forum/viewtopic.php?f=8&t=81 &sid=d3098b39849a9564e6e0b2cac80655c4)*

Vectors of emotion research

> We cannot individuate concepts and beliefs without reference to the environment. The brain and the nervous system cannot be considered in isolation from states of the world and social interactions. But such states, both environmental and social, are indeterminate and open-ended.
>
> *(Edelman, 1992, p. 224)*

Current vectors in emotions studies are necessarily linked to various trends in our societies, disciplines, and technologies. As I write in mid-2017, emotion research is relevant in feminist theories of organic and cultural tendencies and queer studies of gendered states of mind and body. Emotion enters the conversations, codes, and computations of artificial intelligence and is at play in the attempt to make robotics emotional as well as mechanical. Meanwhile, the effects of the possible dehumanization of humankind's emotional processing in a digital world is a matter of concern and argument.

As Edelman and others suggest, the brain's neuroplasticity allows new questions to emerge from the hologram of a universe in which human consciousness participates, not unlike the alchemist's notion of *unus mundus*, a term Jung adopted from the philosophical probing of the universe or multiverse on the margins of our known realities.

Questions arise as to the universality of emotions as an impetus in humanity's interior and external domains, and in the quest to understand the cosmos.

In the schools of emotion studies, neo-Darwinians such as Paul Ekman assert that universal survival emotions can be recognized across space and time, while secondary social emotions are culturally determined, impacted by era and locale. Other emotion theorists hypothesize "that innate emotional temperament, as well as social environment, condition people's moral norms and political stance" (De Sousa, 2017). These notions match Jung's proposal of archetypal dominants akin to universal survival emotions which emerge from or accompany instinct, while social emotions shape the successes and failures of adaptation.

"Horizontal" vectors of shared emotions can be seen within societies and cultures, while "vertical" emotional expressions of epigenetic transmissions are traceable between generations especially in instances of trauma. Generational patterns of perception and response, and the hypothesis of endogenous images also dissolve strict distinctions between nature and nurture, as do the transmitted signals of mirror neuron communication (Ramachandran). The function of "mirror neurons" in imitation and learning in human-animal, person to person and generation to generation transmission of emotional states and styles, as well as knowledge and skill, is traceable among individuals and cultures. There are explicit and implicit norms of customary and expected emotionally determined discharges and behaviors, rituals, and expression. These range from pride in honor killings in one society to Shakespearian dramas about tragic family feuds in another.

The feminist tradition has explored difference and similarity in gender-specific modes and styles of emotional communication and encounter, with some emphasizing the impact of asymmetrical social expectations of women and men, while others posit innate capacities for empathy, sympathy, relatedness, and contextual sensibility.

In his time, Jung stretched toward these views with his notions of the contra-sexual within – a feminine anima in a man and masculine animus in woman, and when he cited alchemical and mythic figures of hermaphrodites and androgynes. He tried to lift our categories of Logos and Eros, masculine and feminine out of biological categorization of male and female. However, he did not reach the radical conclusion he was attempting insofar as he was constricted by the conventional gender-specific norms and asymmetries of context which effect social emotions and roles. His theory sometimes lifts above the projected definitions of a man onto women, and other times falls into the concretizations of his contemporary hierarchal society.

In our era, traditional norms of masculine and feminine are breaking down as we grasp that innate sense of gender is not necessarily based in physical features. Gender studies are upending corporal determinism, allowing for those who do not wish to be defined by birth certificate assignments as to their gender identity, organic self-presentations, emotional processing, and relational links. Embedded social norms, presented as God-given edicts from Eden conflict with rapidly changing framing as to whether morality and ethics, sympathy and empathy or various instincts, affects, and emotions are more or less dominant gendered traits.

Elasticity of gender makes real the seemingly only symbolic hermaphroditic and androgynous images to affirm transgendered and transsexual persons who do not fit into either/or birth determined dualistic categories. Emotional capacities became more individual and psychological.

From homunculus to robot

The cutting edges of research in artificial intelligence (AI) and robotics hearken back to the homunculi, traced through Faust and Frankenstein, perceived in fantasies from zombies to mechanistic aliens.

In a 1932 letter Jung wrote, "My mother drew my attention to Faust when I was about 15 years old. . . . It seems to me that one cannot meditate enough about Faust . . . It is as much the future as the past and therefor the most living present" (Jung, 1973a, Letters, volume 1, pp. 88–89).

In 1955, Jung began the forward of his final opus, *Mysterium Coniunctionis*, with these words: "This book – my last – was begun more than ten years ago. I first got the idea of writing it from C. Kerenyi's essay on the Aegean Festival in Goethe's *Faust*" (Jung, 1971, p. xiii). As already mentioned, he ends by stating that the structure and function of the bodily organs, including the brain, are the same everywhere, and that "the psyche is to a large extent dependent on this organ" (Jung, 1971, p. xix).

In the Aegean Festival of Faust 2, the just formed homunculus, the alchemical "little man" newly produced in a glass retort, sees a statue of Aphrodite in a Cyprus harbor. Besotted with desire and attraction, he hurls his fragile form toward, and is shattered on, her stony shape.

The homunculus, like a fractal of a whole, lives on in brain studies as an imagined form presiding over its various networks and systems. Akin to Damasio's body map in the mind, it is most often represented as a humanoid image superimposed on the brain areas which connect and control various body parts.

Indeed the brain processes perceptual, sensory, and Llinas's endogenous images which rely on body to be conceived. It modulates hunger and appetite, impacts our capacity for incarnation in body's sexual orientation and mind's gender. It "stores" the implicit memories and their images which are both retrieved and sought throughout life in our never-ending quest to realize an innate image of our wholeness.

On its own, the Faustian homunculus' momentary existence does not endure. When incorporated with instinct and emotion when entangled with image and experience as well as idea and thought, it might ultimately allow the lived life and creative expression.

In "A Framework for Consciousness" (2003), Francis Crick and Christof Koch invoke this alchemical creature to describe layered registers of mental process. They posit a nonconscious homunculus, residing in the front of the forebrain, that handles the information stored in the back of the cortex (the sensory regions) and that does all of the "thinking." The front of the cortex is looking at the back. This homunculus is beyond consciousness, the same way that automatic, zombie-like behavior is beyond consciousness, although one is "above" it (supramental) and the other is "below" it (submental). Consciousness is an intermediate level, which is conscious of the homunculus and its work (its "thoughts") as representations of the homunculus in the form of inner speech (Crick & Koch, 2003, p. 120).

The homunculus also inhabits the baseline interest schema of the default emotion state of the brain, its "rest" state. Just as bodies have different metabolisms, so the idling hums at different speeds in different individuals.

With his sense of the affective psyche, Jung grasped that the notion of an only mental brain would crash against those Aphroditic engagements and entanglements which emerge on a spectrum from mild interest, to curiosity, desire, appetite, lust, obsession, compulsion, and possession. The dissociative tendencies of psyche are stretched and can snap with the ambivalences of its attractions and repulsions, conjunctions and disjunctions which inform and monitor our various states of integration and dissolutions.

Yes, Jung described the arc from the infrared of instinct to the ultraviolet of archetypal images, the indivisible dynamics between brain and body. In his scheme, the vectors of instinct and the musings of imagination create the *elan vital* of the experiencing psyche and mind, as well as the archetypal grid of expectation versus which the fulfillment and remorse of life are measured. The homunculus' longing and fleeting quark-like demise is a fitting image for the dead end encountered within a dualistic model of neuroscience which ignores the temperatures and hues inherent in the complex dynamics of emotion.

A summary: context, convergence, and emergence

I have contended that the Swiss psychiatrist C.G. Jung, founder of the depth psychological school of Analytical Psychology, was heir to centuries of Western philosophy's notions of emotion, to 19th-century psychology's and psychiatry's norms for emotional expression, and to early psychoanalytic probing into the liminal emotions in the layers of the human psyche.

While he worked within the frames of his era's intellectual and clinical history, I have suggested that Jung's particular intense and desirous curiosity also took him to the margins of his culture, and to the empirical and imaginal disciplines in the human inheritance. He plumbed the mythopoetic traditions of ancient civilizations, the mind–matter experiments and fantasies of alchemy's proto-science, the Chinese Taoist and Confucian quests for balance and symmetry, and the Zen notions of internal paradoxical mind.

Jung read or met the theorists and theologians, explorers and experimenters, scientists and scholars of his day. Their questions about emotions' source and cause, purpose and value, impact and effect were paramount for those who influenced Jung. They added to Jung's prescient sensibility beyond his time to insights still cogent, operative, or newly framed today.

The naturalist explorer Charles Darwin and the philosopher-psychologist William James especially impacted the focus on emotions in Jungian theory, thought, and practice by augmenting his exposure to the Paris clinic of Pierre Janet and inpatient practice of his psychiatric mentor Eugen Bleuler. These personages, more than Sigmund Freud, had lasting and sustained effects on Jung's grasp of the emotional range of human experience. I have briefly traced their presence in Jung's works, and in some major trends in our current neurosciences of emotion. With his insistence on the human psyche as an affective process with a teleology toward emotional equilibrium, and with his certainty that research on the brain–body continuum would be imperative if his own work was to endure, Jung's perspectives can be juxtaposed with those now emerging or returning via various neuroscientific theses on the nature and function of emotion.

In our time, after years on the margins and fringes of study, emotion is seen as leading to action, stimulating cognition and inspiring imagination. Its chemistry activates body and mind. Hence, emotion emerges in the gestures of body, expressions of language, syntheses of mind, creation of fantasy and invention.

Just as James's margins of consciousness, Freud's psychoanalysis and Jung's Analytical Psychology relativized the rationalistic fantasy of ego mastery, in a return of the suppressed, so too the Enlightenment supremacy of a cognitive intellect is now relativized by a monistic body-mind network of "I feel therefore I am," and "I feel, therefore I think" (Averill, 1994).

Meanwhile the study of emotions has necessarily embraced multiple fields and so has emerged as an interdisciplinary field, including psychiatry and psychology; anthropology, archeology and sociology; chemistry, physics, and evolutionary and developmental biology. It intersects with genetics and epigenetics, morality and ethics, politics and law. It involves gender studies and behavioral economics, as well as computational analysis, robotics, and artificial intelligence.

Biologists trace the impact of emotion in evolution. Physicists ask how and where consciousness fits in the development of the cosmos. Chemists hope to infuse robots with emotion. Theorists emerge, converge, and are impacted by linguistics and aesthetics, art, and music. Emotional factors are perceived in science's observations and the strange loops of brain to brain communication and artificial intelligence as well as outlines of morality and ethics.

No laboratory neuroscience experiment can convey their intensity with the same immediacy. Descriptions of analytic process flesh out and amplify what theory can only estimate as emotion in operation, in the coalesced links between instinct and image in appetites and fantasies, in musings and dreams.

Jung and those Jungians who followed his focus on the psyche as an emotive process have provided the immediate illustrations of how emotion is operative within an individual and between persons, especially in the intense affective retort of the analytic relationship and transference.

It is our good fortune that Jung never saw an analogy he could not evoke. He drew amplifications from the multiple traditions and disciplines of many cultures and eras, leaving us familiar with the abundance of descriptions for emotional states.

The dynamics described in the counterculture proto-sciences of alchemical experiments, the emotional chemistries in the dyads and groups of psycho-therapies can easily conjoin with "theories of other minds," attachment, attunement, mirror neurons, strange-loop exchange, emergence from the complexity, and neural coupling among individuals. All and each of these is ignited, fueled, and propelled by emotion, inhabiting our language, behavior, and comprehension of the lived and experienced life of emotion with powerful and vital images.

Having pursued imagination's constructs, recognizing mind–matter interfaces in dual-aspect monism, they can resonate with the analogies of the material sciences, even when not understanding the mathematical formulas in the background.

Current consensus

Emotional intelligence tells us that any meeting of multiple traditions would be fraught and uneasy. Indeed, in his masterful synopsis of the current states of emotions research in the Stanford Encyclopedia of Philosophy, De Sousa notes that "Even, now, there is fragile agreement on the essences and modes of emotions." Nonetheless, he affirms "a broad consensus has emerged on what we might call adequacy conditions on any theory of emotion, and enumerates the pre-requisites" (de Sousa, https://plato.stanford.edu). Within this scheme, we see Jung's spectrum from instinct to affect to emotion to feeling as a rational faculty:

- Emotions are typically conscious phenomena;
- Yet dispositions to manifest certain emotion types, such as irascibility, are often unconscious;
- Emotions typically involve more pervasive bodily manifestations than other conscious states, but
- They cannot reliably be discriminated on physiological grounds alone;
- Emotions vary along a number of dimensions: intensity, duration, valence, type and range of intentional objects, etc.;
- They are typically, but not always, manifested in desires;

- They are distinct from moods, but modified by them;
- They are reputed to be antagonists of rationality; but also
- They play an indispensable role in determining the quality of life;
- They contribute crucially to defining our ends and priorities;
- They play a crucial role in the regulation of social life;
- They protect us from an excessively slavish devotion to narrow conceptions of rationality;
- They have a central place in moral education and the moral life.

(de Sousa, 2017, pp. 26–27)

In Jung's scheme of depth psychology, we engage both conscious emotion and those subliminal emotions acting as a pre-conscious, proto-conscious, and unconscious sources of identity and memory, assumption and belief, behavior and action. Jung valued the emotions as the hues of the spectrum between the infrared instincts and ultraviolet archetypal images, and as the affective basis of the psyche as states of mind and as a process among multiplicities within a unity. The findings of contemporary neurosciences are amplifying analytic understanding of the emotions as the sources of psychic imagery, of interactive therapeutic process, and of those registries deemed synchronistic. Analytic moments provide the essential living stuff of the theories, while analytic understanding enhances and is enhanced by new confirmations and information.

Jung expanded the psyche as the matrix for resolution of the past, source of appropriate response to the present, and teleological in its focus on the processing what has been for the sake of the future, shaped by final causes as well as efficient cause. Emergent emotions appear in symptom, imagination, and dreams. Emotions infuse or possess, demanding to be recognized and calibrated for the felt and fulfilled life. He wrote:

> The intense emotion that is always associated with the vitality an archetypal idea conveys . . . a premonitory experience of wholeness . . . A better developed understanding can, however, constantly renew the vitality of the original experience. . . . The experience itself is the important thing, not its intellectual representation or clarification, which proves meaningful and helpful only when the road to original experience is blocked.
>
> (Jung, 1970b, paras. 777–778)

Today we trace the emergence of emotion from the embodied life, a source of language and thought. Following C.G. Jung and the physicist Wolfgang Pauli, we pursue the dual-aspected dialogue between mind and matter, placing mind in the middle as the perceiver of time and space. Contemporary philosophers of the mind and neuroscientists are now privileging emotion, and its impact on the felt sense and conception of time and the ongoing reformulations of memory. Inevitably, the observations of psychology function in the sciences, and the sciences impact the realms of psychology. In the psychotherapies, these meet and interact.

If emotion moves, and spirit is that which moves, then the dynamisms of emotion and inspiration may be one and the same in two different guises, for each lend an *elan vital* to the human experience across space and time. Balance remains a matter of intensity and intentionality, dependent on whether one has emotion or emotion possesses one. As Jung observed:

> Emotion is the moment when steel meets flint and a spark is struck forth, for emotion is the chief source of consciousness. There is no change from darkness to light or from inertia to movement without emotion.
>
> *(Jung, 1969, para. 179)*

References

Atmanspacher, H. (2012). Dual-aspect monism à la Pauli and Jung. *Journal of Consciousness Studies*.

Averill, J.R. (1994). 'I feel, therefore I am – I think'. In P. Ekman and R.J. Davidson (Eds.), *The nature of emotion*. New York: Oxford University Press.

Crick, F., & Koch, C. (2003, February). A framework for consciousness. *Nature, Neuroscience*, 6(2).

Damasio, A. (2003). *Looking for Spinoza: Joy, sorrow and the feeling brain*. Orlando, FL: Harcourt.

Darwin, C. (1998 [1896]). *The expression of the emotions in man and animals*. Introduction, Notes and Commentaries by P. Ekman. London: Harper Collins.

de Sousa, R. (1987). *The rationality of emotion*. Cambridge: Massachusetts Institute of Technology Press.

de Sousa, R. (2017). "Emotion". In *The Stanford encyclopedia of philosophy* (Spring ed., E.N. Zalta, Ed.). Winter 2017 edition Retrieved from https://plato.stanford.edu/archives/spr2014/entries/emotion

Edelman, G. (1992). *Bright air, brilliant fire: On the matter of the mind*. New York: Basic Books.

Ekman, P. (1972). *Emotions in the human face*. New York: Pergamon Press.

Ekman, P. (2003). *Emotions revealed: Recognizing faces and feelings to improve communication and emotional life*. New York: Owl Books.

Ekman, P., & Davidson, R. J. (1994). *The nature of emotion: Fundamental questions*. New York: Oxford University Press.

Ekman, P., & Rosenberg, E. (1997). *What the face reveals: Basic and applied studies of spontaneous expression using the Facial Action Coding System (FACS)*. New York: Oxford University Press.

Freud, S., & Jung, C.G. (1974). *The Freud/Jung letters: The correspondence between Sigmund Freud and C.G. Jung* (W. McGuire, Ed.). Princeton, NJ: Princeton University Press.

Hillman, J. (1972). *Emotion: A comprehensive phenomenology of theories and their meanings for therapy*. Evanston, IL: Northwestern University Press.

Hofer, M. (2014). The emerging synthesis of development and evolution: A new biology for psychoanalysis. *Journal of Neuropsychoanalysis*, June.

Hollingdale, R.J. (Trans.). (1960). *Thus spake Zarathustra*. New York: Penguin Books.

James, W. (1884). What is an emotion? *Mind, 9*, 188–205.

James, W. (1890). *The principles of psychology* (2 vols.). New York: Henry Holt. Unaltered republication, New York: Dover, 1950.

Jung, C.G. (1948/1970). On psychic energy. In *Structure and dynamics of the psyche, collected works 8*. Princeton: Princeton University Press.

Jung, C.G. (1965). *Memories, dreams, reflections* (A. Jaffe, recorded, Ed. and R. and C. Winston, Trans.). New York: Vintage Books.

Jung, C.G. (1968/1977). The Tavistock lectures: On the theory and practice of analytical psychology. In *The Symbolic life, miscellaneous writings, collected works 18*. Princeton: Princeton University Press.

Jung, C.G. (1969). *The archetypes and the collective unconscious: Collected works 9.1*. Princeton: Princeton University Press.

Jung, C.G. (1970). *Psychiatric studies, collected works 1*. Princeton: Princeton University Press.

Jung, C.G. (1971). *Mysterium coniunctionis: Collected works 14*. Princeton: Princeton University Press.

Jung, C.G. (1975). *C.G. Jung letters, volume 2* (G. Adler with A. Jaffe, Eds.). Princeton: Princeton University Press.

LeDoux, J. (1998). *The emotional brain: The mysterious underpinnings of emotional life*. New York: Simon and Schuster.

Llinas, R.R., & Churchland, P., Eds. (1997). *The mind-brain continuum*. New York: Carfax Publishing.

Makari, G. (2015). *Soul machine: The invention of the modern mind*. New York: W.W. Norton.

Panksepp, J. (1998). *Affective neuroscience: The foundations of human and animal emotions*. New York and Oxford: Oxford University Press.

Ramachandran, V.S. (2004). *A brief tour of human consciousness*. New York: PI Press.

Schmidt, A. C. (2014). fMRI: Two studies on the neurobiology of repression. *Interdisciplinary Journal for Psychoanalysis and the Neurosciences*, 16(2). Presented at the 15th International Neuropsychoanalysis Congress, New York, July 24.

Solomon, R. (2017). *Encyclopedia Britannica*. www.brittanica.com

Bibliography

Atmanspacher, H. (2011). Quantum approaches to consciousness. In E.N. Zalta (Ed.), *Stanford encyclopedia of philosophy*. Retrieved from http://plato.stanford.edu/entries/qt-consciousness/

Cope, T.A. (2006). *Fear of Jung: The complex doctrine and emotional science*. London: Karnac.

Corrigall, J., Payne, H., & Wilkinson, H. (Eds.). (2006). *About a body: Working with the embodied mind in psychotherapy*. London and New York: Routledge.

Cosmides, L., & Cosmides, J.T. (2000). Evolutionary psychology and the emotions. In M. Lewis and J.M. Haviland (Eds.), *Handbook of emotions*. New York: Guilford Press.

Damasio, A. (1994). *Descartes' error: Emotion, reason, and the human brain*. New York: G.P. Putnam's Sons.

Damasio, A. (1999). *The feeling of what happens: Body and emotion in the making of consciousness*. New York: Harcourt Brace and Co.

Descartes, R. (1984 [1649]). The passions of the soul. In J. Cottingham, R. Stoothoff and D. Murdoch (Trans.), *The philosophical writings of Descartes*, volume 1. Cambridge: Cambridge University Press.

Elster, J. (1999). *Alchemies of the mind: Rationality and the emotions*. Cambridge: Cambridge University Press.

Fisher, H.E. (1992). Anatomy of love the natural history of monogamy. In *Adultery and divorce*. New York and London: W.W. Norton.

Gallese, V., & Alvin, G. (1998). Mirror neurons and the simulation theory of mind-reading. *Trends in Cognitive Sciences*, 2(12), 493–501.

Gilligan, C. (1982). *In a different voice: Psychological theory and women's development*. Cambridge: Harvard University Press.

Goldie, P. (2003). Emotion, feeling, and knowledge of the world. In R.C. Solomon (Ed.), *Thinking about feeling: Contemporary philosophers on emotions*. New York: Oxford University Press.
Goleman, D. (Ed.). (1997). *Healing emotions: Conversations with the Dalai Lama on mindfulness, emotions and health*. Boston and London: Shambhala.
Goleman, D. (2003). *Destructive emotions: How can we overcome them? A scientific dialogue with the Dalai Lama*. New York: Bantam.
Green, A., & Kohon, G. (2005). *Love and its vicissitudes*. London and New York: Routledge.
Griffiths, P. (1997). *What emotions really are: The problem of psychological categories*. Chicago: University of Chicago Press.
Haviland, J.M., & Lewis, M. (Eds.). (1993). *Handbook of emotions*. New York and London: Guilford Press.
Henderson, J.L., & Sherwood, D.N. (2003). *Transformation of the psyche: The symbolic alchemy of the splendor solis*. New York: Brunner-Routledge.
Hofstadter, D. (2007). *I am a strange loop*. New York: Basic Books.
James, W. (1892). A plea for psychology as a 'natural science'. *Philosophical Review, 1*, 146–153.
James, W. (1902). *The varieties of religious experience*. New York: Longmans, Green.
Jung, C.G. (1937/1970). Psychological factors affecting human behavior. In *Structure and dynamics of the psyche collected works v8*. Princeton: Princeton University Press.
Jung, C.G. (1947/1970). On the nature of the psyche. In *Structure and dynamics of the psyche collected works 8*. Princeton: Princeton University Press.
Jung, C.G. (1961). *Psychogenesis of mental disease, collected works 3*. Princeton: Princeton University Press.
Jung, C.G. (1973a). *Visions seminars*, volume 2 (C. Douglas, Ed.). Princeton: Princeton University Press.
Jung, C.G. (1973b). *C.G. Jung letters*, volume 1. (G. Adler with A. Jaffe, Eds.). Princeton: Princeton University Press.
Jung, C.G. (1966a). *The practice of psychotherapy: Essays on the psychology of the transference and other subjects collected works 16*. Princeton: Princeton University Press.
Jung, C.G. (1966b). The psychology of transference. In *The practice of psychotherapy: Essays on the psychology of the transference and other subjects collected works 16*. Princeton: Princeton University Press.
Jung, C.G. (2009). *The red book* (S. Shamdasani, Ed.). New York: W.W. Norton.
Kahneman, D. (2000). Evaluation by moments: Past and future. In D. Kahneman and A. Tversky (Eds.), *Choices, values, and frames*. New York: Cambridge University Press, Russell Sage Foundation.
Kahneman, D. (2011). *Thinking fast and slow*. New York: Farrar, Strauss, and Giroux.
Kast, V. (1991). *Joy, inspiration, and hope* (D. Whitcher, Trans.). New York: Fromm International Publishing.
Levi, D. (2007). *Sex and love with robots*. New York: Harper Collins.
Lewis, M.L. (1993). *Handbook of emotions*. New York: Guilford Press.
Llinas, R.R. (2002). *The I of the vortex: From neurons to self*. Cambridge: Massachusetts Institute of Technology Press.
Meier, C.A. (Ed.). (2001). *Atom and archetype: The Pauli-Jung letters*. Princeton: Princeton University Press.
Minsky, M. (2006). *The emotion machine: Commonsense thinking, artificial intelligence, and the future of the human mind*. New York: Simon and Schuster.
Nussbaum, M. (1990). *Love's knowledge*. Oxford: Oxford University Press.
Nussbaum, M. (2001). *Upheavals of thought: The intelligence of emotions*. Cambridge: Cambridge University Press.

Nussbaum, M. (2006). *Hiding from humanity: Disgust, shame and the law*. Princeton: Princeton University Press.
Pally, R. (2000). *The mind-brain reality*. London: Karnac Books.
Panksepp, J. (2000). Emotion as a natural kind within the brain. In M. Lewis and J. Haviland-Jones (Eds.), *Handbook of emotions* (pp. 137–155). New York: Guilford University Press.
Prinz, J. (2004). *Gut reactions: A perceptual theory of emotion*. Oxford: Oxford University Press.
Rizzolatti, G., & Sinigaglia, C. (2008). *Mirrors in the brain*. Oxford: Oxford University Press.
Rorty, A. (Ed.). (1980). *Emotions*. Los Angeles: University of California Press, pp. 103–126.
Rorty, A. (2003). Enough already with theories of emotion. In R. Solomon (Ed.), *Thinking about feelings: Philosophers on emotions*. New York: Oxford University Press.
Schore, A.N. (1994). *Affect regulation and the origin of the self: The neurobiology of emotional development*. Hillsdale, NJ: Lawrence Erlbaum Associates.
Solomon, R. (1980). Emotions and choice. In A. Rorty (Ed.), *Explaining emotions* (pp. 251–281). Los Angeles: University of California Press.
Solomon, R. (1984). *The passions: The myth and nature of human emotions*. New York: Doubleday.
Solomon, R. (1999). The philosophy of emotions. In M. Lewis and J. Haviland-Jones (Eds.), *Handbook of emotions* (pp. 3–15). New York: Guilford Press.
Solomon, R. (2003). *What is an emotion?* New York: Oxford University Press.
Viola, B. (2003). *The passions*. Los Angeles, CA: Getty Publications.
Viola, B. (2004). *The art of Bill Viola*. London, UK: Thames Hudson.
von Franz, M.L. (1992). *Psyche and matter*. Boston and London: Shambhala.
Zabriskie, B. (2001). A meeting of rare minds. In C.A. Maier (Ed.), *Atom and archetype: The Pauli-Jung letters, 1932–1958*. Princeton: Princeton University Press.
Zabriskie, B. (2004). Imagination as laboratory. *Journal of Analytical Psychology*, *49*, 235–242.
Zabriskie, B. (2014). Time and Tao in synchronicity. In H. Atmanspacher and C. Fuchs (Eds.), *The Pauli-Jung conjecture and its impact today*. Exeter: Imprint Academic.
Zabriskie, B. (2015). Energy and emotion: C.G. Jung's Fordham Declaration. In M. Mattson, F. Wertz, H. Fogarty, M. Klenck and B. Zabriskie (Eds.), *Jung in the academy and beyond: The Fordham lectures 100 years later* (pp. 37–49). New Orleans, LA: Spring Journal Books.

7
JUNG AND MEDITATION
One path toward investigation

Morgan Stebbins

Meditation is a practice with a deep historical tradition and worldwide experience and application. Research into its effectiveness and understanding of its characteristics is a newer phenomenon. One fruitful and important way of looking at meditation is through the lens of Jungian psychology. This chapter will introduce the relationship between Jungian psychology and meditation, summarize the different forms of research in these areas to date, and offer avenues for collaborative research on meditation as both a personal and therapeutic practice using Analytical Psychology tools.

Meditation: a complex and multi-faceted practice

Meditation, however conceived, has been a part of almost all recorded contemplative and mystic traditions. From the famous bas-relief of the yogis of the Indus Valley to Taoist texts and Mayan figures, to the Greek and pre-Greek traditions, there is evidence of an applied reflective process arising in different parts of the world for at least 2,500 years. In the broad sense of *intentional change of consciousness*, meditation covers such diverse practices as shamanic ritual, dance, prayer, and art-making as well as sports, drug use, lucid dreaming, the analytic hovering attention, and of course the silent sitting practice that is the most usual referent. For most of its history, meditation was embedded in local and usually religious praxis, however in the last hundred years or so it has come to be seen as a practice less directly tied to a religious tradition. Two examples of this latest trend are the work of Jon Kabat-Zinn in promoting his *Mindfulness-Based Stress Reduction* at the University of Massachusetts Medical Center in the 1970s (Kabat-Zinn, 2013) and Stephen Bachelor's delinking Buddhist meditation practices from Buddhist context and theology (Batchelor, 1997).

Kabat-Zinn has indicated that

> mindfulness can be considered a universal human capacity that can foster clear thinking and openheartedness, and the goal of mindfulness is to maintain awareness moment by moment, disengaging oneself from strong attachment to beliefs, thoughts, or emotions, thereby developing a greater sense of emotional balance and well-being.
>
> *(Ludwig, 2008, pp. 1250–1352)*

But when we ask more specifically about what meditation is, or the much more complicated question of what meditation is *as a psychic phenomenon*, a complex image arises. Apparently, there are as many answers to the first question as traditions from which different practices emerge. Investigation that focuses on the psyche and its experience of meditation may be a useful starting point for understanding meditation. A brief review of the recent literature on the effects and practice of meditation will then allow us to look at some of the deeper philosophical issues that arise when studying a technology of the mind that has such a wide range of sources and applications. Finally, the problem of meditation from the perspective of the psyche can be approached.

The addition we can make here is to ask what the psyche is doing with a specific meditative activity. Jung asked a similar question about complexes. He said, "I do not want to know the complexes of my patients – that is uninteresting to me. I want to know what a man's [*sic*] unconscious is doing with the complex. I want to know what he is preparing himself for" (Jung, 1977, p. 171). This allows us to wonder what prospective stance a particular meditative activity is aiming to attain.

Most important from a hermeneutic standpoint is that all kinds of meditation have behind them a social and religious context full of myth, practice, and assumption, as well as having in front of them a particular aim or agenda. That is, they arise from a context and so are not neutral in origination or intention. Also, meditation typically involves one or more instructions from a trusted figure which may include assuming a location, a particular body posture (including movement), and attending to something with the mind – the breath, a particular sound or image, what emerges, or nothing at all. In most practices some time limit is also given. It is very hard to define meditation without considering all of these contextual factors as potentially being the single formative factor.

On the other hand, many people have reported benefiting from meditative activity, and my own long experience with different sorts of mental practices – including psychological methods – has shown me that there is a deep interweaving between consciousness, suffering, and individuation. Individuation, the process of becoming consciously what one is unconsciously (the given self) is a central Jungian goal which will be discussed later in the chapter. It is this intersection that seems especially fruitful and leads me to offer *an early working definition of mediation as the fantasy of an intentional state of mind*. It is important to frame this discussion in terms of fantasy for a number of reasons. First is that fantasy refers to imagination and concept, and most references to meditation happen outside of the activity we might call meditation itself. Thus, they participate more as rhetorical tropes that have an effect on recruitment, validation of text or institutional hierarchy than as experimental references. Next, the linkages between consciousness and suffering remain less than causal and it's unclear if insight is related to any given practice or to different feeling states. Finally, we can also further differentiate these fantasies and their corresponding states according to whether they open up or focus down our attention, that is whether they explore and attend to something that arises from beyond conscious intention or rather shape, create, and control an emotional or mental thought or process. This last is a very important consideration in any clinical setting since, psychologically speaking, developing more control is indicated for some people and letting go of control is indicated for others.

This definition seems simple on one level, but since Jung was clear that conscious states are built on and motivated from unconscious ones, we are forced to admit that a conscious intention is often either influenced by or even wholly formed by unconscious factors. Future studies could address different kinds of unconscious structure and agency.[1] That is, meditative practices are chosen by and can be used for different things at both conscious and unconscious levels. If we allow ourselves to travel this path, we have to at least separate meditative practices into the ones with a preferred (conscious) outcome – designated by the individual or by the traditional context of the practice – from ones with an open orientation to the outcome.

Research on meditation: multiple perspectives and approaches

Recent research findings[2] (which overwhelmingly show benefits for any kind of meditation practice but don't control for other activities nor compare practices) can also provide a synopsis of meditation styles.[3] We can look beyond these studies at meditation in three additional ways unique to a Jungian point of view: meditation can be applied within the practices of Analytical Psychology; it can be seen through the lens of the psyche itself and it can be understood in terms of an approach to the unconscious.

In addition, we must take into consideration the recent advent of a wealth of physiological research[4] on meditation especially in the West. This can be seen both as a broad additional source of information and, due to its reliance on and blindness to research context, as an extra level of shadow as well.[5]

The Jungian context

The Jungian hermeneutic is an emergent-field theory of interaction (typically with an analyst) with a particular goal of its own.[6] There are many ways to describe this goal, but we can begin by saying that in general Jungian methods allow the analyst/analysand dyad to investigate autonomous images (that is, unconscious structures, processes, and images) for the purpose of reducing neurotic suffering and potentially to allow the transformation of the whole personality. When examining this interaction, a number of factors must be taken into account. Before even considering those, we have to wonder what the role of research is in personal decision making. What if research showed that your favorite thing was either not valuable in terms of physiology or even slightly harmful? Perhaps you would change your habits, but maybe not – and there are good arguments in both directions.

Along these lines of individual preference and meaning is what Jung called the personal equation – which in hermeneutics is referred to as the hermeneutic circle. It refers to the fact that you cannot make any statement or take a position without at least acknowledging the context. If replying to another, then one must consider the range of intent of the speaker in relation to the subject and the field between them. Furthermore, any psychological statement can be attacked on the grounds that it is the personal experience of the speaker – both of which problems can be mitigated (though not eliminated) by two things: an attempt at transparency in personal agenda and an openness on the side of the reader to see if a given statement rings true experientially apart from the aforementioned bias.[7] Thus, research perspectives in terms of meditation needs to focus on the context of the practice, the focus of the psyche, and the personal equation.

Exploring the nature of meditation

The method used here will be circumambulatory. That is, aspects and images that are relevant to the exploration of meditation will be presented with the hope that a fuller picture of the situation, at least from the psychological viewpoint of the author, might be attained. Jung thought that "A real understanding can, in my view, be reached only when the diversity of psychological premises is accepted" (Jung, 1971, para. 846). This approach is similar to Harvard researcher Ellen Langer's three principles of mindfulness: to acknowledge a wide range of data, to create new categories where needed, and to assume multiple (valid) points of view (Langer, 1997). Langer's understanding of mindfulness diverges considerably from the meditative (and typically religious) approaches in that she focuses almost wholly on outcome (of subject experience) and the experimental factors that influence that outcome. As such, her stance is an important corrective to almost the entire rest of the field.

This multifaceted Jungian approach allows us to see different meditations as illuminating corners of the psyche or fulfilling different psychological needs. Each can therefore be seen as valid but not solely authoritative. Each can be understood, like all collective psychic artifacts, as maps of the psyche and also as tools or paths to enable a relationship with it. Then, like any tool or extension of conscious will, it can be scrutinized in terms of its use in a number of areas: motive, fantasy, outcome, and social context. Finally, we may ask, as Jung does with any complex,[8] what the unconscious intends in choosing this particular mode of psychic functioning. We will also attempt a tentative set of definitions which will enable us to focus our inquiry and not become too mired in generalities.

The personal equation

Jung explored the problem of the individual nature of any observation as well as the impact of the observer on the experimental situation.[9] My own understanding of the impossibility of neutrality requires that I say a few words about my conscious context and agenda. My own long experience with intentional states of mind and psychological methods has shown me, as noted earlier, that there is a deep interweaving between consciousness, suffering, and individuation (and I should add, between those factors and physical and mental performance). This interweaving has been the lodestone of the disparate studies and experiments I have engaged in over 40 or so years.

My exposure to meditation began in martial arts when I was in grade school. It was presented as a way to focus energy and as a tool to enhance training. In my teens I became enamored of Zen practice which (in the form I was engaged in) valued meditation not as means but rather as the process and the manifestation of one's true self, as perplexing as that seemed at the time. In seminary, we practiced the rite of silent morning prayer (with the backing of Psalm 119: "My eyes are awake through the night watches, that I may meditate on Your word."). These are just a few examples of the many forms of meditation and consciousness-change I have experimented with. They come from across the Buddhist landscape as well as from other cultures, including training in hypnosis and shamanistic practices.

In my personal Jungian analysis as well as in my study and practice as an analyst, meditation has come up both as a preparation for active imagination and (not by name) as the process of analysis itself. That is, as the theoretical and experiential change of consciousness that alters one's worldview and changes one experience of suffering. After all, Jung is clear that attitude is everything in terms of making meaning and also in terms of the transformation of neurotic suffering into individuation. Furthermore, to use Freud's term, the "hovering awareness" of the analyst is a finely tuned meditative state itself (Freud, 1924, pp. 325, 327).

I have personally experienced many kinds of changes to my own consciousness – and many of them related to meditation. But should I be pressed, could I say they were (except in certain very particular situations) *directly caused* by meditation, or might I have to admit the possibility that they were instead the effect of some other activity – or that the meditation was not actually caused by some previous insight? Furthermore, could I say that others would have the same benefit that I derived? I have tried to both say and encourage those things, but often to no avail, so I now realize that everyone's needs, aspirations, and particular ways are unique, but also that my way of getting *here* has involved specific meditative practices.

This multifaceted experience has led me to develop a curriculum on contemplative Jungian studies based on an experiential approach to his writings from the Word Association Experiment to active imagination with the overt goal of living through a symbolic understanding. This experience is also the basis of my clinical work and hermeneutic approach to text (including psyche's text). This aligns with Jung's dictum to honor both academic/referential and experiential understanding.

My own stance calls for a four-part view, especially with any topic as emotionally fraught as meditation. The personal and experiential layer includes the personal context embedded in any religious or theological reference in a literalized, belief-oriented sense. The anthropological and linguistic perspective allows us to see how power is wielded within a particular tradition under different guises and what the economics looks like. The historical and textual approach refers the standard academic procedure of text study and historiography.

The Jungian perspective on the psyche

The *psychological stance* refers in my case to the Jungian view that symbols arise as unconscious compensations and as manifestations of individual and group psyche. This process of understanding these symbols proceeds through amplification by exploring at least the five areas of personal history, collective pattern, immediate emotional state, transferential implications, and internal dynamic. It then cycles back around to the immediate personal arising of images (that is the *right now*) and then finally to question personal relevance and conscious choice. After all, we all always land wherever something most *seems to do us good and makes most sense* – as long as we understand making sense to include the numinous overriding of ego function.

This four-part view demands quite a bit from the reader or clinician. It is of course also an ongoing process. However, whatever sector of amplification or study is ignored will then arise as an unconscious attitude and influence one's attitude without such influence being accessible to the ego. The blindness can only be partially countered, but the more aspects or views we can include, the more whole is the amplification. In this way we can continue Jung's project of "considering how certain things could be understood from the standpoint of our modern consciousness," which might lead to a "remedy [of] our philosophic disorientation by shedding light on the psychic background and the secret chambers of the soul" (Jung, 1969b, p. x).

Finally, I have studied the research on meditation and used that as yet another vital point of view – one which is often a corrective to metaphysical claims coming from the same traditions. These areas of experience and bias will be expanded upon – with the transparent claim that there are conflicting languages involved and that my professional and personal identities are embedded in many areas. However, my primary vocabulary comes from a hermeneutically enhanced understanding and practice of Jung as well as the ways in which his view of the psyche creatively weaves into the practice of Zen. Lately I have become aware that both Jung's theory of the psyche and Zen share a stance from philosophy of mind called dual-aspect monism (or in Jung's case, multiple aspect monism). Without going into great detail, this distinction might be helpful here because it dovetails well with the method of amplification, in that we are not pitting one view against another for supremacy but rather trying to create a model which meaningfully relates as many of the sources of data as possible.

To return to our possible working definition of mediation *as the fantasy of an intentional state of mind*, we see that the qualities of intention are not transparent unless we examine the question of the fantasy behind them including the institutional usage. Instead, intention has at least three vectors: the ego state in our fantasy of its autonomy, the social and cultural level that bridges conscious and unconscious, and the unconscious trajectory that arises as either fate or destiny. We can notice as well that states of mind are infinitely varied, though the subjective experience of the reduction of suffering or the attainment of adaptive attitudes can give us some orientation.

Every description of meditation (perhaps by necessity) is couched in the language of some context which then determines the scope, background, and outcome of those descriptions. This is true of analysis as well. The end point evaluation has to come from personal experience and value. "As far as we can discern, the sole purpose of human existence is to kindle a light in the darkness of mere being" (Jung, 1961, p. 326).

Research on meditation techniques

Meditation techniques are legion. A recent article describes 23 kinds of meditation in an effort to help the perplexed figure out his or her best fit.[10] The Meditation Society of America lists 108 types.[11] However, like Maimonides's *Guide for the Perplexed*, it leaves the reader with an even more complex web of practices and religious claims than we began with – while at the same time showing that a symbolic understanding might be beneficial. And this is just a beginning.

Another article describes ten kinds of agnostic or non-theological meditations[12] (which brings up Jung's question about the comparison between natural symbols and cultural symbols).[13] The same article reviews the effects of meditation and claims there are 76 measurable benefits derived from over 3,000 studies. Unfortunately, according to *Scientific American*, those studies almost all have problems that make the findings less robust. It turns out that meditation is hard to study. As stated in the journal *Advances in Mind-Body Medicine*,

> Like other complex, multifaceted interventions in medicine meditation represents a mixture of specific and not-so-specific elements of therapy. However, meditation is somewhat unique in that it is difficult to standardize, quantify, and authenticate for a given sample of research subjects.
>
> *(Advances in Mind-Body Medicine, Spring, 2005, pp. 4–11)*

Studies on meditation have flourished in recent years. A recent Harvard study shows that the brain structure itself changes with meditation.[14] Others have shown improved performance on tasks or changes in brain waves. Jung reported using meditation to prepare for active imagination. Active imagination itself is an altered consciousness.

One recent paper that summarizes research efforts has described meditation in this way: "Meditation can be defined as a family of practices that train attention and awareness, usually with the aim of fostering psychological and spiritual well being and maturity."[15] Of course this throws out embedded assumptions, historical trajectory, and religious context of each of the great meditative traditions whose techniques they summarize.

The foundational research has been oriented toward symptoms and has not taken up the end point goals posited by the traditions: "Researchers primarily have examined meditation's effects as a self-regulation strategy for stress management and symptom reduction."[16] Also these early research efforts are acknowledged to have been plagued by methodological problems which limit their usefulness.

However, research has continued in a number of areas with some promising results nonetheless. These areas are attention, concentration, interpersonal functioning, prevention of depression, comparison with medication use, enhanced empathy, and self-esteem. All areas showed positive correlations, but in almost all cases there were problems with self-selection and attrition. Still, there was a positive connection between meditation (merging all types studied) and some change in all the areas studied.

A very interesting study concerned synesthesia, a neurological syndrome in which one kind of sensory stimulus is experienced as or described in terms of another. There are many forms of this and most have not been studied. Usually synesthesia is thought be quite rare (from 1 in 2,000 to 1 in 2,300) as well as innate and non-trainable. However, in this study meditators met the criteria for synesthesia at more than a 1:2 rate. This study suffered from small sample size (and the research on synesthesia is itself in developmental stages), but it does suggest some tantalizing possibilities.[17]

Some of the physiological effects of meditation include brain-wave coherence, relaxation, and immune system boosting. There have been many more, as researchers use all of the tools of brain investigation to open up new correlations between meditation (or certain kinds of experience within meditation) and measurable body functions.

There is not, as yet, enough evidence to propose any causal relationships nor to make an overarching theory or map of the terrain of meditation and transcendent experience and research. One promising map in the making is Ken Wilber's four quadrant model, with divisions for subjective and objective as well as personal and collective. This would dovetail very easily with Jung's conceptions as well (Wilber, 2000).

Although it is far too early to make any broad conclusions, and while none of the meditative effects of other activities has been comparatively studied (such as the hovering awareness of the analyst or the effect on the brain of active imagination), there do appear to be some non-random results. On the other hand, qualitative research and personal experience point to a much greater effect. The problem may be that, like analysis, a great deal may depend on the relationship with the particular teacher, the setting of the technique, the fluency of the practitioner with the theological context of the technique, the readiness to make a change, and the particular fit of a technique with a particular person.

Participating in an eight-week mindfulness meditation program appears to make measurable changes in brain regions associated with memory, sense of self, empathy, and stress. In a study that appeared in the January 30, 2017, issue of *Psychiatry Research: Neuroimaging*, a team led by Harvard-affiliated researchers at Massachusetts General Hospital (MGH) reported the results of their study, the first to document meditation-produced changes over time in the brain's gray matter.

However with all of these claims and 60 years of studies, nevertheless there still is not a consensus definition of meditation! Furthermore, the research itself is far from conclusive, in fact a recent meta-analysis on 40 years of research states that scientific research on meditation practices does not appear to have a common theoretical perspective and is characterized by poor methodological quality. Firm conclusions on the effects of meditation practices in healthcare cannot be drawn based on the available evidence.

This report reveals that there is no theory of meditation common to all practices that can lead to the building of a hypothesis necessary for testing and evaluating claims. This looks pretty bleak from a research standpoint, and there is other troubling data. Some studies have linked meditation with risk of pain or mental illness (see below), and many meditators are wary of doing any testing at all, claiming that those changes are not the point of meditation – at least not in their particular tradition. In fact, a quick internet search shows many sites promising to reveal the *true* method or understanding of meditation.

This bleakness flies in the face of many personal claims and qualitative research on the effects of meditation and other intentional changes of consciousness, perhaps suggesting some alternative explanations for the effects of meditation or some lessening of the particularly grandiose claims where they occur. I hope to show that the fatasies of and references to intentional changes of awareness – which is my starting definition – come in many forms throughout many areas and time periods without there being much agreement on outcomes, practices or reference. The degree of helpfulness will depend on many factors that link each person with their own context, needs, and style of being in the world.

It is important to remember that meditation is often connected to metaphysical claims which are in turn typically embedded in religious traditions of great variation. So claims for the benefits or end results of a given practice almost invariably include a hidden or overt agenda – as we saw earlier in our internet search – making any claim less than neutral.

In traditional yoga practice,[18] the goal of the physical (*asana*) practice is to enhance meditation as a means to enlightenment. Although much has been written about that goal having been submerged by recent marketing successes of yoga in the West, we can perhaps allow Zizek to remind us that marketing is itself the sublimation and spiritual valuation of the material (Zizek, 2014).

Having mentioned these benefits, it should be said that there are a variety of views on this research. The Dalai Lama encourages scientific study, whereas Donald

Lopez points out that theologically, research is completely against the scriptural tradition of Buddhism.[19]

While mindfulness may work to alleviate certain symptoms of stress, or aid one in living a fuller life, this was not the Buddha's aim in promoting meditative practice. Meditative states were associated with planes of potential existence, and his aim was to gain complete renunciation and escape the cycle of rebirth. So when journalists suggest that research on stress relief demonstrates (or could demonstrate) that Buddhist meditation "works," something has got lost in the translation. Buddhist meditation was never intended simply to relieve stress, and it is hard to figure out how one would go about measuring renunciation.[20]

Furthermore, Lopez shows that the Buddha is described in the sutras in a way that defies either the project or the technique of science: "He has complete recollection of the past, including each of his own past lives as well as the lives of all sentient beings ... The Buddha described in the sutras is more a figure of science fiction than of science" (Lopez, 2012, p. 43). This conundrum is not unique to Buddhism; rather it is a function of approaching the historical claims of any tradition from another point of view, whether that of research science or personal experience. Analytical Psychology (meaning Jungian psychology) is not immune.

It is also important to take note of the research showing that meditation (again broadly defined) can be and has been dangerous.[21] This makes sense if it is a powerful tool of any kind, since all tools have optimum uses and suffer the problem of misuse. For instance there are articles of this type: "Dark Knight of the Soul" (*Atlantic Monthly*), "Recovery," "permanently ruined" – these are not words one typically encounters when discussing a contemplative practice.

It is equally important to remain open to the role of the term experience in traditions that incorporate meditation or other subtle (or claimed) states of mentality. As Robert Scharf has argued,

> While some adepts may indeed experience "altered states" in the course of their training, critical analysis shows that such states do not constitute the reference points for the elaborate Buddhist discourse pertaining to the "path." Rather, such discourse turns out to function ideologically and performatively – wielded more often than not in the interests of legitimation and institutional authority.
>
> *(Scharf, 1995, p. 261)*

Meditation and research: a path toward the future

"Meditation, simply defined, is a way of being aware. It is the happy marriage of doing and being" (Das, 2007). So claims Lama Surya Das, who was one of the first to implement the being and doing trope, which takes us quickly back to a more philosophical stance. Continuing this philosophical bent, meditation can be used to address particular life-philosophy questions such as: Who am I? What is the true purpose of my life? What is my role in this universe? How can I help remove the sufferings of others?

Mindfulness, as developed and practiced by Jon Kabat-Zinn, is "Mindfulness means paying attention in a particular way; on purpose, in the present moment, and nonjudgmentally" (1996). And, according to the yogic traditions,[22] meditation can lead to many enhanced mental states and bodily feats from oneness with the cosmos to fire walking, levitation, omniscience, and eternal bliss.

Olensky writes that meditation is a process of investigation. It involves examining the phenomena of the mind and body with an attitude of curiosity and interest. The first three elements of the seven "factors of awakening" speak to this: mindfulness (*sati*) gives rise to the investigation of states (*dhamma-vicaya*), and this in turn results in greater energy (*viriya*) for making an effort.

We can return for a moment to Dogen, the founder of the Soto school of Zen Buddhism, who instructed his students to practice zazen, or seated meditation, by sitting upright, not thinking of good or bad. Although the word Zen is derived from the Chinese *ch'an*, which again derives from the Sanskrit *dhyana*, meaning meditation, there are relatively few handbooks on meditation and instead a huge literature describing other aspects of Zen.

Dogen, master of the "meditation" school, tries to show that meditation *per se* is not what is intended. Rather he is pointing to a state of mind that is somehow connected to meditation. Other Buddhist texts from the very earliest sources in the Pali canon onward describe enhanced human senses or even superhuman abilities that derive from nuanced awareness linked to meditative techniques. So here we see two diverging lines of thought – one is the question of the role of meditation within a tradition and the other of some "state of mind" goal that can usually only be verified by the master of the particular tradition.

On the other hand, we have (usually more modern) works that appear to separate the more metaphysical or theological aspects of meditation from the physiological or philosophical. Stephen Batchelor is perhaps the best known proponent of this set of views in which meditation, applied philosophy, and humanism are the backbone of the practice rather than ideas of merit, reincarnation, and enlightenment (Batchelor, 1997). This is a so-called atheist or humanistic Buddhist tradition. However, he has run into strong criticism from the well-known scholar of Tibetan Buddhism, Robert Thurman, who insists on a literal belief in reincarnation in order to properly be a Buddhist.[23]

So among the traditional meditation practices as well as modern techniques, one can often see sectarian battles in the background as many of these quotations refer to their own versions as something like *real meditation* or *the true meditation*. These labels can only refer to a sectarian struggle (for market share, as all anthropologists understand), which can also be applied to variations of psychological technique in the absence of well-validated research.

There may not be any prospect of making a sweeping claim about meditation, so instead we will proceed with the understanding that there is not a singular activity or mind-state called meditation but rather that there are meditations embedded within often ritualized contexts that must be taken into account in our four-part hermeneutic investigation.

We can well wonder if there can there be a true phenomenology of meditation and also how various practices are evaluated through the lens of neuroscience. Still, one level of meditation has to do with simple body and often breathing practices that, in themselves, are available to anyone and which typically provide a sense of relaxation, a focusing of the mind, and a lowering of heart rate and breathing rate.

What can a Jungian perspective offer?

At the next level, from a depth psychological perspective, we can ask about the awareness of awareness itself. That is, most people are not aware that they are aware, or if so they are aware in a cursory way; rarely are people aware of *how they are aware*. This attention to the process of mental states is not usually engaged in everyday life. Instead, adaptation to social norms of the mind gives rise to most of the so-called folk psychologies and theories of self.

So a more primordial view of meditation could be the first notice of an awareness itself. This idea dovetails with neuroscientist V.S. Ramachandran's consideration of the nature of the self. In an admittedly speculative gesture, he suggests that an economical (in the evolutionary sense) way of having complex mental functioning would be to have a perception that generalized the other highly complex motor activities and minute perceptions in order to have some kind of bigger picture. This certainly relates to the anthropological idea that humans have a very advanced system of virtual reality – also called imagination – available for testing worldly scenarios.

This virtual aspect of the human mind is what accounts for the incredibly complex network of human relations, including language and symbolic understanding, that also stands in for reality as a concept. This layer of imagination is called, at the collective level, culture. Analysts will know it in its more abstract form: the psyche. The abstract level of functioning remains the same across the globe, whereas the particular references are based on specific cultural experience. Of course, having a virtual scenario that can be changed without recourse to physical reality is also what allows for the problems of many mental illnesses – humans can make up scenarios that help test actions in the world or other scenarios that imply doom and destruction with equal ease and which have equal internal coherence.

The language of the psyche in both cognitive study and depth psychology gives us a useful set of tools with which to investigate meditative states. They are useful in that they are falsifiable (for the most part), they are common to the West and have links to the philosophical traditions that undergird our way of thinking, and they are mostly non-metaphysical. I say mostly from the point of view that all worldview stances are imaginal and collectively co-authored at some level. However I do try to abide by Jung's dictum that

> Since the development of consciousness requires the withdrawal of all the projections we can lay our hands on, it is not possible to maintain any non-psychological doctrine about the gods [or metaphysical claims]. If the historical process of world de-spiritualization continues as hitherto, then everything

of a divine or demonic character outside us must return to the psyche, to the inside of the unknown man, whence it apparently originated.

(Jung, 1970b, para. 141)

Jung clearly feels that the Indian methods head in this direction:

> The Indian conception teaches liberation from the opposites, by which are to be understood every sort of affective state and emotional tie to the object. Liberation follows the withdrawal of libido from all contents, resulting in a state of complete introversion.
>
> (Jung, 1971, para. 189)

Jung continues his evaluation in psychological terms:

> Yoga is a method by which the libido is systematically "introverted" and liberated from the bondage of opposites. The aim of tapas and yoga alike is to establish a mediatory condition from which the creative and redemptive element will emerge.
>
> (Jung, 1971, para. 190)

This in contrast to the Christian myth, which is extroverted and demands an object: "Yoga introverts the relations to the object." However this leads to a problem, in his mind:

> One is inclined to think that ego-consciousness is capable of assimilating the unconscious, at least one hopes that such a solution is possible. But unfortunately the unconscious really is unconscious; in other words, it is unknown. And how can you assimilate something unknown?
>
> (Jung, 1969b, para. 529)

And in the end, the claims of

> a "universal consciousness" is a contradiction in terms, since exclusion, selection, and discrimination are the root and essence of everything that lays claim to the name "consciousness." "Universal consciousness" is logically identical with unconsciousness.
>
> (Jung, 1969b, para. 529)

"For this reason we must look for a different solution. We believe in ego-consciousness and in what we call reality" (Jung, 1969b, para. 529).

One of the big problems from Analytical Psychology (and the question of authority) is the deep assumption that not only (like Tibetan theory) is the true teacher or *guru* within, it shows up *as the perturbation of ego conscious that we attribute to the unconscious*. This is the dividing line. Either some person or tradition has an ultimate authority or the non-ego aspect of ourselves contains, in symbolic form, the necessary information for our own individuation. It is true that in theory images of god coalesce with experiences of the self, and at the bottom the self is a collective entity. However, in practice it makes all the difference whether one looks within or accepts a mass answer of some sort.

In terms of a relationship with the total psyche, Jung writes that

> This means open conflict and open collaboration at once. That, evidently, is the way human life should be. It is the old game of hammer and anvil: between them the patient iron is forged into an indestructible whole, an "individual."
>
> (Jung, 1969b, para. 522)

At the very least it is important to symbolize the metaphysical arena so that a prospective view may be taken of competing cosmic fantasies – including the psychological! From this perspective, this next level of meditation could be thought of as an awareness of the psyche itself. Jung uses the word psyche in a number of ways, but here it is related to the categories of understanding that Kant developed from Aristotle's ten categories or ontological predicates. Jung calls them categories of imagination and they are related to his concept of the archetypes as organs of the psyche. They include concepts like time, space, and causality, which from this perspective are like apertures of the mind rather than aspects of a putative reality.

That is, all that we could experience is the psyche. Or we could say experience is what arises in the psychic field. This perspective is fully supported by what is now quite solid and foundational research on cognition which shows that our idea of the world is constructed by our brains from quite fragmentary sensory data. Evolution demanded a functional system that could help our organism flourish, not an accurate rendition of the world in physical terms. This research indicates, among other things, that we do not directly perceive our own senses, nor are they discrete. Technological advances have allowed otherwise blind people to, for instance, "see" with one's tongue (Twilley, 2017) if certain receptors are linked from a photosensitive material to the nerves of the tongue, showing that any neural signal can be processed by the visual cortex and made into an image. Furthermore, the holographic "picture" that we make of the world has only a tangential and relative relationship with the world that our mechanical sensors find. The usefulness of the humanscape is just that: it is useful for survival and adaptation.

From this point of view (which is a condensation of Jung's neo-Kantian understanding), there is nothing else apart from the mental construction (or psyche) that we have direct access to. Other forms of reality must and need to be inferred from their effects – and this inferential work sometimes leads to adaptation. We draw a fine but important line here in saying both that direct experience is limited and also that there seem to be other aspects or levels of reality available, since our unconscious psyches have the tendency to erupt in disturbing ways when an adaptive change in attitude or perception is needed. Of course, it is impossible to tell whether that other level is an ontic one or is a socially constructed one, so in good

Buddhist and Jungian fashion the question is irrelevant to the question of suffering except insofar as it is treated a pattern of the mind.

A Jungian view on the nature of meditation

The question of patterns of mind brings up the possibility that meditation may have an archetypal, that is, collective propensity and structure. If so, it might be possible to say some things about it that apply in a general sense. I would like to begin by suggesting that meditation – and for that matter depth psychology – begins with the suspicion or insight that one's own mentality may be something other than a transparent beholding of a common reality.

Human thought about mentality has a disturbingly solipsistic flavor, as Jung tirelessly pointed out. Since this kind of thought is similar to an exploration of psychic states, then we have to wonder what we are experiencing – that is, what is the nature of this rhizome-like reality?[24] This reality, in psychological terms, is our common unconscious agreement about the function of language and its relationship to collective values, the idea of individual motive and responsibility, and the fully embedded nature of us in our social context. In a nutshell, this is called the realm of projection. So meditation can be thought of at the next level as a careful consideration of projection and the evidence that allows or forces our adaptive changes. Perhaps the most extensive treatment of projection as a normal, unavoidable, unconscious, and even useful aspect of mental functioning is found in M.L. von Franz's *Projection and Re-collection*. She extends Jung's explanation that since we can only become aware of unconscious dynamics through projection, it is itself both the fabric of reality when everyone agrees on a collective projection and also the means with which an individual reclaims subjective personality by coming to see inaccurate projections as psychic material.

In one sense, then, the psychological project is one of understanding and assimilating projection when the fabric of the projected world (that is, the world we commonly experience) is at odds with an adaptive function of the psyche:

> Projection results from the archaic identity (q.v.) of subject and object, but is properly so called only when the need to dissolve the identity with the object has already arisen. This need arises when the identity becomes a disturbing factor, i.e., when the absence of the projected content is a hindrance to adaptation and its withdrawal into the subject has become desirable.
> (Jung, 1971, para. 789)

Many aspects of meditation can be understood as becoming aware of or working within or across various levels of projection/reality. As mentioned, expanding awareness (through or as meditation) could be described as withdrawing projections. Jung mentions that if we were able to withdraw all projections, we would have divine lucidity. This is very much in agreement with the description of enlightened people in many traditions. If we take a look at this through Von Franz's five stages

(I add two at the end that she describes but does not put in her series), then we get a description of the constant flow of sense and experience from total identification with outer reality to an awareness of it as a psychic substrate and finally to the creation of meaning.

Von Franz uses an unfortunate example, one far removed from our modern or Western sensibility. She uses the example of an African man who hears a tree speak. This is the layer of (the initial) complete identity of subject and object. It is also the normal state of dormant and unremarkable reality. For Westerners, it might be more like the obvious correctness of a political position or the obvious truth of what we "got from our parents." The next level separates the voice from the tree or the platform from the person. The next level evaluates the voice or message on its own merit, apart from the extra authority (or its lack) conferred by the object it is associated with.

At the fourth stage, the voice or message is seen as internal, at least to the extent that we have generated its importance. Usually it is then denuded of importance and a depression sets in. So far we have traced the process of analysis that is common to Analytical Psychology and psychodynamic theory. However, level five is understanding the voice/message as psychically generated and therefore symbolically true and important. Level six is where the message is understood. Level seven has to do with action according to that understanding, which also then eliminates the return of the repressed.

All experience can be described as residing in one of these layers of projection and withdrawal. The rate of withdrawal and the necessity of withdrawal have to do with a person's psychic gradient and the lack of adaptation in a given situation. Since as Jung remarked, reality can be defined as a *consensus gentium*, there is no final reality apart from a relationship with the collective, so individuation is a constant systolic and diastolic movement of psychic material from the psychoid level in which it is embedded in the collective to the fully assimilated level in which it is identical with the individual personality.

Within this description, it is important to remember that passive projection is the world itself as co-arising unconscious matrix (and also mental illness), whereas active projection is the basis of empathy and judgment:

> The active form of projection is, however, also an act of judgment, the aim of which is to separate the subject from the object.
>
> *(Jung, 1971, para. 789)*

The empathy part is important in order to realize the complex relationship between perception and compassion and also to shed some light on the fallacy or at least intricacy of the role of the much maligned ego. At the level of (our fantasy of) a non-differentiated wholeness, there are also no human gestures, ethics, rituals, or artifacts of any kind, including empathy or compassion.

Ritual and symbol emerge out of the psyche's perception of nature and are not *merely metaphors*, as the work by Lakoff and Johnson (and many others) reminds us – rather figures of speech are embedded in the world itself, but through the intervention of the psyche. And as Ricoeur points out in (*Conflict of Interpretations*), as a lovely extension of Gadamer's *Truth and Method*, the *distanciation* of the subject–object divide is precisely what provides for the possibility of communication, rather than being a hindrance.

> All the mythologized processes of nature, such as summer and winter, the phases of the moon, the rainy seasons, and so forth, are in no sense allegories of these objective occurrences; rather they are symbolic expressions of the inner, unconscious drama of the psyche which becomes accessible to man's consciousness by way of projection – that is, mirrored in the events of nature.
> (Jung, 1969b, para. 7)

We now know that much of human evolution has dealt with adapting to the most powerful selecting force on Earth – the human mind. If we go back, in our imaginations, to the first time something became symbolized, to the first flickering of culture as a literally world-changing tool of adaptation, that is the moment that

> Instead of being at the mercy of wild beasts, earthquakes, landslides, and inundations, modern man is battered by the elemental forces of his own psyche. This is the World Power that vastly exceeds all other powers on earth.
> (Jung, 1970b, p. 471)

The problem is that intentional changes to awareness are guided either by an individual conscious mind (leaving aside for the moment the question of whether there is a single conscious mind to speak of), or by a person of authority – who either acts independently or on behalf of a tradition. This means that almost all meditation types are versions of control – which doesn't mean they might not be helpful (to use that word loosely).

That is to say, meditation is a cultural artifact that has the same properties as a tool. Like the image of a tool in a dream, it leverages and extends an ego function into an area of experience that would not otherwise be available. This brings us, again, back to the question of the conscious or unconscious intention of the use of the tool.

The problem of the unconscious remains, and is one of the very major differences between most traditions which prioritize meditation as a kind of mental discipline (versus metaphysical claims), as opposed to traditions in which meditation opens a channel to some other – a god-image of some type. The problem of the unconscious shows itself in two ways. The first is that all masters of meditation are still fallible individuals rather than examples of the perfection of a tradition. This is to speak lightly about the deep shadows of authority I have found in virtually every community based on a hierarchy that I have encountered. The other problem is that if the psyche is somewhat independent of the individual and if the center of the psyche is self-regulating and has, for lack of a better term, a wisdom of some kind for the individual, then controlling it or the symbols that arise from it becomes either a fallacy or at least a hindrance to further psychological growth.

This can occur on a number of levels. One is like the case of Brother Klaus, discussed by Jung in volume 11. It concerns the relationship between natural and traditional symbols. Traditional symbols are the culturally and power-oriented versions of naturally arising symbols that work for the collectively minded people but hinder the creative. Almost all novel religious thinkers have run into problems with traditional authorities because of this.

The next level has been well discussed, not including the problems of the unconscious, in books like *Spiritual Bypassing* (Masters), which show how any spiritual technique (and this is of course applicable to any psychological technique) can be used to hinder growth in some way. That is to say, a tool can be used for good or ill, as well as the problem that the tool can become the master if one is identified with it.

This leads us to the problem of ego consciousness as the only reality:

> With this discovery (of the unconscious) the position of the ego, till then absolute, became relativized; that is to say, though it retains its quality as the centre of the field of consciousness, it is questionable whether it is the centre, of the personality. . . . As I have said, it is simply impossible to estimate how large or how small its share is; how free or how dependent it is on the qualities of this "extra-conscious" psyche. We can only say that its freedom is limited and its dependence proved in ways that are often decisive.
>
> *(Jung, 1969b, paras. 9–11)*

As Jung wrote in the introduction to the Tibetan *Book of the Dead*:

> It is highly sensible of the Bardo Thödol to make clear to the dead man the primacy of the psyche, for that is the one thing which life does not make clear to us.
>
> *(Jung, 1970a)*

From a Jungian point of view, meditation is attention to the psyche. This can take the form of resisting instinctual urges (the level of control, described as the field of the psyche in Aion); playing with arising images (similar to guided meditations but without the guide); holding an emotion until it moves into an image, moving according to a kinesthetic image, noticing what arises (similar to meditations of steady awareness); allowing a psychic impregnation (like Tibetan dream yoga); hovering awareness with attention split between one's own process, the other's process, and the field, and attunement to what changes us (the numinous or devotional aspect). This last is akin to the following:

> We might say . . . that the term "religion" designates the attitude peculiar to a consciousness which has been changed by experience of the numinosum.
>
> *(Jung, 1970b, para. 9)*

So we can see that meditation *and* Analytical Psychology are about the connection of the daily and small to the eternal and cosmic, of the person to meaning, of the mortal to the image-of-god, and of one person to another, that is, to the enhancement of relationships. However from the side of the psyche we can discern four levels of meditational practice. The first is an introjection of the cultural and religious forms that manifest as a particular map of the psyche or meditation technique. Second, related to the focusing aspect of meditation is the skill of staying with a natural image (that is, one not immediately derived from orthodoxy), in both its dynamic and content. Third, relating to the open-awareness aspect is becoming aware of the field of the psyche in general and the mechanism of projection. Also included here would be the prospective aspect of contents that arise in the field and how they are reclaimed as psychic value. Finally is the ability to hold all of those fields for oneself and another and to identify the deepest channels of transformative libido for the other, as happens in true guru-ship and in good analysis.

Notes

1 Unconscious agency can be studied at many levels. Neuroscience studies such as *The New Unconscious* (Hassin et al., 2006) represent the area of tightly controlled foundational research and leads to all sorts of cognitive bias studies and finally to typology and even more difficult multi-variant questions such as the nature of the psyche's "aim."
2 There are many synopses, beginning with a good one in Wikipedia.
3 See the article on 23 styles (http://liveanddare.com/types-of-meditation/), and this is just the beginning. Or for 108 methods, see www.meditationsociety.com/108meds.html.
4 Aion, preface, for a discussion of amplification as a disciplined application of any heuristic approach with the understanding that there are many others, each with its own strengths and weaknesses.
5 Inherent problems with research include but are not limited to funding source bias; many of the acknowledged cognitive biases; the question of paradigm; and the simple fact that there are very few, if any, research programs not run by individuals with particular interests in seeing their own form of meditation become justified in a wider setting.
6 It may seem that I stress the professional and social aspects too much, but it is important to remember from the anthropological side that all *technicians of the sacred* have been a highly paid economic cohort since the beginning of civilization. Their agendas are self-serving – not in a bad way, since everyone has to make a living – and they have that in common with teachers of meditation, priests and healers the world over. For a brilliant discussion of this, see Pascal Boyer's *Religion Explained*.
7 Jung's view was that at the end of the day, the best we can do is to take the various streams of data from all of the functions and hold them in experiential tension, allow this to change our attitude, and act from there.
8 He explored what he called the personal equation in many places, among others in Volume 8, in the brilliant 1925 Seminar which traces the development of his theory *as an aspect of his own personal growth*, and of course in his work with Pauli that lately has become known as the Pauli-Jung conjecture in physics.
9 Atmanspacher and Fuchs (2014), p. 108.
10 http://liveanddare.com/types-of-meditation/
11 www.meditationsociety.com/108meds.html
12 http://thedailymeditation.com/meditation-for-atheists/
13 Jung, natural symbols (Aion).
14 http://news.harvard.edu/gazette/story/2011/01/eight-weeks-to-a-better-brain/

15 www.researchgate.net/profile/Shauna_Shapiro/publication/228583427_An_analysis_of_recent_meditation_research_and_suggestions_for_future_directions/links/54374e6e0cf2dc341db4d514.pdf
16 Ibid.
17 Ibid.
18 At least in terms of Patanjali's classic *Yoga Sutras*.
19 http://info-buddhism.com/Scientific_Buddha_Lopez.html
20 http://secularbuddhism.org/2012/10/10/book-review-donald-lopez-on-buddhism-and-science/
21 www.newscientist.com/article/mg22630210-500-panic-depression-and-stress-the-case-against-meditation/; also www.psychologytoday.com/blog/mindfulness-wellbeing/201603/dangers-meditation
22 Patanjali, *The Yoga Sutras*.
23 https://tricycle.org/magazine/reincarnation-debate/
24 There is an opportunity here to compare Jung's metaphor of the rhizome with research on mirror neurons and even with the Buddhist idea of co-arising reality.

References

Atmanspacher, H., & Fuchs, C. (Eds.). (2014). *The Pauli-Jung conjecture and its impact today*. Exeter, UK: Imprint Academic.
Batchelor, S. (1997). *Buddhism without beliefs*. New York: Riverhead Books.
Batchelor, S. (2010). *Confession of a Buddhist atheist*. New York: Random House.
Boyer, P. (2002). *Religion explained: The evolutionary origins of religious thought*. New York: Basic Books.
Caspi, O., & Burleson, K.O. (2005). Methodological challenges in meditation research. *Advances in mind-body medicine*, *21*(1), 4–11.
Das, S. (2007). The heart-essence of Buddhist meditation. *Tricycle*. https://tricycle.org/magazine/heart-essence-buddhist-meditation/
Freud, S. (1924). *Collected papers II*. The International Psycho-Analytical Library. London: Hogarth Press.
Gadamer, H.-G. (2004). *Truth and method* (2nd rev. ed., J. Weinsheimer and D.G. Marshall, Trans.). New York: Crossroad Publishing.
Hassin, R.R., Uleman, J.S., & Bargh, J.A. (Eds.). (2006). *The new unconscious*. Oxford: Oxford University Press. Introduction and p. 2
Jung, C.G. (1933). *Modern man in search of a soul* (C. F. Baynes with W. Stanley Dell, Trans.). London: Kegan Paul, Trench, Trubner and Company. p. 227
Jung, C.G. (1961). *Memories dreams reflection* (A. Jaffe, Ed.). New York: Pantheon Books.
Jung, C.G. (1969a). *Archetypes and the collective unconscious, collected works vol 9i*. Princeton: Princeton University Press.
Jung, C.G. (1969b). *Aion: Researches into the phenomenology of the self, collected works vol 9ii*. Princeton: Princeton University Press.
Jung, C.G. (1970a). Psychological commentary on 'The Tibetan book of the great liberation' (1939/1954). In R.F.C. Hull (Trans.), *The collected works of CG Jung, volume 11: Psychology and religion: West and east* (pp. 475–508). Princeton: Princeton University Press.
Jung, C.G. (1970b). *Psychology and religion, collected works, volume 11*. Princeton: Princeton University Press.
Jung, C.G. (1970c). *Civilization in transition, collected works, volume 10*. Princeton: Princeton University Press.
Jung, C.G. (1971). *Psychological types, collected works, v6*. Princeton: Princeton University Press.

Jung, C.G. (1977). *The symbolic life: Miscellaneous writings, volume 18* (G. Adler and R.F. Hull, Trans.). Princeton: Princeton University Press.

Kabat-Zinn, J. (1996). Mindfulness meditation: What it is, what it isn't, and its role in health care and medicine. In Y. Haruki, Y. Ishii, & M. Suzuki, (eds.), *Comparative and psychological study on meditation.* Eburon, Netherlands.

Kabat-Zinn, J. (2013). *Full catastrophe living: Using the wisdom of your body and mind to face stress, pain, and illness.* New York: Bantam Dell.

Langer, E. (1997). *The power of mindful learning.* Boston: Lifelong Books, Da Capo Press.

Lopez, Jr., D. (2012). *The scientific Buddha: His short and happy life.* New Haven: Yale University Press.

Ludwig, D.S., & Kabat-Zinn, J. (2008, September). Mindfulness in medicine. *JAMA, 300(11)*, 1350–1352.

Master Robert, A. (2010). *Spiritual bypassing: When spirituality disconnects us from what really matters.* Berkeley: North Atlantic Books.

Patanjali. (2003). *The yoga sutras.* Boulder: Shambhala Publications.

Ricoeur, P. (1974). *The conflict of interpretations: Essays in hermeneutics* (D. Ihde, Ed. and W. Domingo et al., Trans.). Evanston: Northwestern University Press, 1969. p. 121-122

Scharf, R. (1995). Buddhist modernism and the rhetoric of meditative experience. *Numen, 42*(3), 228–283. Republished in *Buddhism: Critical concepts in Buddhist studies*, edited by P. Williams. London: Routledge, 2005, volume 2, pp. 255–298.

Twilley, N. Seeing with Your Tongue, (2017). *New Yorker*, May.

Wilber, K. (2000). *Integral psychology: Consciousness, spirit, psychology, therapy.* Boulder: Shambhala Publications.

Zizek, S. (2014). *Absolute recall: Towards a new foundation of dialectical materialism.* London: Verso Books.

PART V
A complex systems approach to the psyche

8

RESEARCH ON SYNCHRONICITY

Status and prospects

Roderick Main

Introduction

In a letter to Philip Wylie (undated but probably 1949), C.G. Jung referred to synchronicity as one of the best ideas he had ever had (cited in Bair, 2004, p. 551). Elsewhere he indicated its relevance not only for psychotherapy (Main, 2007c), but also for the critique of modern science, religion, and society (Main, 2004, pp. 117–143). Yet Jung only wrote extensively about synchronicity late in life (Jung, 1950, 1951, 1952), and he never clearly or fully integrated the concept into his psychological theory. In the years since Jung's death, there have been many varied attempts to elucidate, apply, and evaluate synchronicity, both within and beyond Analytical Psychology, and these have recently burgeoned to the point where the need for orientation on the topic is pressing. The present chapter therefore provides an overview of existing research on the concept of synchronicity,[1] from which some promising directions for future research are then highlighted under various headings: conceptual, empirical, historical, theoretical, clinical, and cultural. As an example of sustained academic engagement with this topic and to provide additional detail on methodological issues, I include an outline of my own research on synchronicity over the last 25 years.

Jung's definitions and theoretical framing of synchronicity

Before moving to the review of subsequent work on synchronicity, it may be helpful to set out how Jung himself defined and illustrated the concept. Jung defined synchronicity in a variety of ways. Concisely, he defined it as "meaningful coincidence" (1952, para. 827), as "acausal parallelism" (1963, p. 407), as "an acausal connecting principle" (1952), and once, more poetically, as "the 'rupture of time'" (McGuire & Hull, 1978, p. 230). More fully, he defined it as "the simultaneous occurrence of a certain psychic state with one or more external events which appear as meaningful parallels to the momentary subjective state" (1952, para. 850). An example of Jung's, which he presented as paradigmatic (1951, para. 983), will convey what he meant by these definitions as well as, concisely, how he saw the concept of synchronicity fitting into his overall psychological model. The example concerned a young woman patient whose excessive intellectuality made her "psychologically inaccessible," closed off from a "more human understanding" (1951, para. 982). Unable to make headway in analyzing her, Jung reported that he had to confine himself to "the hope that something unexpected would turn up, something that would burst the intellectual retort into which she had sealed herself" (1951, para. 982). He continued:

> Well, I was sitting opposite her one day, with my back to the window, listening to her flow of rhetoric. She had had an impressive dream the night before, in which someone had given her a golden scarab – a costly piece of jewellery. While she was still telling me this dream, I heard something behind me gently tapping on the window. I turned round and saw that it was a fairly large flying insect that was knocking against the window-pane in the obvious effort to get into the dark room. This seemed to me very strange. I opened the window immediately and caught the insect in the air as it flew in. It was a scarabaeid beetle, or common rose-chafer (*Cetonia aurata*), whose gold-green colour most nearly resembles that of a golden scarab. I handed the beetle to my patient with the words, "Here is your scarab." This experience punctured the desired hole in her rationalism and broke the ice of her intellectual resistance. The treatment could now be continued with satisfactory results.
>
> (Jung, 1951, para. 982)

In this example, the *psychic state* was indicated by the patient's decision to tell Jung her dream of being given a scarab. The *parallel external event* was the appearance and behavior of the real scarab. The telling of the dream and the appearance of the real scarab were *simultaneous*. Neither of these events discernibly or plausibly caused the other by any normal means, so their relationship was *acausal*. Nevertheless, the events paralleled each other in such unlikely detail that one cannot escape the impression that they were indeed *connected*, albeit acausally. Moreover, this acausal connection of events both was symbolically informative and had a deeply emotive and transforming impact on the patient, and in these senses was *meaningful*.

Jung attempted to account for synchronistic events primarily in terms of his concept of *archetypes*. For this purpose, he highlighted the nature of archetypes as "formal factors responsible for the organization of unconscious psychic processes: they are 'patterns of behaviour.' At the same time they have a 'specific charge' and develop numinous effects which express themselves as *affects*" (1952, para. 841). They "constitute the structure" not of the personal but "of the *collective unconscious* [. . .] psyche that is identical in all individuals" (1952, para. 840; emphasis added). Jung further characterized archetypes as *psychoid* on account of their being irrepresentable (1952, para. 840) and able to manifest in outer physical processes as well as inner psychic ones (1952, para. 964). Also relevant for Jung was that archetypes typically expressed themselves in the form of *symbolic images* (1952, para. 845). He considered that synchronistic events tended to occur in situations in which an archetype was active or "constellated" (1952, para. 847). Such constellation of archetypes in the life of a person was governed for Jung by the process of *individuation* – the inherent drive of the psyche toward increased wholeness and self-realization. Individuation in turn proceeded through the dynamic of *compensation*, whereby any one-sidedness in a person's conscious attitude was balanced by contents emerging from the unconscious, which, if successfully integrated, contributed to a state of greater psychic wholeness.

Relating these psychological structures and dynamics to his example, we can note Jung's suggestion that it had "an archetypal foundation" (1952, para. 845) and, more specifically, that it was the archetype of rebirth that was constellated. Jung wrote that "Any essential change of attitude signifies a psychic renewal which is usually accompanied by symbols of rebirth in the patient's dreams and fantasies. The scarab is a classic example of a rebirth symbol" (1952, para. 845). The emotional charge or numinosity of the archetypal event was evident from its having "broke[n] the ice of [the patient's] intellectual resistance." The compensatory nature of the experience was also clear: the patient's one-sided rationalism and psychological stasis were balanced by an event that both in its symbolism and in its action expressed the power of the irrational and the possibility of renewal. Finally, that all of this promoted the patient's individuation was implied by Jung's statement that "The treatment could now be continued with satisfactory results."

The features of synchronistic events that Jung's definitions and discussions most emphasized were the simultaneity of their component events, their acausality, their improbability, and their meaning. He frankly acknowledged that the first of these features, simultaneity, was not straightforward. For there were other events that he wanted to designate as synchronistic where the element of simultaneity was not so apparent, events that either could not at the time be known to be simultaneous (as, for example, with apparently clairvoyant visions) or seemingly were not simultaneous at all (as, for example, with apparently precognitive dreams). In order to account for these further kinds of coincidences, Jung presented, in his 1951 Eranos lecture "On Synchronicity," the following three-pronged definition:

> All the phenomena I have mentioned can be grouped under three categories:
>
> 1   The coincidence of a psychic state in the observer with a simultaneous, objective, external event that corresponds to the psychic state or content (e.g., the scarab), where there is no evidence of a causal connection between the psychic state and the external event, and where, considering the psychic relativity of space and time, such a connection is not even conceivable.

2   The coincidence of a psychic state with a corresponding (more or less simultaneous) external event taking place outside the observer's field of perception, i.e., at a distance, and only verifiable afterward [...].
3   The coincidence of a psychic state with a corresponding, not yet existent future event that is distant in time and can likewise only be verified afterward.

In groups 2 and 3 the coinciding events are not yet present in the observer's field of perception, but have been anticipated in time in so far as they can only be verified afterward. For this reason I call such events *synchronistic*, which is not to be confused with *synchronous*.

(1951, paras. 984–985)

Overview of some of the main approaches to researching synchronicity

In his principal essay on the topic, "Synchronicity: An Acausal Connecting Principle" (1952), Jung adopts a broad, multidisciplinary approach to making sense of synchronistic experiences. The disciplines and perspectives on which he draws include mainstream sciences such as physics and biology; newer or aspiring sciences such as psychical research and parapsychology; philosophy and intellectual history; analysis and psychotherapy; and the study of religion and spirituality, including divination and esoteric traditions (Main, 2004, pp. 65–90). Subsequent works on synchronicity have also tended to engage with several disciplines and perspectives, even while focusing on one or on selected relationships among them.

Jung published his principal essay on synchronicity in a co-authored volume alongside an essay by the Nobel Prize–winning physicist Wolfgang Pauli (Jung & Pauli, 1952), and this alliance is reflected in the predominantly scientific framing of Jung's essay (Main, 2004, pp. 104–105). Not surprisingly, much subsequent work has also reflected on the status of synchronicity in relation to science. Among the most substantive contributions with a predominantly scientific focus are publications by Marie-Louise von Franz (1974, 1992), David Peat (1987), Victor Mansfield (1995, 2002), Suzanne Gieser (2005), Lance Storm (2008), Joseph Cambray (2009), George Hogenson (2005, 2009, 2014), John Haule (2011), and Harald Atmanspacher (2012). The scientific discipline most discussed is physics, though Von Franz and Peat in their different ways survey a range of historical and contemporary developments in science, Cambray explores complexity theory, and Haule takes account of evolutionary biology before moving on to field theories in physics. All of these works, however, also connect synchronicity to conspicuously non-scientific frameworks, whether psychotherapy, divination, esotericism, ancient or modern philosophy, mythology, Buddhism, politics, or shamanism. None treats synchronicity as of exclusively scientific interest.

Jung's work on synchronicity was also inspired by psychical research and especially by the work of Joseph Banks Rhine in the new discipline of parapsychology. These newer or aspiring sciences have provided significant foci within the work of

Mansfield (1995, 2002), the present author (1997b, 2012), Storm (2008), and Haule (2011). But again the focus never remains exclusive for long, with religious, psychological, anthropological, and other perspectives also being invoked.

Jung's own grasp of philosophy and intellectual history, in relating synchronicity to the rest of his thought, was impressive in scope but sometimes unreliable, as his primary aim was usually to amplify his own thought rather than to understand the thought of others on its own terms. Later attempts to situate Jung's concept of synchronicity philosophically or in relation to intellectual history have included wider-ranging books by Ira Progoff (1973) and the present author (2004), and more focused studies. Paul Bishop (2000) considers Jung's preoccupation with the mind–body problem and the notion of intellectual intuition in German Idealist philosophy. Several other authors, including David Lindorff (2004), Gieser (2005), Arthur Miller (2009), and Atmanspacher and Christopher Fuchs (2014) and their contributors, closely examine Pauli's influence on and collaboration with Jung. Cambray (2009, 2014a, 2014b, 2014c) has also traced the influence on Jung of the aesthetic and holistic perspectives of German Romantic scientists.

One field by which Jung was clearly influenced but within which he explored the significance of synchronicity surprisingly little was psychotherapy. A few subsequent books contain substantial discussions of synchronicity in relation to therapy, notably those by Jean Shinoda Bolen (1979), Robert Aziz (1990, 2007), and Robert Hopcke (1997). Mostly, however, the existing in-depth discussions of synchronicity in the therapeutic context have appeared in journal articles. The present author (2007c) reviews both Jung's limited clinical discussions of synchronicity and the more extensive clinical discussions by later analysts published in a variety of articles between 1957 and 2005. Since 2005, important articles on the clinical significance of synchronicity have continued to appear (Reiner, 2006; Hogenson, 2009; Colman, 2011; Carvalho, 2014; de Moura, 2014; Connelly, 2015; Atmanspacher & Fach, 2016).

At the other end of the spectrum from the consideration of synchronicity in relation to science is its consideration in relation to religion and spirituality. Jung himself seems to play down the religious sources and significance of synchronicity in his principal essay (1952; Main 2004, pp. 105–107), though these are easy enough to detect or extrapolate. Aziz (1990, 2007), Mansfield (1995, 2002), and the present author (2004, 2007a) specifically address the religious implications of synchronicity. Some of the works of these authors focus almost exclusively on religion and spirituality (Main, 2007a), sometimes with a psychotherapeutic inflection (Aziz, 1990, 2007). Others explicitly address the dual religious and scientific influences on and significance of the concept of synchronicity (Mansfield, 1995, 2002; Main, 2004).

Prospects for future research

Despite all of this work, the concept of synchronicity, while fairly widely diffused within popular culture, especially within holistic science (Combs & Holland, 1994) and holistic spirituality (Main, 2004, pp. 144–174), has so far achieved very little integration within mainstream academic and intellectual fields. It is not that the concept has been decisively disproven or discredited – it tends to be too poorly understood and too cursorily evaluated for this – but rather that it has been disregarded. Part of the reason for this mainstream neglect may be the multidisciplinary complexity, incompleteness, and at times confusion of Jung's expositions of synchronicity (Main, 2004, pp. 36–62). Also off-putting is the frequent superficiality of the more popular uses and presentations of the concept. But a further factor likely inhibiting its wider serious consideration is that, with its propositions that there are uncaused events, that matter has a psychic aspect, that the psyche can relativize time and space, and that there may be a dimension of objective meaning accessible to but not created by humans (Main, 2004, p. 2), synchronicity challenges the positivist, realist, and humanist epistemological assumptions that predominate in the sciences and social sciences. Because it presents this challenge, the concept resists being proven, or perhaps even rendered plausible, in terms of these dominant epistemologies.

There do, however, seem to be some prospects for improving the understanding and possibly the credibility of synchronicity. In the following sections I note some of the promising directions that have been opened up by existing research. For convenience I have identified different strands within this research as primarily conceptual, empirical, historical, theoretical, clinical, or cultural. Many studies, of course, could be included under several of these headings. For, as we have seen, in their attempt to get to grips with the topic, subsequent researchers, like Jung, have drawn on a plurality of disciplines from both the sciences and the humanities and have deployed a corresponding plurality of methods.

Conceptual

Despite his efforts to be precise, Jung's definitions, characterizations, and illustrations of synchronicity leave many issues unclear. A number of subsequent, overarching studies have attempted to identify and resolve these issues in ways that remain consistent with Jung's own theoretical framework (Von Franz, 1974, 1980, 1992; Aziz, 1990; Mansfield, 1995; Main, 2004; Cambray, 2009; Haule, 2011; Atmanspacher, 2012). Within as well as beyond these studies, each of the main concepts informing Jung's definitions of synchronicity – time, acausality, probability, and meaning – has been scrutinized, and some directions for future research have emerged.

In particular, the role of time in synchronicity has been repeatedly questioned in view of Jung's qualifications regarding simultaneity in his more elaborate definitions (Pauli in Meier, 2001, pp. 38–39; Koestler, 1972, p. 95; Aziz, 1990, pp. 71, 149). Other difficulties relate to his characterization of synchronicity sometimes in terms of qualitative time, whereby "whatever is born or done at this particular moment of time has the quality of this moment of time" (1930, para. 82), and other times in terms of "a psychically conditioned relativity of space and time," whereby "space and time are, so to speak 'elastic' and can apparently be reduced almost to vanishing point" (1952, para. 840; Aziz, 1990, pp. 71–72; Main, 2004, pp. 51–53, 110–111; Yassemides, 2014). To some extent these difficulties can be resolved by taking account of the different frameworks, predominantly religious or predominantly scientific, within which Jung at different times considered synchronicity (Main, 2004, pp. 110–111). But the difficulties also point to the need for deeper metaphysical reflection on the relationship of synchronicity to time. A stimulating attempt at such reflection has compared Jung's thinking about time in synchronicity with Henri Bergson's notion of duration, including how Bergson's notion has been later adapted in the philosophy of Gilles Deleuze (McMillan, 2015).

In relation to acausality, one recurrent issue has been the need to specify what kind of causality it is that acausality negates, and specifically whether acausality is still an appropriate term if other kinds of causes than efficient causes (for example, final causes) are invoked in explaining synchronicity (Mansfield, 1995, pp. 72–83; Main, 2004, p. 54). Jung's choice of the term acausality might also be examined in the light of Paul Forman's thesis about how in the interwar years this and related terms were taken up by German physicists for non-scientific reasons relating to cultural and intellectual climate (Gieser, 2005, pp. 57–60; Asprem, 2014, pp. 128–139, 142). Another issue is Jung's use of acausality to refer on the one hand to one-off synchronistic events at the level of ordinary human experience and on the other hand to statistically analyzable forms of orderedness in microphysics (Gieser, 2005, pp. 272–298).

The role Jung ascribes to probability in synchronicity has been criticized in light of general statistical considerations relating to the law of very large numbers (Diaconis & Mosteller, 1989; Main, 2004, pp. 27–29). The applicability of this law to synchronistic events has been challenged, including by pointing to limitations and problems within probability theory itself (McCusker & Sutherland, 1991; Combs & Holland, 1994, pp. 155–159). Closer examination of synchronicity in relation to the theory of probability might therefore be valuable, especially in view of Jung's innovative if not idiosyncratic use of statistics (Main, 2004, pp. 58–61, 113). More recently, probability has also been the focus of some speculations relating synchronicity to power-law distributions such as Zipf's law (Hogenson, 2005, 2009, 2014), and this work has in turn prompted a proposal for scientifically testing synchronicity (Sacco, 2016).

Finally, there have been many discussions of meaning in synchronicity. Among the issues discussed have been the relationship between meaning and order (Von Franz, 1992, pp. 267–292), the complementarity between causality and meaning (Atmanspacher, 2014b), whether the meaning in synchronicities is found or created (Bright, 1997; Colman, 2015), and what kinds or levels of meaning might be involved in synchronicities (Aziz, 1990, pp. 64–66, 75–84; Colman, 2011, 2012; Giegerich, 2012; Main, 2004, pp. 56–58, 112–113, 2014c; Atmanspacher, 2014a, pp. 192–193). Advancing these discussions is particularly important because it is the involvement of meaning that ties synchronicity to the rest of Jung's psychological model and constitutes the real challenge of synchronicity to prevailing philosophy of science.

In general, there remains in the case of each of the above concepts – time, acausality, probability, and meaning – a need for further clarification of what Jung's understanding of the concept was, whether a modified understanding might actually serve Jung's purposes better, and how either Jung's understanding or a modification of it can be related to mainstream discussions of the concept in philosophy and other relevant disciplines. In particular, such further clarification will need to take account of attempts to define and conceptualise the same broad range of phenomena from other theoretical perspectives: for example, those of psychoanalysis (Devereux, 1953; Faber, 1998; Williams, 2010); psychical research (Johnson, 1899; Koestler, 1972; Henry, 1993; Kelly et al., 2007, 2015); psychology (Watt, 1990–1991); psychiatry (Beitman, 2016); and statistics (Hardy et al., 1973; Diaconis & Mosteller, 1989). Some of the work from these alternative perspectives has explicitly taken issue with central aspects of Jung's concept of synchronicity (Koestler, 1972; Faber, 1998; Williams, 2010).

Empirical

Notwithstanding the difficulties surrounding Jung's own attempt at an "astrological experiment," reported in the second chapter of his principal essay on synchronicity (1952, paras. 872–915; Main, 2004, pp. 58–61), it may be possible to conduct at least some levels of experimental testing of synchronicity (Sacco, 2016). The possibilities may be greatest in those respects where synchronistic phenomena resemble parapsychological phenomena (Braud, 1983; Thalbourne et al., 1992–1993; Palmer, 2004; Atmanspacher & Fach, 2013; but note Mansfield, 2002, pp. 161–179). Indeed, for anyone who construes synchronistic and parapsychological phenomena to be in important respects the same, there already exists in parapsychology a considerable body of relevant experimental research (Kelly et al., 2007). Data from this research could be re-examined from the perspective of the concept of synchronicity.

Again, rigorous social scientific methods of data gathering could be used to accumulate both larger, better organized databases, on which more quantitative analyses could be performed, and richer synchronistic case studies, which would be more sensitive than existing accounts of synchronistic experiences to psychological, sociological, and other contexts. At least one project aimed at the systematic collection of synchronistic data within psychotherapy is indeed currently underway (Roesler, 2014; see also present volume).

Historical

Detailed historical and comparative studies could be undertaken to test the extent to which the pre-modern, non-Western, and esoteric sources that influenced Jung's formulation of the concept of synchronicity really were, as Jung claims, based on similar principles. Deeper study of the esoteric influences on Jung could be especially valuable in light of the recent burgeoning of high-quality scholarship on Western esotericism (Hanegraaff, 2012; Asprem, 2014; Partridge, 2015, Magee, 2016). Similarly, the relationship of synchronicity to Chinese thought, especially to the *I Ching*, has been sympathetically, if briefly, addressed by a number of distinguished Sinologists (Peterson, 1982, 1988; Smith, 2008, pp. 211–217). This could help to provide a securer scholarly basis both for advancing existing understanding of Jung's relationship to the *I Ching*, including his friendship with Richard Wilhelm (Clarke, 1994, pp. 89–102; Karcher, 1999; Main, 1997a, 1999, 2007a, pp. 141–187; Zabriskie, 2005), and for fuller comparison of the concept of synchronicity with ancient Chinese theories of correlative cosmology and cosmic resonance (Main, 2007a, pp. 162–172; Smith, 2008, pp. 32–36, 248–249). Jung's interest in archaic thought, which is even more removed from modern Western culture, can also be fruitfully reconsidered as an influence on his concept of synchronicity (Bishop, 2008).

In addition to esoteric, Eastern, and pre-modern thought being examined as influences on the concept of synchronicity, insights derived from the study of synchronicity might in turn provide a useful tool for understanding the intellectual worlds of esoteric, Eastern, and pre-modern thought. Divination has already been the site for a number of scholarly explorations along these lines (Hanegraaff, 2012, p. 362, citing the work of Kocku von Stuckrad; Redmond & Hon, 2014, pp. 205–214).

There also remains scope for further historical and contextual studies of Jung's engagement with the more contemporary influences on him, such as physics and parapsychology, including his friendships with Pauli and Rhine (Gieser, 2005; Atmanspacher & Fuchs, 2014; Mansfield et al., 1998; Asprem, 2014). And finally an important piece of work remains to be done in systematically tracking, historically and sociologically, the various receptions and transformations of the concept of synchronicity in clinical practice, in academic work, and in both popular and elite culture.

Theoretical

There have recently been several illuminating and suggestive attempts to relate the concept of synchronicity to theoretical frameworks that already have intellectual purchase beyond Analytical Psychology. Chief among these frameworks are emergence, process philosophy, and dual-aspect monism.

The relation of synchronicity to emergence has been explored especially by Cambray (2004, 2009), Hogenson (2005, 2009), Warren Colman (2011, 2015), and Robert Sacco (2016). Among the features that make this approach promising are that emergence is consistent with, even if challenging to, current mainstream science; applies at different scales and hence, like synchronicity, draws on and could potentially be relevant to a wide range of disparate disciplines; and provides scope for treating synchronicity both as an object of study (through exploring its phenomenological and theoretical connections to complexity theory) and as a method of study (through applying it in ways analogous to how complexity theory is applied). However, further work still needs to be done to clarify the exact relationship between synchronicity and emergence. If, for instance, emergence is ultimately understood as a causal phenomenon and if synchronicity is understood as a form of emergence, this would seem to undermine Jung's claims for the acausal character of synchronicity. It is also important to note that there are different positions on emergence, ranging from those that presuppose materialism to those that presuppose some form of panpsychism or even idealism (Kelly et al., 2015, pp. 513–515).

There have also been several discussions of synchronicity in relation to Whiteheadian process philosophy, with varying judgements about how fruitful the connections might be. Steve Odin (1982, pp. 171–187) finds synchronicity, along with other Jungian concepts, helpful for framing his comparison of Hua-Yen Buddhism with Alfred North Whitehead's process metaphysics, especially the notion of the "atemporal envisagement of all possibilities" common to Hua-Yen visionary experience and Whitehead's conception of the primordial nature of God (1982, pp. 5–6). Such atemporal envisagement he considers to be regulated by synchronicity and to have been "empirically verified by the testimony from subjects with retrocognitive and premonitory dreams or inner visions" (1982, pp. 6). In contrast, David Ray Griffin (1989, pp. 1–76), while generally very positive about the possibilities of connecting Jung's and Whitehead's work, singles out synchronicity as "probably the weakest element in Jung's speculations [. . .] an element that will forever prevent Jungian psychology from being integrated with the rest of science" (1989, pp. 27). He has reservations in particular about the notions of acausality and of a psychic relativity of time that could permit precognition (1989, pp. 27–36). More recently, Haule (2011, pp. 152–155, 171–178) has drawn on Whiteheadian process philosophy to support his science-based account of synchronicity as the expression of psychoid processes operating at all levels of animate and inanimate nature. His account is elegant but makes no attempt to engage with the problems presented by apparently precognitive synchronicities, on which Odin and Griffin differ. Both the extensive connections and the unresolved issues suggest that further fruitful work could be done in examining synchronicity vis-à-vis process thought.

Another framework to which synchronicity has recently been related in ways that seem both theoretically and empirically promising is dual-aspect monism. Focusing on Jung's collaboration with Pauli, Atmanspacher (2012) has presented synchronicity in terms of a model whereby psyche and matter are seen as dual epistemic manifestations of an underlying psychophysically neutral ontic monism, the *unus mundus*. Some strengths of the model are that it is has been elaborated out of explicit statements by Jung and Pauli; openly addresses the need to provide metaphysical grounding for Jung's thought, including his concept of synchronicity; is compatible with modern physics; elegantly solves problems in consciousness studies; and fits neatly with empirical data in areas as diverse as exceptional (i.e., paranormal) experiences and order effects in surveys and questionnaires (Atmanspacher, 2014a). Interesting attempts have already been made to apply the model to illuminate the states of mind involved when synchronicity occurs in psychotherapy (Connolly, 2015). However, the model has also been criticized: for example, from an emergentist and phenomenological perspective for retaining epistemological dualism and relegating "the living reality of an *unus mundus* [. . .] to a far-off abstract hypothetical domain removed from the world of knowledge and experience altogether" (Colman, 2015, pp. 320–321). This criticism may be at least partly addressed by the concept of "relative onticity" that Atmanspacher has introduced into his refinements of what he calls the "Pauli–Jung conjecture" (2014a, pp. 186–188).

Each of the above frameworks recognizes the importance of taking seriously the philosophical underpinnings of Jung's thought. Several other attempts to illuminate synchronicity from philosophical perspectives, in some cases partially overlapping with the above, can also be noted, including work drawing on speculative realism (Haworth, 2012) and the philosophy of Deleuze (McMillan, 2015). A major challenge for future research would be to test and compare how satisfactorily each of the theoretical frameworks mentioned in this section accounts for the full range of data that can reasonably be subsumed under the concept of synchronicity.

Clinical

As noted earlier, research exploring how synchronicity can be applied in psychotherapy has continued unabated. Much of this research consists of individual clinicians' reflections on single cases where synchronistic phenomena have appeared during therapy. Where implications have been drawn from more systematic programs of research, this research has usually been carried out initially in other areas or on other topics than synchronicity. Cambray (2009, pp. 68–87), for example, has applied insights from neuroscience, especially concerning mirror neurons, in his discussion of synchronicity in relation to empathy and the analytic field. Hogenson (2009) draws on the findings of the Boston Process of Change Study Group and links their notion of "moments of meeting" to the way meaning can be experienced in the form of synchronicity during psychotherapy. And Colman (2015) invokes phenomenological biology to explain the meaning-making that occurs in synchronicity in terms of embodied intentionality in the world. Even the project of the Berlin Research Group reported by Hans Dieckmann (1976), which resulted in some important findings about synchronicity – including "an astonishing increase in the phenomena of synchronicity" when the participating analysts "started to keep more accurate records of [their] subliminal perceptions" (1976, p. 27) – was primarily investigating not synchronicity but transference and countertransference. In addition to such interdisciplinary inspirations and secondary findings, it can be hoped that with the collection of larger and richer sets of data specifically on synchronicity it may become possible for programs of research to be pursued where synchronicity during therapy is the primary object of research rather than a phenomenon secondarily illuminated by research in other areas (Roesler, 2014).

Cultural

As well as taking synchronicity as an object of research, primary or secondary, it may be worth exploring ways in which synchronicity could be deployed as part of a method of research. Of course, in the field of psychotherapy this already occurs insofar as synchronistic experiences are used in analysis as one means of finding out about the unconscious states of analysands. A greater challenge is to find ways of applying synchronicity in social and cultural research. This might involve researchers, if only experimentally, stepping into the assumptive world of synchronicity and attempting to find ways of using that perspective to analyze social and cultural phenomena; that is to say, looking at the phenomena in terms of the acausal patterns of meaning they exhibit instead of, or in addition to, looking at them in terms of their causes and effects. The test of such an exercise would be whether it yielded insights that would not otherwise or so readily have been available. To date only a few attempts at this have been made (Main, 2006c; Cambray, 2009, pp. 88–107), from which the difficulties of the venture are apparent. Some modern approaches to divination, which are explicitly grounded in a synchronistic understanding of reality, could possibly be added to this (Hyde, 1992; Cornelius, 1994; Karcher, 1998; Tarnas, 2006). There are also a few hints of how synchronicity might be applied in the study of literature (Rowland, 2005, pp. 146–147, 175–177; Hammond, 2007; Mederer, 2016), as well as in business and leadership studies (Jaworski, 2011; Laveman, 2014). Efforts along all these lines are worth continuing, for it is difficult to see how synchronicity could ever be considered integrated into mainstream thought until it forms not just an object of inquiry but part of a method of inquiry.

A multidisciplinary and polymethodological approach

Given the wide diversity of research on synchronicity, it is impossible within the space of a short chapter to give an adequate account of the range of methodologies that researchers have deployed. As a way of illustrating at least some of the approaches that can be taken, I shall note some of the principal methods involved in my own attempts to get to grips with this topic.

Synchronicity has been one of the principal topics of my own research for about 25 years. I have had two main foci. On the one hand, with particular attention to Jung's writings, I have tried to clarify how synchronistic experiences can best be described, classified, and theorized. With these aims I have looked at synchronicity in relation to the practice of psychotherapy (Hall et al., 1998; Main, 2007c), paranormal or anomalous experiences (1997b, 2012), religious or spiritual experiences (2001, 2007a), and myth (2001, 2007b, 2013). I am interested in theoretical perspectives that can accommodate the full range of synchronistic phenomena, respecting all of their physical, psychological, and spiritual aspects. I share the view of Edward Kelly and colleagues (2015), expressed in relation to anomalous phenomena generally, that such theoretical perspectives might be illuminatingly viewed as underpinned by panentheistic metaphysics (Main, 2015b, 2017).

On the other hand, I have attempted to explore the possible cultural significance of synchronicity. I have discussed synchronicity in relation to late 19th and early 20th-century tensions between science and religion (2000, 2004, 2014c), with particular attention to the problem of disenchantment (2007b, 2011, 2013) and meaning (2004, 2012, 2014c). Related to these issues, I have also examined the role of synchronicity in contemporary holistic spirituality (2002, 2004, 2006a) as well as in both traditional and contemporary uses of the *I Ching* (1997a, 1999, 2007a).

Recently my interests have focused on looking in greater depth at synchronicity vis-à-vis Western esotericism (2010a, 2014b, 2015a). All of the preceding work is part of a broader exploration of the social and cultural significance of synchronicity (Main, 2006b, 2006c, 2014a), especially of its potential as a tool for the critique of modern Western culture (Main, 2004, 2011). In relation to this exploration, I think Jung and Pauli's co-publication (Jung & Pauli, 1952) and correspondence (Meier, 2001) especially warrant further study (Main 2014a, 2014c).

Linking physical, psychological, and arguably spiritual aspects of reality, synchronicity seems to require to be studied by a multidisciplinary approach. Jung himself, as we have seen, drew on both scientific disciplines such as physics, biology, psychology, and parapsychology, and humanities disciplines such as philosophy, theology, and history of religions. My own approach has also been multidisciplinary and, as a consequence, polymethodological. Drawing on my background in classics (especially literature and philosophy), religious studies (especially psychology of religion), and psychoanalytic studies (involving history and sociology), I have mainly approached synchronicity from the perspectives of the humanities and social sciences.

The principal methods I have used have been historical (2000, 2004), textual (2004, 2014c), and comparative (1997a, 2002, 2007a, 2011), especially for the task of elucidating and culturally locating Jung's writings on synchronicity. For assessing the coherence and philosophical implications of Jung's and others' thoughts on the topic I have additionally undertaken conceptual and theoretical research (2004, 2007a, 2014c), both scrutinizing the various concepts implied in synchronicity (time, acausality, meaning, and probability) and considering how effectively different theoretical frameworks (statistical, psychological, parapsychological, scientific, and theological) can account for the phenomena (2004, 2007a). I have also undertaken a number of hermeneutic studies (2001, 2007a, 2012) in order to explore more deeply the senses in which synchronistic experiences can be interpreted as meaningful, as proposed by Jung.

The data I have studied have consisted of accounts both of synchronistic experiences themselves and of how such experiences have been responded to, including how they have been theorized and applied. In relation to synchronistic experiences themselves, I have extracted numerous narratives of one-off or short series of experiences from published works, variously clinical and non-clinical, Jungian and non-Jungian in orientation (2007a, 2007b, 2007c, 2013). In addition, I have examined a couple of longer series of synchronicities centering on a single individual (Main, 2001; 2007a, pp. 63–79, 81–140). One of these series had already been published (Thornton, 1967, pp. 124–133). The other series was made available to me in journal form by the experiencer and had not been published at the time of my initial work on it, though he published some of it subsequently (Plaskett, 2000). The responses to, and theorizations and applications of, synchronicity that I have studied have been drawn from the whole range of literature on the topic to which I have had access (Main, 2004, 2007a).

I should also note one unsuccessful attempt to gather data on synchronicity. In 1998 some colleagues and I sent a questionnaire inviting accounts of synchronicities to every Jungian analyst and trainee in the United Kingdom and then to every member of the International Association for Analytical Psychology (Hall et al., 1998). However, only a handful of responses was received, with no returns at all in the United Kingdom, despite analysts there having received the questionnaire twice.

The principal methods I have used to analyze the data obtained by these means are, variously, taxonomical: classifying different kinds of experiences, influences, and explanations (2004, 2007a); phenomenological: providing a richer picture of how synchronicities are actually experienced (1997b, 2004, 2007a, 2007b, 2013); hermeneutic: eliciting what specific synchronistic events might mean, predominantly but not exclusively within the theoretical framework of Jungian psychology (2001, 2007a, 2007b, 2012, 2013); abductive: seeking the best-fitting theory to account for the full range of data of synchronicity (1997b, 2004, 2007a, 2011, 2012, 2014c; cf. Kelly et al., 2015); and, tentatively, acausal: using synchronicity as the basis for a method of research (2006c).

Despite being stretched in all these different methodological directions, I am acutely aware that there are many approaches to the study of synchronicity that, for want of the necessary training, time, or aptitude, I have not pursued but that could be, and in some cases already have been, fruitfully pursued by others. These approaches might include, for example, experimental research, archival research, textual analyses in the original German, the methodical tracking of the cultural diffusion and transformations of the notion of synchronicity following Jung's publications, and heuristic or auto-ethnographic research.

Conclusion

Jung described his essay "Synchronicity: An Acausal Connecting Principle" as "an attempt to broach the problem [of synchronicity] in such a way as to reveal some of its manifold aspects and connections, and to open up a very obscure field which is philosophically of the greatest importance" (1952, para. 816). The problematic, manifold, and obscure nature of synchronicity is amply attested by the quantity and diversity of research to which Jung's essay has subsequently given rise, as well as by the lack of decisive outcomes from this research. Synchronicity is, unsurprisingly, well established as a concept within Analytical Psychology, and also has fairly wide currency within popular culture. However, it is still rarely if ever deployed as part of a method of research by academics who are not already self-consciously Jungian in orientation.

Greater interest in synchronicity within wider academic and scientific communities is most likely to arise where the problems being addressed by other academics and scientists are similar to those that the concept of synchronicity has aimed to address. One set of problems that immediately stands out in this respect concerns the mechanistic and physicalist biases in contemporary science and the efforts that have been made to redress these imbalances by drawing attention to more holistic perspectives. There are strong parallels, for instance, between the kind of thinking in terms of whole patterns of meaning that is characteristic of synchronicity and the type of holistic attention to the world that characterises right hemispheric brain activity according to some contemporary neuroscientists (McGilchrist, 2009). Again, as Cambray has noted, current theorists of complexity and emergence have taken renewed interest in the kind of holistic German Romantic science that was also a major influence on Jung and his concept of synchronicity (2014a, 2014c), and it is possible that specific viewpoints inspired by that earlier holistic tradition, such as the relationship between environmental and genetic factors in epigenetics, could be illuminatingly compared to synchronicity in at least some contexts (2014c, pp. 23–25).

A related set of problems that played its part in spurring Jung's conceptualization of synchronicity is encapsulated in the term "disenchantment" (*Entzauberung*): problems relating to the excessive rationalization of modern Western culture and its loss of a sense of sacredness and meaning. Recent research into disenchantment from a "problem history" (*Problemgeschichte*) perspective has shown how the associated epistemological problems of the scope of empirical and rational knowledge, the possibility of metaphysics, the relations between facts and values, and the separation of science from religion were variously responded to within physics, chemistry, biology, and psychology, as well as within less mainstream disciplines and knowledge cultures such as psychical research, parapsychology, and occultism (Asprem, 2014). These responses, occurring in the very decades during which Jung was developing the thoughts that would eventually be formulated as synchronicity (1900 to 1939), both could be illuminated by the analogous case of synchronicity and in turn could provide a wealth of opportunities for further contextualising and comparing Jung's concept.

Despite Jung's ambivalence about philosophy (Main, 2010b), there are aspects of his work on synchronicity that could interest professional philosophers. As an alternative to materialism, idealism, and dualism, the philosophical position of dual-aspect monism, to which both Jung and Pauli seem to have been led by their reflections on synchronicity (Atmanspacher, 2012), is in the same camp as the neutral monism that Thomas Nagel considers the best-supported framework for understanding how mind relates to matter (Nagel, 2012, pp. 4–5, 56–58, 61–65). Jung and Pauli's dual-aspect monism has some distinctive and empirically promising features, such as the way the mental and material aspects are specified in terms of complementarity (Atmanspacher, 2012), that might especially repay further philosophical attention. Within a different philosophical tradition, exploration of the conceptual and contextual connections between Jung's psychology, including the concept of synchronicity, and Deleuze's philosophy (McMillan, 2015), not least their shared interest in esoteric currents of thought (Kerslake, 2007, pp. 159–188; Ramey, 2012), is likely to be as fruitful for scholars of Deleuze as for scholars of Jung.

Another way of eliciting wider scholarly interest in synchronicity might be to draw attention to ways in which it has been and arguably still is implicitly present right at the heart of numerous cultures. Most obviously, since almost all cultures before the modern period, Western and Eastern, have relied on one or another form of divination, synchronicity, as one of the most sophisticated attempts to understand divination, could have enormous significance as a tool for understanding the thought processes informing decision making within those earlier cultures. More surprisingly, perhaps, it has also been argued that one of the staples of contemporary academic scholarship, the comparative method, is "a very close cousin of synchronicity," since "What comparison is *always* about [. . .] is identifying meaningful connections between apparently separate events or things, that is, between seeming coincidences" (Kripal, 2010, p. 74). Here in particular, if this relationship is indeed as close as suggested, there may be opportunities for elucidating how synchronicity might become part of a method of research through enriching existing comparative practices.

The above possibilities for eliciting wider academic and scientific interest in synchronicity are some of the ones that currently appear most promising to me, and the list largely reflects my own preoccupations and limitations. I shall end at a more general level by suggesting that there are at least five questions that might help to guide further work on synchronicity:

First, what is the full range of phenomena that the concept of synchronicity is designed to capture?

Second, how adequate is Jung's psychological framework for explaining the full range of synchronistic phenomena, firstly in its own terms and then compared with other possible explanatory frameworks?

Third, how adequate is Jung's hermeneutic strategy for interpreting synchronistic experiences, that is, for eliciting their specific meaning, again firstly in its own terms and then compared with other possible hermeneutic strategies?

Fourth, what is the broader cultural significance of synchronicity?

And fifth, how can the concept of synchronicity be applied, not just in psychotherapy and personal development but also in academic research and in social and cultural analysis?

For me, the sign that synchronicity will have been properly established as a concept within Western, or indeed global, culture will be that it starts being invoked and operationalized by researchers, academics, and non-therapeutic professionals who are not initially working within the ambit of Jungian thought. That synchronicity has not, after more than 60 years, achieved this status to any notable extent does not mean that it has been refuted as a concept. The dissonances between synchronicity and the assumptions of mainstream scientific and academic cultures are not insignificant, and it may be that there need to be major shifts to those assumptions themselves before whatever potential the concept of synchronicity may have can be realized. My suspicion is that as well as being the beneficiary of such shifts the challenging concept of synchronicity may also be one of the agents of them.

Note

1 For previous surveys of work on synchronicity, each inflected to its immediate purposes, see Main (2004, 2007a, 2007c, 2011). Parts of the present chapter are an updating of material from those earlier works.

References

Asprem, E. (2014). *The problem of disenchantment: Scientific naturalism and esoteric discourse 1900–1939.* Leiden: Brill.

Atmanspacher, H. (2012). Dual-aspect monism à la Pauli and Jung. *Journal of Consciousness Studies, 19*(9/10), 96–120.

Atmanspacher, H. (2014a). Notes on psychophysical phenomena. In H. Atmanspacher and C. Fuchs (Eds.), *The Pauli-Jung conjecture and its impact today* (pp. 181–199). Exeter, UK: Imprint Academic.

Atmanspacher, H. (2014b). Roles of causation and meaning for interpreting correlations. *Journal of Analytical Psychology, 59*(3): 429-34.

Atmanspacher, H., & Fach, W. (2013). A structural-phenomenological typology of mind-matter correlations. *Journal of Analytical Psychology, 58*(2), 219–244.

Atmanspacher, H., & Fach, W. (2016). Synchronistic mind-matter correlations in therapeutic practice: A commentary on Connolly (2015). *Journal of Analytical Psychology, 61*(1): 79-85.

Atmanspacher, H., & Fuchs, C. (Eds.). (2014). *The Pauli-Jung conjecture and its impact today.* Exeter, UK: Imprint Academic.

Aziz, R. (1990). *C.G. Jung's psychology of religion and synchronicity.* Albany, NY: State University of New York Press.

Aziz, R. (2007). *The syndetic paradigm: The untrodden path beyond Freud and Jung.* Albany, NY: State University of New York Press.

Bair, D. (2004). *Jung: A biography.* London: Little, Brown.

Beitman, B. (2016). *Connecting with coincidence: The new science for using synchronicity and serendipity in your life.* Deerfield Beach, FL: Health Communications Inc.

Bishop, P. (2000). *Synchronicity and intellectual intuition in Kant, Swedenborg, and Jung.* Lampeter: Edwin Mellen.

Bishop, P. (2008). The archaic: Timeliness and timelessness. *Journal of Analytical Psychology, 53*(4), 501–523.

Bolen, J. (1979). *The Tao of psychology: Synchronicity and the self.* New York: Harper and Row.

Braud, W. (1983). Toward the quantitative assessment of 'meaningful coincidences'. *Parapsychology Review, 14*(4), 5–10; reprinted in Storm (2008).

Cambray, J. (2004). Synchronicity as emergence. In J. Cambray and L. Carter (Eds.), *Analytical psychology: Contemporary perspectives in Jungian analysis* (pp. 223–248). Hove and New York: Routledge.

Cambray, J. (2009). *Synchronicity: Nature and psyche in an interconnected universe.* College Station: Texas A&M University Press.

Cambray, J. (2014a). The influence of German romantic science on Pauli and Jung. In H. Atmanspacher and C. Fuchs (Eds.), *The Pauli-Jung conjecture and its impact today* (pp. 37–56). Exeter, UK: Imprint Academic.

Cambray, J. (2014b). 'The red book': Entrances and exits. In T. Kirsch and G. Hogenson (Eds.), *The red book: Reflections on C.G. Jung's liber novus* (pp. 36–53). London and New York: Routledge.

Cambray, J. (2014c). Romanticism and revolution in Jung's science. In R. Jones (Ed.), *Jung and the question of science* (pp. 9-29). London & New York: Routledge.

Carvalho, R. (2014). Synchronicity, the infinite unrepressed, dissociation and the interpersonal. *Journal of Analytical Psychology, 59*(3), 366–384.

Clarke, J.J. (1994). *Jung and eastern thought: A dialogue with the orient.* London: Routledge.

Colman, W. (2011). Synchronicity and the meaning-making psyche. *Journal of Analytical Psychology, 56*(4), 471–491.

Colman, W. (2012). Reply to Wolfgang Giegerich's 'A serious misunderstanding: Synchronicity and the generation of meaning'. *Journal of Analytical Psychology*, *57*(4), 512–516.

Colman, W. (2015). Bounded in a nutshell and a king of infinite space: The embodied self and its intentional world. *Journal of Analytical Psychology*, *60*(3), 316–335.

Connolly, A. (2015). Bridging the reductive and the synthetic: Some reflections on the clinical implications of synchronicity. *Journal of Analytical Psychology*, *60*(2), 159–178.

Cornelius, G. (1994). *The moment of astrology: Origins in divination*. London: Penguin Arkana.

de Moura, V. (2014). Learning from the patient: The East, synchronicity and transference in the history of an unknown case of C.G. Jung. *Journal of Analytical Psychology*, *59*(3), 391–409.

Devereux, G. (Ed.). (1953). *Psychoanalysis and the occult*. London: Souvenir Press, 1974.

Diaconis, P., & Mosteller, F. (1989). Methods for studying coincidences. *Journal of the American Statistical Association*, *84*(408), 853–861.

Dieckmann, H. (1976). Transference and countertransference: Results of a Berlin research group. *Journal of Analytical Psychology*, *21*(1), 25–35.

Faber, M. (1998). *Synchronicity: C.G. Jung, psychoanalysis, and religion*. Westport, CT: Praeger.

Giegerich, W. (2012). A serious misunderstanding: Synchronicity and the generation of meaning. *Journal of Analytical Psychology*, *57*(4), 500–511.

Gieser, S. (2005). *The innermost kernel: Depth psychology and quantum physics: Wolfgang Pauli's dialogue with C.G. Jung*. Berlin: Springer.

Griffin, D. (Ed.). (1989). *Archetypal process: Self and divine in Whitehead, Jung, and Hillman*. Evanston, IL: Northwestern University Press.

Hall, J., Main, R., & Marlan, J. (1998). Synchronicity in Jungian analysis. *The Umbrella Group Newsletter*, *3*, Spring/Summer, 17–18, 38–39; partly reprinted in the *International Association for Analytical Psychology Newsletter*, *18*, 146–149.

Hammond, B. (2007). Coincidence studies: Developing a field of research. *Literature Compass*, *4*, 622–637.

Hanegraaff, W. (2012). *Esotericism and the academy: Rejected knowledge in western culture*. Cambridge: Cambridge University Press.

Hardy, A., Harvie, R., & Koestler, A. (1973). *The challenge of chance: Experiments and speculations*. London: Hutchinson.

Harrington, A. (1996). *Reenchanted science: Holism in German culture from Wilhelm II to Hitler*. Princeton, NJ: Princeton University Press.

Haule, J. (2011). *Jung in the 21st century, volume 2: Synchronicity and science*. London and New York: Routledge.

Haworth, M. (2012). Synchronicity and correlationism: Carl Jung as speculative realist. *Speculations*: 189–209.

Henry, J. (1993). Coincidence experience survey. *Journal of the Society for Psychical Research*, *59*, 97–108.

Hogenson, G. (2005). The self, the symbolic, and synchronicity: Virtual realities and the emergence of the psyche. *Journal of Analytical Psychology*, *50*(3), 271–284.

Hogenson, G. (2009). Synchronicity and moments of meeting. *Journal of Analytical Psychology*, *54*(2), 183–197.

Hogenson, G. (2014). Are synchronicities really dragon kings? In H. Atmanspacher and C. Fuchs (Eds.), *The Pauli-Jung conjecture and its impact today* (pp. 201–215). Exeter, UK: Imprint Academic.

Hopcke, R. (1997). *There are no accidents: Synchronicity and the stories of our lives*. London: Macmillan.

Hyde, M. (1992). *Jung and astrology*. London: Aquarian Press.

Jaworski, J. (2011). *Synchronicity: The inner path of leadership* (2nd ed.). San Francisco, CA: Berrett-Koehler.

Johnson, A. (1899). Coincidences. *Proceedings of the Society for Psychical Research, 14*, 158–330.
Jung, C. G. (1930). Richard Wilhelm: In memoriam. In *Collected works, volume 15, The spirit in man, art and literature*. London: Routledge and Kegan Paul, 1966.
Jung, C. G. (1950). Foreword to the 'I Ching'. In *Collected works, volume 11, Psychology and religion: West and east* (2nd ed.). London: Routledge and Kegan Paul, 1969.
Jung, C. G. (1951). On synchronicity. In *Collected works, volume 8, The structure and dynamics of the psyche* (2nd ed.). London: Routledge and Kegan Paul, 1969.
Jung, C. G. (1952). Synchronicity: An acausal connecting principle. In *Collected works, volume 8, The structure and dynamics of the psyche* (2nd ed.). London: Routledge and Kegan Paul, 1969.
Jung, C. G. (1963). *Memories, dreams, reflections* (A. Jaffé, recorded and Ed., and R. and C. Winston, Trans.). London: Fontana, 1995.
Jung, C. G., & Pauli, W. (1952). *The interpretation of nature and the psyche* (R. F. C. Hull and P. Silz, Trans.). London: Routledge and Kegan Paul, 1955.
Karcher, S. (1998). Divination, synchronicity, and fate. *Journal of Religion and Health, 37*(3), 215–228.
Karcher, S. (1999). Jung, the 'Tao' and the 'Classic of Change'. *Harvest: Journal for Jungian Studies, 45*(2), 60–83.
Kelly, E. F., Crabtree, A., & Marshall, P. (2015). *Beyond physicalism: Toward reconciliation of science and spirituality*. Lanham, MD: Rowman and Littlefield.
Kelly, E. F., Kelly, E. W., Crabtree, A., Gauld, A., Grosso, M., & Greyson, B. (2007). *Irreducible mind: Toward a psychology for the 21st century*. Lanham, MD: Rowman and Littlefield.
Kerslake, C. (2007). *Deleuze and the unconscious*. London: Continuum.
Koestler, A. (1972). *The roots of coincidence*. London: Hutchinson.
Kripal, J. (2010). *Authors of the impossible: The paranormal and the sacred*. Chicago, IL: University of Chicago Press.
Laveman, D. (2014). Business leadership, synchronicity, and psychophysical reality. In H. Atmanspacher and C. Fuchs (Eds.), *The Pauli-Jung conjecture and its impact today* (pp. 275–305). Exeter, UK: Imprint Academic.
Lindorff, D. (2004). *Pauli and Jung: The meeting of two great minds*. Wheaton, IL: Quest Books.
Magee, G. (Ed.). (2016). *The Cambridge handbook of western mysticism and esotericism*. Cambridge: Cambridge University Press.
Main, R. (1997a). Synchronicity and the 'I Ching': Clarifying the connections. *Harvest: Journal for Jungian Studies, 43*(1), 51–64.
Main, R. (Ed.). (1997b). *Jung on synchronicity and the paranormal: Key readings selected and introduced by Roderick Main*. London: Routledge and Princeton, NJ: Princeton University Press.
Main, R. (1999). Magic and science in the modern western tradition of the 'I Ching'. *Journal of Contemporary Religion, 14*(2), 263–275.
Main, R. (2000). Religion, science, and synchronicity. *Harvest: Journal for Jungian Studies, 46*(2), 89–107; reprinted in L. Storm (Ed.), *Synchronicity: Multiple perspectives on meaningful coincidence* (pp. 25–41). Pari, Italy: Pari Publishing, 2008.
Main, R. (2001). *Putting the Sinn back into synchronicity: Some spiritual implications of synchronistic experiences*. 2nd Series Occasional Paper 28. Lampeter: Religious Experience Research Centre.
Main, R. (2002). Religion, science, and the new age. In J. Pearson (Ed.), *Belief beyond boundaries: Wicca, Celtic spirituality and the new age* (pp. 173–222). Aldershot: Ashgate and Milton Keynes: Open University Press.
Main, R. (2004). *The rupture of time: Synchronicity and Jung's critique of modern western culture*. Hove and New York: Brunner-Routledge.
Main, R. (2006a). New age thinking in the light of C. G. Jung's theory of synchronicity. *Journal of Alternative Spiritualities and New Age Studies, 2*, 8–25.

Main, R. (2006b). The social motivation of C.G. Jung's critique of scientific rationalism. *Transpersonal Psychology Review*, *10*(1), 3–13.
Main, R. (2006c). The social significance of synchronicity. *Psychoanalysis, Culture, and Society*, *11*(1), 36–53.
Main, R. (2007a). *Revelations of chance: Synchronicity as spiritual experience*. Albany, NY: State University of New York Press.
Main, R. (2007b). Ruptured time and the re-enchantment of modernity. In A. Casement (Ed.), *Who owns Jung?* (pp. 19–38). London and New York: Karnac.
Main, R. (2007c). Synchronicity and analysis: Jung and after. *European Journal of Psychotherapy and Counselling*, *9*(4), 359–371.
Main, R. (2010a). Jung as a modern esotericist. In G. Heuer (Ed.), *Sacral revolutions: Cutting edges in psychoanalysis and Jungian analysis* (pp. 167–175). London and New York: Routledge.
Main, R. (2010b). Jung's uncertain separation of psychology from philosophy: A response to Segal. *Journal of Analytical Psychology*, *55*(3), 385–388.
Main, R. (2011). Synchronicity and the limits of re-enchantment. *International Journal of Jungian Studies*, *3*(2), 144–158.
Main, R. (2012). Anomalous phenomena, synchronicity, and the re-sacralisation of the modern world. In S. Kakar and J. Kripal (Eds.), *Seriously strange: Thinking anew about psychical experiences* (pp. 1–27, 275–283). New Delhi: Penguin Viking.
Main, R. (2013). Myth, synchronicity, and re-enchantment. In L. Burnett, S. Bahun and R. Main (Eds.), *Myth, literature, and the unconscious* (pp. 129–146). London: Karnac.
Main, R. (2014a). The cultural significance of synchronicity for Jung and Pauli. *Journal of Analytical Psychology*, *59*(2), 174–180; also published in E. Kiehl (Ed.). (2014). *Copenhagen 2013–100 years on: Origins, innovations and controversies: Proceedings of the XIXth Congress of the International Association for Analytical Psychology*. Einsiedeln, Switzerland: Daimon, pp. 148–155.
Main, R. (2014b). Foreword. In M. Mather (Ed.), *The alchemical Mercurius: Esoteric symbol of Jung's life and works* (pp. X-XII). London and New York: Routledge.
Main, R. (2014c). Synchronicity and the problem of meaning in science. In H. Atmanspacher and C. Fuchs (Eds.), *The Pauli-Jung conjecture and its impact today* (pp. 217–239). Exeter, UK: Imprint Academic.
Main, R. (2015a). Psychology and the occult: Dialectics of disenchantment and re-enchantment in the modern self. In C. Partridge (Ed.), *The occult world* (pp. 732–743). Abingdon and New York: Routledge.
Main, R. (2015b). Theorizing rogue phenomena. Essay review of E. Kelly, A. Crabtree and P. Marshall (Eds.), *Beyond physicalism: Toward reconciliation of science and spirituality* Lanham, MD: Rowman and Littlefield, 2015, *Mind and Matter: An International Interdisciplinary Journal of Mind-Matter Research*, *13*(2), 249–256.
Main, R. (2017). Panentheism and the undoing of disenchantment. *Zygon*, 52(4), 1098–1122.
Mansfield, V. (1995). *Synchronicity, science, and soul-making: Understanding Jungian synchronicity through physics, Buddhism, and philosophy*. Chicago and La Salle, IL: Open Court.
Mansfield, V. (2002). *Head and heart: A personal exploration of science and the sacred*. Wheaton, IL: Quest Books.
Mansfield, V., Rhine-Feather, S., & Hall, J. (1998). The Rhine-Jung letters: Distinguishing synchronicity from parapsychological phenomena. *Journal of Parapsychology*, *62*(1), 3–25.
McCusker, B., & Sutherland, C. (1991). Probability and the psyche I: A reproducible experiment using Tarot, and the theory of probability. *Journal of the Society for Psychical Research*, *57*(822), 344–353.

McGuire, W., & Hull, R.F.C. (Eds.). (1978). *C. G. Jung speaking: Interviews and encounters*. London: Thames and Hudson.

McMillan, C. (2015). *The 'image of thought' in Jung's whole-self: A critical study*. Unpublished Ph.D. thesis, University of Essex, UK.

Mederer, M.-L. (2016). *Making chance meaningful: Exploring links with creativity and its culturally subversive application*. Unpublished Ph.D. thesis, University of Essex, UK.

Meier, C.A. (Ed.). (2001). *Atom and archetype: The Pauli/Jung letters 1932–1958*. London: Routledge.

Miller, A. (2009). *Deciphering the cosmic number: The strange friendship of Wolfgang Pauli and Carl Jung*. New York: W.W. Norton.

Nagel, T. (2012). *Mind and cosmos: Why the materialist neo-Darwinian conception of nature is almost certainly false*. Oxford: Oxford University Press.

Odin, S. (1982). *Process metaphysics and Hua-Yen Buddhism*. Albany, NY: State University of New York Press.

Palmer, J. (2004). Synchronicity and psi: How are they related? *Proceedings of Presented Papers – Parapsychology Association Papers 2004, 173*–184.

Partridge, C. (Ed.). (2015). *The occult world*. Abingdon and New York: Routledge.

Peat, F.D. (1987). *Synchronicity: The bridge between matter and mind*. New York: Bantam.

Peterson, W. (1982). Making connections: 'Commentary on the attached verbalizations' of the 'Book of change'. *Harvard Journal of Asian Studies, 42*(1), 67–116.

Peterson, W. (1988). Some connective concepts in China in the fourth to second centuries BCE. *Eranos Yearbook, 57,* 201–234.

Plaskett, J. (2000). *Coincidences*. Hastings: Tamworth Press.

Progoff, I. (1973). *Jung, synchronicity, and human destiny*. New York: Julian Press.

Ramey, J. (2012). *The hermetic Deleuze: Philosophy and spiritual ordeal*. Durham, NC: Duke University Press.

Redmond, G., & Hon, T.-K. (2014). *Teaching the 'I Ching (Book of changes).'* Oxford: Oxford University Press.

Reiner, A. (2006). Synchronicity and the capacity to think. *Journal of Analytical Psychology, 51,* 4, 553–573.

Roesler, C. (2014). Investigating synchronistic events in psychotherapy. In H. Atmanspacher and C. Fuchs (Eds.), *The Pauli-Jung conjecture and its impact today* (pp. 241–254). Exeter, UK: Imprint Academic.

Rowland, S. (2005). *Jung as a writer*. Hove and New York: Routledge.

Sacco, R. (2016). The Fibonacci life-chart method (FLCM) as a foundation for Carl Jung's theory of synchronicity. *Journal of Analytical Psychology, 61*(2), 203-222.

Smith, R. (2008). *Fathoming the cosmos and ordering the world: The Yijing (I-Ching, or classic of changes) and its evolution in China*. Charlottesville, VA and London: University of Virginia Press.

Storm, L. (Ed.). (2008). *Synchronicity: Multiple perspectives on meaningful coincidence*. Pari, Italy: Pari Publishing.

Tarnas, R. (2006). *Cosmos and psyche: Intimations of a new world view*. New York and London: Penguin Viking.

Thalbourne, M., Delin, P., Barlow, J., & Steen, D. (1992–1993). A further attempt to separate the yins from the yangs: A replication of the Rubin-Honorton experiment with the 'I Ching'. *European Journal of Parapsychology, 9,* 12–23.

Thornton, E. (1967). *The diary of a mystic*. London: George Allen and Unwin.

von Franz, M.-L. (1974). *Number and time: Reflections leading toward a unification of depth psychology and physics* (A. Dykes, Trans.). London: Rider and Company.

von Franz, M.-L. (1980). *On divination and synchronicity: The psychology of meaningful chance*. Toronto: Inner City.
von Franz, M.-L. (1992). *Psyche and matter*. Boston and London: Shambhala.
Watt, C. (1990–1991). Psychology and coincidences. *European Journal of Parapsychology, 8*, 66–84.
Williams, G. (2010). *Demystifying meaningful coincidences (synchronicities): The evolving self, the personal unconscious, and the creative process*. Lanham, MD: Jason Aronson.
Yassemides, A. (2014). *Time and timelessness: Temporality in the theory of Carl Jung*. London and New York: Routledge.
Zabriskie, B. (2005). Synchronicity and the 'I Ching': Jung, Pauli, and the Chinese woman. *Journal of Analytical Psychology, 50*, 223–235.

9
COMPLEXITY, ECOLOGY, SYMBOLISM, AND SYNCHRONICITY

Joseph Cambray

At the heart of traditional Analytical Psychology is the notion that the *symbol* serves as the mediating factor between the interplay of conscious and unconscious dynamics. In defining the symbol, Jung stressed the importance of it being "alive" in the sense of containing a vibrant inclusion of the unknown. Symbols are seen as having collective relevance, transcending the individual's psychology and reflecting both a timeless component from the depth and more immediately the zeitgeist or time period in which they live: "Since, for a given epoch, it is the best possible expression for what is still unknown, it must be the product of the most complex and differentiated minds of that age" (Jung, 1971, p. 819).

Subsequent generations of Jungian analysts and scholars have embraced and amplified the focus on symbolic understanding. While Jung's interest in developments in contemporary science persisted through some of his correspondences, the incorporation of this facet of cultural development was in partial eclipse. More recently a group of researchers has been applying new concepts from scientific studies, as through the adaptation of neurobiological studies applied to corollary states of consciousness. This has in turn led to interest in the wider field of complexity studies in the Jungian community.

A complex systems approach to the psyche requires accessing multiple research vertices to contribute to our fund of knowledge in ways that transgress traditional academic disciplinary lines. New perspectives demonstrating the interconnectedness of many facets of reality previously treated in isolation support the need for new theories and methods for describing these phenomena. The tools developed in studying systems of increasing complexity have begun to reveal a profound ecological basis for experience. This chapter will seek to articulate efforts to include this approach within the Jungian perspective.

An introduction to complexity

Complexity science is an amalgam of various disciplines, with origins in general systems theory, cybernetics, and dynamic, non-linear systems theory, with indirect incorporation of components from artificial intelligence, fractal geometry, and chaos theory, as well as various subspecialties that evolved in each domain (see Castellani & Hafferty, 2010, for a brief history of the field especially as applied to sociology). The field of "complexity" (shorthand for the broad discipline including theory, practice, and science) has itself undergone a series of developments that have had increasing applicability to the human and information sciences. Human psychological development from birth on has been revised by applications of complexity studies, for example from the field of social neuroscience. Network theory has been shown to have tremendous applications across all fields involved with information process (whether it be tracking the spread of diseases, stock market fluctuation, explorations of "big data" for marketing purposes, or 10,000 other uses). The most important subset of networks are those that are deemed "scale-free" (homologous at 3 or more levels of scale), as these are known to exhibit self-organization usually with emergent phenomena and hence are an aspect of complexity studies. Further, complexity studies have been successfully applied to the arts and humanities. Thus it appears to be the new overarching paradigm for the early 21st-century intellectual life.

The non-linear features of systems displaying complexity generally require forgoing precise algorithmic mathematical description, as are usually sought by reductive approaches, in the modeling of subjects under investigation. However, with the advent of high-speed computers, simulations and perturbation modeling have produced some remarkable discoveries.

The class of complex systems that operate in competitive environments, known collectively as "complex adaptive systems" (CAS), are of particular interest to Analytical Psychology research. Complex systems, for example, describe much of evolutionary biology and have been shown to spontaneously self-organize. In general, as local "agents"[1] interact with each other in an open complex system (subject to environmental forces), the self-organization they manifest often has "emergent" properties. These properties are only found in the aggregate, that is, they are holistic features that arise from the interactions between the agents; they are not discoverable in the agents themselves and cannot be reduced to them. Emergent phenomena are found throughout all of nature, from the quantum world to the cosmological; living creatures are exquisite examples. A few examples: the liquidity of water at room temperature – with its low molecular weight, water might be expected to be gaseous at temperatures needed for life if one looked solely at an individual molecule of H_2O; it is the hydrogen bonding between molecules that serves as the glue that keeps the aggregate molecules in liquid form; the spiral form of hurricanes and many galaxies; the shape of snowflakes and so on are all emergent properties. More directly related to the topic of this chapter, the mind is considered to be an emergent property of the brain-body interacting in a human (narrative) environment, that is, it is not reducible to explanation based on neural phenomena, no matter how complicated.

The introduction of complexity concepts into Jungian psychology began during the 1990s, after the work of the savants of the Santa Fe Institute became known through a series of books and publications (e.g., Cambray, 2002). The inaugural Jungian paper was by David Tresan (1996) and was followed by a number of other contributions, which re-examined key Jungian concepts in terms of complexity science. These include theoretical reconsideration of archetypes and complexes (Hogenson, 2001; Saunders & Skar, 2001; McDowell, 2001; Knox, 2003), synchronicity and the Self, Jungian analytic methods, and individuation (Cambray, 2002, 2004, 2009; Hogenson, 2004, 2005). These were complemented and followed up by studies on the clinical, developmental, and dynamic use of the reconsidered concepts (Martin-Vallas, 2006, 2008; Knox, 2004a, b; Merchant, 2006, 2009; Hogenson, 2009; Cambray, 2006, 2011). While broadly embracing a shared paradigm, many of the authors articulated clear differences between their positions, as on archetypes, from the radically emergent (Hogenson, Saunders, and Skar) to those attempting to retain more of a place in genetics as a physical locus for the archetypes-as-such (Knox, Merchant). The recent rise in epigenetics seems to have widened the possibilities for non-DNA heritable pathways for certain patterns and will likely require reassessment of the archetypal hypothesis (Cambray, 2015). The field remains in dynamic tension among various models, all contributing but none being unilaterally embraced.

These lines of development have also led into questions about related topics, such as the mind–body or mind–matter relationship as envisioned from within this new paradigm. An exciting new formulation based on a philosophical stance traceable to Spinoza (dual-aspect monism), but reshaped with 20th-century quantum logic, which Wolfgang Pauli introduced in discussions with Jung on synchronicity and the psychoid archetype, has led to the Pauli–Jung conjecture. For psychophysical systems the hypothesis proposes correlations between mind and matter based on meaning rather than causation (Atmanspacher & Fuchs, 2014, p. 5). There has also been some experimental verification of this formulation, with the additional observation of negative correlations, that is, where connections as between mind and matter would be expected but are not found, as in certain dissociative ruptures of body–mind links (Atmanspacher & Fach, 2013).

Complex networks in Jungian psychology

The use of networks to graphically describe amplificatory processes was initiated by Jung in the mid-1920s, the period in which Jung was giving seminars to his students. Jolande Jacobi presents an example of this in her 1942 book on *The Psychology of C. G. Jung* (1973, p. 87). Jacobi's graphic form is of a completely ordered rigid network and would not be expected to have scale-free properties if taken as an accurate representation. However, in the next generation of Jungians, Edward Edinger developed a series of alchemical amplificatory networks (shown at the start of each chapter based on one particular alchemical operation) for his book *Anatomy of the Psyche* (1985). These networks were marked in such a manner as to suggest varying strengths of links and were not fully interconnected into a lattice. The greater flexibility implicit in the graphics was moving in the direction of increasing scale-free properties. These studies all occurred long before the development of the World Wide Web and the types of network analyses that have now become familiar in many disciplines. The pioneering work of Albert-László Barabási and colleagues, summarized in Barabási's popular book *Linked* (2002), is one of the best introductions to the study of contemporary network science.

In retrospect, a scale-free model of the psyche appears to have been an inherent feature of the Jungian vision. The notion of a collective unconscious with complexes formed around archetypal cores as nodal points is consistent with such a model. This gains further support when the idea of individuation is superimposed on this view of the psyche. Large hubs with high density of links would be anticipated to be associated with the primary complexes of early childhood. In fact, one could see psychoanalytic object-relations theory as a powerful articulation of this central aspect of the developmental personality network. Jungian interest in the second half of life could in turn be articulated as an exploration of resonant archetypal nodes to which a person may have had limited exposure beforehand, but which have become activated (or constellated) through life experience often enhanced through undergoing a Jungian analytic process.

Analyses of scale-free networks have revealed the crucial role of weak links allowing larger scale transformation in networks (Csermely, 2006). Weak links are those that are more easily broken or disrupted, for example the wetness of water being due to the weak links between water molecules (hydrogen bonding) versus the strong link within the molecules themselves. Therefore, the analytic working through of complexes may reduce the excessively strong linkages of some hubs (such as those emanating through transference expectations, such as a mother complex) while connecting in and integrating more isolated nodes explored in a long-term analysis with a series of moderate and weak links that entails growth of the personality. The consequences of such analytically facilitated transformations would be a larger, more robust, and dynamic personality network with emergent holistic features.

Rhizomatic networks in Jungian psychology[2]

There was an ecological network image that Jung was especially fond of: the rhizome. Derived from the Greek term "*rhiza*" translated as root; according to the Merriam-Webster dictionary, a rhizome is "a somewhat elongate usually horizontal subterranean plant stem that is often thickened by deposits of reserve food material, produces shoots above and roots below, and is distinguished from a true root in possessing buds, nodes, and usually scale-like leaves" (www.merriam-webster.com/dictionary/rhizome). The most well-known quote regarding this concept is from *Memories, Dreams, Reflections*:

> Life has always seemed to me like a plant that lives on its rhizome. Its true life is invisible, hidden in the rhizome. The part that appears above ground lasts

only a single summer. Then it withers away – an ephemeral apparition. When we think of the unending growth and decay of life and civilizations, we cannot escape the impression of absolute nullity. Yet I have never lost a sense of something that lives and endures underneath the eternal flux. What we see is the blossom, which passes. The rhizome remains.

(Jung, 1961, p. 4)

The term was first introduced into modern science by botanists and gardeners of the mid-19th century. Typical, well-known rhizome plants are bamboo, ginger, aspen trees, and so on.

The dense underground network of a rhizome can be quite extensive, with many smaller roots in a network converging in spots to produce the nodes which are associated with the aboveground, observable growth. The rhizome also tends to interact with numerous other root systems in its vicinity. Thus Jung's use of this analogy for an image of the psyche suggests a complex network of unconscious connections extending and supporting various individual representatives above ground, that is, in conscious expression. The psyche then is analogized by a highly entwined, non-local network that is invisible at the surface level but beneath is profoundly distributed across and embedded in a larger ecological system.

The ecological network can be imagined to function at multiple levels, starting with the psychoid. The individual human aspects of the psyche would at this deep level be connecting not only to our somatic experience but more broadly into the world of energy and matter usually treated as non-living, or inorganic, such as the non-biological aspects of our environment. The metaphor of entangled roots might here be described in terms of the entwining of fundamental or psychoid archetypal patterns. A consequence of such interconnections suggests the possibility of grasping truths about nature through empathy and intuition. However, the sharp distinctions between subjective and objective aspects of these phenomena no longer hold sway at this level, as the network transcends this apparent division of inner and outer. Similarly, the usual parsing of the world by ego consciousness, a convenient and even necessary fiction, can now be seen as an isolated focus on what has emerged from the rhizomatic world, while secretly being tethered to it.

At biological levels, our ecological networks begin with our microbiome the sum of all the viral, fungal, microbial, and even multicellular beings which engage with our human cells to constitute our biological being. This network generally operates wholly outside ordinary consciousness, yet at biochemical and biophysical levels we fully participate as an active member. In the last decade researchers have learned that even various functions of consciousness are indeed susceptible and influenced by the human microbiome (for example see Bharwani et. al., 2016; Carpenter, 2012). While many life forms are not formally sapient, the complexities of biological intelligences exhibited by them is impressive. Our dawning awareness and ecological engagement with these intelligences is burgeoning though still in its infancy. The study of interspecies communications, from parasitism to symbiosis, or predation to play, is revealing a host of networks previously unimagined, though many of these are intuited in the imagery of dreams and symbols, but a fuller exploration of this is beyond the scope of this short chapter.

Returning to the root metaphor, rhizomatic interactions can serve multiple purposes, many of which are currently being investigated in botany. For example, dying trees are now known in certain circumstances to "download" their essential nutrients to mycorrhizal networks (fungi), which have infiltrated tree roots without injuring them. In fact, the trees regularly "make and deliver food to the fungus; the fungus, in turn, dramatically increases the plant's water and mineral absorptive powers via its vast network of filaments. They provide far more surface area for absorption than the meager supply of short root hairs the tree could grow alone" (Frazer, 2015). The mycorrhizal networks also serve as a conduit and communication pathway between trees, even of different species. They can transmit warnings about predation, pathogens, as well as nutrient distribution, allowing cooperative coordination previously undetected between the various components of the network. Thus, older trees have been shown to support the growth and health of seedlings. Frazer cites the work of Suzanne Simard who is studying the role of mycorrhizas in stabilizing the forest soils in the face of climate change and how their networks have scale-free topologies and act as fundamental agents of self-organization in the CAS of forest ecosystems (e.g., Simard & Austin, 2010; Simard et al., 2012). These studies have been expanded and popularized by Peter Wohlleben in his 2016 international bestseller, *The Hidden Life of Trees*.

From these detailed, scientific explorations on plants, we can come to appreciate how profoundly complex the psyche must be – if fungi and trees have such a rich, interconnected life, what then of sapient beings? Should we not be learning from the ground up about the way biological intelligence has evolved methods of communication that foster cooperative, integrated modes of engaging with others? If we are able to suspend our knowing sufficiently to open to an appreciation of these ways of being, I believe our models of the psyche will be enriched beyond our current imagination, and that this was implicit in Jung's intuition when he turned to the rhizome as his metaphor for the psyche.[3]

In addition to the passage quoted earlier, Jung makes historical links to the concept of "rhizomata," back through the alchemist and ultimately to Empedocles in his article "The Spirit Mercurius" (Jung, 1967b). Speaking about impressive trees in forests that function as a symbolic "prototype of the *self*" which "conceals a great secret," he says:

> The secret is hidden not in the top but in the roots of the tree; and since it is, or has, a personality it also possesses the most striking marks of personality – voice, speech, and conscious purpose, and it demands to be set free by the hero. It is caught and imprisoned against its will, down there in the earth among the roots of the tree. The roots extend into the inorganic realm, into the mineral kingdom. In psychological terms, this would mean that the self has its roots in the body, indeed in the body's chemical elements. Whatever this remarkable statement of the fairytale [the spirit in the bottle] may mean

in itself, it is in no way stranger than the miracle of the living plant rooted in the inanimate earth. The alchemists described their four elements as *radices*, corresponding to the Empedoclean *rhizomata*, and in them they saw the constituents of the most significant and central symbol of alchemy, the *lapis philosophorum*, which represents the goal of the individuation process.

(Jung, 1967, para. 242)

Even without explicit knowledge of forest ecology, Jung's orientation toward the secret held in the roots seems a powerful intuition guided by his growing awareness of the role of the psychoid level of reality.

The four *rhizomata* of Empedocles are usually understood as the four root principles or "*archai*" (primordial rulers; gods; fundaments; origins) of ancient philosophy: water, fire, air, and earth. Empedocles was the pre-Socratic philosopher who articulated the tetrad, adding earth as the fourth principle to that of Thales (water), Heraclitus (fire), and Anaximenes (air) to complete this cosmology in a synthesis of earlier visions. For Empedocles, these principles are eternal and uncreated.[4]

This model or variants served as the fundamental background for the study of alchemy from the ancient through the medieval periods, which is what Jung is referring to in the passage quoted earlier. The synthesis of the four elements into a unified whole was the goal of alchemy and where "gold" was to be obtained. The portrayal of the fundaments of the world as the four elements persisted in Western thought until the rise of modern science, especially the rise of atomic theory. However, the scientific description became increasingly focused on elements solely as physical realities, the metaphoric aspects and philosophical use of the elements were discarded and replaced by a reductionist, literal search for the basic substances of reality.

One of the gifts of depth psychology has been to return meaning to our pursuit of the nature of reality and the realities of nature. Jung's psychological, symbolic approach to alchemy in particular breathed new life into these ancient archetypal ideas. The transformations pursued by the alchemists take on a contemporary relevance when reflected through a psychology of the unconscious. The personality becomes the "material" undergoing the transformations, and in a deeper sense this also alters the nature of the world in an interconnected, if incremental, manner at the same time. In a novel synthesis, the chemist-philosopher Gaston Bachelard has explored the application of depth psychology to the elements in a series of books, which have been translated into English: *La psychanalyse du feu* (*The Psychoanalysis of Fire*, 1964); *L'eau et les rêves* (*Water and Dreams*, 1994); *L'air et les songes* (*Air and Dreams*, 1988); *La terre et les rêveries du repos* (*Earth and Reveries of Repose*, 2011); and a second book on earth: *La terre et les rêveries de la volonté* (*Earth and Reveries of Will*, 2002).

According to philosopher David Macauly, a fuller explication of Empedocles's views would include:

> Rhizomata, first, serve as the name for earth, air, fire and water; secondly, refer to the visible masses in the world corresponding to these names, and, thirdly, indicate what we might now call a mythic or symbolic dimension, as

when Empedocles associates fire with the sun, or the sea (water) with "Earth's sweat" (fr. 55). In terms of this characterization, rhizomata are: (a) eternal, (b) uncreated (ageneta) and (c) constitutive of what the world is made – "for these are all" (fr. 26).

(Macauly, 2005, p. 286)

As a "theory of everything," it is one of the earliest to present a holistic synthesis integrating four principles as equal contributors striving for harmony and balance. In this there is an eco-political philosophy, as Macauly notes:

> Wellbeing relies on a relative equality, diversity of forms, and dynamic equilibrium, principles that generally operate in mature ecosystems or stable ecological communities in the case of human societies.
>
> *(Macauly, 2005, p. 288)*

He goes on to link these pre-Socratic views to the person who coined the term ecology, Ernst Haeckel, who as I've shown had a significant influence on Jung not only from the perspective of natural philosophy, but also artistically, as found in *The Red Book* (Cambray, 2014). Of Haeckel's approach to ecology, he remarks that it is:

> the science of relations between organisms and their environment. Like Empedocles, he tended to characterize the cosmos as unified, placing humans and non-human animals on the same biological and moral levels and depicting the natural world as a relatively benevolent source of wisdom.
>
> *(Cambray, 2014, p. 295)*

Macauly is also intrigued by the developments in forest ecology, especially the way trees interact in beneficent ways with their environments.

From this, we can see that a nascent eco-orientation attended the transformation documented in *The Red Book* (1914–1930), which were so key to Jung's mature views on the psyche.[5] Key in Jung's move out of *The Red Book* was his turn to alchemy, initiated by his receipt of the manuscript translation of *The Secret of the Golden Flower* from Richard Wilhelm. Within the scope of Jung's alchemical writings an eco-oriented perspective can be found by 1937, when he gave his Eranos lecture on "The Vision of Zosimos." There he remarks:

> The psychology of the unconscious has to reckon with long periods of time like this, for it is concerned less with the ephemeral personality than with age-old processes, compared with which the individual is no more than the passing blossom and fruit of the rhizome underground.
>
> *(Jung, 1967c, para. 120)*

The further amplification of the symbol of the rhizome then came in his 1942 Eranos paper, "The Spirit of Mercurius," just mentioned. And it is perhaps no accident that the next paper in *CW 13* after the Mercurius paper is his great study of "The Philosophical Tree," published in 1945, which had been written in preparation for a *Festschrift* for Gustav Senn, a professor of botany at the University of Basel, (*CW 13*, p. 251). It is as if the strife and destruction of the Second World War, with the advent of atomic weaponry, had begun to produce a compensatory response, a turning toward the endangered life of the planet as an integrated whole.[6] Images of deep interconnectedness, below the level of ordinary awareness were arising, perhaps from more collective, psychoid levels of reality. More generally, we can consider Jung's writing and methods as rhizomatic. This is an extension of the recognition of his approach to the psyche as a form of complexity, especially the identifying, tracking, and enlivening of what is emergent (Cambray, 2015; Rowland, 2016). In essence the formulation of individuation could be seen as a rhizomatic exploration of the endless pathways of the psyche. For most people this requires a long life as at least one dimension of the process, hence the alchemical goal of longevity could be read as one of the ingredients needed for rhizomatic individuation.

Ecological networks and the expansion of symbolic approaches

As network science has developed and expanded over the last several decades, applications of networks to ecological systems have grown apace. According to Borrett and colleagues, who surveyed the ecology literature from 1936 through 2012, they found more than 29,000 relevant articles with an exponential rise since 1985, so that by 2012 papers on networks comprised over 5% of the total number of articles published on ecology for the year (Borrett et al., 2014). Qualitatively the network approach in ecological studies can be traced back to Darwin at least, as Ings et al. note:

> Ever since Darwin contemplated the interdependence of the denizens of his "entangled bank" (Darwin 1859), ecologists have sought to understand how this seemingly bewildering complexity can persist in nature. . . . The study of the nexus of interactions among organisms that comprise ecological networks has consequently played a central role in the development of ecology as a scientific discipline.
>
> *(Ings et al., 2009, p. 254)*

They also envision a shift from focusing on specific key species to a more inclusive understanding of ecosystems:

> Ecological network theory could also stimulate a revision of many current conservation strategies by shifting the emphasis away from charismatic species towards a more holistic perspective, where both species and links matter.
>
> *(Ings et al., 2009, p. 262)*

This more integrated approach seeks to include both top-down and bottom-up views of ecosystems to build the most accurate and sophisticated models possible. A potential consequence of this more complex view of natural systems which encompasses the patterns of interaction is the need to develop a more expansive view of our symbolic reading of natural phenomena and the capacities of organisms in environments. For purposes of space, two abbreviated examples are offered.

One of the most frequently told stories is about the reintroduction of gray wolves into Yellowstone National Park in the United States. After the wolves were hunted to local extinction more than 75 years ago, they were deliberately reintroduced into the park in 1995–1996. As one of the top (alpha) predators, the elimination of the wolf had a "trophic cascade" effect, which according to the Encyclopedia Britannica is an "ecological phenomenon triggered by the addition or removal of top predators and involving reciprocal changes in the relative populations of predator and prey through a food chain, which often results in dramatic changes in ecosystem structure and nutrient cycling" (www.britannica.com/science/trophic-cascade, March 20, 2016), or a skewing of the ecological network. In the case of Yellowstone, the loss of this key predator produced a cascade in which ungulates descended into lower elevations eating many seedlings, for example aspens, which had reverberating effects, including grasslands and wetlands. The reintroduction of the wolf has to some degree begun to rebalance the ecosystem. Most notable has been the return of beavers, building dams and expanding wetlands, the return of songbirds and increased diversity of vegetation, among other changes, all indirectly attributable to the reconfigured network (Smith et al., 2003).

The symbolism usually associated with the wolf reflects the anxiety of encounters with a feared predator. The entry for wolf in De Vries's *Dictionary of Symbols and Imagery* is primarily oriented toward negative affects, though with an acknowledgement of being sacred to the Great Goddess because it howls to the Moon and its eyes light up in the dark, often linked with witches. The wolf is seen to represent:

> *untamed nature*: general evil as the chaotic, destructive element in the universe and man, with a possible triumph in the end; Inversion. . . . it feeds on corpses; its haunts wooded mountains.
>
> *(De Vries, 1984, p. 507)*

Further amplifications focus on:

> cruelty, murderer . . . avarice, greed, a thief . . . the Devil . . . poverty, hunger, melancholy . . . corruption, heresy, cowardice, hypocrisy . . . darkness, night, winter.
>
> *(De Vries, 1984, pp. 507–508)*

A few more positive notion are cited as exceptions, such as protection of children as in the Romulus and Remus story of the founding of Rome, but the affects associated with the symbolism are so negative that hunting it to extinction is not surprising.

If our understanding of the psychological significance of imagery associated with a creature such as the wolf is to keep pace with our increasing knowledge of the ecological complexity associated with these figures, then it is incumbent on the analytic community to expand our knowledge of these networks and to address the projections replacing them with more complete views. This does not require a wholesale abandonment of the cultural, historical use of this imagery, but does highlight the need to contextualize the affective environments in which symbolic understandings evolved. As the environments in which we live change and our understanding of how they operate increases, older layers of psychic perception need careful reconsideration, or interpretive views become stagnant. Generally, when less negative affect is stirred by something in nature, richer, more benign symbolism flourishes and can contain great intuitive insight into the way nature functions.

A second anecdote involves a non-local field event observed in a plant. To human observers it has a synchronistic touch to it. This drew attention when NPR journalist Robert Krulwich told the story of a wild coffee plant that almost disappeared on air. On "All Things Considered" on March 28, 2006, he reported the following story about the plant:

> Called "cafe marron," it lived on one island, Rodrigues, in the middle of the Indian Ocean in what is now part of Mauritius. As plants go, it was nothing special. Its leaves were green, its height average (about 5 or 6 feet), its flower white, its existence ignorable.
>
> In 1877, a European visitor, passing through Rodrigues, made a drawing of it and that is the only image we had of this plant, because after that, goats and pigs began to multiply on Rodrigues, and the plant began to disappear. By mid-century, it was presumed to be extinct.
>
> Then in 1979, a biology teacher on Rodrigues handed out copies of that 1877 drawing to a group of 12-year-olds, and one of the boys raised his hand and said, "Please, sir, I've got one near my house."
>
> The teacher was dubious, but he took a sample branch, sent it to the Royal Botanical Gardens in Kew, in London, where it was identified. It was wild.
>
> I happened on... [a] description while reading... *Last Chance to See*. Wondering how the story ended, I began making calls, found a botanist, Wendy Strahm..., Margaret Ramsay, a plant specialist from Kew ... and Richard Payendee, a conservation worker on Rodrigues ... and pieced together the rest of the story, which, very briefly, involves:
>
> - An international rescue mission that rushed two fragile bits of plant to London.
> - A 20-plus-year attempt by some of the most sophisticated botanists in the world to get this plant to create a seed so it could have a future.
> - A daring experiment in 2003 that produced a breakthrough.
> - And, most important, and most dramatically, an unanticipated, unexplainable and utterly mysterious conclusion.

The conclusion was only available on the NPR audio story. It included the fact that not another one of these plants could be found; this was the last one in the world. The botanists wanted to clone the plant, but a seed was required. However, the Kew Garden plant wouldn't cooperate, nor would the original plant. Finally, using plant hormones, the botanists induced seed formation. Remarkably, at just that moment a cutting from the original plant, without any hormones, also spontaneously seeded.

The human–plant engagement in an "eco-tech" interactive field seems to have been involved in the non-local emergence of seeds, a moment of archetypal rebirth at the brink of extinction, punctuated by synchronistic resonance in the sole surviving members of the species. I believe this offers a glimpse of how we might broaden our exploration of synchronistic phenomena as outcomes of CAS undergoing transformations. I believe it could be considered as an induced correlation above the baseline in the sense that Atmanspacher and Fach discuss (2014). How might the involvement of the ecological aspects of the field have contributed? The intentionality was clearly local, but the results were non-local; a larger vision of biological intelligence and responsiveness is required to truly go further in these studies. As mentioned earlier, recent work on trees and fungi in forest networks are shown previously unimagined interconnectedness and the generation of intelligence and intention in systems that had been seen as lacking anything more than the most rudimentary forms, yet now in aggregate generating actions with a sort of teleological outcome.

Conclusions

The science of complexity emerged in the late 20th century, and with technological advance in information processing has expanded to become one of the most important contemporary directions in scholarly studies. The application to Jungian and depth psychologies has developed in parallel, primarily through applications to theoretical understandings of core concepts. In this chapter I have endeavored to extend these studies in a way that indicates a revision is needed of the way in which concepts such as symbolism are viewed and applied against the backdrop of increased knowledge and understanding of our world. Human beings' implicit separation from their environments, the planet, and even the cosmos is no longer tenable, even within scientific formulations. I would urge a broad and thorough reconsideration of all of the basic assumptions in light of evolving understandings offered through complexity studies. Further discussion of new directions in this research will be postponed until the final chapter.

Notes

1 The term agents is used here in a very broad, general manner for any set of components that interact with one another, whether atoms, molecules, or galaxies; insects in colonies, herds of animals, schools of fish, flocks of birds; humans in collective behavior as in traffic jams or fluctuating stock markets, to give just a few obvious, well-studied examples.
2 Selected aspects of this section have been recently published (Cambray, 2017).

3 Philosopher Gilles Deleuze openly acknowledged his debt to Jung in borrowing the concept of the rhizome for his own critical, decentering approach. Deleuze and co-author Guttari reject what they refer to as "arborescent culture" (using "trees" as a hierarchical metaphor, top-down structures, such as "decision trees" in medical diagnosis) that they see as pervasive and completely dominant in the Western intellectual tradition, across most academic disciplines (Delueze & Guttari, 1987). Their rhizomatic view is of radical interconnectedness that is acentric, antigenealogical, non-hierarchical, and non-signifying, but in favor of multiplicity and diversity.
4 Because of these attributes of Empedocles, Deleuze could not fully adopt Jung's use of the rhizome metaphor. In effect the Empedoclean reading of the *rhizomata* is ultimately hierarchical, and so Delueze rejected this and Jung's elaboration of the rhizome associated with this viewpoint.
5 As I've shown previously, Alexander von Humboldt was a significant unnamed influence on Jung in his assimilation of his *Red Book* experiences. For many scholars, Von Humboldt is now seen as one of the first environmentalist in the West (Cambray, 2015; Wulf, 2015).
6 Macauly discusses the ancient Greeks' distress over pollution as both moral and environmental danger. In his reading of Empedocles, he concludes:

> Empedocles suggests that a culpable individual (daimon) will be hounded by the four elements: "Air hunts them onward to the Sea" which "disgorges them on Land" and then "Earth will spue toward beams of radiant Sun" which "will toss them back to whirling Air" (fr. 115). Like their cosmic rule, the four rhizomata take turns in exacting justice for polluting deeds against the natural world and, in essence, against the four divine and personified elements themselves.
>
> *(Macauly, 2005, p. 302)*

References

Atmanspacher, H., & Christopher, F. (2014). *The Pauli Jung conjecture and its impact today* (H. Atmanspacher and C. Fuchs, Eds.). Exeter, UK: Imprint Academic.
Atmanspacher, H., & Wolfgang, F. (2013). A structural-phenomenological typology of mind-matter correlations. *Journal of Analytical Psychology, 58*, 219–244.
Bachelard, G. (1964). *Psychoanalysis of fire* (A.C.M. Ross, Trans.). Boston: Beacon Press.
Bachelard, G. (1988). *Air and dreams* (E. R. Farrell and C. Frederick, Trans.). Dallas, TX: Dallas Institute of Humanities and Culture.
Bachelard, G. (1994). *Water and dreams* (2nd printing). Trans. E. R. Farrell. Dallas, TX: Pegasus Foundation.
Bachelard, G. (2002). *Earth and reveries of will* (K. Halman, Trans.). Dallas, TX: Dallas Institute of Humanities and Culture.
Bachelard, G. (2011). *Earth and reveries of repose* (M. McAllester Jones, Trans.). Dallas, TX: Dallas Institute of Humanities and Culture.
Barabási, A.-L. (2002). *Linked: The science of networks*. New York: Perseus Books Group.
Bharwani, A., Firoz Mian, M., Foster J.A., Surette, M.G., Bienenstock, J., & Forsythe, P. (2016). Structural & functional consequences of chronic psychosocial stress on the microbiome & host. *Psychoneuroendocrinology, 63*, 217–227.
Borrett, S., Moody, J., & Edelmann, A. (2014). The rise of network ecology: Maps of the topic diversity and scientific collaboration. *Ecological Modelling, 293*, 111–127.
Cambray, J. (2002). Synchronicity and emergence. *American Imago, 59*(4), 409–434.
Cambray, J. (2004). Synchronicity as emergence. In J. Cambray and L. Carter (Eds.), *Analytical psychology: Contemporary perspectives in Jungian analysis*. Hove and New York: Brunner-Routledge.

Cambray, J. (2006). Towards the feeling of emergence. *Journal of Analytical Psychology*, 51, 1–20.
Cambray, J. (2009). *Synchronicity: Nature & Psyche in an interconnected universe (Fay Lecture Series)*. College Station: Texas A&M University Press.
Cambray, J. (2011). Moments of complexity and enigmatic action: A Jungian view of the therapeutic field. *Journal of Analytical Psychology*, 56, 296–309.
Cambray, J. (2014). *The red book: Entrances and exits: The red book: Reflections on C. G. Jung's liber novus* (T. Kirsch and G. Hogenson, Eds.). New York and London: Routledge.
Cambray, J. (2015). Jung, science, German romanticism: A contemporary perspective. In M. E. Mattson, F. J. Wertz, H. Fogarty, M. Klenck and B. Zabriskie (Eds.), *Jung in the academy and beyond: The Fordham lectures 100 years later*. New Orleans, LA: Spring Journal Books.
Cambray, J. (2017). The emergence of the ecological mind in 'Hua-Yen/Kegon' Buddhism and Jungian psychology. *Journal of Analytical Psychology*, 62(1), 20–31.
Carpenter, S. (2012). That gut feeling. *Monitor on Psychology*, 43(8), 50.
Castellani, B., & Hafferty, F.W. (2010). *Sociology and complexity science*. Berlin, Heidelberg: Springer Verlag.
Csermely, P. (2006). *Weak links: Stabilizers of complex systems from proteins to social networks*. Berlin: Springer-Verlag.
de Vries, Ad. (1984). *Dictionary of symbols and imagery*. Amsterdam and London: North Holland Publishing Company.
Deleuze, G., & Guattari, F. (1987). *A thousand plateaus: Capitalism and schizophrenia*. Minneapolis, MN: University of Minnesota Press.
Edinger, E. (1985). *Anatomy of the psyche*. La Salle, IL: Open Court.
Frazer, J. (2015). Dying trees can send food to neighbors of different species via 'Wood-Wide Web'. *Scientific American*, May 9, 2015.
Hogenson, G. (2001). The Baldwin effect: A neglected influence on C.G. Jung's evolutionary thinking. *Journal of Analytical Psychology*, 46, 591–611.
Hogenson, G. (2004). Archetypes: Emergences and the psyche's deep structure. In J. Cambray and L. Carter (Eds.), *Analytical psychology: Contemporary perspectives in Jungian analysis*. Hove and New York: Brunner-Routledge.
Hogenson, G. (2005). The self, the symbolic and synchronicity: Virtual realities and the emergence of the psyche. *Journal of Analytical Psychology*, 50, 271–284.
Hogenson, G. (2009). Synchronicity and moments of meeting. *Journal of Analytical Psychology*, 54, 183–197.
Ings, T.C., Montoya, J.M., Bascompte, J., Blüthgen, N., Brown, L., Dormann, C.F., . . . Lauridsen, R. B. (2009). Review: Ecological networks – beyond food webs. *Journal of Animal Ecology*, 78(1), 253–269.
Jacobi, J. (1973). *The psychology of C. G. Jung*. New Haven, CT: Yale University Press.
Jung, C.G. (1961). *Memories, dreams, reflections*. New York: Pantheon Books.
Jung, C.G. (1967a). The philosophical tree. In *Alchemical studies, collected works 13*. Princeton, NJ: Princeton University Press.
Jung, C.G. (1967b). The spirit mercurius. In *Alchemical studies, collected works 13*. Princeton, NJ: Princeton University Press.
Jung, C.G. (1967c). The vision of zosimos. In *Alchemical studies, collected works 13*. Princeton, NJ: Princeton University Press.
Jung, C.G. (1971). *Psychological types, collected works 6*. Princeton: Princeton University Press.
Knox, J. (2003). *Archetype, attachment, analysis: Jungian psychology and the emergent mind*. New York and Hove: Bruner-Routledge.
Knox, J. (2004a). Developmental aspect of analytical psychology: New perspectives from cognitive neuroscience and attachment theory. In J. Cambray and L. Carter (Eds.),

Analytical psychology: Contemporary perspectives in Jungian analysis. Hove and New York: Brunner-Routledge.

Knox, J. (2004b). From archetypes to reflective function. *Journal of Analytical Psychology*, 49, 1–19.

Macauly, D. (2005). The flowering of environmental roots and the four elements in presocratic philosophy: From Empedocles to Deleuze and Guattari. *Worldviews*, 9(3), 281–314.

Martin-Vallas, F. (2006). The transferential chimera: A clinical approach. *Journal of Analytical Psychology*, 51, 627–641.

Martin-Vallas, F. (2008). The transferential chimera II: Some theoretical considerations. *Journal of Analytical Psychology*, 53, 37–59.

McDowell, M. (2001). Principle of organization: A dynamic-systems view of the archetype-as-such. *Journal of Analytical Psychology*, 46, 637–654.

Merchant, J. (2006). The developmental/emergent model of archetype, its implications and its application to shamanism. *Journal of Analytical Psychology*, 54, 339–358.

Merchant, J. (2009). A reappraisal of classical archetype theory and its implications for theory and practice. *Journal of Analytical Psychology*, 51, 125–144.

Rowland, S. (2016). *Remembering Dionysus: Revisioning psychology and literature in C.G. Jung and James Hillman.* London and New York: Routledge.

Saunders, P., & Skar, P. (2001). Archetypes, complexes and self-organization. *Journal of Analytical Psychology*, 46, 305–323.

Simard, S., & Austin, M. (2010). *The role of Mycorrhizas in forest soil stability with climate change.* INTECH Open Access Publisher, pp. 275–302.

Simard, S.W., Beiler, K.J., Bingham, M.A., Deslippe, J.R., Philip, L.J., & Teste, F. P. (2012). Mycorrhizal networks: Mechanisms, ecology and modelling. *Fungal Biology Reviews*, 26(1), 39–60.

Smith, D.W., Peterson, R.O., & Houston, D.B. (2003). Yellowstone after wolves. *BioScience*, 53(4), 330–340.

Tresan, D. (1996). Jungian metapsychology and neurobiological theory. *Journal of Analytical Psychology*, 41, 399–436.

Wohlleben, P. (2016). *The hidden life of trees: What they feel, how they communicate – Discoveries from a secret world.* Vancouver, BC: Greystone Books.

Wulf, A. (2015). *The invention of nature: Alexander von Humboldt's new world.* New York: Alfred A. Knopf.

10

THE TIBETAN BOOK OF THE DEAD NEEDS WORK

A proposal for research into the geometry of individuation

George B. Hogenson

Introduction

This chapter is a response to a proposition put to me over 40 years ago, at the beginning of my initial study of Jung's system of psychology. Briefly put, I was at the time exploring possible dissertation topics in the Department of Philosophy at Yale University. In a discussion with Professor Rulon Wells, with whom I hoped to work, he remarked, "The Tibetan *Book of the Dead* needs work." Wells was known for rather oracular pronouncements, so I asked him what he was referring to, to which he replied, "don't you think it is odd that Jung reads it backwards?" I replied that I was aware of Jung's essay on the *Book of the Dead* or *Bardo Thödol*, but that I was reluctant to undertake studying the matter at that time. We moved on, and I completed my early work on Jung and Freud under his direction, but his comments have remained with me ever since. In 2015, I finally took a pass at examining Jung's treatment of the *Book of the Dead* at the joint conference of the International Association for Analytical Psychology, and International Society for Jungian Studies, held at Yale. What follows is a refinement of that paper.

The Tibetan Book of the Dead

The argument of the paper rests on an examination of the structure of elements in the *Book of the Dead* and in Jung's *Red Book*. To that end, I will briefly discuss both books, beginning with Wells's second comment, Jung's backwards reading of the *Book of the Dead*.

Jung's psychological commentary was appended to the translation of *The Book of the Dead* – so-called – as presented by W.Y. Evans-Wentz, a theosophist associated loosely with Madam Blavatsky and others in the theosophical movement. He was educated at Stanford and Oxford, where he did a degree in anthropology. His family, while not exceptionally wealthy, provided sufficient resources for Evans-Wentz to undertake a personal journey in search of wisdom, particularly in the study of East Asian religious and mystical traditions. In the course of these travels he acquired a Tibetan text intended to provide guidance for the soul of the deceased through a period of transition that could either result in release from the cycle of rebirth or lead to rebirth and a continuation of the cycle. In collaboration with a Tibetan Lama, Kazi Dawa-Samdup, Evans-Wentz produced a translation of the book and saw it published in 1927. To his credit – for he does seem to have been a very modest and frankly honest man – he listed Dawa-Samdup as the translator and himself as editor (Lopez, 2011). Jung published his commentary in the German edition of the *Bardo* in 1935, and R.F.C. Hull's translation of the commentary appeared in the 1957 English edition. It can now be found in Volume 11 of Jung's *Collected Works* (Jung, 1969a).

The material Evans-Wentz acquired is one text among many that deal not only with the individual's transition following death, but also a variety of meditation and ritual practices undertaken throughout life, in large measure as preparation for the experiences of the after death transitional state. These materials are now available in a translation by Gyurme Dorje, still under the title of *The Tibetan Book of the Dead*, of which the Evans-Wentz materials make up Chapter 11 (Dorje, 2005). Jung also engages some of the elements of this larger literature in his other commentaries, particularly the "Psychological Commentary on *The Tibetan Book of the Great Liberation*" (Jung, 1969a). What is important in these other texts is that they involve meditation practices that in fact lay the groundwork for the visionary events of the *Bardo*, and the encounter with the terrifying experiences of the post-death journey. It is the successful navigation of this period that allows the individual to escape the cycle of rebirth. In the *Great Liberation* commentary Jung explicitly associates this preparatory process with his own notion of the transcendent function, the emergence of symbolism that acts to unite elements of the psyche. In the *Bardo*, this visionary process is assumed to have taken place prior to death, thereby equipping the individual with the resources to recognize the appearance of terrifying phenomena as expressions of the mind.

In other words, if the dying person recognizes the fundamental nature of the illusions perpetrated by the mind, the brilliant illumination of emptiness they encounter at the beginning of the afterlife journey will result in their transition out of the cycle of rebirth. Unfortunately this does not always result in release, and yet another stage sets in where still another opportunity to recognize the emptiness of the bright light presents itself, but the soul of the deceased is again frequently so overwhelmed by that light that he or she gravitates instead toward a softer, smokier light that brings on an immersion in the thangkas or representations of the 42 Peaceful Deities and the 58 Wrathful Deities and so on, confronting states where they must deal with the residue of their actions while alive – karmic material if you will – both good and bad. The conclusion of this process is to descend to the point where the soul perceives and becomes fascinated by an act of sexual intercourse in the material world, thereby reentering the cycle by entering the newly conceived body.

Jung's reading of the Evans-Wentz translation of *The Tibetan Book of the Dead* (Karma-Glin-Pa, Evans-Wentz, & Lopez, 2000) is indeed backwards, in the sense that he sees the psychological importance of the book for the Tibetan running from psychic unity to sexuality in the moment of rebirth, while the Western psychoanalytic reading, beginning with Freud, moves from sexuality to Jung's own notion of the unity of opposites. Jung characterizes a possible Freudian reading of the book – had there been one – as being trapped in the last stage of the process described in the book:

> Freudian psychoanalysis, in all essential aspects, never went beyond the experiences of the *Sidpa Bardo*; that is, it was unable to extricate itself from sexual fantasies and similar "incompatible" tendencies which cause anxiety and other affective states. Nevertheless, Freud's theory is the first attempt made by the West to investigate, as if from below, from the animal sphere of instinct, the psychic territory that corresponds in Tantric Lamaism to the *Sidpa Bardo*.
>
> *(CW 11:843)*

For Jung, the Freudian focus on sexuality, which ties it to the last stage of the process described in the *Book of the Dead*, nevertheless opens the door to a deeper reading of the book, if one in fact takes the notion of reading backwards seriously:

> This [Freudian] knowledge also gives us a hint of how we ought to read the *Bardo Thödol* – that is, backwards. If, with the help of our Western science, we have to some extent succeeded in understanding the psychological character of the *Sidpa Bardo*, our next task is to see if we can make anything of the preceding *Chönyid Bardo*.
>
> *(CW 11:844)*

Jung correctly refers to the *Chönyid Bardo* as the stage of karmic illusion (CW 11:845) and he compares it to the domain of his own theory of the archetypes, which he here refers to as "categories of the imagination." Importantly, Jung remarks that "the products of imagination are always in essence visual, their forms must, from the outset, have the character of images and moreover of typical images" (CW 11:845). However, Jung's view that sexuality is the central feature of the *Sidpa Bardo*, is misleading from a Buddhist point of view in that the carnality that leads to rebirth is more a matter of entry into the world of illusion and suffering, the world of, as we will see, chaotic multiplicity. To avoid this fate, and achieve release from the cycle of rebirth, the individual will have trained their mind while alive to recognize the illusory nature of the imaginal states they will encounter after death through contemplation of the two orders of peaceful and wrathful deities.

FIGURE 10.1 The peaceful deities

Source: Courtesy of Gyurme Dorje

FIGURE 10.2 The wrathful deities

Source: Courtesy of Gyurme Dorje

FIGURE 10.3 Kalachakra Mandala
Source: WikiCommons

Other meditation practices focus on the great cosmic mandalas of wholeness such as the Kalachakra. Mandala images, needless to say, occupy a central place in Jung's system, and play a critical role in the process of individuation, as outlined, inter alia, in his paper, "A Study in the Process of Individuation" in Volume 9i of the *Collected Works*. Mandala imagery, of course, also plays an important role in Jung's *Red Book*. To enlarge the horizon of our inquiry, therefore, I now want to turn briefly to an examination of some aspects of the images in that central work.

The Red Book

Among the commentaries on *The Red Book* that have appeared since its publication in 2009, surprisingly little attention has been paid to the illustrations or to its format as an illuminated manuscript. As we have already seen, however, for Jung the visual is of central importance for his understanding of the archetypal, or, to use his expression from the commentary on the *Book of the Dead*, the categories of the imagination. An exception to this is Joseph Cambray's paper, "*The Red Book*: Entrances and Exits" (Cambray, 2014), originally presented at the San Francisco conference on *The Red Book* in 2010. I will not try to reproduce Cambray's entire argument, but rather focus on his reconstruction of the source for much of the imagery in the book. Cambray begins with two of Jung's dreams that likely date from 1894, just as Jung was about to enter university and was debating what course of study to undertake. Here are the dreams as they appear in *Memories, Dreams, Reflections*:

> I was in a dark wood that stretched along the Rhine. I came to a little hill, a burial mound, and began to dig. After a while I turned up, to my astonishment, some bones of prehistoric animals. This interested me enormously, and at that moment I knew: I must get to know nature, the world in which we live, and the things around us.
>
> (Jung, 1965)

Then the second dream:

> I was in a wood; it was threaded with watercourses, and in the darkest place I saw a circular pool, surrounded by dense undergrowth. Half immersed in the water lay the strangest and most wonderful creature: *a round animal, shimmering in opalescent hues, and consisting of innumerable little cells, or of organs shaped like tentacles. It was a giant radiolarian*, measuring about three feet across. It seemed to me indescribably wonderful that this magnificent creature should be lying there undisturbed, in the hidden place, in the clear, deep water. It aroused in me an intense desire for knowledge, so that I awoke with a beating heart.
>
> (Jung, 1965, Cambray's emphasis)

It is likely that the second of these two dreams is memorialized on the first page of *The Red Book* in the landscape illustration where we see the anomalous presence of jellyfish in what appears to be a Swiss lake:

Cambray's argument regarding the imagery, particularly in the second dream, is that Jung was likely familiar with the illustrations of the German naturalist Ernst Haeckel, whose extraordinary studies of aquatic creatures began to appear as early as the 1860s. In this regard, Cambray points to Haeckel's painting of jellyfish as a likely inspiration for both Jung's dream, and his illustration. Equally compelling are other illustrations in *The Red Book* that bear a remarkable resemblance to illustrations that appeared in Haeckel's monumental *Kunstformen der Natur*, published in 1899 (Haeckel & Klier, 2003). See Haeckel paintings starting on p. 180.

What interests us for present purposes, however, is less the sources of Jung's illustrations, but rather the structure of the organisms he used as models for many of his illustrations. What Haeckel did not realize, as neither did Jung, is that the radiolarians in his illustrations are fractal in structure, displaying precisely those elements of self-similarity and scaling that define the emergent properties of fractal geometry as developed by Benoit Mandelbrot. As Mandelbrot has demonstrated, the

FIGURE 10.4 *The Red Book*, p. 1: From *The Red Book* by C.G. Jung, edited by Sonu Shamdasani, translated by Mark Kyburz, John Peck, and Sonu Shamdasani

Source: Copyright © 2009 by the Foundation of the Works of C.G. Jung Translation 2009 by Mark Kyburz, John Peck, and Sonu Shamdasani. Used by permission of W.W. Norton & Company, Inc.

FIGURE 10.5   Ernst Haeckel, 1880; *Kunstformen der Natur* (1904), plate 8: Discomedusae

fractal structures found in organisms such as Haeckel's radiolarians are ubiquitous in nature (Mandelbrot, 1983). On the one hand, this characteristic of natural phenomena might lead us to simply infer that any depiction of a natural phenomenon is likely to entail a fractal structure. While true – trees have fractal structures, so an accurate rendering of a tree is likely to have a fractal structure – I would argue that

The Tibetan Book of the Dead needs work **181**

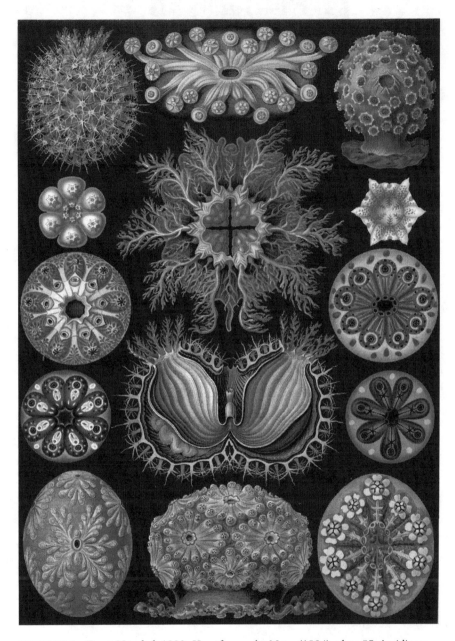

FIGURE 10.6   Ernst Haeckel, 1880; *Kunstformen der Natur* (1904), plate 85: Ascidiacea

this fact is trivial. What is more interesting is whether the truly symbolic is in fact defined by fractal patterns, or more precisely, whether the fractal dimensions of a given symbolic moment tells us something about the nature of a symbol and what that symbol reveals about the psyche. I will now try to put a bit more substance into this last comment.

FIGURE 10.7 Detail, Ernst Haeckel, 1880; *Kunstformen der Natur* (1904), plate 85: Ascidiacea

FIGURE 10.8 *Red Book*, p. 125: From *The Red Book* by C.G. Jung, edited by Sonu Shamdasani, translated by Mark Kyburz, John Peck, and Sonu Shamdasani

Copyright © 2009 by the Foundation of the Works of C.G. Jung Translation 2009 by Mark Kyburz, John Peck, and Sonu Shamdasani. Used by permission of W.W. Norton & Company, Inc.

From the emergence model of archetypes to symbolic density

In 1999 I presented a paper at the meeting of the North American Societies entitled "The Baldwin Effect: A Neglected Influence on C.G. Jung's Evolutionary Thinking," subsequently published in 2001 (Hogenson, 2001). Building on earlier work by David Tresan (Tresan, 1996) and John van Eenwyk (Eenwyk, 1991) and followed by several other authors, including Jean Knox, Joseph Cambray, John Merchant, and Maxson McDowell (Knox, 2004; Cambray, 2002; Merchant, 2006; McDowell, 2001), these papers marked the beginning of a discussion of archetypes as emergent phenomena rather than expressions of pre-existing templates derived from evolution or other sources. In essence, the emergence model focused on the appearance of archetypal phenomena – the archetypal image – by way of the dynamics of complex systems, including cultural, biological, and other environmental factors, and either relativized or completely eliminated the idea of the archetype in itself. In 2001 I debated some of these points with Anthony Stevens (Stevens & Hogenson, 2003), at that time the foremost advocate for an evolutionary understanding of archetypal theory (Stevens, 1983, 2015), and there followed a series of papers and responses addressing the question of an evolutionary model (Goodwyn, 2010; Knox, Merchant, & Hogenson, 2010; Roesler, 2012) which largely concluded with a rejection of an evolutionary, pre-set modular model of archetypal theory in the tradition of evolutionary psychology.

An important question nevertheless remained: how were we to characterize the nature of the archetypal image? Jean Knox, in her important book *Archetype, Attachment, Analysis* (Knox, 2003), adapted the work of cognitive scientists such as George Lakoff's theory of image schemas (Lakoff & Johnson, 2003) and Annett Karmiloff-Smith's argument for representational recapitulation (Karmiloff-Smith, 1996) to the question of the fundamental structure of archetypal phenomena. My own work on this question took a different direction, however, focusing on a program of research emanating from the complex systems program of the Santa Fe Institute and computer simulations of language structure and the nature of generalized or simulated symbol systems. As I will describe in this chapter, the initial elements of this research paradigm extend back into the early years of the 20th century, but come to fruition only with the advent and application of digital computers, which also provided the technical resources need to finally study the nature of fractal geometry in detail. Overarching these elements in the research program has been the recognition of the significance of scaling phenomena in the structure and behavior of natural and artificial systems.[1]

The combination of these linked elements in contemporary thinking gave rise to what I have termed "symbolic density" as a way of understanding the nature of archetypal images and other symbolic formations. The term "symbolic density" refers to a measure of what might be called the psychological carrying capacity or hermeneutical depth of a given symbolic structure. The notion begins with an early mathematical analysis of word frequency in texts undertaken by a Harvard University professor by the name of George Kingsley Zipf (1900–1950), whose *Human Behavior and the Principle of Least Effort* (Zipf, 1949) proposed a theory of language development based on the interaction between a speaker and a listener.

Zipf's analysis actually began with a study of the relative size of cities. Taking the population of the largest city in a given region and comparing it to other populations, Zipf discovered that the next largest city was approximately one half the size of the largest, and the third city was about one half the size of the second largest. Turning to language, Zipf found that in a given textual set, say the Bible, the same proportions applied to the frequency of words used. The most common word, usually "the," was approximately twice as frequent as the next most common word. The rapid falling off of frequencies when graphed in order of frequency yielded a distinctive pattern, commonly referred to as a long tail graph.

Typically the analysis of these curves entails their normalization on a double logarithmic scale that allows for more precise analysis of the phenomena due to the fact that any two elements in the data set vary as a power or exponent of one another. This characteristic is reflected in a logarithmic chart known as a power law distribution.

The analysis leading to this pattern came to be known as Zipf's law, and was eventually recognized to account for an unusual variety of phenomena, including not only the frequency of words in a text or city populations, but the intensity of earthquakes, the distribution of visits to websites, and the rate of ion transfers in the nervous system among many other phenomena. It appears that Zipf's law – or the somewhat refined version known as the Zipf–Mandelbrot law – is one of those odd artifacts of nature, another being Fibonacci numbers, that seemingly link otherwise disparate phenomena by way of some underlying mathematical structure.

At the IAAP Congress in Barcelona in 2004 I presented a paper titled "The Self, The Symbolic and Synchronicity" (Hogenson, 2005), where I outlined the idea of symbolic density, arguing that what we categorized as a complex, an archetype, or a synchronicity were in fact moments on a single symbolic continuum defined by Zipf's law, where the symbolic structure in question moved to positions of ever greater phenomenological saturation or psychological carrying capacity. This

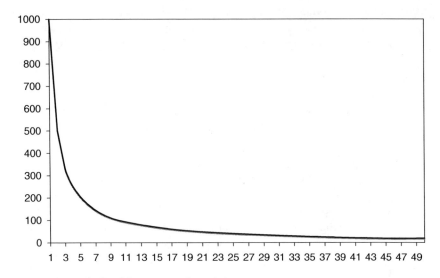

FIGURE 10.9 Idealized frequency of words in a text

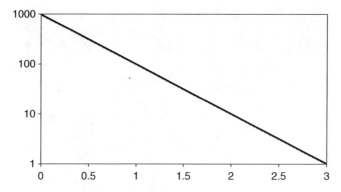

FIGURE 10.10   Idealized double logarithmic distribution

notion can be illustrated by Jung's discussions of specific archetypal images, such as the divine child where the list of metaphors, epithets, and characteristic events – magical birth, prodigies of infancy, and so forth – proliferate seemingly without limit. Symbolic density can be seen as the underlying characteristic of the archetypal image that allows Jung's hermeneutical method of amplification to go forward.

To a large degree this argument is based on research by a group of theoretical physicists connected to the Santa Fe Institute and other similar research groups who were examining the implications of Zipf's law, not only for language but also for the behavior of a variety of systems that display what in complex dynamic systems theory is referred to as scaling phenomena (Bak, Tang, & Wiesenfeld, 1990; Bak & Chen, 1989; Bak, 1999; Ferrer i Cancho & Solé, 2003; Ferrer i Cancho, Riordan, & Bollobás, 2005; Sornette, 2003; Saichev, Malevergne, & Sornette, 2008; Saichev, Malevergne, & Sornette, 2009). In particular, the work of Ferrer i Cancho and Solé was relevant to the question of symbolic density because their conclusion, based on a carefully constructed computer simulation, was that the appearance of Zipf's law was intrinsic to any symbolic system. Paul Vogt of Tillburgen University reached a similar conclusion in 2004 with the addition of a hierarchical category structure associated with the emergence of the Zipf–Mandelbrot law (Vogt, 2004; Vogt, 2005; Vogt & Divina, 2005). Interestingly, Vogt also referred to the phenomenon as one of symbolic density.

To summarize my argument in 2004, and in several other papers up to and including a recent paper, which slightly modified the original argument (Hogenson, 2004; Hogenson, 2014), I am suggesting that the symbolic function falls under the same fundamental scaling laws that are manifested in a variety of other natural phenomena, and that this aspect of the symbolic gives rise to dense symbols as the psychological carrying capacity of the symbol increases. The corollary to this conclusion is that the symbolic acts not only as a system of signification, but also reveals deeper levels of structure within the larger environment. Jung, in his important 1916 paper, "The Transcendent Function" (Jung, 1969b), argues that the symbol serves to mediate between the conscious and unconscious. I now want to suggest that this mediating function takes place by way of the emergence of a structural pattern that is shared by both the conscious and the unconscious as they relate to the symbol

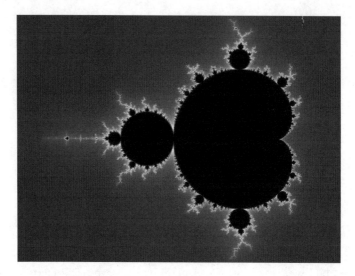

FIGURE 10.11 The Mandelbrot set
Source: WikiCommons

itself. To put it another way, the system conscious/unconscious can be said to self-organize around the mediating symbol, which itself already displays the elements of a fractal structure. To illustrate how this may happen in relation to *The Tibetan Book of the Dead* and *The Red Book* will require some speculative engagement with the underlying processes that lead to certain aspects of the structure of mandalas, and a return to the question of why Jung reads the *Book of the Dead* backwards.

The Mandelbrot set

The image of the Mandelbrot set is one of the most widely reproduced mathematical graphs, not the least due to the fact that with the addition of some parameters related to the color of different points on the graph, that have nothing to do with the construction of the graph itself, an array of extraordinary beauty can be constructed with the aid of a computer. Nevertheless, the Mandelbrot set as we typically see it is essentially a graph of the output of a recursive formula that takes the result of one iteration of the formula as the input to the next iteration. It is also the case that as a recursive formula, the Mandelbrot set is in principle infinite in its mathematical depth, a feature that has led to increasingly deep renderings of the intricate patterns of the set.

The Mandelbrot set is generated by the iterative repetition of an equation, in simplified form, $z = z^2 + c$, where c is a complex number that cycles through a process that generates the graph. What concerns us here, however, is the simple fact that with every iteration the value of z changes. This has consequences as we look at other possible graphs of similarly parameter-bounded formulas. A notable case of such a recursive graph that is strongly linked to the Mandelbrot set is a bifurcation graph, also known as a logistic map, which is often used to understand the behavior of populations.

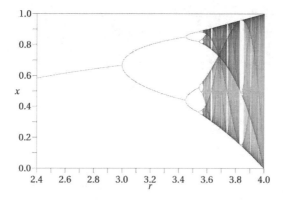

FIGURE 10.12 Logistic bifurcation map

Source: WikiCommons

The bifurcations in the logistic map – from which it gets it other name – correspond to critical inflection points on the Mandelbrot set. Essentially, what is happening is that as the formula for the Mandelbrot set evolves, the value of z – in this simplified example – reaches critical points where the graph changes dramatically. If these values are transposed to the logistic map, and used as parameter values in that graph, they correspond to critical bifurcation points in the graph, as can be seen in this illustration:

FIGURE 10.13 The Mandelbrot set and the logistic bifurcation map I

Source: WikiCommons

One can go a step further, as the bifurcation map has a corresponding graphical representation in what is known as a cobweb plot.

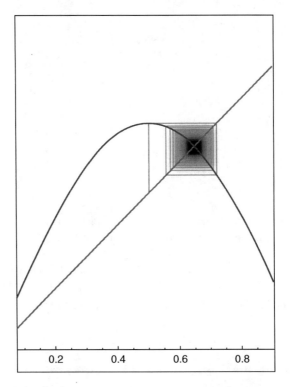

FIGURE 10.14   Cobweb plot

Source: "Fractal Geometry," Yale University, Michael Frame, Benoit Mandelbrot (1924–2010), and Nial Neger

I want to focus on one moment in the process when the relationship between the Mandelbrot set and the bifurcation diagram results in the first bifurcation where the iteration of the generating equation moves from a singular outcome to a cycle pattern of two outcomes.[2]

This particular point in the iteration of the three graphs constitutes a critical inflection point where a fundamental unity splits (bifurcates) into the first duality, going further with the iterative process results, ultimately in the emergence of a chaotic regime to the right-hand side of the bifurcation diagram. The proposal I now want to make is that the fractal structure of the bifurcation diagram represents precisely that point which so fascinated Jung, the move from unity to duality – the problematic of the unity of opposites. Additionally, the pattern in the cobweb plot, at precisely this instant, is a quaternity, precisely as described by Jung in his discussions of the unifying elements of mandalas and other symbols of wholeness. Returning for a moment to the Kalachakra mandala, as well as other major

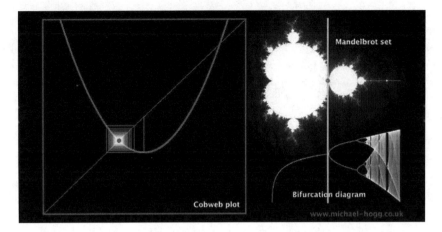

FIGURE 10.15   The Mandelbrot set and the logistic bifurcation map II
Source: Courtesy of Michael Hogg

mandala images, we can see this quaternary structure at the center of the structure. With these thoughts in mind, we can now return to the question of Jung's reading *The Tibetan Book of the Dead* backwards, that is from chaos to unity, and the deep function of the symbolic in Jung.

De-integrates, re-integrates and the dissociative psyche

By way of Pierre Janet, Jung's early model of the psyche relied heavily on fragmentary elements – partial personalities – that contributed in important ways to his development of the theory of complexes. As I argued in 2004, and as has also been suggested by the Jungian analyst Patricia Skar and the mathematician Peter Saunders (Saunders & Skar, 2001), the aggregation of complexes, or the formation of denser patterns of complex interaction, may be avenues to the emergence of archetypes. As the title of this section suggests, Michael Fordham's more developmental notion of infant de-integration and re-integration (Fordham, 1969) in the formation of the self also originates in the complexity of Jung's dissociative model. With these elements in mind, I would suggest that the patterns that evolve within the fractal geometry of the Mandelbrot set, the bifurcation diagram and the cobweb plot, all serve to illustrate the correspondence that might exist between these models of the psyche and the fractal structure of nature and the mandalas of Tibetan Buddhism and Jung's *Red Book*.

Jung, almost in passing, addresses *The Tibetan Book of the Dead* from the cultural point of view established by the history of psychoanalysis – that is the sexual theory of Freud – and then argues that if one continues to read the book backwards, one eventually comes to his own theory of a deep unity underlying the diversity of the psyche. Far better, it would seem, to begin with his original position on the dissociative foundation of the psyche and work backwards from there. What we then would have is a movement from the dissociative position to the opposites and finally to unity. I would suggest, in that vein, that Jung's own fascination with the unifying and containing function of the mandala could then be seen as a natural outcome of the more general fractal structure of mandala imagery. Remember that meditation on mandalas such as the Kalachakra is intended to prepare the individual for the after death journey in just such a way as to avoid falling back into the cycle of rebirth which is essentially a fall into multiplicity, a fall into de-integration.

Conclusion

The particular insight of Benoit Mandelbrot was to open the door to a rigorous mathematical investigation of the structure of the natural world. The peculiarity of fractal geometry is that it appears to describe the structure of phenomena that move from the branches of a tree to the patterns formed by blood vessels, the shores of Norway, and the patterns that appear to define the structure of dark matter (Cambray, 2016), the so far undefined material that makes up the bulk of matter in the universe. His work began, however, with the insights of a dilettante scholar at Harvard University who was counting the frequency of words in a text. The symbol stands, in some degree, at the beginning of this process, and it would seem inconsistent with the degree to which fractal analysis of the natural world has progressed for those of us who traffic daily in the symbolic to overlook the insight that we can gain from reading back to the symbolic the larger insights provided by the geometry of fractals.

There is a growing body of literature that lends additional insight into the relationship of the fractal structure of visual images and the deep structure of the psyche. In 1997 the physicist Richard Taylor published a small essay on the fractal structure of Jackson Pollock's drip paintings (Taylor, 1997). This paper was followed by a more sustained and technical examination of Pollock's paintings in 2002 (Taylor, Micolich, & Jonas, 2002). Taylor has continued to examine the relationship between fractal structures and psychology (Taylor, 2006; Taylor, 2012; Taylor, Martin, Montgomery, & Smith, 2017) and the study of fractal patterns in perception and other psychologically significant phenomena continues to grow (Street, Forsythe, Reilly, Taylor, & Helmy, 2016; Spehar, Walker, & Taylor, 2016; Strudwick, 2010; Moon et al., 2014). Research in Analytical Psychology needs to address this literature in the context of an examination of Jung's focus on visual imagery as the fundamental expression of the deep psyche, and his interest in the role of the mandala in the process of individuation. The intent of this chapter has been to suggest elements of what a focus on fractal geometry might reveal about the workings of the psyche.

Notes

1 For an accessible but comprehensive overview of scaling phenomena, see Geoffrey West, *Scale: The Universal Laws of Growth, Innovation, Sustainability, and the Pace of Life in Organisms, Cities, Economies, and Companies* (2017).

2 An animation of the iterative development of these three patterns produced in 2010 allows us to understand in greater detail the relationship of the Mandelbrot set to the bifurcation diagram and the cobweb plot: https://vimeo.com/13566850 (Hogg).

References

Bak, P. (1999). *How nature works: The science of self-organizing criticality*. New York: Copernicus.
Bak, P., & Chen, K. (1989). The physics of fractals. *Physica D: Nonlinear Phenomena, 38*, 5–12.
Bak, P., Tang, C., & Wiesenfeld, K. (1990). Self-organized criticality. *Physical Review A, 163*, 403–409.
Cambray, J. (2002). Synchronicity and emergence. *American Imago, 59*, 409–434.
Cambray, J. (2014). 'The red book': Entrances and exits. In T. Kirsch and G. Hogenson (Eds.), *The red book: Reflections on Jung's liber novus* (pp. 36–53). London: Routledge.
Cambray, J. (2016). Darkness in the contemporary scientific imagination and its implications. *International Journal of Transpersonal Studies, 35, 2*, 75–87.
Dorje, G. (2005). *The Tibetan Book of the Dead: Complete Translation* (G. Dorje, Trans.). New York: Penguin Books.
Eenwyk, J.R.V. (1991). Archetypes: The strange attractors of the psyche. *Journal of Analytical Psychology, 36*, 1–25.
Ferrer i Cancho, R.F., Riordan, O., & Bollobás, B. (2005). The consequences of Zipf's law for syntax and symbolic reference. *Proceedings of the Royal Society, B, 272*, 561–565.
Ferrer i Cancho, R.F., & Solé, R.V. (2003). Least effort and the origins of scaling in human language. *Proceedings of the National Academy of Sciences, 100*(3), 788–791.
Fordham, F. (1969). Some views on individuation. *Journal of Analytical Psychology, 14, 1*, 1–12.
Goodwyn, E. (2010). Approaching archetypes: Reconsidering innateness. *Journal of Analytical Psychology, 55*, 502–521.
Haeckel, E., & Klier, M. (2003). *Kunstformen der Natur*. Munich: Prestel.
Hogenson, G.B. (2001). The Baldwin effect: A neglected influence on CG Jung's evolutionary thinking. *Journal of Analytical Psychology, 46*, 591–611.
Hogenson, G.B. (2004). What are symbols symbols of? Situated action, mythological bootstrapping and the emergence of the self. *Journal of Analytical Psychology, 49*, 67–81.
Hogenson, G.B. (2005). The Self, the symbolic and synchronicity: Virtual realities and the emergence of the psyche. *Journal of Analytical Psychology, 50*, 271–284.
Hogenson, G.B. (2014). Are synchronicities really dragon kings. In H. Atmanspacher and C.A. Fuchs (Eds.), *The Jung-Pauli conjecture and its impact today* (pp. 201–216). Exeter: Imprint Academic.
Hogg, M. *Mandelbrot set: From order to chaos*. Retrieved from https://vimeo.com/13566850
Jung, C.G. (1965). *Memories, dreams, reflections*. New York: Vintage.
Jung, C.G. (1969a). Psychological commentary on 'The Tibetan book of the great liberation' (1939/1954). In R.F.C. Hull (Trans.), *The collected works of CG Jung, volume 11: Psychology and religion: West and east* (pp. 475–508). Princeton: Princeton University Press.
Jung, C.G. (1969b). The transcendent function (1916/1957). In R.F.C. Hull (Trans.), *The collected works of CG Jung, volume 8: The structure and dynamics of the psyche* (pp. 67–91). Princeton: Princeton University Press.
Karma-Glin-Pa, Evans-Wentz, W.Y., & Lopez, D.S. (2000). *The Tibetan book of the dead: Or the after-death experiences on the Bardo plane, according to Lama Kazi Dawa-Samdup's English rendering*. San Francisco: Oxford University Press.
Karmiloff-Smith, A. (1996). *Beyond modularity: A developmental perspective on cognitive science*. Cambridge: Massachusetts Institute of Technology Press.

Knox, J. (2003). *Archetype, attachment, analysis: Jungian psychology and the emergent mind.* London: Routledge.
Knox, J. (2004). From archetypes to reflective function. *Journal of Analytical Psychology, 49,* 1–19.
Knox, J., Merchant, J., & Hogenson, G. (2010). Responses to Erik Goodwyn's approaching archetypes: Reconsidering innateness. *Journal of Analytical Psychology, 55,* 522–549.
Lakoff, G., & Johnson, M. (2003). *Metaphors we live by.* Chicago: University of Chicago.
Lopez, D.S. (2011). *The Tibetan book of the dead: A biography.* Princeton: Princeton University Press.
Mandelbrot, B.B. (1983). *The fractal geometry of nature.* New York: W.H. Freeman.
McDowell, M.J. (2001). Principle of organization: A dynamic-systems view of the archetype-as such. *Journal of Analytical Psychology, 46,* 637–654.
Merchant, J. (2006). The developmental/emergent model of archetype, its implications and its application to shamanism. *Journal of Analytical Psychology, 51,* 125–144.
Moon, P., Muday, J., Raynor, S., Schirillo, J., Boydston, C., Fairbanks, M.S., & Taylor, R.P. (2014). Fractal images induce fractal pupil dilations and constrictions. *International Journal of Psychophysiology, 93*(3), 316–321.
Roesler, C. (2012). Are archetypes transmitted more by culture than biology? Questions arising from conceptualizations of the archetype. *Journal of Analytical Psychology, 57, 2,* 223–246.
Saichev, A.I., Malevergne, Y., & Sornette, D. (2010). *Theory of Zipf's Law and Beyond.* Berlin: Springer-Verlag.
Saunders, P., & Skar, P. (2001). Archetypes, complexes and self organization. *Journal of Analytical Psychology, 46,* 305–323.
Sornette, D. (2003). *Why stock markets crash: Critical events in complex financial systems.* Princeton: Princeton University Press.
Spehar, B., Walker, N., & Taylor, R.P. (2016). Taxonomy of individual variations in aesthetic responses to fractal patterns. *Frontiers in Human Neuroscience, 10,* 350.
Stevens, A. (1983). *Archetypes: A natural history of the self.* New York: William Morrow and Co.
Stevens, A. (2015). *Archetype revisited: An updated natural history of the self (Routledge Mental Health Classic Editions).* London: Routledge.
Stevens, A., & Hogenson, G.B. (2003). Debate: Psychology and biology. In *Cambridge 2001: Proceedings of the Fifteenth International Congress for analytical psychology* (pp. 367–377). Einsiedeln: Damon Verlag.
Street, N., Forsythe, A.M., Reilly, R., Taylor, R., & Helmy, M.S. (2016). A complex story: Universal preference vs. Individual differences shaping aesthetic response to fractals patterns. *Frontiers in Human Neuroscience, 10,* 213.
Strudwick, L. (2010). Infinite space and self-similar form in alchemy and fractal geometry. *Mythological Studies Journal, 1*(1), 1–22.
Taylor, R. (1997). Jack the dripper: Chaos in modern art. *Physics World,* November edition, 76–81
Taylor, R. (2006). Reduction of physiological stress using fractal art and architecture. *Leonardo, 39*(3), 245–251.
Taylor, R. (2012). The transience of virtual fractals. *Nonlinear Dynamics, 16*(1), 91–96.
Taylor, R., Martin, T.P., Montgomery, R.D., & Smith, J.H. (2017, February). Seeing shapes in seemingly random spatial patterns: Fractal analysis of Rorschach inkblots. *PloS One, 14,* 1–17.
Taylor, R., Micolich, A.P., & Jonas, D. (2002). The construction of Jackson Pollock's fractal drip paintings. *Leonardo, 35*(2), 203–207.
Tresan, D.I. (1996). Jungian metapsychology and neurobiological theory. *Journal of Analytical Psychology, 41,* 399–436.

Vogt, P. (2004). Minimum cost and the emergence of the Zipf-Mandelbrot law. *Artificial Life IX: Proceedings of the Ninth International Conference on the Simulation and Synthesis of Living Systems*, 214–219.

Vogt, P. (2005). Meaning development versus predefined meanings in language evolution models. *Proceedings of IJCAI-05*, 1154–1159.

Vogt, P., & Divina, F. (2005). Language evolution in large populations of autonomous agents: issues in scaling. In *Proceedings of the Joint Symposium on Socially Inspired Computing at AISB 2005*, 80–87.

West, G.B. (2017). *Scale: The universal laws of growth, innovation, sustainability, and the pace of life in organisms, cities, economies, and companies*. New York: Penguin Press.

Zipf, G.K. (1949). *Human behavior and the principle of least effort: An introduction to human ecology*. Eastford, CT: Martino Fine Books.

PART VI
Cross-cultural research

11

THE LOSS AND RECOVERY OF TRANSCENDENCE

Perspectives of Jungian psychology and the Hua-Yen School of Buddhism

Toshio Kawai

Introduction

Transcendence has been defined as being in a state that goes beyond the ordinary experience and world. In Analytical Psychology, the transcendent function is central to understanding the psyche and inner life.

This chapter explores the nature of the experience of the loss and recovery of transcendence from a Jungian perspective and from the perspective of the Hua-Yen School of Buddhism and offers some ways that this Buddhist perspective can be a useful therapeutic tool. Because the Hua-Yen School of Buddhism understands transcendence as nothingness that is at the same time potential energy, this understanding can shed new light on Jung's focus on the loss and recovery of transcendence.

We will begin exploring the development of the concept of transcendence in Jungian thought by presenting some early experiences of C.G. Jung and how they helped to develop his concept of transcendence and its role in Jungian psychology.

Jung's youthful experience of Communion led to the loss of a personal myth

Jung reported his first experience of Communion when he was 15 years old. He was full of expectation for religious mystery and transcendence:

> I [Jung] prepared myself for Communion, on which I had set my last hopes.... he [Lord] had let fall certain hints such as, "Take, eat, this is my body," meaning that we should eat the Communion bread as if it were his body, which after all had originally been flesh. Likewise we were to drink the wine which had originally been blood. It was clear to me that in this fashion we were to incorporate him into ourselves. This seemed to me so preposterous an impossibility that I was sure some great mystery must lie behind it, and that I would

> participate in this mystery in the course of Communion, on which my father seemed to place so high a value.
>
> (Jung, 1961, p. 53)

But his experience in Communion was disappointing, even disastrous.

> Suddenly my turn came. I ate the bread; it tasted flat, as I had expected. The wine, of which I took only the smallest sip, was thin and rather sour, plainly not of the best. Then came the final prayer, and the people went out, neither depressed nor illumined with joy, but with faces that said, "So that's that."
>
> (Jung, 1961, p. 54)

It is clear that Jung already had lost his naïve belief and lived in a disenchanted world. Jung reflected on his experience and wrote:

> Only gradually, in the course of the following days, did it dawn on me that nothing had happened. . . . this ceremony contained no trace of God – not for me, at any rate. . . . Slowly I came to understand that this communion had been a fatal experience for me. It had proved hollow; more than that, it had proved to be a total loss. I knew that I would never again be able to participate in this ceremony. "Why, that is not religion at all," I thought. "It is an absence of God; the church is a place I should not go to. It is not life which is there, but death."
>
> (Jung, 1961, p. 55)

As he wrote that he experienced "a total loss" and "an absence of God," his failure in the ritual indicated the loss of or inability to establish connection with the transcendent and the dominance of emptiness. The Christian belief and myth had lost meaning for him.

Later, the loss of Christian myth became a more abstract question for Jung. When he was writing "Symbol and Transformation of Libido," he raised the following issues about individual belief:

> But in what myth does man live nowadays? In the Christian myth, the answer might be, "Do you live in it?" I asked myself. To be honest, the answer was no. For me, it is not what I live by. "Then do we no longer have any myth?" "No, evidently we no longer have any myth." "But then what is your myth – the myth in which you do live?" At this point the dialogue with myself became uncomfortable, and I stopped thinking. I had reached a dead end.
>
> (Jung, 1961, p. 171)

As Jung's disappointing experience of Communion made evident, he did not live in the Christian myth anymore and was looking for the myth in which he did live. His crisis which started just after the publication of his book, *Symbols of Transformation*, and his self-experiment using active imagination had to do with this task of finding his own myth. As Jung described it: "Myth, says a Church Father, is 'what is believed always, everywhere, by everybody'; hence the man who thinks he can live without myth, or outside it, is an exception" (Jung, 1956, p. xxiv).

In his confrontation with a personal mental crisis which had started with his terrible vision of Europe full of flood and blood, Jung recorded his active imagination in *The Black Book* and wrote down his imagination with comments and pictures in *The Red Book*. I will now discuss how Jung tried to recover his relationship to the transcendent in the course of development of *The Red Book*.

Jung's personal journey seemed to go through three or four stages. Each stage has to do with a different understanding of psychology and individuation. The final one, which appears in "Scrutinies," will lead to my topic here, Hua-Yen Buddhism.

Liber Primus and Jung's rebirth of God

The first trial in the recovery from the loss of transcendence was shown in the mythic story depicted in the first book, *Liber Primus* of *Liber Novus*. In the first book, the death and rebirth of God is experienced through Jung's active imagination. Chapter 5, "Descent into the Hell in the Future," shows this death and rebirth of God. In his imagination, Jung sank into great depths. He saw in a dark cave that someone wounded, someone slain floated and a huge black scarab passed. A red sun streamed in the deep and dark water. Jung commented "the black beetle is the death that is necessary for renewal" (Jung, 2009, p. 151).

In Chapter 7, "Murder of the Hero," Jung and a youth lurk beside a narrow rocky path, fire at Siegfried, and kill him. After this chapter, "The Conception of the God" follows. Jung mentions the ambiguity of God. After this chapter the prophet Elijah and a blind woman Salome appeared.

In the last chapter Jung himself is sacrificed, being wounded by a black snake. But suddenly blind Salome can see the light; the serpent falls from Jung's body and lies on the ground. Elijah says "Your work is fulfilled here." This is Jung's own myth showing the death and rebirth of God. His image of God is a mixture of Christian and non-Christian symbols. In this sense this is a rather arbitrary, personal myth and story. Jung is both the one making the sacrifice and the one being sacrificed, which is important for the union with the transcendent.

Liber Secundus and experiencing transcendence as physical

Obviously the rebirth of God as an arbitrary, personal myth and fantasy was not enough for Jung. He continued his work with active imagination and started the second book, *Liber Secundus*. One characteristic in the second book is that the union in transcendence was depicted as a physical experience which has already appeared in a milder form in the last scene of the first book (Kawai, 2012). For example, the chapter "The Sacrificial Murder" in the second book is very impressive. Jung was compelled to eat a piece of liver from a dead girl. A woman who is supposed to be the soul of this girl asks Jung: "Step nearer and you will see that the body of the child has been cut open; take out the liver." She asks further: "Take a piece of the liver, in place of the whole, and eat it" (Jung, 2009, p. 290). Jung was reluctant and tried to avoid it, but finally he ate a piece of liver:

> I kneel down on the stone, cut off a piece of the liver and put it in my mouth. My gorge rises – tears burst from my eyes – cold sweat covers my brow – a dull sweet taste of blood – I swallow with desperate efforts – it is impossible – once again and once again – I almost faint – it is done. The horror has been accomplished.
>
> (Jung, 2009, p. 290)

I would like to mention one more scene of physical experience. This is a scene of self-dismemberment which reminds me of the vision of Zosimos. Jung trampled upon himself using a winepress machine:

> I have trodden the winepress alone and no one is with me. I have trodden myself down in my anger, and trampled upon myself in my fury. Hence my blood has spattered my clothes, and I have stained my robe. For I have afforded myself a day of vengeance, and the year to redeem myself has come.
>
> (Jung, 2009, p. 300, citing Isaiah 63:3–4)

These scenes are tremendous. But I have the impression that Jung was not satisfied by the mythical story and symbolism in the first book and needed more direct, physical images to express the nature and importance of the process of transcendence. They remind me of the many novels of the Japanese writer Haruki Murakami. In his stories, violent and cruel scenes are frequently described that could be connected with pre-modern cults and rituals (Kawai, 2006).

For example in *The Wind-Up Bird Chronicle* (2005 [2002]), Lieutenant Mamiya told of his experience in Mongolia during the Second World War. His superior was caught and skinned alive. The description in the novel was horrible. But it reminded me of Jung's paper "Transformation Symbolism in the Mass," in which Jung mentions the symbolism of skinning. The extraordinary popularity of Haruki Murakami's books in Japan and in other countries shows that transcendence can probably no longer appear in either a ritual or through the symbolic, but in direct physical violence and sexuality.

The process of experiencing transcendence used to be mediated by rituals and symbols which were carried out and shared by the community. But because historical rituals and symbols have lost their power in the modern community, transcendence can only appear directly through violence. This physical aspect and image seems to be not fully worked out in Jungian psychology, although it is clearly emphasized in Jung's *Red Book*.

In the face of the loss of God and transcendence, Jung tried to rediscover them first by creating a personal myth in the first book and then by physical experiences of the transcendence in the second book of *The Red Book*. Because these direct trials were insufficient, Jung was compelled to propose a further solution of internalization.

Liber Secundus and rebirth of God as phantasy

Jung's position in the second book was to recover the ontological loss of transcendence as an inner psychological experience of image. Internalization is a key concept in recovering a relationship with the mythical world. Jung seems to be aware that he does not live in the pre-modern world with a living myth. He confesses, for example, that he does not know how to pray to the sun: "I should not forget my morning prayer – but where has my morning prayer gone? Dear sun, I have no prayer, since I do not know how one must address you" (Jung, 2009, p. 271). He invented some afterwards. But the emphasis seemed to be laid on the loss of the prayer. In this sense there is no God anymore because God is not an independent, objective being but appears only in a concrete prayer or ritual. This passage from the *Liber Secundus* makes Jung's loss of God and myth evident despite his trial in *Liber Primus*.

While the death and rebirth of God were seriously and literally made a theme of the first volume of *The Red Book*, the rebirth of God was realized in the second book as the internalization of God. After the bull God Izdubar had collapsed, Jung had to help and transport him. In order to carry the gigantic God Izdubar, Jung made him into a mere fantasy. "I am basically convinced that Izdubar is hardly real in the ordinary sense, but is a fantasy" (Jung, 2009, p. 282). Because the fantasy "takes up no space" and Jung can "squeeze Izdubar into the size of an egg and put him in the pocket," Jung can transport him easily. When Izdubar came out of the egg again, this was understood as the rebirth of God. But for us it is more important to notice that the rebirth of God became possible by way of internalization. As Jung writes, God "did not pass away, but became a living fantasy. . . . If we turn the God into fantasy, he is in us and is easy to bear" (Jung, 2009, p. 283). While the death and rebirth of God are performed literally as stories in the first book, these are realized in the second book more psychologically through the idea of internalization.

This is the achievement of *The Red Book*. Due to this internalization, Jung could establish his psychology, which deals with God and rituals as an inner archetypal reality. So the rebirth of God was for Jung not a literal rebirth, but rather the birth of a psychology which is based on the idea of internalization and the reality of fantasy.

In "Psychological Types," Jung declares his famous motto which is quoted often by James Hillman: "The psyche creates reality every day. The only expression I can use for this activity is fantasy" (Jung, 1921, p. 78). With this internalization Jung could cope with the problem of God and transcendence. We could relate to God as an image in the psyche. But in the face of metaphysical and scientific critics Jung could argue that he had only to do with psychological images and not with metaphysical entities. But this position could also cause a kind of dissociation.

The *Scrutinies* and nothingness

Jung finished his experiment concerning *Liber Primus* and *Liber Secundus* in 1914, but started to write again in *The Black Book* in 1915. This may indicate that his trials to find his own myth and recover access to transcendence were not yet sufficient for him. At the beginning of 1916 Jung experienced a mysterious event in his house, which led to "*Septem sermones ad morteos*" and the third part of *The Red Book*, "Scrutinies." Jung's house was said to be filled with the spirits. They cried out in chorus, "We have come back from Jerusalem where we found not what we sought" (Jung, 1961, p. 216). Jung said, that is the beginning of the Septem Sermones.

In this experience, Jung's previous idea of internalization is not adequate. When Jung was writing the first and second books of *The Red Book*, he saw his patients during the day and spent family life normally. Only during the night did he continue his self-experiment with active imagination. It was held within his internal space, so there was no sign of psychosis which often disturbs and even destroys the capacity to function in outer reality. But now the dead flowed out from internal space to external space. Not only he but his children noticed the presence of the dead. Such an experience made it necessary for him to later revise his theory and to create such concepts as synchronicity and psychoid.

In the third part of *The Red Book*, Philemon taught the dead: "I begin with nothingness. Nothingness is the same as the fullness. In infinity full is as good as empty" (Jung, 2009, p. 346). In these phrases there is a hint at understanding nothingness not as negative loss, but as creative nothingness. As Jung felt a total loss and an absence of God after his failure in Communion, Jung was struggling with the absence of God and his own myth. In this sense the emptiness and the nothingness were terrible and destructive for him. But here nothingness is the same as the fullness.

The Hua-Yen School of Buddhism

Since this understanding of the principle of nothingness is very close to that of the Hua-Yen School of Buddhism, I would like to show how Jung's trial in "Scrutinies" can be understood in this context. But is it legitimate to understand these phrases in reference to the Hua-Yen School? This school is based on the Hua-Yen (Avatamska, Flower Garland) sutra and the practice of meditation. It belonged to Mahayana Buddhism in China from the 6th to 9th centuries and later came to Japan. Its basic idea is the interconnection of all things in the world.

Among major schools of Mahayana Buddhism, Madhyamika School with its outstanding figure of Nagarjuna emphasizes the emptiness, while the Vijnanavada School or Yogacara School lays stress on being and imagination. The Hua-Yen School is situated between two extreme positions and can mediate both. Jung's idea in the sermons of Philemon also has an affinity to Gnosticism. Is it possible and meaningful to compare Jung's idea with East Asian philosophy which at first seems totally out of its cultural and historical context? I will explore the legitimacy of this comparison in the following sections.

East and West

Just before the beginning of the "Septem Sermones ad Morteos," there are introductory words: "The seven Sermons to the Dead written by Basilides in Alexandria, the City where the East touches the West" (Jung, 1961, p. 378).

In 1918–19 Jung was in Chateau d'Oex as commandant and sketched every morning in a notebook a small circular drawing. He learned much later through reading the Chinese book *The Secret of Golden Flower*, translated and sent to him by Richard Wilhelm in 1928, that these drawings could be regarded as mandalas. But even without this later knowledge Jung seemed to be aware of the influence from the East in case of "Septem Sermones ad Morteos."

The Hua-Yen School was not exclusively formed in the context of the East like other texts and schools of Mahayana Buddhism. According to Toshiko Izutsu's (1981) Eranos lecture, "The Nexus of the Ontological Event," the Hua-Yen sutra was part of a group of smaller scriptures written at different times and in different places, and arranged into a single sutra in India. It took its final form in Central Asia between AD 200 and 350. It was translated and brought to China twice from Central Asia (418–420; 659–699). So it was neither a purely Indian nor Chinese product but was established first in Central Asia where the East touches the West. Central Asia at that time was under strong influence by Iranian and Greek culture.

Moreover, the most famous Buddhist priest and philosopher in the history of the Hua-Yen School, the third patriarch Fa Ts'ang (法蔵 643–712), was Iranian. He was born and grew up in China, but was of Iranian ethnicity. Izutsu noted the Iranian influence on the Hua-Yen School through its emphasis on aspects of sun and light. The emptiness or fullness in which all things interpenetrate each other and coagulate is experienced as light. In the Hua-Yen mandala there is Vairocana Buddha. He is situated in the center of the Hua-Yen mandala. The Sanskrit word Vairocana derives from the word which means the radiance of the sun. Izutsu suggests that it would not be a pure accident that Fa Ts'ang chose a sutra which has an illuminating Buddha in the center.

Izutsu assumes that there must have been a reminiscence of Ormazd or Ahura Mazda, the brilliant Lord of Light of Zoroastrianism. Izutsu and other Buddhist philosophers point out that Plotinus's Enneades has a similarity to the Hua-Yen sutra. There,

> all is transparent, nothing resistant; every being is lucid to every other, in breadth and depth. Light runs through light. And each of them contains all within itself, and at the same time sees all in every other. So that everywhere there is all, and all is all and each is all, and infinite indeed is this world of glorious light. Each of them is great. The small is great. The sun, there, is all the stars, and every star, again, is all the stars and sun.
>
> *(Plotinus, V. 8, p. 425)*

So although Jung's cosmology in "Septem Sermones ad Morteos" was based on Gnosticism, it would not be totally out of historical context if we relate Jung's

"Septem Sermons" to Hua-Yen philosophy. Both were born out of the exchange between the West and the East. Concerning the experience of light or sun, we could say that this is a universal one. Very often patients depict the sun or report a strong experience of sun either at the onset of or recovery from schizophrenia. The sun depicted by Norwegian painter Edvard Munch is a typical example. It is the same for the mandala, since it means either integration of psyche or failed defense.

Emptiness and transcendence in the Hua-Yen School

Philemon begins his first sermon with the following words:

> Now hear: I begin with nothingness. Nothingness is the same as the fullness. In infinity full is as good as empty. Nothingness is empty and full. You might just as well say anything else about nothingness, for instance, that it is white, or black, or that it does not exist, or that it exists. That which is endless and eternal has no qualities, since it has all qualities. "We call this nothingness or fullness the Pleroma."
>
> *(Jung, 2009, p. 346)*

I would like to show how this Pleroma which is nothingness and fullness at the same time can be understood in reference to the Hua-Yen School. In the following quotation from the 17th chapter of "Hua-Yen sutra," it is claimed that one single pore contains the whole universe:

> Enlightening beings, in a single pore, manifest the infinite lands of the ten directions: Some are defiled, some are pure, made by various deeds – all do they comprehend. In a single atom, infinite lands, with infinite Buddhas and their offspring; The lands are each distinct, not mixed up: As of one, all they clearly see. In one pore they see all the worlds In the space of the ten directions. There is not a single place where there is no Buddha; Thus are the Buddha-lands all pure. In a pore they see Buddha-lands And also see all sentient beings: The three times and six dispositions are not the same – Day and night, month and hour, bondage and freedom. Thus do enlightening beings of great knowledge Single-mindedly head for the sovereignty of truth.
>
> *(Cleary, 1993, p. 420)*

I made this one long quotation intentionally to give a feeling for the style and atmosphere of this sutra even in translation. There are a lot of repetitions which can lure us into meditating consciousness. There are many similar expressions to be found in the Hua-Yen sutra. In this quotation spatial metaphors are conspicuous, but it is also said that one single instant contains eternity, that is, past, present and future. This can be explained by the theory of Four Domains of Reality (*dharmadhatsu*) proposed by the fourth Patriarch of the Hua-Yen School, Ch'eng Kuan (澄観738–839).

I follow here with the explanation made by Izutsu. The first Domain consists of sensible things (Chinese: *shih*, 事). This corresponds to our normal state of consciousness. Everything has its essence (self-sufficiency, 自性) and clear shape. But with deepened consciousness things lose their essence and contour. All things become undifferentiated, which is the second Domain of the absolute metaphysical Reality (Chinese: li, 理, principle). "Being the all-pervading, all-comprising oneness of metaphysical non-articulation, it is the pre-phenomenal ground of reality out of which arise all phenomenal thing. Its being non-articulated implies at the same time that there is in it absolutely nothing" (Izutsu, 1981, p. 382).

This Domain of absolute metaphysical Reality has two fundamental aspects, all-nullifying and all-creating. We can notice its similarity to Jung's pleroma which is at the same time nothingness and fullness. I quote a related passage from "Scrutinies." Jung's words are not as precise as the Hua-Yen sutra, but are very similar.

> Yet because we are parts of the Pleroma, the Pleroma is also in us. Even in the smallest point the Pleroma is endless, eternal, and whole, since small and great are qualities that are contained in it. It is nothingness that is whole and continuous throughout. Only figuratively, therefore, do I speak of creation as part of the Pleroma. Because, actually, the Pleroma is nowhere divided, since it is nothingness. We are also the whole Pleroma, because, figuratively, the Pleroma is the smallest point in us, merely assumed, not existing, and the boundless firmament about us. But why then do we speak of the Pleroma at all, if it is everything and nothing?
>
> *(Jung, 2009, p. 347)*

But the Domains of Reality in the Hua Yen School still have third and fourth expressions. The third Domain is "that of free, unobstructed interpenetration of li (principle) and shih (thing)." The absolute metaphysical principle, li, is a kind of cosmic energy which emerges and differentiates itself as various phenomenal beings. "All the different things in the empirical world are one and the same in that each of them (every shih, thing) embodies the one absolute Reality (the li) totally and perfectly" (Izutsu, 1981, p. 382).

This is why one single pore contains the whole universe and one single moment has the eternity in itself because it derives from this metaphysical reality. With this understanding, everything is differentiated but loses its ontological substance and essence, in Buddhistic terms self-sufficiency. So everything becomes a unique ontological event.

The fourth Domain is that of interpenetration of thing and thing, *shih* and *shih*. This can be seen as return to the initial daily consciousness with a subtle difference. Daisetsu Suzuki describes this state in his paper on the Hua-Yen School: that in the Dharmadhatsu, therefore, there is an interfusion of all individual objects, each of which, however, retains the full individuality that there is in it (Suzuki, 1953, p. 147).

It is characteristic for the Hua-Yen School that the true world or transcendence is not postulated in the beyond, but in this reality. The metaphysical principle of nothingness which is at the same time potential energy interpenetrates reality. Jung's problem was that he still looked for transcendence as separate substance in the beyond. Jung tried to restore the Christian God and to find his own myth. But his experience of the haunted spirits means that the differentiation in reality is being lost. His "Septem Sermones" emerged out of a fusion with the dead.

If we understand Jung's experience and writing after his encounter with the dead according to Hua-Yen School's interpretations, we could formulate Jungian psychology differently. It may be useful to see how Jung's psychology could be slightly differently understood from the Hua-Yen point of view.

Union and emergence

For Jung, *conjunctio* was the central theme of his psychology and individuation. In *The Red Book*, conversations and relationships with figures in the imagination were important. These are reflected in his work "Relations between the Ego and the Unconscious" (Jung, 1966). Psychotherapeutic work consists in integration of and union with unconscious figures. Later in alchemy, union was the main theme, as the title "Mysterium Conjunctionis" shows. The *conjunctio* can be regarded as goal of individuation.

Union and Hua-Yen

Union plays also an important role in the Hua-Yen School. In the Domain of *li* principle, things are fused together. Daisetsu Suzuki described this state of fusion, translating personally some phrases from Sanskrit: Sudhana the young pilgrim felt as if both his body and mind completely melted away; he saw that all thoughts departed away from his consciousness; in his mind there were no impediments, and all intoxications vanished (Suzuki, 1953, p. 148).

The Japanese monk Myoe, who was an outstanding figure in the history of the Hua-Yen School in Japan, reported a dream of "coagulation of body and mind" just before his death. It is interesting to notice that physical image plays an important role for union in both examples from the Hua-Yen School as was also the case in *Liber Secundus*. Although union as losing differentiation in reality is very important in the Hua-Yen School, this is not the goal of its practice and philosophy. As was described earlier, there are still third and fourth stages of Reality and something more emerges out of this fusion. Hua-Yen School calls it *hsing ch'i* 性起 (Japanese: *shoki*), "the arising or emergence of the Buddha-Reality."

So according to the Hua-Yen School, individuation is not a process which leads to a goal of union, but an event or a movement between undifferentiated fusion and emergence. Or to put it differently, the way from out from union is more important than the way into it. Concerning the all-illuminating light of Vairocana, I mentioned the experience of the sun in the case of schizophrenia. We can also experience a total fusion and emergence in therapy with autistic spectrum disorder (ASD) patients.

As we live in the world of language, the world is in its normal state differentiated. In the case of ASD patients, very often this differentiation is lacking. That is why they have difficulty with language capacity and relationship with others. In successful therapy with ASD patients, emergence of a subject can occur after a total fusion. In this case, the capacity of the therapist to be able to enter in the state of fusion and to separate from it becomes important.

Internalization and interiority

In the second book of *The Red Book*, Jung tried to save and recover God by internalizing it in his psyche. The bull God Izdubar was made smaller and put in the pocket, then turned into a fantasy. Internalization is a very Christian and modern strategy which leads to individual inner life and gave rise to psychotherapy. This made it possible for Jung to be involved with images of an internalized God instead of being bothered by metaphysical and theological questions.

In this sense Jung has a very modern structure of mind though the contents of his interest are very archaic. In the case of Hua-Yen, the ruling principle is not internalization but interiority. Everything, the whole universe is contained in each thing. It is said in the Hua-Yen sutra, for example, "even in a particle of dust the whole universe is seen reflected." But concerning alchemy Jung expresses the same idea: "not to mix anything from outside with the content of the Hermetic vessel, because the lapis 'has everything it needs'" (Jung, 1968, para. 220).

This logic can be adapted to the dream as Wolfgang Giegerich proposes, an internal approach to images and dreams. A dream is not the internalized world of a human subject, but it has its own world in which everything, even the human subject, is contained. This would change our attitude toward the image fundamentally. The image is emergence and interiority. This seems to be congruent with the Jungian way of working with images. We do not try to manipulate and lead images or personality in a certain direction or toward goals as tends to be the case in cognitive behavioral therapy. Instead we prefer to be surprised by a new emergence of image and to be influenced and guided by the potential of image.

Interdependence and individuality

According to the Hua-Yen School, everything does not have its essence but is based on nothingness. Everything is emergence from the emptiness and consequently "depends for its phenomenal existence upon everything else." In this way everything is an interrelated, ontological event. This "dynamic, simultaneous and interdependent emergence and existence of all things" is called *yuan ch'i* 縁起 (Japanese: *engi*). This is an ontological understanding of reality not as substance but as relationship. From this point of view synchronicity is not an exceptional happening, but a normal state of interconnectedness with only various degree of intensity.

With this understanding of interconnectedness of all things, it is difficult to differentiate one thing from the other since each thing contains everything. To overcome this difficulty, the Hua-Yen School uses the concept of "powerful" and "powerless" with a matrix of components. For example, A, B, and C contain all components.

A (a, b, c, d, e, . . .)
B (a, b, c, d, e, . . .)
C (a, b, c, d, e, . . .)

In this matrix there is no difference among A, B, and C. But for A, certain components, a and f, are powerful while others are powerless. For B, b and g are powerful while others are powerless. In this way they appear individually differently, although their components are the same.

While the Hua-Yen School is based on the idea of interrelated events, psychotherapy tends to focus on a certain related fact. For example, psychotherapy tries to work out and through a mother complex or a trauma. But such a trial may reinforce a momentary powerful component and substantiate an ontological event to a fact.

From the Hua-Yen point of view, especially in the fourth stage of reality, things are seen "as if." Things are differentiated but not fixed. If a patient criticizes his or her mother, the therapist has to listen to it, but "as if he or she is criticizing his or her mother." After immersing into fusion or nothingness, something different may emerge as powerful.

Consequence for psychotherapy and individuation

This chapter is concerned with the loss and recovery of transcendence in Jungian psychology and hopefully in our present time. Therefore I have tried to show how the lost transcendence can be found immanently in reference to Hua-Yen School of Buddhism. God or transcendence is neither dead nor lost, but has been absent from the beginning. This absence is, however, at the same time fullness which flows into the reality as energy and light.

I have already made some comments concerning psychopathology and psychotherapy since Jungian psychology is keenly connected with the practice of psychotherapy. As concluding remarks, I would like to show some further consequences for psychotherapy and individuation.

As interdependence and emergence are ontological events according to the Hua-Yen School's understanding, individuation is not a goal or process, but rather an event. This is a performance done to be able to reach the undifferentiated state and let something emerge from this state. It is of course important to reach the state of consciousness without differentiation as deeply as possible. But the Hua-Yen School has a unique position in presuming the enlightened standpoint. So even if we have never consciously reached the undifferentiated, eliminated state of *li* or emptiness, we can presuppose this position to be taken by the therapist. So we can be present in the therapy as li or emptiness or pleroma which would enable the patient's verbalization, imagination, and transformation.

References

Cleary, T. (1993). *The flower ornament scripture: A translation of the Avatamsaka sutra*. Boulder, CO: Shambhala.
Izutsu, T. (1981). *The nexus of ontological events: A Buddhist view of reality: Eranos-Jahr Buch 1980*, pp. 357–392. Frankfurt: Insel Verlag.
Jung, C.G. (1921). *Collected works, v 6, psychological types* (G. Adler, Ed. and R.F.C. Hull, Trans.). Princeton, NJ: Princeton University Press.
Jung, C.G. (1956). *Collected works, v. 5, symbols of transformation* (G. Adler, Ed. and R.F.C. Hull, Trans.). Princeton, NJ: Princeton University Press.
Jung, C.G. (1961). *Memories, dreams, reflections*. New York: Pantheon Books.
Jung, C.G. (1966). Relations between the ego and the unconscious. In G. Adler and R.F.C. Hull (Ed. and Trans.), *Collected works, v. 7, two essays on analytical psychology* (2nd ed.). Princeton, NJ: Princeton University Press.
Jung, C.G. (1968). *Collected works, v 9ii, Aion* (2nd ed., R.F.C. Hull, Trans.). Princeton, NJ: Princeton University Press.
Jung, C.G. (2009). *The red book* (S. Shamdasani, Ed.). New York: W.W. Norton.
Kawai, T. (2006). Experience of the numinous today: From the novels of Haruki Murakami. In A. Casement and D. Tacey (Eds.), *The idea of the numinous: Contemporary Jungian and psychoanalytic perspectives* (pp. 186–199). London and New York: Routledge.
Kawai, T. (2012). The red book from a pre-modern perspective: The position of the ego, sacrifice and the dead. *Journal of Analytical Psychology*, *57*(3), 378–389.
Plotinus. (1956). *Enneades* (2nd ed., S. McKenna, Trans., revised by B.S. Page). London: Faber and Faber.
Suzuki, D. (1953). The *Bodhisattva's* abode. In *Essays in Zen Buddhism* (3rd series, pp. 108–163). London: Rider and Company.

12
PSYCHOTHERAPY RESEARCH IN TIMES OF CHANGE

Grazina Gudaitė

Introduction

Analytical Psychology offers an unique perspective on and a valuable tool for psychological research into personal transformation. Because of its basic definition of the unconscious as including multiple levels internally and having a collective nature, Jungian principles can be used to investigate both cultural and individual transformations. The central mechanism of opposition, with the capacity to hold two opposites until an emergent third appears, provides an important framework that can be used for analysis of both cultural and individual change and development. This is particularly useful when examining the individual journey in the light of a given culture. Both cultures and individuals change and transform. Analytical Psychology principles can provide important means for exploring the interaction between the two, culture and the individual, and demonstrating how those interactions inform individual growth and transformation.

This chapter will examine how Analytical Psychology tools can parse the relationship between culture and change to help understand the process of an individual's transformation experience. Two studies will be presented, one examining the individual experience of psychotherapy and the second examining the relationship of an individual to authority as part of the therapeutic process. We begin with a discussion of the nature of research into psychotherapy, tools that Analytical Psychology offers researchers, and how they can both support and help to understand the individual transformation process.

Psychotherapy research in the context of the transformation process

Psychotherapy research is a rapidly developing area of study that is important for solving practical questions about psychotherapy application and for developing a deeper understanding of an individual's transformation process as well. Multidimensional transformations are an inherent part of modern life for individuals. Examples of such transformations include the transition from an authoritarian system to a democratic one, migration and integration in different cultures, changes within social structures. The learning of new roles and the development of new models of relationship, fostering of an individual's initiative and responsibility are all important tasks for individuals of our time. Some societies need to confront the consequences of an authoritarian regime or to heal wounds left by cultural trauma. Research conducted during the last two decades at Vilnius University has documented such consequences of cultural trauma as the loss of significance of male roles within society and family, a high prevalence of self-destructive behaviors, excessive alcohol consumption, suicides, and destruction of personal initiative (Gailienė & Kazlauskas, 2005; Gailienė, 2015). The confrontation of destructive consequences stemming from the past embrace of many tasks left by the authoritarian regime has induced a wide spectrum of inner changes of personality. While this research has highlighted the specific cultural shifts in Lithuania correlated with the resultant transformation individuals have undergone, other societies may experience cultural trauma or changes with the resultant impact on individual well-being and growth from their own societal perspective. The issues resulting in cultural trauma may vary by society or culture, but the process of change is universal.

The Analytical Psychology of C.G. Jung is a good guide for acquiring a deeper understanding of the influence of historical heritage and for healing wounds from the past. The Jungian hypothesis of different layers of the unconscious and the articulation of the presumption of a cultural complex (Singer & Kimbles, 2004), as well as ideas on the transformation process and a variety of ways to work with symbolic material, are all very useful in seeking to more fully understand the manifestation of an individual's difficulties and when pursuing the psychotherapy process.

Studies of cultural trauma have shown that by exploring the family history of an individual with its secrets, understanding can emerge of the role of culture in an individual's life, which can in turn be helpful in understanding defensive attitudes toward authority and self-destructive and regressive behavior in that individual's life (Gudaitė, 2005). Kalsched writes that an intensive trauma may "incarcerate" the essential aspects of the Self, not letting them become manifest, thus limiting a person's growth and expression. In dreams or in other states of consciousness when Ego control is weakened, trauma appears as compulsive striving for repetition, resistance to being identified, connections to the experiences of death, the feeling of inner emptiness, and frightening inner figures (Kalsched, 1996). These symptoms may be components of different affective and personality disorders.

Our studies showed that rigid and primitive defenses, an authority complex or complexes accompanied by fear or aggression could be rooted in cultural unconsciousness (Gudaitė, 2014; Kalinenko & Slutskaya, 2014). The confrontation with an authority complex and authoritarian attitude, regressive behavior, and other consequences of an authoritarian regime are part of the tasks that an individual must face in the time of transition. It seems that Jung's reflection, made more than 60 years ago, still fits our time.

> We are living in a time the Greeks called "metamorphosis of the gods" of the fundamental principles and symbols. The peculiarity of our time, which is certainly not of our conscious choosing, is the expression of the unconscious man within us who is changing.
>
> *(Jung, 1957, p. 60)*

Facing and bringing the shadow into consciousness, be it personal or cultural, is part of the work an individual needs to do in a time of change.

Analytical psychotherapy may play an important role in such a process. It assists an individual in facing and containing the shadow aspects of history and in discovering new possibilities for the future as it reveals the ways of the phenomenology of transformation. Psychotherapy research can be useful for supporting the growth of personal as well as cultural consciousness. Transformation and renewal are archetypal themes; their expression depends on historical circumstances, the cultural context, and the psychology of the individual. We need to explore these themes to better understand their expression in modern society. For example, research to clarify the manifestations of symbolic material can reveal the multidimensional possibilities of the process of transformation. Or scientifically planned analysis of a dream series can be a reliable source of information for a deeper understanding of the dynamics of the inner relationships.

This aspect is closely related to the question about the effectiveness of analytical psychotherapy in the process of healing the past wounds sustained by an individual. A considerable number of studies are now available which detail a wide spectrum of the consequences of cultural trauma or the impact of an authoritarian regime (Barocas & Barocas, 1980; Rowland-Klein & Dunlop, 1998; Yehuda & Bierier, 2007; Weisath, 2005; Gailienė, 2015; Rasche & Singer, 2016). At the same time, only a few studies address the value of psychotherapeutic approaches that integrate historical heritage. The reflections of numerous practitioners and studies of psychotherapy cases definitely show that analytical psychotherapy can be effective in healing wounds of the past (Wirtz, 2009; Hill, 2014; Schellinski, 2014). We still need more research on scientifically based understanding of the healing factors and conditions for positive transformation, and on the mechanisms involved together with the entire healing process through analytical psychotherapy.

Research and Analytical Psychology in Lithuania

The Department of Clinical Psychology at Vilnius University conducted research on historical heritage and psychotherapy based on the theory of Analytical Psychology. A portion of those studies was directed toward deeper understanding of psychopathology as a consequence of trauma or an authoritarian regime. Another aspect of these studies was focused explicitly on psychotherapy research.

In Lithuania, interest in the practice and theory of Analytical Psychology is growing along with the number of Jungian psychotherapists and internationally recognized analysts. The development of analytical psychotherapy practice has opened the possibility and the need for conducting research in this field as a separate discipline. With the rapid development of different psychotherapeutic approaches to healing, the need for research on the effectiveness of analytical psychotherapy became evident in the last decade.

A group of Jungian-oriented clinical psychologists and researchers of Vilnius University have jointly conducted research on the effectiveness of this form of psychotherapy. The Science Council of Lithuania supported two research projects based on the paradigm of Analytical Psychology. "Effectiveness in Psychotherapy: An Analysis of Personality Change and the Underlying Factors" (2011–2013) and "The Revelation of Personality's Integrity: Problem of Relation with Authority and Psychotherapy" (2014–2016) were completed in Lithuania. Two dissertations were defended in the context of those projects, several articles were published in scientific journals, and two books have been published: *Efficiency of Psychotherapy: Therapeutic Factors and Subjective Experience of Change* and *Relationship with Authority and Issues of Personal Power*.

The focus of our research was to develop a deeper understanding of the psychotherapy process from the perspective of a client. The measurement of objective parameters, such as symptoms or features of character, the analysis of a patient's subjective reflections, the development of depth presumptions of change – were the main elements of our research. We combined quantitative and qualitative research and integrated the material into the case analysis, which helped with observing the systematic process of psychotherapy. We concentrated on effectiveness of psychotherapy in exploring the relationship to authority, but experience of trauma came out in the process of research.

The following sections describe the results of two studies from our research. One summarizes the variety of subjective experiences occurring during analytical psychotherapy, including the role of imagery in the evaluation of the therapy. The other study reveals the possibilities of successfully using analytical psychotherapy in the context of confronting the consequences of an authoritarian regime.

The role of image in qualitative psychotherapy research

The evaluation of dynamic factors in therapeutic work and the exploration of the subjective experience of therapy are complex processes. Identifying different sources for gathering data can be helpful in revealing the complexity of the whole process. Qualitative research or a combination of quantitative and qualitative principles of analysis are important in such a process. In our studies we used the usual structure of qualitative research: data were collected by using a semi-structured interview. We used the method of thematic analysis (Boyatzis, 1998), which was helpful in articulating the themes of the psychotherapy process as found in the reflections of patients (Bieliauskienė, 2014; Lozovska, 2014), in part by combining visual and verbal material in the course of collecting the data (Gudaitė & Rukšaitė, 2014). The authors discussed the use of visual material and they felt strongly that the image is unjustly forgotten in qualitative research (Prosser, 2005; Bryman, 2011). Such research findings support the central place of the image in Analytical Psychology. Jungian analysts always accepted the image as an important way of self-expression and communication. "The image is a condensated expression of the psychic situation as a whole, and not merely, or even predominantly, of unconscious contents pure and simple" (Jung, 1954b, p. 445). Image expression is related to emotional life and that is very important for a deeper understanding of subjective experience.

Our study

What experiences are accepted as being really healing moments in therapy? How do clients understand what healing is for them and what are the conditions of the therapeutic action? The answer to these questions could reveal the subjective understanding of healing factors that are important for the evaluation of the effectiveness of psychotherapy. The aim of our study was to analyze the most important psychotherapy episodes (as identified below) and reveal the emotional context of such an experience. Students enrolled in postgraduate psychotherapy studies took part in this research. One hundred and seventy-two individuals participated in the 120-hour course of group sessions on dream analysis combined with elements of gestalt therapy. Participants ranged in age from 25 to 35 years. They identified problems with interpersonal relationships and emotional difficulties such as anxiety, depression, or fears at the beginning of therapy. The widening awareness of complexes, the discovery of new ways for dealing with them, and the development of the inner and outer relationship systems were described as the tasks of psychotherapy. The course of psychotherapy took a year and a half. In the final stage of therapy, clients were asked to answer several questions: Was psychotherapy useful for them? If yes, then what episodes were the most important to them? Participants were asked to identify the most important episode from the whole course and to draw a picture symbolizing the experience of healing or growth.

The analysis of data was qualitative, using the inductive thematic analysis, that is, differentiation of the main themes describing the subjective experience of a healing episode. The majority of participants (98.8%) evaluated psychotherapy as a positive experience. Among the positive effects they mentioned an improvement of their emotional state, increased self-confidence, an improvement of interpersonal relations, and a better awareness of needs. For them, psychotherapy extended the options for emotional regulation and offered a more constructive way to work with anger. An analysis of the pictures opened a wider experience of therapy and showed the multidimensional field of experiencing healing or growth. No pictures were similar among the 172 participants. Each drawing was different, and that is very important in revealing the authentic experience of each individual. When participants named what they wanted to express by drawing, several themes arose, which all revealed the variety of healing or growing processes:

- Awareness of the flow of life energy versus the feeling of being stuck;
- Experience of the variety of relatedness versus isolation and loneliness;
- Ability for self-regulation versus being dependent or controlled by others;
- Discovery of new aspects of life and surprise versus an experience of repeated pattern;
- Openness to risk new possibilities versus a defensive attitude;
- Integration of the opposites versus an identification with a one-sided position;
- Egocentrism versus relatedness with the spiritual dimension of life.

The emotional context of the most important episodes was described as an experience of hope, surprise, relief, and a sense of being safe. Nobody mentioned aggression, sadness, or anxiety, although therapists described many such emotional experiences during the therapy course.

Our study suggested that the awakening of hope is important and that clients accept it as the most important healing moment in therapy in a majority of the cases. Psychotherapy researchers accept the awaking of hope as one of the most important signs of effective psychotherapy (Frank, 1971, 1991). In our study, the experience of hope was related to the sense of continuity and to the experience of energy flow. For example, a participant drew a picture of a river and explained the image saying "for me therapy was as the cleaning up of a river stream, that was polluted by trash" (No. 9). Hope may be related to the perspective of the future and to the acceptance of life cycles. "I name my picture "*Spring*" . . . The ice had melted and nature began to flourish. That is the most important moment in therapy" (No. 33). The other emotion reflected upon in describing the healing moment was an experience of surprise. Sometimes that was related to the experience of a paradox or a miracle. "I experienced therapy as meeting Kierkegaard in Kernavė (Kernavė is first capital of Lithuania, a small town near Vilnius). It was possible and it happened within the space of psychotherapy" (No. 87). Sometimes surprise can be related to the discovery of unexpected signs. "I had lost my way in the desert. You know there are no paths to follow in the desert, but a star appeared in the sky and we were able to move further" (No. 69).

These examples suggest that healing moments and the experience of hope or surprise cannot be explained only by a deterministic point of view. A certain number of the clients had accepted the healing moment as a moment of emergence of something with qualities of an impersonal nature. Such reflections fit well the theory of Emergence which opens *another door* for finding analogies and archetypal patterns of psyche manifestation. Perhaps a deeper understanding of the Emergence theory and the principle of synchronicity (Cambray, 2010) can be helpful in the comprehension of the phenomenology of psychotherapy and transformation, which are all important in evaluating the effectiveness of psychotherapy.

Our clients reflected that the use of drawings was helpful for most of them. It widened the possibilities of self-expression and helped to represent different layers of the process. Combining nonverbal and verbal information is important for modern qualitative research. Drawing a picture opens a separate dimension of experience and reflection that can serve as an appropriate tool for nonverbal material. For example, it is not easy to express in words the experience of the integration of polarities or relatedness to a supernatural or spiritual dimension of life: an individual needs symbolic language and drawing pictures can be a good way to express that.

We understand that our conclusions are rather limited because all of the research participants were students. They are creative and do not suffer from serious clinical psychopathology. It may be that patients with serious clinical issues would respond differently and that their expression of subjective experience could involve other emotional qualities and other themes of therapy. It would be important to do such research in the future. On the other hand, different methods of drawings have always been used as an important source of information in clinical assessment.

We believe that Analytical Psychology can be helpful in the further development of qualitative research, especially with the integration of visual material. Such integration can open new opportunities for the evaluation of effectiveness of psychotherapy.

The psychotherapy process: moving from authority complex toward a sense of inner authority

In this section we will introduce a second study that examines an important cultural context for personal transformation: the relationship to authority. The relationship of an individual toward authority is generally ambivalent. When it is associated with an authoritarian regime and its repressive influence on the individual, it may be characterized by obedience, weakness, and a lack of freedom (Grigutytė & Rukšaitė, 2016). In the process of achieving freedom, individuals must liberate themselves from old models of relationship toward authority and find new ones, as the relationship with authority is important in one's values system, self-esteem, and even self-realization.

Ambivalence toward authority is described in psychotherapy literature too. Authority is connected to the power principle, to repression and limiting of spontaneous reactions of the individual. Authority usually is perceived as a power that is projected to the outer world and psychotherapy facilitates taking back these projections. Psychotherapy practice reveals that the healing process of an individual is closely related to the growth of inner authority at the center of personality. There are a few studies in Analytical Psychology concerning this phenomenon, though Dieckmann has emphasized that "individuation especially in the analytical situation, can bring about not only a changing, and rebirth, of the inner nature of man, but, to the same degree, a change and rebirth as regards structure and authority" (Dieckmann, 1977, p. 236).

"*Auctoritatas*" in Latin denotes the power and influence to direct the actions of other people; some linguists also include the ability to be an author (one who can create and produce). Authority may be either personal or impersonal. Personal authority is based on real superiority in relation to other people, be it of greater strength, position, or wisdom. Impersonal authority is based on a social hierarchy system, such as the differences between generations, the degree of experience, or an ability to connect to a transcendental reality. Therefore, when we speak about the relationship with authority, we mean the relationship with somebody who has power, who can regulate the life of an individual and who is also the author of some of life's scenarios or of life itself. The relationship with authority is a very dynamic one: both the experience of obedience and of resistance to authority are necessary for individual growth (Morselli & Passini, 2011). Depending on the stage of development of an individual the connection with authority can be realized in relationships with other people (parents, teachers, etc.), with social structures as well as in relationships with transcendental forces, with God or gods, or with supernatural forces whose images depend on culture, history, and the individual.

Our study

We explored the representation of authority in the initial stage of psychotherapy and how these representations developed in the analytical process. Our research included 48 cases of long-term (three or more years) analytical therapy. Clients ages ranged from 30 to 50 years old. They represented a wide spectrum of social positions and professions (teachers, medical doctors, specialist of law, artists, etc.). All were patients in psychotherapy and included a wide spectrum of clinical issues. Different personality disorders (narcissistic, avoidant, borderline, dependent, histrionic, schizoid), anxiety, and other affective disorders were common for the patients when they came to psychotherapy.

At the conclusion of Analytical Psychology therapy, we analyzed the dynamics of the relationship toward authority. With permission of the therapist and the client, we analyzed the case histories which were documented by the therapists. Case analysis has always been accepted as one of the main forms of research in clinical psychology. It helps to observe the systematic process of development and transformation (Haynes, 1983). Case study is a recognized scientific method if used in an appropriate way. It is important to have a clear subject of research, a theoretical background for the analysis of data and multiple sources of data about the phenomena (Yin, 2003). Multiplicity is the principle which makes this method valid. In our study we analyzed case histories with special focus on the relationship with authority as manifested in interpersonal relationships, in the development of the therapeutic relationship and in symbolic material. Our analysis included personal or family history, complex episodes and their manifestation in a transference relationship, dreams and dream series, and the dynamics of images.

Initial representations of authority

We found that in a majority of cases (56%), authority was perceived as dangerous and destructive in the initial stage of psychotherapy. In one-third of the cases, there was an ambivalent relationship with authority. In a small number (12%) of cases we found that relationship with authority was seen as helpful. The authority complex, consisting of the feeling of being unsafe with expectations of danger was rather common at the beginning of therapy, regardless of age, profession, social status of the client, or experience of the therapist.

An analysis of dreams and remembered episodes showed that cultural trauma and living under conditions of political repression played an important role in the formation of the inner models of relationship to authority. Authority figures that appeared in dreams or memories were communist leaders, KGB officials, or military officers from the Soviet or Nazi armed forces. They were recognized as dangerous because they were able to kill, torture, or persecute. Another group of images that represented authority figures took the form of mythical or fantastic figures, also perceived as dangerous in their unpredictability or in their ability to destroy daily life and bring chaos. When facing such figures, the ego of the client felt inferior and powerless. As a result of such interactions, the individual was feeling inferior or invalid and not permitted to move forward.

Defense strategies such as denial, projection, dissociation, avoidance, and so forth were common in the connection with authority. Dreams and remembered episodes illustrated the complicated picture of this relationship. For example, in many participants' dreams we find the figure of a soldier. The soldier was associated with an instrument of authority understood as an enemy or a hostile figure. The analysis of family history indicated that many clients had the experience of being some kind of soldier, being an instrument in somebody's hands. Moreover, the identity of a soldier was an important part of *Homo Sovieticus*; being a soldier meant total obedience and having some certain function in the big mechanism of an authoritarian regime. It meant being an object. Returning back to subjectivity, the developing of an inner world of relationship, particularly a relationship with authority in a positive sense, are the tasks of confronting the consequences of an authoritarian regime.

The dynamic of images in a psychotherapy process

Our analysis of the psychotherapy cases in our study revealed several important aspects of reestablishing a mature relationship with authority.

1. One aspect was an awareness of the defensive attitude toward authority which manifested as maladaptive rebellious behavior or excessive emphasis on self-importance, an understanding of the role of projections of an authority complex, and the differentiation between inner and outer authority were all important insights that provided relief and a sense of freedom, as well as the awareness that authority could be a source of life and not destruction.

2   Another aspect of forming a mature relationship with authority was the actualization of inner authority in the psyche of an individual. Identification and disidentification with a position of authority, the feeling of personal initiative, the ability to follow the guidance of others, and a feeling of dignity are important signs of the formation of inner authority. This actualization of inner authority was especially helpful in healing depression, helplessness, or passivity.
3   The development of the relationship with authority also includes awareness about its shadow. Being in a superior position (relationship with authority is described as being a vertical axis of relationship, and superiority is part of that experience) could mean the ability to use others, to humiliate, to ignore, or even to destroy the life of others. People who survived an authoritarian regime recount many examples of such destructive behavior of authority.

Our study showed that the survivors of cultural trauma had rather defensive attitudes and sometimes used tricky strategies in their relationship with authorities. Hiding himself or herself, changing identity, unpredictably appearing or disappearing, being passive and pretending to be foolish – such were the strategies we found employed in the relationship with authority in many family histories of our case studies. To trick the system, to trick the authority was an important survival strategy. Perhaps it be necessary for some time. But an individual needs to be careful and conscious about his relationship with authority, not only in the actual experience toward authority, but also when the authoritarian regime ends. Representations of a defensive, regressive, or even destructive relationship toward authority may remain at an unconscious level for many years and can manifest in an individual's life under a democratic regime as well.

Clinical practice shows that the boundary between tricking the authority and tricking oneself is a thin one. If someone is not conscious about it, the "Trickster" can take on demonic characteristics and the destruction can turn onto the self. We presume that the high suicide rate in Lithuania and a variety of regressive behaviors could well be related to a lack of awareness of the Trickster's energy. According to Jung, the Trickster's nature is dual and contradictory. It has an ability to change its shape, and that can be important in confronting rigid defense systems. The trickster deity in mythology breaks the rules of the gods of nature; it can exert positive effects, but it can also lead to psychopathology as it is closely related to the dissociation and splitting of a personality (Jung, 1954a). Developing awareness of shadow aspects of the relationship toward authority is important stage in the maturation process of an individual.

4   Being conscious of a transcendental aspect of authority, a fourth aspect was discovered in our research on the development of the relationship with authority. The actualization of one's own creativity and the respect for the Creator's manifestations were important moments in analysis. As one of the clients expressed, "analysis was moving from being a soldier toward being a musician." Soldier and musician – both are instruments of authority. Being a soldier

means to obey and to follow the directions of authority without personal choice. Musicians can make choices about what they play, they are guided by the esthetic principle which is close to the Eros principle, and that can be helpful for liberation oneself from the Power principle.

A mature relationship with authority includes many aspects of an individual's experience. He or she is able to be in a superior position, but can also leave it; one is able to be an author, but is open to being a figure in someone else's scenario; he or she is able to play, but is conscious about rules and structure; he or she can self-realize yet recognizes and respects the creation of others and the Other at the same time.

Our research demonstrated that psychotherapy can be helpful in the process of moving from an authority complex toward the development of an inner authority. We distinguished several criteria that characterize such a process: recognition versus defensiveness, inner authority versus an authority complex, experience of authorship versus dependency and control by an other, awareness of dynamics versus a one-sided attitude toward authority, ego-centered versus direction toward the transcendental. These criteria can be a useful in assessing the effectiveness of psychotherapy.

Conclusions

Psychotherapy effectiveness research is a multidimensional process where practice, theory, and science meet (Lambert & Archer, 2006). This meeting seems rather complicated when we try to realize it. Psychotherapy practice and theory involve with a multifaceted process. There is a large variety of psychotherapy directions, methods, and conceptions which describe the therapeutic processes and its results in different terms. There is need for integration and finding common therapeutic factors, methods, and mechanisms (O'Brien & Houston, 2000). A literature review shows that the problem of evaluation of psychotherapy effectiveness and some resulting controversial conclusions depend not only on the diversity of psychotherapy approaches, but also on the problem of what is the subject of effectiveness research itself. It is important to measure observable characteristics of an individual's behavior (the so-called objective parameters), their manifestation and changes, which are so important for evidence-based psychotherapy (Wampold, 2001).

A human being is not only one who can learn many functions used to adopt the world; he is a subject and he has his way of making meaning. He has fantasies, dreams, creativity – a rich inner world that is the main subject of psychotherapy. Thus when we explore the effectiveness of psychotherapy, it is important to uncover the subjective experience of individual who is in psychotherapy. A third dimension for exploring psychotherapy is to understand that force which stands beyond behavior and beyond subjective experience. Depth presumptions of inner structures and an inner system of relationship are the most familiar examples of psychodynamic therapy discussed in psychotherapy research. The role of culture, cultural complexes, and awareness of cultural identity can be very important in understanding all three dimensions I mentioned above. An appropriate use of theory may be helpful for integrating the results of research and also for revealing new perspectives for understanding the transformation process. Deeper understanding of the emergence of hope and inspiration is an important theme for further research in psychotherapy effectiveness as well as in exploring the multidimensional picture of a sense of identity. Further studies of cultural identity and the relationship of the individual to culture can be an important theme in revealing healing sources for that individual and culture as well. It seems to us that Analytical Psychology can be a good basis for integrating psychotherapy practice, for planning research and for being a good enough basis for psychotherapy itself.

References

Barocas, H., & Barocas, C. (1980). Separation – Individuation conflicts in children of holocaust survivors. *Journal of Contemporary Psychotherapy*, *11*(1), 6–14.

Bieliauskienė, I. (2014). *Qualitative study of the effectiveness of psychotherapy: Therapeutic factors from the perspective of male and female clients*. Summary of Doctoral Dissertation. Vilnius: Vilnius University.

Bryman, A. (2011). *Visual methods in psychology: Using and interpreting images in qualitative research*. London: Routledge.

Boyatzis, R.E. (1998). *Transforming qualitative information: Thematic analysis and code development*. London: Sage Publications.

Cambray, J. (2010). Emergence of the self. In M. Stein (Ed.), *Jungian psychoanalysis: Working in the spirit of C.G. Jung*. Chicago and La Salle, IL: Open Court.

Dieckmann, H. (1977). Some aspects of the development of authority. *Journal of Analytical Psychology*, *22*(3), 230–242.

Frank, J.D. (1971). Therapeutic factors in psychotherapy. *American Journal of Psychotherapy*, *25*, 350–361.

Frank, J.D., & Frank, J.B. (1991). *Persuasion and healing: A comparative study of psychotherapy*. Baltimore and London: Johns Hopkins University Press.

Gailienė, D. (Ed.). (2015). *Lithuanian faces after transition: Psychological consequences of cultural trauma*. Vilnius: Eugrimas.

Gailienė, D., & Kazlauskas, E. (2005). Fifty years on: The long – term psychological effects of Soviet repression in Lithuania. In D. Gailienė (Ed.), *The psychology of extreme traumatization: The aftermath of political repression* (pp. 67–108). Vilnius: Akreta.

Grigutytė, N., & Rukšaitė, G. (2016). Lithuanian historical heritage: Relationship with authority and psychological well-being. *The European Proceedings of Social and Behavioral Sciences*, pp. 274–284.

Gudaitė, G. (2005). Psychological aftereffects of the Soviet trauma and the analytical process. In D. Gailienė (Ed.), *The psychology of extreme traumatization: The aftermath of political repression* (pp. 108–126). Vilnius: Akreta.

Gudaitė, G. (2014). Restoration of continuity: Desperation or hope in facing the consequences of cultural trauma. In G. Gudaitė and M. Stein (Eds.), *Confronting cultural trauma: Jungian approaches to understanding and healing*. New Orleans, LA: Spring Journal Books.

Gudaitė, G., & Rukšaitė, R. (2014). Awakening the hope: Images of psychotherapy process and analysis of subjective experience. In G. Gudaitė (Ed.), *Efficiency of psychotherapy: Therapeutic factors and subjective experience of change*. Vilnius: Vilnius University. Printed in Lithuanian language.

Hayes, S. (1983). The role of individual case in the production and consumption of clinical knowledge. In M. Heisen, E. Kazdin and S. Bellack (Eds.), *The clinical psychology handbook*. New York: Pergamon.

Hill, J. (2014). Dreams don't let you forget: Cultural trauma and its denial. In G. Gudaitė and M. Stein (Eds.), *Confronting cultural trauma: Jungian approaches to understanding and healing*. New Orleans, LA: Spring Journal Books, pp. 31–47.

Jung, C.G. (1954a). On the psychology of the trickster figure. In *The collected works (volume 9) The archetypes of the collective unconscious*. Princeton: Princeton University Press, 1990, pp. 255–275.

Jung, C.G. (1954b). Definitions. In *The collected works (volume 6) psychological types*. Princeton: Princeton University Press, 1990, p. 445.

Jung, C.G. (1957). *The undiscovered self*. Princeton: Princeton University Press, 1990, p. 60.

Kalinenko, V., & Slutskaya, M. (2014). 'Father of the people versus enemies of the people': A split-father complex as the foundation for collective trauma in Russia. In G. Gudaitė and M. Stein (Eds.), *Confronting cultural trauma: Jungian approaches to understanding and healing*. New Orleans, LA: Spring Journal Books.

Kalsched, D. (1996). *The inner world of trauma: Archetypal defenses of the personal spirit*. London: Routledge.

Lambert, M.J., & Archer, A. (2006). Research findings on the effects of psychotherapy and their implications to practice. In C. Goodheart, A. Kazdin and R. Stenberg (Eds.), *Evidence-based psychotherapy: Where practice and research meet*. Washington, DC: American Psychological Association.

Lozovska, J. (2014). *Reflecting on psychotherapeutic changes: Therapeutic factors and the transformation of anger expression*. Summary of Doctoral Dissertation. Vilnius: Vilnius University.

Morselli, D., & Passini, S. (2011). New perspectives on the study of the authority relationship: Integrating individual and societal level research. *Journal for the Theory of Social Behaviour, 41*(3), 291–307.

O' Brien, M., & Houston, G. (2000). *Integrative psychotherapy*. London: Sage Publications.

Prosser, J. (2005). *Image-based research – A sourcebook for qualitative researchers*. London: Taylor and Francis Group.

Rasche, J., & Singer, T. (2016). *Europe's many souls: Exploring cultural complexes and identities*. New Orleans, LA: Spring Journal Books.

Rowland-Klein, D., & Dunlop, R. (1998). The transmission of trauma across generations: Identification with parental trauma in children holocaust survivors. *Australian and New Zealand Journal of Psychiatry, 32*(3), 358.

Schellinski, K. (2014). Horror inherited: Transgenerational transmission of collective trauma in dreams. In G. Gudaitė and M. Stein (Eds.), *Confronting cultural trauma: Jungian approaches to understanding and healing*. New Orleans, LA: Spring Journal Books.

Singer, T., & Kimbles, S. (Ed.). (2004). *The cultural complex: Contemporary Jungian perspectives on psyche and society*. New York: Brunner-Routledge.

Wampold, B.E. (2001). *The great psychotherapy debate: Model, methods, and findings*. Mahwah, NJ: Lawrence Erlbaum Associates.

Weisath, L. (2005). Psychotraumatology: An overview from a European perspective. In D. Gailienė (Ed.), *The psychology of extreme traumatization: The aftermath of political repression*. Vilnius: Akreta, pp. 26–67.

Wirtz, U. (2009). The symbolic dimension in trauma therapy. In *Spring 82: Symbolic life* (pp. 31–52). New Orleans, LA: Spring Journal Books.

Yehuda, R., & Bierier, L. (2007). Transgenerational transmission of cortisol and PTSD risk. *Progress in Brain Research, 167*, 121.

Yin, K. (2003). *Case study research: Design and methods*. London: Sage Publications.

13
THE LOSS OF PSYCHOLOGICAL INFRASTRUCTURE IN THE "UBIQUITOUS" SELF-CONSCIOUSNESS OF OUR TIMES

Yasuhiro Tanaka

Developed as an essential way of understanding the human experience and psychopathology based on the new perspective of "modernism," psychology was created using the idea of observation of the self. In particular, self-observation became a central tenet of Analytical Psychology, and its vision of the *self* as its psychological infrastructure. This chapter will examine this central tenet from the standpoint of postmodern thought and apply Jungian principles to cultural and personal issues in Japan. The role of psychological infrastructure in the age of the "ubiquitous" self-consciousness or today's internet will form the basis for our discussion.

Modern? Contemporary? – The concept of "modern"

The German philosopher, Jürgen Habermas, described the concept "*Moderne*" in his article "Modernity: An Unfinished Project" (Habermas, 1980). He noted that the word "modern" was first employed in the late 5th century in order to distinguish the present, now officially Christian, from the pagan and Roman past. This definition is confirmed by the origin of word "modern," namely, it was derived from the Latin word *modernus*, which is a cognate with *modo*, meaning "just now." Essentially, the word "modern" does not denote a specific time, but "the expression 'modernity' repeatedly articulates the consciousness of an era that refers back to the past of classical antiquity precisely in order to comprehend itself as the result of a transition from the **old** to the **new**" (p. 39). This concept of modernity emerged at a time of cultural change and tends to be used as a marker reflecting this shift.

In the 19th century Western Europe after going through the (French) Enlightenment, formulated modernity in terms of opposites: "in opposing the classical and the romantic to one another, modernity sought its own past in an idealized vision of the Middle Ages" (p. 39). Moreover, "in the course of the nineteenth century (in which this Romanticism ceased to idealize a specific age) *this* Romanticism produced a radicalized consciousness of modernity that detached itself from all previous historical connection" (p. 39). After that, the prevailing understanding of the term modernity was solely the "abstract opposition to tradition and history as a whole" (p. 39).

Habermas described that thusly "what was considered modern was what assisted the spontaneously self-renewing historical contemporaneity of the *Zeitgeist* to find its own objective expression" (p. 40). Modern consciousness contains "this forward orientation, this anticipation of an indefinite and contingent future, the cult for the New" (p. 40) in itself, and in this context, it had to be characterized by the unremitting "self-negating movement" (p. 40). This movement was inescapably intertwined with its self-renewing act of separating and differentiating from the past, in which even the current forms of the self are always being nullified or at least relativized.

We can thus say that such modern consciousness, which was established in the middle of the 19th century by detachment from history as a whole and by the acquisition of its own abstractness, was a totally *new* consciousness. That is to say, consciousness that is self-aware tends to vulnerably focus on itself setting the stage for the emergency of a concomitant experience of dissociation of self. The development of psychology was to serve as a significant asset in dealing with this new experience of self, this new reality, as seen below.

Duplication, or replication, of the "I" in "the century of psychology"

As described above, the unremitting "self-negating movement" was integrated into modern consciousness by the mid-1800s. This shift in consciousness was closely related to and maybe a precursor for the birth of psychology as an academic discipline in the second half of the 19th century.

Psychology emerging out of philosophy in its earliest days adopted self-observation or introspection as its own methodology. This well reflects that psychology was originally a discipline of self-consciousness, or self-relation. That is to say, "self-consciousness" was both the subject and methodology of psychology.

This dual aspect of self-consciousness is further articulated in the development of psychotherapy in the 20th century called "the century of psychology." Psychoanalysis as invented by Freud first paid attention to the psychical mechanism of "repression" in patients with conversion hysteria. He had the idea that hysteric patients would *repress* negative emotions they could not accept in themselves. This was mainly related to the problems of self-relation in neurotics. The same could be said for the various "defense mechanisms" that the school of ego-psychology conceptually developed afterwards.

Moreover, as seen more clearly in the conceptions of "transference" and "archetype," what was dealt with in analytical psychotherapy was always "the other as self" or "self as the other." In that sense, we can say that a *simple* "other" does not exist in such therapeutic modalities as psychoanalysis and Analytical Psychology.

In this context, the prominent feature of what is called "modern consciousness" is that it is consciousness reflecting on itself, or being "self-consciousness." It cannot avoid creating *dissociation* when shifting between the reflecting self and the reflected self without interruption. It is not a coincidence that psychology was born in the second half of the 19th century. This is clearly shown in the fact that the classic methodology of psychology was self-observation or introspection, as stated earlier. The dissociative nature of modern consciousness acutely needed psychology to explicate these experiences through the study of such self-relationships.

As noted earlier, the concept of "modern" as a consciousness that rests on an inflection point in time rather than being statically located in a historical context developed in the 18th century paved the way for the development of psychology. Concerning this simultaneity, or oneness, of becoming conscious and being dissociated, Jung states in "The Meaning of Psychology for Modern Man" (Jung 1933), "When man became conscious, *the germ of the sickness of dissociation* was planted in his soul, for consciousness is at once the highest good and the greatest evil" (Jung, 1933, para. 291), or "*the sickness of dissociation* in our world is at the same time a process of recovery, or rather, the climax of a period of pregnancy which heralds the throes of birth. . . . that which brings division ultimately creates union" (Jung, 1933, para. 293, my italics).

In that sense, we may say that psychoanalysis, founded by Freud at the end of the 19th century, was a *vaccination therapy* against the sickness of dissociation as a psychological virus whose host was modern consciousness. In another paper (Tanaka, 2009), I described the process of self-development of this sickness: (1) psychoanalysis as a vaccination therapy for the virus of dissociation, (2) "borderline cases" as a next-generation virus, (3) multiple personality disorder as a third-generation virus. This is tantamount to the process of duplicating, splitting, and replicating "I" in the 20th century, "the century of psychology."

However, in the 21st century, the "I" has become no longer duplicating, splitting, and replicating in such a way, but rather being unevenly distributed as information in the outer world, as will be discussed in the next section.

Externalization and ubiquity of the "I" in the postmodern world

In the 20th century, the so-called century of psychology, the "I" was doubled and then multiplexed by the "dissociation virus," where we can no longer find the features of "modernity" that were shown before. As we will discuss here, from the end of the 20th century to the 21st century, the "I" seems to have stopped its movement, that is, being doubled and multiplexed, *inside* itself, and now it appears to take on a ubiquitous aspect, *outwardly* seeking its field in this world. In this sense, we can say that contemporary consciousness is "non-modern" consciousness in the postmodern world.

I shall first describe the general human condition of the contemporary world in this section and then present two clinical cases well expressing the state of the contemporary consciousness in comparison with other two neurotic patients living in the modern world in the next section.

Ubiquitous — the "I" defined by the externalized self as information

The word "ubiquitous" is derived from a Latin word *ubique*, meaning "existing or being everywhere." Traditionally, this word was used in monotheistic cultural eras to express "the ubiquity of God," that is to say, God imagined as the one and only fundamental reality can be at all places simultaneously. However, it is today generally used to mean the "ubiquity" of computers ("ubiquitous computing").

In Japan, this feature of the computing environment was first clearly visualized in TRON (The Real-time Operating system Nucleus) project by Ken Sakamura in 1984, who was at that time an assistant professor in the School of Science at the University of Tokyo. After that, the technology based on this idea became popular on a worldwide scale under the names of "Computing Everywhere," "Calm Computing," and "Invisible Computing." In 1991, Mark Weiser, who was at that time the head of the computer science laboratory at the Palo Alto Research Center of Xerox in the United States, declared in his article "The Computer for the 21st Century" that what they called ubiquitous computing would gradually emerge as the dominant mode of computer access over the next 20 years (Weiser, 1991).

The history of ubiquitous computing summarized above will enable you to figure out what "ubiquitous computing" means today: existing or being everywhere, computers embedded in the actual environment that will automatically judge and decide the behavior of various things. Of course, this kind of technology brings invaluable convenience to human beings. Regardless of being aware or unaware of it, we are now receiving and enjoying the full benefit of the conveniences far and wide. On the other hand, could we say the function of computers as an automatic judgment or decision maker means that human beings will have diminishing needs for judgement by themselves and suffer an atrophy of the capacity for judgment, ironically even in the moment it has reached its most refined form as "a tool"?

The best example of the interaction of convenience and personal decision-making can be found on the Amazon website: "Customers Who Bought This Item Also Bought," "Special Offers and Product Promotions," "Inspired by Your Browsing History." Or, we can also find another example in hard disc recorders equipped with an automatically programmed recording function. On one hand, it is true that they will present unknown or unconscious choices for us to consider; on the other hand, they also create the possibility that any choices other than their recommendations or any other futures are taken away or hidden.

Using the example described above, we can see that we are surrounded by such accumulated information on individuals and the "I" as externalized information which will appear ahead of "me" everywhere. A Japanese sociologist, Kensuke Suzuki, summarized this situation and expressed the following thought-provoking opinion: "two paradoxical events will occur at the same time, that is to say, one chooses a future regarding one's own life, in parallel with that, one receives the future as already decided, as if it were one's fate" (Suzuki, 2007, p. 57).

Virtual reality and neurosis

In Weiser's article mentioned earlier, there is also one more interesting point of note. He thought that diametrically opposed to "ubiquitous computing" was the notion of "virtual reality," which was becoming prevalent by 1991.

"Virtual reality" was a technology that attracted lots of attention throughout the 1980s and 1990s. It created a pseudo world, so-called cyberspace "in" the computer, where people could play various active roles. As represented by online gaming, the features of "virtual reality" were sometimes criticized with the words "people cannot distinguish such a world from reality." However, considering the contrast with "ubiquitous computing" *embedded in our environment*, we can say that a partition between the "Real" as the world "this side" and the "Net" as the world "the other side" was established therein, *somehow or other*.

Thinking of "virtual reality" in this sense, it would be possible to say that some remnants of the modern worldview could be still found there. We can primarily discuss this issue in relation to "neurosis," as follows.

The English word "virtual" has meanings "imaginary, idol," therefore, in Japan, "virtual reality" is often translated to the word "仮想現実 (the meaning of these Chinese characters in English: imaginary reality or fictional reality)." However, the word "virtual" also has meanings "effective, practical" because it is derived from the Latin word *virtualis* meaning "potency, efficacy."

The French philosopher Pierre Lévy (1995) sees "the virtual" as a component of "the actual." Employing his idea, we can say that the virtual would be a certain practical possibility composed for any purpose in each case. Namely, it could be also said as "a practical sense of reality composed for a certain purpose, though it is different from the actual reality" (Suzuki, 2007).

In this regard, we can find that "virtual reality" has a similarity to neurosis that Jung recognized as real but unreal. He noted "the neurosis is manufactured anew every day" (Jung, 1911, para. 655). In this meaning, neurosis is considered as the "practical sense of reality composed for a certain purpose, though it is different from the actual reality," which is created by a patient.

In terms of the collective connection that transcends individuals, we can also find a structural similarity in the relationship between "collective unconsciousness" and "internet." Here, while "virtual reality" is no longer considered to be "inner" but "outer," it appears that the two-world "structure" of "modern consciousness" is brought within as it is, which creates "neurosis" by containing "dissociation" as its own premise of the existence, as described earlier.

In contrast, such "structure" can no longer be found in "ubiquitous computing." As such, all things are defined by the "I" as the computerized self. In this sense, the world bubbles over with horizontally and unidimensionally externalized, or ubiquitously distributed, the "I" as information. From this perspective, we can say that "virtual reality" is the technology that was created during the transitional period from modern to the postmodern time (today) as "the intermediate."

A case study of self-consciousness in Japan: ubiquitous self-consciousness and loss of psychological infrastructure

As described at the end of last section, what was brought into the "contemporary consciousness" from the "modern consciousness" was not its two-world "structure," but rather a style of "self-consciousness."

As mentioned earlier, "modernity" itself is a concept of the self-relationship in regard to opposition or transition, which itself is unsubstantial. Being detached from history as a whole in the modern age, what the abstract "individual" sought was nothing but "self." Therefore, "modern consciousness" can be considered as self-related consciousness. "Contemporary consciousness," however, does not have such reflectedness as folding back or looking back any more. It is the "ubiquitous" self-consciousness, that is, the consciousness that is *merely* composed of, or *outwardly* oriented toward, the "I" being externalized or existing ubiquitously as information which bubbles over horizontally and unidimensionally in the world.

Negative self-consciousness in anthropophobia

In order to see the features of this "ubiquitous" self-consciousness, here we will look at the negative self-consciousness in anthropophobia. Anthropophobia has been described as a peculiar neurosis in Japan and regarded as a clinical state that occurs frequently during puberty and adolescence. We can generally define anthropophobia as a form of neurosis, where one backs away from interpersonal relationships as much as possible, due to patients experiencing unreasonably high levels of anxiety and mental strain in their interpersonal situations, and worry about being looked down upon by others, causing discomfort to others and being disliked by others. In addition, in the 1960s and 1970s, many researchers pointed out that the style of Japanese interpersonal relationships was well reflected by this clinical state (Tanaka, 1992).

The investigation by Ogawa et al. should be noted as an empirical and quantitative approach to studying "consciousness of interpersonal anxiety" among these patients. Ogawa (1974) first clarified "consciousness of interpersonal anxiety" based on the actual "worries" of patients with anthropophobia and then designed the "Interpersonal Anxiety Questionnaire" revised by Hayashi et al. (1981) as the "Interpersonal Relationship Questionnaire." Both instruments attempted to focus on "negative self-consciousness" as the quintessence of anthropophobic mentality in a series of investigations.

In 1994, I published an article with my colleagues, "Longitudinal Changes of Characteristics and Structure of Anthropophobic Tendency in Adolescence" (Tanaka et al., 1994). In it, data from university students completing the "Interpersonal Relationship Questionnaire" collected in 1981 and 1991 were compared quantitatively, using multivariate analytical methods over time. I obtained the following interesting results: in the data from 1991, (1) "consciousness of interpersonal anxiety" itself was quantitatively very much reduced; (2) their worry <*feeling strain in interpersonal relationships*> was no longer extracted as an independent factor, although it was extracted as the first factor that formed "consciousness of interpersonal anxiety" in the data of 1981; (3) instead, their worries <*being unable to fit in with a group*> and <*concerns about others*> were extracted as the first and the second factors, respectively.

Based on these findings, it is obvious that among university students the "consciousness of interpersonal anxiety" exhibited remarkable quantitative and structural changes over the course of one decade (between 1981 and 1991). How can we interpret these changes?

First, it should be pointed out that what composes the major portion of "consciousness of interpersonal anxiety" is no longer "strain" that one feels *inside*, but rather a consciousness toward the *outside*, such as "group" or "others," has appeared. The major worry <*being unable to fit in with a group*> are as follows: "being unable to fit into a group" and "not being good at getting along in a group." In contrast, the major worry <*concerns about others*> are "concerns about how others regard me" and "concerns about how colleagues in the workplace, classmates, and neighbors regard me." From these findings, it is presumed that the subjects tend to have a "biased view" that is related to other people's perception of them, rather than to their own "self." Furthermore, it could be said that many university students have difficulty in taking part in gatherings or groups due to this "biased view."

In addition, the worry <*being regarded as a strange person*> was not extracted as an independent factor in 1991, although it was extracted as the 12th factor in 1981. This factor showed such a degree of anxiety that "one single-mindedly wants to conceal his or her own pathology and thus worries over whether or not his or her *timid* attitude will be known to his or her friends or acquaintances." When Ogawa developed the "Interpersonal Anxiety Questionnaire" (1974), this factor was considered as "a particular worry of patients with anthropophobia from its contents." In other words, we could imagine that, although this factor expressed the essence of their worries, based on the "negative self-consciousness," such "self-consciousness," or psychological structure, could no longer be formed *naturally*, as of 1991. As will be discussed in the next section, this longitudinal change of anthropophobic tendency well reflects the state of "self-consciousness" today in Japan.

The state of "self-consciousness" today in Japan

Today, more than 20 years have passed since 1991, and now we rarely see patients with this kind of psychological structure in our practice. Of course, many patients come to us to deal with their worries regarding interpersonal relationships, but it is relatively rare that they complain about so-called interpersonal strain. Their chief complaint has become more *concrete*, like a problem in their extremely "narrow" interpersonal relationships, as Keiko Iwamiya, a Japanese clinical psychologist who specialized in psychology of puberty and school counseling, described (Iwamiya, 2009): "How can I be accepted in my class?" "What kind of position, or role, should I take therein?" "How can I manage to fit in with this or that group of classmates?" Among their concretized complaints, it is difficult for us to see their abstract or psychological themes, that is, "the others locked in their subjectivity" and "self-consciousness." In other words, "others" and "groups" in anthropophobic worries were always *not specified but general*, namely, abstract and psychological.

I will present another example. Today, there are many *Bocchi* who do not fit in with any peer groups at Japanese universities. *Bocchi* is an abbreviated form of "*Hitori-bocchi*," which in Japanese means "all on one's own." *Bocchi* students *act by themselves* at universities (in many cases, students act as a group); quickly and separately moving throughout their university campus, sitting in the front row of the lecture halls, all on their own, having lunch alone, and not having conversations with any other students. You might associate only with their loneliness or sadness from these descriptions, but in actuality, it seems to me, they have already obtained so-called *citizenship* at Japanese universities or culture. As Chihiro Hatanaka pointed out, there are special seats for *Bocchi* (*Bocchi-seki*) in student cafeterias, and they have a kind of "meal code" for themselves, that is, they should not eat alone at McDonald's, but rather should buy a *Bento* (Japanese lunch box) at a convenience store and then take it to eat at a nearby park (Hatanaka, 2013).

Of course, *Bocchi* have problems with interpersonal relationships, but among them we cannot imagine the intervention of "the others as self" or "self as the others," which is the premise of therapeutic psychology, as noted earlier. In contrast with anthropophobic patients, the others, or the others' gaze, for *Bocchi* are always concrete and objective, not at all abstract or subjective; the others for them are never locked in their subjectivity. Therefore, the screens in *Bocchi-seki* function substantially as a boundary from the others and as a shield from the others' gaze.

As I mentioned before, "self-consciousness" *was* both the subject and methodology of psychology in modern times. Psychology developed as a discipline of such modern consciousness always reflecting on itself. In that sense, we can also say that this "self-consciousness" *was* the sole "psychological infrastructure" upon which our "psychology" was exclusively based, and that anthropophobic patients still maintained this "self-consciousness" as their "psychological infrastructure"; although it was one-sidedly in negative form, that is, "*negative* self-consciousness."

However, as indicated by their complaints in the school counseling office and their problems in interpersonal relationships that was expressed in *Bocchi* as a cultural phenomenon, among today's Japanese students during puberty and adolescence, whose mentality used to be regarded as closely connected to anthropophobic tendency, we can no longer find any *trace* of such psychological infrastructure. *They have no psychology* in its former sense any longer.

In this manner, I have the impression that this psychological "base structure" or infrastructure has already been lost in postmodern times. The state of "ubiquitous" self-consciousness is closely related to such a loss of "psychological infrastructure."

Ubiquitous as invisible "information infrastructure"

Here our discussion returns to "ubiquitous computing." We already mentioned Sakamura, who was the project leader of TRON. He considered "ubiquitous computing" as "information infrastructure" and described it as the social foundation through which, from moment to moment and from place to place, a user can utilize various information and services that have been optimized for him/her *without bearing the burden of conscious operation* (Sakamura, 1987, 1988). As one can infer from this description, the definition of "infrastructure" in the dictionary is the generic term for what forms social economic bases and social production bases, in which road, port and harbor, rivers, rail, communications and information system center, sewerage system, school, hospital, park, public housing, and so forth are included.

Sakamura (2007b) says that it is important to take an approach of "tagging (putting tags one after another)" to build an "information infrastructure." The definition of "tagging" is "to put tags on actual things and to use them as [a] cue for extracting information." According to him, "this could be one of the important concepts to connect the virtual and actual worlds" (Sakamura, 2007a).

Namely, the aim of "ubiquitous computing" is to promote a seamless and barrier-free world. The tag to be placed is named "u-code," which is a colorless and transparent identifier that has no relationship with the social administration system; in other words, non-meaningful code. Furthermore, the design concept is "the externalization of [the] network." It is very natural that this kind of concept reaches such a conclusion that "ubiquitous computing" is planned as so-called open-architecture and can be expanded to the world as open and universal infrastructure.

As described earlier, we cannot define the value of the convenience that we receive and enjoy through promoting seamless and barrier-free exchange between the virtual and actual worlds. So I never deny this trend, but I have some questions regarding such current technology. How does it influence our mind or psyche? Through it, what intent will the soul have and what kind of trial will the soul impose on us?

First, we need to consider "de-signification" of the world itself through "tagging" u-codes. As we can infer from the words "open architecture," the concept of "possession" or "ownership," for example, "patent" or "brand," which characterizes the modern age, in a sense, will lose the traditional meaning there. Although Sakamura provides an example of "address" (residence indication), there is no town name or street name in it, because the indication using "u-code" is composed only of meaningless numbers. From a certain perspective, it would discard and abstract the history accumulated in the name of place. Furthermore, it goes without saying that "ubiquitous computing" as "information infrastructure" is not as visible a form of infrastructure as "road, port and harbor, rivers, rail, communications and information system center, sewerage system, school, hospital, park, public housing." Although we would no longer be aware of it, our judgment in each case would undoubtedly reflect the "information" accumulated by various forms and methods.

In that sense, we may say that the establishment of "social foundation that a user can utilize without bearing a burden of conscious operation" concludes that people have no need for making any decision by themselves but lose their power of judgement. As noted earlier, the more this "information infrastructure" is established, the more people lose the "infrastructure" within themselves. This is what I call "the loss of psychological infrastructures" in the "ubiquitous" self-consciousness.

How do we see, or experience, the loss of psychological infrastructure in our practice?

To help understand what "psychological infrastructure" means, I will first present one sandplay and one dream from two patients with anthropophobia whom I saw for psychotherapy in the first half of the 1990s.

Boy A was a male high school student who came to see me, complaining about interpersonal strain. Since he could not speak well during sessions, he brought a short report in each session to summarize what he wanted to say; he made me read these reports out loud in every session. Figure 13.1 shows his first sandplay expression. A green sheet was spread over the sand as if it would prevent the force from the realm of "under." In addition, the surrounding area was enclosed by bushes, as if to protect the realm of "inside."

As shown in Figure 13.2, on the boundary, a "grave" and a "shrine" were set, which likely symbolized his fear and longing for the realm of "outside." In this manner, we can easily imagine that there is a "base structure" that is shown by this patient's expression, which allows us psychotherapists able to read psychological "meaning." Here we call it "psychological infrastructure."

FIGURE 13.1 Sandplay by Boy A

FIGURE 13.2 Sandplay by Boy A

Another case, Ms. B, was in her early twenties when she came to see me with her chief complaint of "extreme interpersonal strain." She soon started to report some dreams in her psychotherapy. The following dream was reported in the second session, as one of her initial dreams.

> *I had an appointment for a date with a man. Our meeting point was in a sewer tunnel (underground passage inside a manhole). I felt uneasy because dirty water was flowing around my feet and was dripping from above. My partner stood leaning against a wall. I spoke a few words with him. Suddenly, he started to speak in language used by women, and before I knew it, his breasts became bigger. I asked her, "Who are you?" She answered, "I am his sister. My brother could not come because of his illness, I came here in his place."*

Her associations for this dream were as follows; the sewer tunnel was cold and dirty, vague and dark. I felt, "Why am I here in this place?" The sewer tunnel has often appeared in my dream. I have never been exposed to the sun. I feel it is unpleasant, but I think that it is appropriate for me. No place more beautiful than a sewer tunnel would be suitable for me. The man in the dream was my acquaintance and was the same age as me. He was not unique, just an ordinary person. The person had his face, but when I noticed it, his appearance changed. Until then, I was happy, but then felt disappointed. I asked "who are you?" strongly, meaning *it's awful*. In dreams, I can frankly say what I want to say. I stamped my feet in frustration as if I were a child, or in anger. I had anticipated his transformation. Because I am a pessimist, I generally think the worst. This dream was the most impressive compared with the other dreams.

In this manner, any *meaningful* association comes from the patient, which is characteristic of image equipping "psychological infrastructure." As Jung pointed out, "The division into two was necessary in order to bring the 'one' world of the state of potentiality into reality. Reality consists of a multiplicity of things. But one is not a number; *the first number is two, and with it multiplicity and reality begins*" (*CW* 14, para. 659; my italics); the emergence of "two" is essential to psychological differentiation and development. This "two" has already been established in her dream; <above (light)/under (dark)>, <beautiful/dirty>, <uncommon/ordinary>, <joy/disappointment>, etc. These divisions and differentiation happen *within* her "anticipation." In this context, we can say that she lives in the world after the emergence of "two," in other words, in the world where the "two" forms its *inside*; the psychological infrastructure has already been established in her psyche even at the beginning of psychotherapy.

In contrast, we psychotherapists in Japan have many opportunities to realize the loss of "psychological infrastructure" in our daily practice. However, in the 1990s, in addition to Boy A and Ms. B mentioned above, I also met Ms. C, whose sandplay had such a unique image that we psychotherapists were unable to read its psychological "meaning," In other words, there was no "psychological infrastructure," as will be shown below.

Ms. C was in her late thirties, and came to see me saying that she wanted to undergo sandplay therapy, after having undergone four years of treatment with a psychoanalytical-oriented psychotherapist. Her chief complaint was "my interpersonal relationships are not good. I cannot understand myself."

In her sandplay sessions, she stood in front of the shelf lined with items and placed whatever attracted her attention each time into the tray. Figures 13.3 and 13.4 show her sandplay expressions half a year and a year and a half after our psychotherapy was started.

This course of action in sandplay was important for Ms. C to make her "subject" stand up *in every moment* (even if slightly) during the psychotherapy, despite the fact

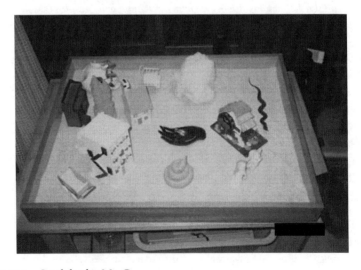

FIGURE 13.3 Sandplay by Ms. C

The loss of psychological infrastructure **235**

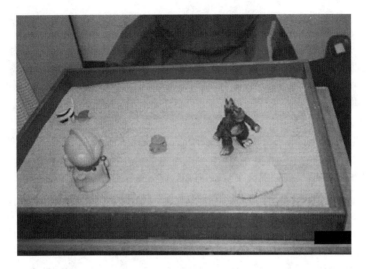

FIGURE 13.4 Sandplay 2 by Ms. C

that she was extremely lacking in initiative and subjectivity. On the other hand, it was obvious that as her therapist I experienced difficulty in reading the *meaning* and the *development* of her sandplays because her sandplays had no structure, no division, and no intention from her inside at all. At that time, I had no idea of the concept of adult autistic spectrum disorder, therefore I did not see through her state as such. Today, looking back on this case, I think that she was in this category. Within my limited clinical experience, such a kind of adult patient was almost nonexistent, except for rare cases such as Ms. C in the 1990's.

To conclude, I would like to describe one dream. This dream was reported by Mr. D, a man in his late thirties, who had a tendency toward ASD, when the psychotherapy was initiated. I met him in the 2000s:

> *I urinate in the toilet. My urine does not stop and is very yellow. From the toilet bowl, something mixed with the water and the urine pours out. At first, I try to avoid it, but the volume becomes bigger. The water gradually pools, and it becomes a square puddle and finally becomes bigger and bigger, like a pool. My daughter starts to swim in it. I also swim, but say that we should stop swimming because it is dirty. Both of us get out of the pool, but my daughter seems to want to swim some more.*

This dream properly suggests that the "psychological infrastructure" has not been built in his psyche.

The sewage disposal system cannot help his endless urination. Furthermore, from the toilet bowl, "something mixed with the water and urine pours out," eventually it becomes "*like* a pool." His daughter started to swim in this "pool that is not a pool." At first, the dreamer also swims in this pool, but finally says, "we should stop swimming because it is dirty," and both of them get out of the pool.

Today, we psychotherapists need to be involved with this kind of patient. It is difficult for them to establish a "vessel" inside themselves, and they live in a world where "oneself" extends endlessly and expands without clear "separation" between "oneself" and "urine," or between "oneself" and "daughter." In this context, it is necessary for us to stop dreaming of the "good old days" of psychotherapists that are symbolized in such sandplay and dream of anthropophobic patients as presented herein. We should begin with the fact at hand: the loss of "psychological infrastructure."

Conclusion

Analytical Psychology, which was also born in modern times, is based on the premise or "base structure" of self-relation, that is, "psychological infrastructure," in its therapeutic practice. However, this premise has already been broken down. Thus, through our own clinical experiences of psychotherapy for patients whose sandplays or dreams have no "psychological infrastructure," like adult patients with ASD (Tanaka, 2015), we need to learn that even our sense of "oneself," or construction of our "self-consciousness," may vary in the tide of the times. As discussed earlier, the "ubiquitous" self-consciousness may be the dominant manner of our current culture. Furthermore, it might be inevitable that we psychotherapists must open ourselves to such a *new* modality of "oneself" (otherwise, it might be too *old* for us to fit in), insofar as we want to be *clinical* in its truest sense.

References

Habermas, J. (1980/1996). Modernity: An unfinished project. In M. Passerin d'Entrèves and S. Benhabib (Eds.), *Habermas and the unfinished project of modernity* (pp. 38–55). Cambridge: Polity Press.

Hatanaka, C. (2013). Hattatsushogai no Jidai niokeru Jiko no Genjo to Hensen—Mixi kara Facebook he (The actual situation and change of self in the age of developmental disorder—From Mixi to Facebook). In T. Kawai and Y. Tanaka (Eds.), *Otona no Hattatsushogai no Mitate to Shinriryoho (Diagnosis and psychotherapy of adult developmental disorder)* (pp. 218–234). Osaka: Sogensha.

Hayashi, Y. et al. (1981). Taijn-fuan-ishiki Shakudo-kosei no Kokoromi (An experiment to scale consciousness of interpersonal anxiety). *Yokohama Kokuritsu Daigaku Hokenkanri-Ceter Nenpo*(1), 29–46.

Iwamiya, K. (2009). *Futsu no Ko no Shishunki ('Ordinary' boys and girls in puberty)*. Tokyo: Iwanami Shoten.

Jung, C.G. (1911). *Symbols of transformation: Collected works 5*. Princeton, NJ: Princeton University Press.

Jung, C.G. (1933). The meaning of psychology for modern man. In *Civilization in transition, collected works 10*. Princeton, NJ: Princeton University Press.

Jung, C.G. (1955). *Mysterium coniunctionis: Collected works 14*. Princeton, NJ: Princeton University Press.

Levy, P. (1995). *Qu'est-ce que le virtuel?* Paris: La Découverte (Virtual to wa nanika? – Digital jidai ni okeru Reality (M. Yoneyama, Trans.), 2006. Tokyo: Showado).

Ogawa, K. (1974). Iwayuru Taijinkyofushosha niokeru 'Nayami' no Kozo nikansuru Kenkyu (A study of the structure of 'worries' that what is called anthropophobic patients have). *Yokohama Kokuritsu Daigaku Kiyo, 14*, 1–33.
Sakamura, K. (1987). *Create TRON (TRON wo Tsukuru)*. Tokyo: Kyoritsu Shuppan Co., Ltd.
Sakamura, K. (1988). *Introduction to TRON (TRON Gairon)*. Tokyo: Kyoritsu Shuppan Co., Ltd.
Sakamura, K. (2007a). *What is ubiquitous – Information, technology, human (Ubiquitous towa nanika – Jouhou, Gijutsu, Ningen)*. Tokyo: Iwanami Shoten.
Sakamura, K. (2007b). *Japan, toward the country that can change – Innovate Nippon (Kawareru Kuni – Nihon e – Innovate Nippon)*. Tokyo: ASCII Books.
Suzuki, K. (2007). *Thought in internet society – How to live 'Ubiquitous I' (Web-shakai no Sisou – 'Henzaisuru Watashi wo dou ikiruka –)*. Tokyo: NHK Publishing, Inc.
Tanaka, Y. (2009). On dissociation as a psychological phenomenon. *Psychologia, 51*(4), 239–257.
Tanaka, Y. (2015). Do adult PDD patients dream of papier-mâché sheep? In *Copenhagen 2013–100 years on: Origins, innovations and controversies: Proceedings of the 19th Congress of the International Association for Analytical Psychology*. Einsiedeln: Daimon.
Tanaka, Y. et al. (1992). Taijikyohusho Ron – Sono Bunkenteki Kosatsu (Historical development of theories and investigations of anthropophobia). *Jochi Daigaku Shinrigaku Nenpo, 16*, 7–18.
Tanaka, Y. et al. (1994). Seinenki niokeru Tijin-fuan-ishiki no Tokusei to Kozo no Jidaiteki-suii (Longitudinal changes of characteristics and structure of anthropophobic tendency in adolescence). *Shinri-rinshogaku Kenkyu, 12*(2), 121–131.
Weiser, M. (1991). The computer for the 21st century. *Scientific American, 265*, 3, 94–104. This article can be found at the website: www.ubiq.com/hypertext/weiser/SciAmDraft3.html

14
CULTURAL COMPLEXES AND CULTURAL IDENTITY IN BRAZIL
The development of an individual identity

Walter Boechat

The interaction between the individual and the culture in which he/she lives in is a core question when discussing the development of personal identity. This chapter examines the interplay between individuals and their culture and how culture can affect the development of individual identity. As a case in point, we will analyze Brazil and the symbols and culture complexes that belong to the country's history. Individuals are always subject to the influence of cultural complexes and symbols. To understand the individual, we must also understand the culture to which he or she belongs.

Luigi Zoja, in an interview with Gustavo Barcellos, *Cadernos Junguianos*, No. 2 (2006), offers a valuable perspective on why such a focus is important:

> Latin America is the only truly new culture in history to be created by man. Asia is a continuation of the old Asia, with the addition of technology but no other radical changes. Africa has not modernized and is still unable to overcome the trauma of colonialism. Europe is a continuation of itself, and North America is a continuation of Europe dressed up in hyper-technology. Latin America alone represents a new complexity.

This statement by Zoja deserves a careful examination. In fact, Latin American culture has a unique structure. In some ways its history may resemble that of North America, which also suffered the trauma of slavery and had waves of immigration. But the multicolored social tissue of Brazil and Latin America as a whole is a very peculiar one. One fact deserves special attention: the strong racial blending in Brazil. This blending produced a population of various shades of skin color and is a special feature of Brazilian culture. We shall discuss these process in greater detail ahead, but the way indigenous population and Afro-descendants are present in Brazilian culture is a very peculiar one.

This cultural influence may be felt in language, food, religion, and cultural habits in general. The African religious rites in Bahia and other locations are a special example of this. Since the arrival of the African slaves in the 18th century, their religious traditions did not compete with Christianity; rather a unique phenomenon of *religious syncretism* occurred through which the African deities gradually became identified with the Christian saints, so the two religious faiths could coexist side by side. Another peculiarity is how in Latin America the civilization built up by European immigrants is, in some ways, still close to the values and symbols of traditional societies. Indigenous religious symbolism, mainly Shamanism, is still alive in cults in special locations. These cults may be found even near large cities.

In today's complex societies centered around modern-day communications, we can no longer consider individuals as existing in isolation, but must see each person as emerging within a context of social and cultural relationships. Individuals, nations, peoples, and cultures make up the fabric of interactions and interpenetrations, which have been accelerated by communications, trade, and the porosity among cultures. This age of openness to information, symbols, and values from a wide range of cultures, the arts, and commerce has led to a movement of reflection and a need for self-recognition and discovery: *Who are we?* What are the cultural processes at work that influence or shape the development of individual identity? Questions surrounding cultural identity are now more urgent than ever. Psychology currently has a fundamental role in this search for identity, where individuals, cultures, and social exchanges are part of a single dynamic in constant interaction.

It is becoming increasingly clear that an understanding of the Brazilian soul is essential in order to better comprehend each individual's personal characteristics. At this time in which the postmodern paradigm, the *complexity paradigm* (Morin, 1999) is emerging, different disciplines are no longer being compartmentalized and psychologists must reach out to sociologists and anthropologists in order to understand the complexity of the Brazilian soul.

Investigating Brazil's roots may be compared to looking at the specific case history of a single individual, complete with personal traumas, discoveries, transformations, and possibilities. Understanding the Brazilian soul is not an easy task due to its fundamentally multicultural nature. Our identity as a people is still incomplete, and is in fact much more of an ongoing process. What is the future of this process? Perhaps its changeable character is the cause of the fascination that the Brazilian soul holds for many both at home and abroad. While Western European culture is generally seen as fully complete, Latin America, and Brazil in particular, still maintains a character associated with potential and development, albeit with a range of serious problems.

One fascinating aspect of Brazilian social structure is the manifest crossbreeding of its population. The colonization of North America took place through families that followed the rigorous principles of Protestant Puritanism, while excluding native populations and slaves. In Brazil, however, crossbreeding was the dominant trend. Although historically we have always been far from reaching a racial democracy, Afro-descendants and Brazilian Indians constituted the majority from relatively early on, creating a largely mixed-race population.

Although most of the indigenous population was devastated soon after the country's discovery, Brazilian culture has always maintained some proximity with tribal societies and their oral traditions, customs, and myths. The African influence, which has been part of Brazil's heritage for centuries and has also been a fundamental part of our history, has contributed to the soul of Brazil and its diet, religion, customs, and language. This inheritance is fixed in Brazil's cultural unconscious and affects our behavior, dreams, and ambitions in various ways, despite the fact that Brazilians may not be aware of it.

We will now take a deeper look at Brazilian roots and at how our origins were established. This exploration is important because one of the most striking characteristics of Brazilians is their absence of memory of the historical past of the nation and their lack of contact with their own identity. This lack of cultural identity leads to a dangerous phenomenon whereby role models from North America or Europe are copied and our own unique originality is forgotten.

Europe passed through the long Middle Ages before experiencing the extraverted Renaissance, during which period the overseas discoveries of land were made. Brazil at this time, however, was home to a wide variety of indigenous ethnicities with a completely different social reality. The country's identity formed over time from the beginning of African forced immigration in the 17th century to the heavy influx of white Europeans from the 19th century, and still continues today. The Brazilian process of growth and development was entirely different from that in Europe, creating different identities and potential solutions that need to be considered in their original form. The conclusion we reach is that we often forget that Brazil is an example of the new complexity that Jungian analyst Luigi Zoja referred to earlier.

The distancing of our original identity is undoubtedly associated with Brazil's inferiority complex, previously addressed by a range of authors. Our nation's values are always seen as inferior to those of other countries, the latter being more in line with modern standards of order, organization, and planning. Brazilians, however, are disorganized, spontaneous, and without method. Does our typical hero figure Macunaíma simply lack character? Or does his improvisation represent a creativity that brings with it new vitality? With our depressive outlook, we can be extremely critical of our reality and fail to realize our creative capacity, losing out on the chance to rejuvenate ourselves through improvisation.

The old legend says that the city of Lisbon was founded by Ulysses, who ended up there after ten years fighting the battle of Troy. This is where the old name of the city *Ulyssippo*, meaning *city of Ulysses*, comes from. What Achilles did not manage over ten long years through brute force, Ulysses managed through cunning with his idea of the Trojan Horse. All descendants of the Iberian people in this mythic imagining have inherited this element of trickery and deceit. This Trickster is one of the symbolic figures of the Brazilian collective psyche, and there is a range of representations of this in our folklore, including Pedro Malasartes, Macunaíma, Exú, and the *Carioca malandro*, a typical rogue from Rio.[1] We have an overall negative view of these characters that are truly dominant in Brazil's cultural unconscious, and we do not value their creative and transformative character. The story of Zé Pelintra, one of our most famous *malandros* or rogues, illustrates this creative potential for transformation. His story begins in Lapa, the bohemian center of Rio de Janeiro, as a dangerous *malandro* who was quick in a fight. He was killed one night after being slashed with a blade in a brawl. Zé Pelintra then magically appeared in the rituals of the *Catimbó* religion of Brazil's northeast region in the guise of a powerful healer, skilled doctor, and wounded healer, much like Asclepius, the ancient Greek god of medicine. The *malandro* appears as a phantom whose character oscillates between dangerous psychopath and extremely positive. The musician Chico Buarque expressed the ambiguities of this figure brilliantly in his musical play *A Ópera do Malandro* ("The Opera of the Malandro"). Does the mutability of these stereotypes in our cultural unconscious not also say something about its enormous creative potential?

Jungian psychology and the study of the Brazilian soul

Over 60 different peoples have migrated to Brazil since the arrival of the Portuguese, and together these make up a highly complex multiracial society with unique characteristics, even compared to our Latin American brothers. The indigenous population, the original Brazilians, suffered what Leonardo Boff called a truly Latin American holocaust (of which not much is said in the history books).[2] Some of these populations remain to this day in isolated form in the Amazon region; other groups are spread all over Brazilian territory undergoing a process of adaptation to the white society in various degrees. Due to this unique, original process, reflecting on Brazilian identity presents a great challenge.

Jung's psychology may contribute in some way to this reflection on the nature of the Brazilian soul and its related issues. Some may say, "Oh, studying Brazil is a job for sociologists, historians, and economists. The psychology of the unconscious has very little to contribute to this matter." But following the state of crisis of our current paradigm, as identified by North American physicist Thomas Kuhn, the sciences can no longer be considered on an individual basis. The Brazilian soul in its vast complexity can only be examined using a range of integrated disciplines, and Analytical Psychology has a lot to say on the matter.

In his extensive theoretical works, C.G. Jung's fundamental proposal focused on humanity's collective unconscious, the archetypes and the manifestation of these in the myths of a wide variety of peoples. During his many voyages from 1920 onwards, he researched a range of peoples and tribal societies on the Ivory Coast, the Pueblo Indians of New Mexico, and the Shivaists with their temples in India. In all of these locations he sought the same goal: to observe the spontaneous appearance of the archetype in the mythological images of the local culture. This research had a highly cultural basis, although Jung seldom formulated a theoretical model for the cultural psyche of the peoples he studied, despite their being unique, each with their own individual characteristics.

According to Thomas Singer, the only instance in his work in which Jung sought to articulate culture with the collective unconscious was in his Seminar on Analytical Psychology, lecture 16 (Jung, 1925/1989, apud Singer, 2012, pp. 3, 4). In this seminar, Jung proposed a model of different planes or layers of the psyche, comparing these to geological bands.

Jung explained then the different layers of the (individual) psyche as: (1) individual, (2) family, (3) clan, (4) isolated nation, (5) wider group (Latin American, for example), (6) primate predecessors, (7) general animal predecessors, and (8) "central fire."

This was one of Jung's most important links between the personal unconscious and the collective unconscious, and in it we can see that the layers of culture and nation are well defined and associated with humanity's collective unconscious. Jung returned a few times to this theme on the relationship between the cultural unconscious and the collective unconscious as a whole. One of his few texts on this relationship was *Wotan* (1936), in which he makes use of the Teutonic god Wotan, or Odin, the god of storms, wind, prophecy, and the battlefield, in order to describe the rapid social and political changes in Germany at the time, when the National Socialists had risen to power just three years previously in 1933.

A range of Jungian researchers has sought to identify the relationship between individual and cultural identity. Joseph Henderson developed the concept of *cultural unconscious*, meaning the layer of the collective unconscious belonging to a determined people, country or culture (1990, pp. 103–113). This is one of the most important theoretical references that seek to explain the challenge of cultural identity. Vannoy-Adams (1996) discusses the *stereotypes* and *stereotypical images* of a culture and the values and references that guide behavior in a social group. Finally, Kimbles and Singer (2004) developed the concept of *cultural complex*, an important theoretical tool used to understand the social structure of cultures and their history.

The notion of cultural complex is an expansion on Jung's original concept of the *feeling-toned complex*, a center of representations in the individual's psyche cemented by emotion. The cultural complex conceptualizes nuclei of conflict in the social psyche of peoples and social groups, which are generally the result of traumas in their history and conflicts of identity. I will now discuss some cultural complexes found in Brazil, including the inferiority complex that has been described by a range of national and foreign authors, the lack of hero figures and the trauma caused by slavery. However, with the gradual development of Jungian psychology in Latin America, interest in the application of Jungian concepts to cultural phenomena in this part of the continent has increased a lot. This interest is visible at the Latin American Congresses of Analytical Psychology that happen every three years, gathering large number of Jungians from this region and abroad.

The proceedings of these congresses, besides the usual clinical papers, contain a large number of articles concerned with social identity in Latin America and cultural problems. Some Brazilian authors have published important research on culture issues from the Jungian perspective. Gambini (1999, 2016) has for some years published on the question of the aforementioned Latin American holocaust and its implications for Brazilian identity. Ramos (2004, p. 102) wrote about an important cultural complex in Brazil: corruption. Wahba (2012, p. 75) studied cultural complexes of the city of São Paulo expressed in the numerous graffiti in its walls. Feldman (2012, p. 109) worked with the Amazon Indians, developing the concept of *cultural skin* through the study of Indian skin painting, also developing some infant observation among Indians from the Amazon.

These examples are just some instances of various applications of Jungian concepts to a complex multiracial culture. In this chapter, I will use the psychological perspective of the shadow psychodynamics and repression in the individual to evaluate how these mechanisms also work at a social level. I will then approach the role of two basic culture complexes in Brazilian society: the slavery cultural complex and the lack of a hero figure in this country's history.

Jung in his writing demonstrated how the collective often appears in the individual, for this he developed his theory of the archetypes and the collective unconscious. I am following in this chapter an opposite way already trodden by Jungian authors interested in political and social issues: I will try to understand how psychological mechanisms that appear in the individual patient in the consulting room also have a social dimension. We shall describe how the repressed cultural complex needs expression as much as the individual pathological complex so one can reach a healing effect, as much in the individual patient as in the culture.

Another important psychological element in understanding Brazilian social roots is Myth. As much as Jung, Freud and many after them emphasized the importance of Myth to understand the individual, I shall here approach the mythic phantasies the Portuguese and other navigators projected onto Brazil and the New World as a whole and what these projections have to do with the identity of the country.

Brazilian identity, history, and cultural memory

In order to discover the cultural identity of a nation, it is essential that we consider its history and memory. It is no coincidence that various books on the history of Brazil have appeared recently, some are best sellers, covering a range of different angles and including one with the curious title *The Politically Incorrect Guide to Brazilian History*. Brazilian cinema, having recently undergone significant commercial expansion, has made an important contribution to the recovery of our country's past. There now exists an intense exchange of information with other cultures, and their images, issues, and possibilities are constantly on display across the full range of media, perhaps provoking this moment of reflection on our own identity. All of the above point to one unquestionable fact: Brazilian history and heritage are almost totally unknown, even to Brazilians themselves. It could be said that Brazilians *are a people without memory or references*, and are therefore currently going through an *identity crisis*. This leads us on an almost obsessive search for references outside of our own history. The exclusive and one-sided value some Brazilians give to researching European origins in order to carve out a personal identity is one notorious example.

This process reveals a significant cultural complex within our identity that the Brazilian playwright Nelson Rodrigues defined as Brazil's *complexo de vira-latas* ("mongrel complex"). When writing about corruption as a cultural complex in Brazil, the Jungian analyst Denise Ramos also explored the Brazilian population's feelings of inferiority. Everything related to the first world is seen as superior. Trapped within this perspective, Brazilians tend to overlook their own creative potential. This clear inferiority complex has also been noticed by outside observers, such as the North American Brazil specialist, Thomas Skidmore:

> Brazil has practically lost its identity [. . .] Brazilians think that only foreigners have the solution. Brazil is rich in resources [. . .] its self-esteem needs to be recovered. I have spent 40 years studying Brazil, principally this matter of optimism and pessimism [. . .] this habit of saying that Brazil is a waste of time.
> *(Skidmore, cited by Ramos, 2004, p. 107)*

How can Brazil's identity be sought in its origins? The cornerstone of our identity is geography and the nature of the tropics. *Soul and Earth*, the poetic title of one of Jung's books, names the elements that are essential when considering Brazilian identity. In this book, Jung cites an Aboriginal belief that colonizers never really manage to appropriate the land they conquer, as it is home to ancestral spirits that are reincarnated in newborn children. Jung believed this contained a great psychological truth: "the foreign land assimilates its conqueror" (Jung, 1927, §103). In the case of Brazil, its luscious natural beauty and almost unending stretches of forest, rivers, and mountains were the basis for various archetypical projections by the navigators arriving at *terra brasilis*.

The meeting of European and Native American peoples was a huge cultural event for the Western world. It is generally viewed from an ethnocentric perspective. A range of very different cultures, including the Aztecs in Mexico and the Incas in Peru, had a mythological perception of the Europeans, as was the case when Hernán Cortes was believed to be the Aztec god Quetzalcoatl, meaning "feathered serpent." However, the majority of historians do not mention the fact that the European vision of the people of the Americas was also permeated with mythological projections. Europe at the end of the 15th century was dominated by millenarian archetypal fantasies. These fantasies, including one in which the then age of renewal could lead to the discovery of new worlds, were the driving force behind the voyages that led to their discoveries. Various myths were projected by the Europeans onto the newly conquered lands, such as the mythical image of Eldorado, the mysterious Amazonas and the fabled lands of Prester John. Mythological projection therefore occurred *on both sides*. Cambray (2009) discusses impressive synchronicity phenomena that occurred during the conquest of Aztecs by Spanish navigator Hernán Cortés (see Cambray, 2009, chapter 5 for details). Zoja (2004, p. 78) also approached the cultural trauma involved in the conquest of Mexico by the Spaniards from the mythological perspective. There is a natural tendency of the psyche through which the unknown always causes some degree of mythological projection according to the circumstances. I therefore propose that we abandon the ethnocentric perspective that mythologization took place just on the part of the American native populations and that the colonizer had a concrete and objective perspective.

The huge cultural *mélange* that Brazilian culture would later become was in its beginnings, and today it is still an unfinished project. The enslavement of the Indians during colonization lasted for just the first century, this being substituted by the African slave trade from the 17th century onwards.

This first encounter between the cultures of Europe and the Americas took place at great cost, involving sacrifice, wars, and death. The mechanism by which diseases are transmitted was still completely unknown, and naturally there was no knowledge of viruses and bacteria. Louis Pasteur would only make his discoveries in the 19th century. The explanation at the time for the transmission of disease was that this was caused by malign winds. Since antiquity, winds have been personified and associated with spirits that influence people and their destinies. In Ancient Greece, the *Boreas* wind was responsible for fertility, and the *Hiperboreans*, the immortals, inhabited the region of the *Hiperborea*. This magical attribution to the winds still remains in Europe. In Switzerland, the hot wind that blows from the Ticino region in the south, known as the *Föhn*, is considered responsible for all illnesses and sudden feelings of malaise. The word *malaria* comes from *males-ares* ("bad airs"), as the disease was understood to be caused by bad winds.

The story of the Portuguese navigators commanded by Martim Afonso de Sousa that anchored off the island of Queimada Grande, on the coast of São Paulo, is very well known. There was a hot wind blowing in from the island, and the sailors set fire to the ship in order to protect themselves from the malign winds that could contaminate them with fatal illnesses (Narloch, 2013). At the beginning of the colonization of the New World, there was just a vague notion that venereal disease was transmitted through sexual contact. This led to many of these diseases being taken back to Europe and plaguing the royal courts. Just as Europe contaminated the first inhabitants of the Americas with lethal epidemics of influenza, decimating entire groups of indigenous people, diseases from the Americas were transported to the Old World by the first navigators. It seems as though this was the price that was paid as a result of these two great societies meeting (Narloch, 2013).

The search for the origins of identity: three myths on our origins

Brazilian psychologist José Oswaldo de Meira Penna, citing the work of Sérgio Buarque de Holanda, organized the myths surrounding the origins of Brazil into three main categories: the myth of paradise on earth, the myth of the green inferno, and the myth of Eldorado (Meira Penna, 1974). Each of these myths will now be addressed.

Medieval man inherited the Homeric belief from classical antiquity in the original golden age, a time of lost perfection and nostalgia for lost origins to be recovered. The medieval mentality expressed this feeling of nostalgia for a return to uterine origins. With the powerful and extraverted renaissance, this desire to return to the past was projected into the future and became concrete. For instance, the Far West started to represent paradise on earth in the here and now. The myth of paradise, previously the ideal of a past golden age, started to be projected into the future and literalized. In his book *Visão do Paraíso* ("Vision of Paradise"), Sérgio Buarque de Holanda discusses the mythological fantasies of the Portuguese navigators before the discovery of Brazil (Buarque de Holanda, 1997). The idea of a paradise on earth dominated these fantasies. One of the legends of the time about a paradise on earth located in the Far West is of particular interest: the Irish legend of *Hy Brasil*, or *Bresail*, a blissful paradise island that was believed to exist at the very edge of the Far West (Meira Penna, 1974, p. 98). This mythological legend that preceded the discovery of our country raises serious doubts about the origins of its name.

Sérgio Buarque de Holanda describes the accounts given by Christopher Columbus to the Catholic kings as permeated with visions of paradise (Buarque de Holanda, 1997, p. 14ff). He told of his desire to explore the paradisiacal lands to the north of the river Amazon as a part of paradise on earth. In order to do this, he requested that the Spanish kings provide him with three fully equipped ships. Américo Vespúcio also spoke of the innocence of the naked Indians and their perfect form as something from a kind of earthly paradise.

The fantasy of paradise on earth dominates Brazil's cultural unconscious and constellates the powerful image of the Great Mother archetype, the lady of our origins who Pero Vaz de Caminha described in his oft-cited letter on the discovery: "if it were rightly cultivated, it would yield anything" (Meira Penna, 1974, p. 100) The Great Mother, the lady of pleasures and origins, has a counterpart in the national economy: the country that continuously provides raw materials, commodities, and the fruits of its earth so that other countries can develop manufactured products. The Great Mother creates in the national character the figure of the child who doesn't want to grow up and who depends on the handouts of the protective Great Mother-State, where positions are offered as a sort of sponsorship and not according to merit. This is one of the important shadows of the Brazilian soul, the *puer aeternus* archetype who is eternally dependent on the protective Great Mother-State.

Our discoverers would never have been able to take the country as their colony without the help of their allied Indians, such were the dangers of the Green Inferno, the second myth of our origins according to Meira Penna (1974, p. 109). The density of the forest, its venomous animals and enemy tribes would have presented an almost insurmountable obstacle. This impenetrably dense vegetation has always held a mythical character. Our folklore and legends based on a mixture of both our indigenous and African roots contain one of the most striking universal symbols of the devouring mother-figure: the *serpent*. She appears in the form of *Boiúna*, an indigenous name meaning "big snake," one of the most significant myths from the Amazon region. One of our most important folklorists, Câmara Cascudo, says that unlike the serpent myths of African origin, the legend of Boiúna is not the basis of any form of worship, nor is it associated with sexual seduction. Her purpose, originating from the night and the beginning of time, is simply to destroy, threaten, and devour people, reducing them to nothing. She swims across the surface of the water, her eyes like two flares illuminating the night. While she moves, she lets out a terrifying sound (Cascudo, 1972, p. 173).

Meira Penna cites another powerful dream as the only way of overcoming the lethargy of searching for the Great Mother's breast and avoiding the Green Inferno and its dangers: the search for gold and diamonds (Meira Penna, 1974, p. 125). According to the old indigenous legend disseminated throughout Latin America, with varying versions in each country, there was an ancient nation with a capital full of palaces, some of which covered in precious gemstones and others with gold roofs. This kingdom was ruled by a man called El Dorado, as his body shined like gold as though it were a star-scattered sky. The mythical country of Eldorado was searched for by the Spanish and English on countless occasions across various countries in South America: Venezuela, Colombia, Peru, the region of the Guianas, and the Brazilian state of Roraima. The myth of Eldorado contains a strong alchemical element. But while the medieval alchemist searched for philosophical gold in his laboratory – this gold often, in fact, symbolic – the gold of Eldorado was just as concrete and immediate as the other myths associated with the formation of the New World: it needed to be found in the here and now, providing immediate enrichment and material comfort. *Aurum nostrum non est aurum vulgi*, goes the old alchemist saying. This statement could certainly have never been applied to Eldorado, where concrete material gold was situated and became the underlying cause of the ambition and death of many.

The search for gold and emeralds was the driving force of an important phenomenon in the construction of Brazil's identity, the *Bandeiras* (typical expeditions to inland Brazil). Sérgio Buarque de Holanda considered these expeditions to be one of the important roots of Brazilian identity (Buarque de Holanda, 1995, p. 101). A new character known as the *bandeirante* emerged, an ambitious and fearless type whose expeditions would cross over the line established by the Treaty of Tordesillas and shape Brazil's current borders. The expeditions of Fernão Dias Paes Leme, Raposo Tavares, and others would not have been successful in overcoming the incredible difficulties of the unexplored land of inland Brazil if it hadn't been for the help of their allied Indians. Historical accounts describe the Bandeiras as including a much greater number of Indians than of white people. In addition, there was an Indian influence present in the *bandeirantes* themselves: their tenacity and resistance revealed their indigenous blood, a result of the miscegenation that is manifest in our constitution and has been typical of Brazil's identity since the country's origins.

Crossbreeding and identity

Darcy Ribeiro discussed at length the formative role of crossbreeding in Brazil's identity (Ribeiro, 1995, pp. 106–111). The *mameluco* is a classic example of the first stage of the mixture of races in Brazil between the whites and the Indians. *Mamelucos*, born from Portuguese and indigenous parents, had incredible physical strength.

They could cover huge distances and helped the *bandeirantes* to complete their civilizing missions. The word *mameluco* originates from Arabic and was used to describe slaves who were taken by their Arab masters from those they defeated. These slaves were taken from their parents by their conquerors and then trained to manage and control other slaves. The term was used to describe Brazilian Indians by the Jesuits, who were scandalized by the primitive savagery of these men who were capable of capturing and enslaving their own people.

At a later stage, the African element was integrated into the national character after the start of the Atlantic slave trade in the 17th century. This would come to an end only in 1895, making Brazil the last country in the Western Hemisphere to eliminate slavery! This led to slavery forming a huge cultural complex within Brazil's identity. Darcy Ribeiro recalls:

> No people passing through this as the routine of their life over the centuries would come out of it without being indelibly marked. All of us Brazilians are the flesh of this flesh of those tortured blacks and Indians. All of us Brazilians are, likewise, the mad hand that tortured them. The tenderest softness and the most atrocious cruelty come together here to make us the sensitive and long-suffering people that we are and the insensitive and brutal people that we also are.
>
> *(Ribeiro, 1995, p. 120)*

Ribeiro affirms from an anthropological point of view what is also an important realization from a psychological perspective. What he describes here is the significant cultural complex of the Brazilian psyche, the scars of a period of slavery that lasted for over three centuries. Images of the sadistic overseer and the suffering slave can be viewed as an important cultural stereotype present in Brazilian collective psyche that is responsible for the extremely stratified social class system in Brazil.

The long period of slavery remains in the cultural unconscious of this country as a powerful cultural complex. Its effects on collective psyche are still present. One of its manifestations is the cruel social class system mentioned earlier. As with all cultural complexes, its action on the cultural unconscious is similar to a personal complex in the unconscious of the individual. At a personal level, dissociation of complexes is a key element in psychopathology. Also the cultural complex of slavery and exploitation of a large group of people remain disassociated in the cultural unconscious of Brazil. The disassociated element continues to act, although denied and repressed. As long as the dissociated complex remains in the unconscious, it will produce continuing pathological effects at the conscious level.

Recently efforts have been developed to deal with this disagreeable past. A museum in tribute to the slaves who died shortly after arriving at Brazil was built at a central district in Rio de Janeiro, next to the Valongo Port, the location of arrival. The museum is just at the spot where a cemetery of slaves was discovered (Boechat, 2016, p. 125). There are other movements for the recovery of repressed memories, like the quota system for blacks and mestizos at public universities and various political movements in favor of black identity. At the cultural level, as well as at a personal level, *the role of memory* is fundamental in the transformation and integration of the repressed complexes in the shadow.

Parallel to the enormous suffering and exploitation of slave labor, the continuous flow of Africans resulted in the introduction of intense cultural influences. African culture contributed its gods, food, customs, and language to the national collective psyche. Since its beginnings, Brazil has been a country that is mixed by nature. At the beginning of the 19th century, the population was predominantly mixed-race and black. Under the guise of apparent assimilation of differences and the freedom and integrated coexistence of very different groups, a sort of underlying racism was allowed to develop within the country's culture from the very outset. I will refer to this here as *cordial racism*.

I borrow this term from an excellent survey performed by the newspaper *A Folha de S. Paulo* (1998), with the title of the same name, which sought to demonstrate that racism was present in Brazilian society. Even Gilberto Freyre was mistaken when he said that we coexist in Brazil under a *racial democracy*. Today it is commonly agreed that racism exists in Brazil, although this is different from Anglo-Saxon racism as it is closely linked to social class.

The term cordial racism refers to the notion of cordiality defined by Sérgio Buarque de Holanda. In his book *Raízes do Brasil*, he writes:

> Brazil's contribution to civilization will be cordiality. We will give to the world the *cordial man*. The affability in dealing with other people, hospitality, generosity, virtues so praised by foreigners who visit us, represent, in effect, a defined feature of the Brazilian character [. . .]. It would be a mistake to suppose that these virtues mean "good manners," "civility." Above all they are legitimate expressions of extremely rich and overflowing basic emotions.
> (Holanda, 1936/1999, p. 146ff., my translation.)

The author later states that this polite attitude is an attempt to disguise any truly spontaneous manifestations that may appear in the behavior of the cordial person. Spontaneity here is converted into a formula. Politeness works as a way of defending oneself from society, and as a disguise that allows people to keep their feelings and emotions intact (Holanda, 1936/1999, p. 147, my translation).

Buarque de Holanda's description of the cordial man in his 1936 book is of great importance to psychology. In his text on the sociology and history of Brazil, he provides a vivid description of how the archetype of the Brazilian persona works as a system of defense, a true cultural stereotype. Now we have a better understanding of the term cordial racism. Aware of the implications and contrasts that Buarque de Holanda indicated with his use of the word cordial, we get a better idea of how cordiality can be used as a disguise for violence, rejection, hatred, attitudes of superiority, and principally a lack of openness toward equal opportunities, better salaries, and the right to a university education for blacks, mixed-race, and indigenous individuals.

This question of apparent integration and concealed exclusion has been present in Brazil since the abolition of slavery. The half million slaves liberated in 1888 entered a complex multiracial system in which the archetype of the persona acquired one particular feature that I will call here *racial persona*. This became extremely important in the social placement of each individual.

It is important to remember here that Brazil was not a biracial society from the beginning like the United States or South Africa. There was intensive miscegenation from the beginning of the colonial era between the Portuguese and the Indians, and later with the Africans. There was always a large majority of the population with Indian or African blood. In terms of the resulting phenotypes, this multiracial society included every possible degree of color from white European to black African, with the later introduction of an Asian influence. Skin color, hair texture and other characteristics, or the *racial persona*, would go on to help individuals to climb the social ladder.

Mixed-race people have a great deal of mobility on the social scale as a result of their racial persona, and a surprising phenomenon occurs with this change in social class: the person's own *perception of the color of their skin* changes as they change their social status. It is as if a rise in the social scale leads to the person's skin miraculously lightening. A clear example of this mixing of social class and skin color can be seen in an account by Darcy Ribeiro (1995, p. 225), demonstrating that this attitude goes back to colonial times. It describes how Henry Koster, an Englishman traveling in Brazil in the 19th century, was surprised when he saw a mixed-race man dressed in a chief captain's uniform – not a common sight at the time. He was offered the following explanation: "Yes, he is mixed-race, but now as Chief Captain he can only be white."

Prejudice against skin color in the past in Brazil included the powerful fantasy known as the whitening of the race. According to Thomas Skidmore (1974/1989), the encouragement of white European immigration at the end of the 19th century was not just a decision based on economics. The country's intellectual elite was heavily influenced by racist ideas coming from Europe at the time and actually wanted to whiten the race. This theory maintained that through repeated generations of mixing with white genes, which were dominant and stronger than African or indigenous genes, a generation of whites would be produced. The incredible part of this racist theory is that it proposed to achieve ethnic purity in Brazil through racial mixing, not through exclusion! This was unique to Brazil and has never been seen anywhere else. The first ethnologist to defend race whitening was João Batista de Lacerda during the First Universal Races Congress in London in 1911 (see Skidmore, 1974/1989, p. 81ff.).

The alchemical idea of *whitening of the race* was combatted by another movement that started in Brazil in the 1930s: cultural anthropology and cultural syncretism led by Gilberto Freyre and others. Freyre was a strong critic of the race whitening theory and argued that environment and culture were the main agents forming the country's identity, with race being an etiological factor of lesser importance. From

1933 on, with the rise of Nazi fascism in Europe and its fanatical emphasis on racial purity, Freyre's approach was clearly the most appropriate. Old ideas about race disappeared in Brazil and racist scientific theories became anachronistic in South America. However, the idea that non-white ethnic groups were inferior remained, exemplified by the idea that Blacks and Indians could only achieve social success though sport or music, not through academic professions. Thankfully these ideas remain among just a few people.

The cultural complex in the consulting room

Clinical practice is the territory where the complexes are constellated and confronted. The psychoanalyst cannot avoid the fact that he treats patients in a given culture in a given place. In my practice in Rio de Janeiro I came across the emergence of the cordial racism that played an important role in the development of some clinical cases. I can remember well one of this cases, the patient I shall name Carlos, a Catholic priest, black, 42 years old. Various reasons led him to search for analysis; the main reason, at a conscious level, was his guilt feelings for the death of a brother. As he related to me, once he was driving a car accompanied by his brother after consuming alcohol. They suffered a serious accident and the brother died. He never forgave himself for that. Although this complaint occupied a lot of time in the beginning of the analysis, other shadow contents gradually became important in our discussions. Among these, the topic of "race" and persecution gained importance. He had a deep interest in his Africans roots, assisting in African religious rituals and developing research on interreligious studies. He was particularly interested in religious syncretism, so typical of Brazil, between Catholicism and *Candomblé*, a religion of African origin. His superiors in church strongly opposed these studies. When he applied to become a professor at a well-known Catholic University in town, he was stopped by the board of directors, who, as he said, had connections with the Church. The ecclesiastic authorities, although showing signs of friendship and admiration toward Carlos, were opposed, in a secret way and with *cordiality*, to his admission to the University. He became depressed and angry seeing this resistance to his approach to African religion signs of racism. At this time he had a very interesting dream:

> *Carlos is in a large square, where there is a kind of meeting or festival with many people, most of them Black. It seems to be a festival with religious undertones of Black religion. Then he sees an altar, typical of an African religion, with the statue of a god. (It is not clear for him which god is present at the dream). Suddenly he sees a powerful and numinous tree at the center of the square, and he is filled with awe. He awakes with feelings of peace and happiness.*

Carlos associated this tree with the representation of the goddess *Iroko*, a deity connected to a powerful tree. This was the first tree to grow, a tree through which all the *Orishás* (gods in the *Candomblé* African religion) descended to earth. Iroko represents ancestry. I told Carlos the dream was showing that he needed to be connected to his deepest values and symbols so to resist any kind of pressure from his superiors or from society in general. The dream happens in a kind of mandalic square, a festival with black people. This also demonstrates a need to be in contact with his own group within a social context. His emotions at the end of the dream are quite reassuringly positive. This positive effect of the dream showed up in his life. In the weeks that followed the dream, Carlos fought courageously, writing his superiors a manifesto defending his right to study and write about African deities. He made a strong claim that this would not contradict the practice of celebrating the Catholic Mass and conducting Catholic rituals.

We must emphasize an important feature of the central symbol of this dream, and probably the central symbol for the whole clinical case. The tree *Iroko* is a living symbol in the cultural unconscious of Brazil. Its symbolism is very similar to other pagan trees representing the *axis mundi*, roots, origins, identity, soul of the tribe, like Yggdrasil and many others. But in this case it pertains to a living mythology of an oppressed social group and coming from the cultural unconscious, it brings meaning to the dreamer.

The appearance of myths in the search for identity

An overview of Brazil's history since its discovery clearly demonstrates that the pre-colonial era, miscegenation, the huge trauma left behind by slavery and race whitening theory have all left their mark on the country's cultural unconscious and powerful images in our traditions, influencing our psyche and behavior. The scars left by our history on our character include a striking feeling of inferiority and an obsessive search for values in European and North American culture (Ramos, 2004).

This lack of cultural identity is a reflection of the lack of role models and references in Brazilian history. The myth of the hero is a fundamental reference in the organization of the individual and collective conscience. If the myth of the hero is present during the organization of a child's psyche, this is also a basic reference for the cultural identity of the whole population. In Brazilian culture, we can observe a significant absence of role models that could be used in the organization of the collective consciousness. With the exception of sports and music, there is a huge vacuum in terms of role models. Perhaps this is why recent experiences at the 2014 World Cup hosted in Brazil were so painful for the collective consciousness: an important model of heroism and success, the hero soccer player, was unexpectedly knocked to the ground in a way that had never before been imagined.[3]

One of the most important hero figures in Brazilian history emerged during the colonial era in Vila Rica, the capital at the time. This was a famous sculptor, who is an important example of genius and resilience, called Antonio Francisco Lisboa and nicknamed Aleijadinho. The work attributed to him and his life story has always been the focus of controversy. Philosopher and historian Guiomar de Grammont recently published some research on the much-discussed life of Aleijadinho, backing up the thesis that the story of Antonio Francisco Lisboa is a myth. Grammont actually went further than previous supporters of this theory, showing links between the myth of Aleijadinho and typical figures found in historical tales (Grammont, 2004). The figure of the repulsive monster, worthy of pity but also creative and searching for redemption, can be seen in various fairy tales such as "Beauty and the Beast," in which the beast has to be rescued and owns treasures in a magic castle. Another example of this model is the novella written in 1818 by the English author Mary Shelley, *Frankenstein, or The Modern Prometheus*. This story describes the creation of an artificial monstrous creature by the young medic Viktor Frankenstein. Ethical issues and moral dilemmas are important conflicts for this half man/half machine, and the book discusses the matter of beauty derived from monstrosity. A third example of the similarity between monstrosity and beauty mentioned by Grammont is the memorable figure of Quasimodo, the hunchbacked bell keeper of Notre Dame in the book by Victor Hugo, *The Hunchback of Notre-Dame*. The hunchback is ugly, reclusive, deformed and obsessed by his genuine love for the gypsy girl Esmeralda (Grammont, 2004).

These models that spontaneously appeared in literature follow genuine archetypal patterns. Even in Ancient Greece we can see an association between physical deformity and beauty in the figure of the god Hephaestus, the lame god of crafts and *techne* (from the Greek "do as nature does"). Hephaestus's monstrosity came from when his parents Zeus and Hera threw him from Olympus into the ocean. This fall left him lame, and yet he married Aphrodite. Could it be argued that the moving legend of Aleijadinho is based on a Greek archetypal figure? Where is the line between the historical Antonio Francisco Lisboa and the mythical Aleijadinho who wandered the alleyways of Vila Rica, Mariana, São João del Rey, and the other cities of the Brazilian gold rush?

At the time of the gold rush, there was a legend about an artisan and sculptor who decorated baroque churches and worked for the religious brotherhoods, and who stood out for his physical deformity. His name was again Antonio Francisco Lisboa, and one of his hands had been paralyzed by an undetermined illness. In 1858, lawyer and director of teaching in Ouro Preto, Rodrigo Ferreira Bretas, became captivated by this mysterious figure and decided to write his biography. He found very little concrete information other than the name Antonio Francisco Lisboa, which was associated with a baroque artisan who worked decorating the churches of Minas Gerais and who lived around 50 years previously. There were vague references to his disability, although these were not documented. However, Bretas went ahead and wrote a biography rich in detail. The sculptor was supposed to have suffered from a serious illness, probably tuberculosis or leprosy, which had deformed his hands and left him with a repulsive appearance. Despite everything, in a remarkable example of overcoming the odds with creativity, the artist managed to produce beautifully moving sculptures. Bretas described the terrible deformities that Antonio Lisboa suffered as a result of his illness. He also gave him the name

Aleijadinho, which cannot be traced in the historical records (Grammont, apud Narloch, 2013).

As Grammont realized, the similarities between the fascinating figure of Aleijadinho and the characters of famous works such as Quasimodo are significant. The lame god Hephaestus has many similarities to Aleijadinho. We can safely say that this is a mythical character in the Brazilian cultural unconscious, a mythological legend that emerged from the cultural unconscious. These legends appear because culture needs their images as a reference. It is interesting that a legend could be produced as a result of the conscious effort of a lawyer 50 years after the life of Antonio Lisboa. Based on rumors about the disability of this artisan, Bretas created a mythological figure who is referred to in many books on the history of Brazil and in school curricula. Like any myth, Aleijadinho has archetypal roots and interesting similarities with the artisan god Hephaestus and literary characters. As an authentic creative hero who is genuinely national, it was inevitable that Aleijadinho be mixed-race. A mythical genealogy was created for him, as he was supposed to be the son of a Portuguese architect, Manuel Francisco Lisboa, and his African slave. These mixed origins would later impress some artists from the modernist movement, who saw Aleijadinho as a genius and a representative of our genuinely national creativity.

Which of the sculptures attributed to Aleijadinho are actually his? Today we know that many originate from the atelier of Antonio Francisco Lisboa but were created by other masters. Most of them are also of rather dubious quality (Grammont, cited by Narloch, 2013). But is the historical existence of Aleijadinho really so important? Are not other heroes always to a certain extent fabricated or a product of our own individual and collective psychological needs? As Jung once said in one of his most important statements, "the psyche creates realities every day" (Jung, 1921/1974, §78).

Notes

1 One of the worse aspects of the Brazilian trickster phenomenon is corruption, which has appeared widely in the press in recent years. Some Jungians have dealt with this phenomenon. See, for example, Ramos (2004, p. 102).
2 Leonardo Boff, in conversation with Lugi Zoja, and a group of Jungians, Rio de Janeiro, March, 2012.
3 In the 2014 World Cup, the German team beat Brazil easily in the semifinals.

References

Boechat, W. (2016). Racism, an unwelcome guest in Brazilian culture identity. In E. Kiehl, M. Saban and A. Samuels (Eds.), *Analysis and activism: Social and political contributions of Jungian psychology*. London: Routledge.
Buarque De Holanda, S. (1936/1999). *Raízes do Brasil*. Sao Paulo: Companhia das Letras.
Buarque De Holanda, S. (1997). *Visão do Paraíso*. São Paulo: Brasiliense.
Cambray, J. (2009). *Synchronicity: Nature & psyche in an interconnected universe*. Texas: Texas A&M University Press [Brazilian edition (2013) consulted: *Sincronicidade: Natureza e Psique num Universo Interconectado*. Petrópolis: Vozes. Translation by Caio Liudvik from the original edition of Texas A&M University Press.]

Cascudo, Luis da C. (1972). *Dicionário do Folclore Brasileiro*. São Paulo: Ediouro.
Feldman, B. (2012). The cultural skin of Latin America. In *Listening to Latin America: Exploring cultural complexes in Brazil, Chile, Colombia, Mexico, Uruguay and Venezuela*. New Orleans, LA: Spring Journal Books.
Folha de s. Paulo/ datafolha. (1998). *Racismo Cordial* (2ª ed.). Sao Paulo: Ática.
Gambini, R. (2016). Our future lies hidden in our roots. In E. Kiehl, M. Saban and A. Samuels (Eds.), *Analysis and activism: Social and political contributions of Jungian psychology*. London: Routledge.
Gambini, R., & Dias, L. (1999). *Outros 500: Uma Conversa sobre a Alma Brasileira*. São Paulo: Editora do Senac.
Grammont, G. de (2004). *Aleijadinho e o Aeroplano*. Sao Paulo: Civilização Brasileira.
Henderson, J. (1990). The cultural unconscious. In *Shadow and self*. Selected Papers in Analytical Psychology. Wilmette, IL: Chiron Publications.
Jung, C.G. (1921/1974). *Psychological types: Collected works: Volume VI*. Princeton: Princeton University Press.
Jung, C.G. (1925/1989). *Analytical psychology: Notes on seminar given in 1925*. Amazon: Kindle e-books.
Jung, C.G. (1927/1971). *Soul and earth: Collected works: Volume X*. Princeton: Princeton University Press.
Jung, C.G. (1936/1971). *Wotan: Collected works: Volume X*. Princeton: Princeton University Press.
Meira Penna, J.O. (1974). *Em berço Esplêndido: Ensaios de Psicologia Coletiva Brasileira*. Rio de Janeiro: José Olímpio.
Morin, E. (1999). Por uma reforma do pensamento. In Pena-Vega, A. e Pinheiro do Nascimento (org.), *O pensar complexo: Edgar Morin e a crise da modernidade*. Rio de Janeiro: Garamond.
Narloch, L. (2013). *O Livro Politicamente incorreto da História do Brasil*. Amazon: Kindle e-Books.
Ramos, D. (2004). Corruption: A cultural complex in Brazil? In T. Singer and S. Kimbles (Eds.), *The cultural complex: Contemporary Jungian perspectives on psyche and society*. New York: Brunner-Routledge.
Ribeiro, D. (1995). *O Povo Brasileiro*. Sao Paulo: Companhia das Letras.
Singer, T. (2012). Introduction. In *Listening to Latin America*. New Orleans: Spring Books.
Singer, T., and Kimbles, S. (Ed.). (2004). *The cultural complex: Contemporary Jungian perspectives on psyche and society*. New York: Routledge.
Skidmore, T. (1989). *Preto no Branco* (2ª ed.). Rio de Janeiro: Paz e Terra.
Vannoy-Adams, M. (1996). *The multicultural imagination: 'Race, colour and the unconscious'*. London: Routledge.
Wahba, L. L. (2012). São Paulo and the cultural complexes of the city: Seeing through graffiti. In *Listening to Latin America: Exploring cultural complexes in Brazil, Chile, Colombia, Mexico, Uruguay and Venezuela*. New Orleans: Spring Books.
Zoja, L. (2004). Trauma and abuse: The development of a cultural complex in the history of Latin America. In T. Singer and S. Kimbles (Eds.), *The cultural complex: Contemporary Jungian perspectives on psyche and society*. New York: Brunner-Routledge.
Zoja, L. (2006) A Psique da América Latina. [The Psyche of Latin America] Zoja interviewed by Gustavo Barcellos. In *Cadernos Junguianos, Journal from de Jungian Association of Brazil*, No. 2, 2006, 48–60.

PART VII
A glance towards the future

15
GOING FORWARD

Joseph Cambray

The present volume has hopefully provided the researcher interested in Analytical Psychology with a survey of current areas of research in a number of key domains. This was not intended to be an exhaustive review but a selection of some of the more salient topics being pursued nowadays by analysts and scholars of the subject. It is also complemented by a second volume on empirical research.

In this final chapter, I will not summarize the findings presented by the various authors here, nor attempt to draw conclusions directly from their work. Rather, I will look for possible trajectories from these offerings into imagings about potential areas of study going forward. This can be facilitated by considering recent developments in the study of innovation, especially how societies evolve creative projects. In particular this can be examined in the spirit of advancing a research agenda based on the notion of the "adjacent possible" as first articulated by Stuart Kauffman, one of the key contributors from the Santa Fe Institute with its groundbreaking work on complexity studies[1] (Kauffman, 2016). As research tends to best answer well-articulated questions, meaningful conclusions often raise even more fruitful areas for future exploration. The choices made in pursuing lines of inquiry then shape not only the next round of discoveries but also the possibilities which can be attended to or which slip into the background. Here we will attempt a few tentative suggestions for nearby possible topics.

History and methods

Research methods have been evolving throughout the history of discovery and have been increasingly codified with the rise of the sciences. As these have been extended from studies of the natural world to the realms of social and cultural phenomena, methods have necessarily complexified. Quantitative studies have been complimented by qualitative approaches, including narrative analysis which has been especially germane to clinical and analytic studies. Often combining approaches, in various ways, for example, sequentially or in parallel, has led to increasingly rich mixed methods forms of research. Depth psychological ideas such as the "wounded researcher" (Romanyshyn, 2007) have brought additional value to subjective, countertransferential relations to one's "subject" as integral to research itself. Attending to the psychoactive dimensions to research, how we are "called" by a subject, the deeper layers of our being that are mobilized by a specific topic help bridge the personal-subjective factors with the more objective dimensions of our studies.

Depth psychological research necessarily engages far more than the conscious mind, or ego functions of the researcher. Inevitably research topics evoke a parallel to the clinical phenomena of countertransference and we are drawn to those materials that in some ways (often neither obvious nor explicit on the surface) captivate us with compelling emotional force. The strength of these desires tends to provide clues to what is being activated in our psyches by the subjects of research – they seem to choose us as much as we choose them.

As information technology's sophistication continues to develop, we can anticipate new ways to envision and interact with "data"; perhaps even the nature of data itself will be transformed. Internal experience and virtual simulations have already begun to intersect and this will likely expand exponentially. The value of this growth will not only be found in the entertainment industry, its most obvious home as already witnessed by augmented and mixed realities layered on our daily, perceptual reality as emerging forms of entertainment, but also in education. For example, electronic information technologies in the experiential delivery of knowledge, and in our interactions and relationship with one another as well as with the world. Similarly, huge, searchable databases of dreams, gathered from dreamers around the world, will allow large-scale thematic analyses. This will help us articulate collective phenomena from the multiplicity of data points, perhaps yielding greater substantive evidence to support anecdotal reports of the non-local dimensions of the psyche and supraordinate aspects of its functioning.

Examining the details of correspondences, as in Chapter 2, helps us not only to see through the formal published presentations of ideas, getting to their origins and evolution within a set of exchanges, but can also deconstruct time. Recognizing more of the adjacent possibilities that lurked at the margin of the correspondences can retrospectively allow appreciation of the depth of intuitive insights that were not given full substance, perhaps due to lack of adequate resources to flesh them out. At the same time other ideas that perhaps should have withered but were erroneously pursued can be tracked as part of any genuine discovery process. In this way we can cultivate a lens for our own intuitive gropings and perhaps refine our felt sense of when and what to pursue – how to mine our intuitions for the truths they may reveal and to recognize the influences that bear upon us, consciously or unconsciously, in formulating our thought.

More broadly, can historical documents help us to revision our approaches and the questions we pursue? Certainly the history of research is filled with examples of new ideas, often at the onset of a paradigm shift, which are subjected to ridicule.

Hence, a naïve sense of scorn should alert us to the possibilities of unconscious enactment. Where we are inhibited for creative explorations by our "blind" spots (where unconscious emotional constraints do not allow us to see what is in front of us), "dumb" spots (where we lack adequate knowledge to make adequate judgments), and "hard" spots (where our current theories constrain our imaginations; see McLaughlin, 1998). Similarly, history teaches us to attune to the conditions which facilitate the emergence of the truly innovative. Often a syncretic flux contributes to the melding of ideas into substantial innovations; recognizing the conditions from historical analysis which have fostered this can lead us individually and collectively to important creative breakthroughs.

Archetype, culture, and consciousness

As the large, proto-theoretical conceptions of traditional Jungian psychology are critically examined and refined, a richer, more nuanced view of the psyche is emerging. At least three layers are available for further articulation: social and cultural realms as emergent from individual and their interactions; the neuroscientific, now no longer restricted to examining the internal workings of the individual through social and anthropological neuroscientific studies; and the ecological as descriptive of interactive and relational fields comprised of multiple organisms contributing to larger systems capable of displaying adaptive intelligence. These lines of inquiry offer pathways to hone and even transform our understanding of symbolism, and in the process helping us to more fully appreciate indigenous traditions with their profound local knowledge.

The recent renewed interest in altered states of consciousness from a research perspective provides valuable opportunities for analytical psychologists who have been examining unconscious dynamics stemming from various states such as dreams, active imagination, synchronistic events, and transference/countertransference field phenomena. Recent employment of psychoactive substances inducing altered states for healing purposes, for example ketamine for the treatment of depression which has otherwise proved refractory (Matthews & Zarate, 2016), is just one additional area. In general, the transformative potential of altered states has been known for millennia but has remained until recently at the periphery of mainstream scientific research.

As tools and skills develop for exploring "anomalous" states of consciousness, the potential for employment in clinical work and social research will expand. This will require thorough re-examination of theoretical models of mind, culture, and nature, and will challenge the binary logic of subjective versus objective descriptions as all too limiting. Likewise, synchronistic phenomena, linking psyche and world, cannot be handled within binary constructions. Neither can the remarkable instances of artistic renderings of complex phenomena well in advance of scientific comprehension of those phenomena (Cambray, 2016). We can look forward to more art-based research grounded in complexity studies to open up the realm of the "excluded middle" from Aristotelean logic under which we still tend to labor.

Paradigm shifts

Complexity studies are bringing about a paradigm shift from reductive toward holistic understandings of the world. Both viewpoints have contributions to make, but by including and embracing complexity we are challenged to revision many aspects of our lives. Thus in cross-cultural studies the value of bidirectionality of influence is increasingly revealed, altering the learning environment and the interactive field between peoples from different groups. This has important clinical implications as well: traditional power differentials need careful scrutiny to avoid abuse.

Theoretical frames require careful appreciation of the factors operating at their onset. As one example, consider the colonial formulations of the mind of "primitive" people in describing "archaic" mental states associated with early mental life. The decolonializing of the depth psychologies can bring renewal and appreciation for what these approaches were, returning to Western civilization at the end of the 19th and early 20th centuries without embracing the ethnocentric hierarchy of cultural value implicitly being imposed.

Appreciation of the role of somatic contributions to expressions of consciousness, even if largely remaining unknown to the individual, is also underscoring the complexities involved in the formation of mind for organisms in environments.

Thus we can look at the microbiome (the sum of all of the organisms, viral, bacterial, multicellular, which live in and on the human body) and its impact on mental functioning, including moods, appetites, and cognition. We can also look at mind as ecological emergent from interactions with caregivers and the world. Mind is not generated in a vacuum but gradually forms and comes into being from internal pressures meeting a receptive metabolizing environment which gives articulate meaning to the internal urges and reactions. Our minds are thus formed in the interactive field of engagement with caretakers who are in turn impacted by their engagements with those in their care. Mind emerges in a bidirectional field of interactions embedded within natural and cultural worlds. We can also turn to the study of microaggressions, those slights of power and privilege that largely operate outside of our awareness yet impact our felt sense of self to the point of engendering dysphoric moods and even outright illnesses in the recipients. These pathways for communication and the extent of impact are yet to be fully explicated.

The advent of epigenetics has provided a somatic base for recognizing multigenerational trauma. These injuries have been tracked with data verifying their transmission biologically from parents to children and even to grandchildren (Carey, 2012). While neo-Lamarckian mechanisms have been demonstrated and the results have been verified, the modifications are not of the genetic materials (DNA/RNA) themselves, but of the biochemicals within which they are encased. These findings hold the potential for a reassessment of archetypal theory in terms of epigenetic mechanisms. Research linking the epigenetic effects with states of consciousness have not yet been undertaken, though they remain enticing possibilities.

The fluid aspects of identity emerging from revisioning of bodies, genders, cultures, power dynamics, and social justice provide rich, fertile ground for a liberating expansion of seemingly sedentary identities. The psyche and the self (perhaps a necessary illusion) will continue to undergo transformations in the field of these revelations and will likely lead not only to increased valuing of diversity (internally as well as with others and the world) but also to recognition of its necessity for ecological survival.

The tenets of analytic psychology will most likely undergo a number of significant changes in the face of the types of explorations currently underway. Openness to this will ensure viability and allow the radical exploratory impulses that spawned the depth psychologies to find rebirth in the 21st century. This volume is hopefully a small step in that direction.

Note

1 Applying quantum logic, in a manner similar to that proposed by Atmanspacher in the Pauli/Jung hypothesis (mentioned in our companion book), Kauffman has sought to bring attention to the pathways of the discovery process. He's coined the term the adjacent possible in a quantum based reappraisal of the realm of possibles in relationship to actuals. This has led him to propose a new dualism that emerges from possibles becoming actuals through decoherence without total collapse, retaining the realm of possibles, so that they remain as *ontologically real*. Furthermore because the loss of (wave function) phase information in decoherence is acausal, these two realms, the actuals and the possibles are acausally related. This opens new ways to consider the significance of synchronicity as an important element in a wide variety of discovery processes. While this cannot be explored in detail here future publications will articulate the value of this approach for Analytical Psychology.

References

Cambray, J. (2016). Intuizione artistica e immaginazione psicoide: un ponte tra realta simboliche e ecologiche. *Enkelados, 4*, 117–133.

Carey, N. (2012). *The Epigenetics revolution: How modern biology is rewriting our understanding of genetics, disease, and inheritance*. New York: Columbia University Press.

Kauffman, S. A. (2016). *Humanity in a creative universe*. New York: Oxford University Press.

Mathew, S. J., & Zarate Jr., C.A. (Eds.). (2016). *Ketamine for treatment-resistant depression: The first decade of progress*. Cham, Switzerland: Adis, Springer International Publishing.

McLaughlin, J. T. (1998). Clinical and theoretical aspects of enactment. In S.J. Ellman and M. Moskowitz (Eds.), *Enactment: Toward a new approach to the therapeutic relationship*. Northvale, NJ: Jason Aronson, Inc.

Romanyshyn, R. (2007). *The wounded researcher: Research with soul in mind*. New Orleans, LA: Spring Journal Books.

INDEX

Note: Page numbers in *italics* indicate figures on the corresponding page.

adjacent possible 259
alchemy 62, 95–96, 163–164
altered states of consciousness 261
Analytical Psychology 4–6; *see also* depth psychology
Answer to Job (Jung) 38
anthropophobia 228–236, *232–233, 234–235*
antinomial stance 21, 30
a priori 52–53
Archetypal Psychology 6
archetypal theory 9, 50–54
archetypes: as categories of imagination 174, 177–178; as complex systems 57–62, *61*; emergence model of 183–186, 189–190; Great Mother 246; hero figures 252–253; models of 53; synchronicity and 136–137; teleology and 62–63
authoritarian regimes and cultural trauma 211–212, 218
authority, relationships with 216–220
autistic spectrum disorder 207, 235–236
auto-organization and strange attractors 56–57
awareness 122–123
axis mundi 31–32

"The Baldwin Effect" 183
bandeirante figure 247
bandeiras 247
Bardo Thödol see *The Tibetan Book of the Dead*

bifurcation graphs 186–188, *187*
biological level of ecological networks 161–162
The Black Book (Jung) 202
Bleuler, Eugen 50, 90
Bocchi students 230
The Book of the Dead see *The Tibetan Book of the Dead*
boundaries in complex systems 55–56
Brazil: culture of 239–240; identity, history, and cultural memory in 243–245; inferiority complex of 240, 244; myths in search for identity in 252–254; myths of origins of 245–247; racial blending in 238, 239–240, 247–251; study of soul of 241–243; Trickster figure in 240–241
Buddhism *see* Hua-Yen School of Buddhism
Buddhist meditation 121

case analysis 217
C. G. Jung Institute 37, 97
childhood psychosis 59
Chönyid Bardo 174
Christian myth, Jung loss of 197–198
cobweb plots *188*
coffee plant, wild 167–168
collective psyche and cultural complexes 70–71
collective unconscious 9, 96, 241–243; *see also* archetypes; psyche

compensation 137
complex adaptive systems (CAS) 158, 168
complexes 51, 90; *see also* cultural complexes
complexity paradigm 239
complexity studies and paradigm shifts 262–263
complex systems: archetypes as 57–62, *61*; overview 158–159; in physics 54–56; psyche as 6, 10–12, 54, 56–58, 157; scaling phenomena in structure and behavior of 183, 185; *see also* networks in Jungian psychology
conjunctio 206–207
conscious intention 114
consciousness: altered states of 261; defined 20–21; homunculus and 103–104; meditation as intentional change of 112, 116; modern 223–225, 228
conscious-unconscious dialectic 96–97
contrasexual within 102–103
cordial racism in Brazil 249, 251
correspondences of Jung: with Kirsch 39–42; with Neumann 42–43; overview 35, 44–45; with Pauli 36–37; with Schmid-Guisan 43–44; with White 37–39
corruption, as cultural complex in Brazil 244
creationism 62, 63, 70
cross-cultural research 12–14
cultural anthropology and cultural syncretism in Brazil 250–251
cultural complexes: in Brazil 242–243, 248–249; in Brazilian consulting rooms 251–252; characteristics of 72–74; courses of action with 80; overview 9, 69, 70–71, 242; research on 71–72, 74–80; as universal and specific 75
cultural identity of Brazil 239–240, 243–245, 252–254
cultural significance of synchronicity 145–147, 149–150
cultural trauma 211–212, 218
cultural unconscious 71, 96, 242, 252
culture, role of, on individual development 13–14

daimon 25–26
Darwin, Charles 54, 62, 70, 87–88
death: desire for 52; of God 199, 201; Grail myth and 30; Kalachakra mandala and 190; transition following 173–174; *see also The Book of the Dead*
de-integration 189–190

depth psychology: Bachelard and 163; emotion in 91, 107; overview 4–7; postmodernism and 20–21; psyche and 19; subjectivity in research and 26–27
Descartes, René 87
discourse and social production of knowledge 25–26
disenchantment 149
dissociation virus 225
dissociative model of psyche 189–190
drawings during psychotherapy 216
"Dream Symbolism in the Individuation Process" (Jung) 36–37
dual-aspect monism: alchemy and 95; emotion and 106; overview 8; synchronicity and 144–145, 149; Zen and 117

East Asian philosophy 202–204
ecological networks: expansion of symbolic approaches and 165–168; rhizomatic 160–165
ecology: ecological crisis and 28; Haeckel and 164
Eidgenossische Technische Hochschule (ETH) 36, 92
Einstein, Albert 92
Eldorado, myth of Brazil as 247
emergence: *conjunctio* and 206; idea of 54; *a priori* state and 63; relation of synchronicity to 143–144; simultaneous and interdependent 207–208
emergence model of archetypes 183–186, 189–190
emergent properties of complex systems 158–159
emotion: in consulting rooms 96–98; cultural complexes and 74; current consensus on 106–108; in history 86–87; history of experience of 9–10; homunculi and 103–104; as image in psyche and neuroscience 98–100; Jung and 90–91, 93–94, 105, 108; multiple domains of experience of 91–93; overview 85–86; psycho-psychic energy and 100–101; scientific inquiry on 87–88, 105–106; theories of 89–90; vectors in studies of 101–103
Empedocles 163–164
emptiness in Hua-Yen School of Buddhism 204–206
epistemology of Jung *61*
etymology 23–24, 29
Evans-Wentz, W. Y. 172–173
extraversion 44

feeling-toned complexes 242
field research 11
fractal geometry 178, 180–181, 188–190
free association 94
Freud, Sigmund: complex thought and 57; Jung and 35, 90, 92; libido concept, incest taboo, and 50–51, 52; repression and 224
Freudian reading of *The Book of the Dead* 174
Freud–Jung letters 35

Galton, Francis 50
gender and emotion 102–103
Gesammelte Werke (Jung) 61
Gestalt Psychology 95
Gnosticism 202, 203
God, death and rebirth of 199, 201
Goering, Matthius 40
Grail myth 30
Great Mother archetype 246
Green Inferno myth of Brazil 246–247

Habermas, Jürgen 223–224
Haeckel, Ernst, illustrations of 178, *180, 181, 182*
healing moments, themes of 214–215
hermeneutic circle (personal equation) 114–116
hero figure myth in Brazil 252–254
Hestian focus 31
Hillman, James 6, 24, 27–29, 90, 201
historical documents, examination of 8, 260–261; *see also* correspondences of Jung
history, emotion in 86–87
history and methods of research 259–261
homunculi 103–104
hope, awakening and experience of 215
Hua-Yen School of Buddhism: Central Asian origins of 203; emptiness and transcendence in 204–206; individuation in 208–209; interdependence and 207–208; interiority in 207; overview 12, 202; understanding of transcendence in 197; union in 206–207

"I": in century of psychology 224–225; as externalized information 225–228
I Ching, relationship of synchronicity to 142, 146
image, role of: in psychotherapy process 218–220; in qualitative psychotherapy research 213–214
incest taboo 51–52

individual identity, development of, in Brazil 238–241
individuation: compensation and 137; as goal 113; Hua-Yen School of Buddhism and 206–207; mandala images in 174, 177; as movement of psychic material 127; transcendence and 208–209
information infrastructure, ubiquitous computing as 231–232
interdependence and individuality 207–208
internalization 201, 202, 207
internalization of God 201
International Association for Analytical Psychology 3
International General Medical Psychotherapy Association 40
introversion 44
Izutsu, Toshiko, "The Nexus of the Ontological Event" 203, 205

James, William 88–90, 91, 95
Janet, Pierre 90, 105, 189
Japan: experience of loss of psychological infrastructure in *232–233*, 232–236, *234–235*; self-consciousness in 228–232
Jewish-Christian dialogue 39–42
Jung, Carl Gustav: birthday of 3; creativity 26; death of 41; development of theories of 4–5; image 30; life of 35; loss of transcendence of 197–199; psychosis of 59–60; symbol 5, 157; travels of 241; *see also* correspondences of Jung; *specific works*
Jungian approach to scientific method and research 69–70
Jungian community 6–7
Jungian International Congress 76
Jungian research community 3–4, 7
Jung–Pauli letters 36–38

Kalachakra mandala 174, *177*, 188–189, 190
key informants 77–80
Kirsch, James, Jung correspondence with 35, 39–42
knowledge: discourse, and social production of 25–26; ways of knowing 76–77

language: autistic spectrum disorder and 207; importance of, in postmodern thought 23–25; of psyche 30–32
Latin America, culture of 238, 239
Latin American Congresses of Analytical Psychology 242

libido, nature of 51–52, 92
Lithuania: cultural shifts in 211; research and Analytical Psychology in 212–216
logistic maps 186, *187*
long tail graphs 184, *184*

Mahayana Buddhism 202
mandala imagery: fractal structure of 189–190; in Hua-Yen Buddhism 203; in individuation 174, 177; Kalachakra mandala *177*
mandalas, meaning of 204
Mandelbrot, Benoit 178, 180, 190
Mandelbrot set *186*, 186–189, *187*
maypole dance 31–32
meaningfulness 21
meaning in synchronicity 141
"The Meaning of Psychology for Modern Man" (Jung) 225
meditation: as attention to psyche 10, 124–125, 129–130; in *The Book of the Dead* 173, 174; as cultural artifact 128; as intentional state of mind 113, 118–119; Jungian perspective on 114–115, 122–130; levels of practice 129–130; on mandalas 190; nature of 115, 125–130; overview 112–114; personal equation in 115–116; psyche in 116–117; research on 114, 118–122; techniques of 118–119
Memories, Dreams, and Reflections (Jung) 92–93, 160–161, 178
mentality, human thought about 125–126
mindfulness ness, 121–122
mindfulness meditation programs 120
mirror neurons 100, 102
modern/modernity, concept of 223–224
monism 117; *see also* dual-aspect monism
Murakami, Haruki 200
mycorrhizal networks 162
Mysterium Conjunctionis (Jung) 103, 206
mythological projection 244–245
mythopoetic way of knowing 76–77
myths: of origin in Brazil 245–247; in search for identity in 252–254

narcissism of Jung 60
negative self-consciousness 228–229
networks in Jungian psychology: complex 159–160; expansion of symbolic approaches and 165–168; rhizomatic 160–165
network theory 158
Neumann, Erich, Jung correspondence with 35, 42–43

neuroscience: emotion and 98–100; free association and 94; synchronicity and 145
neurosis: in Japan 228–229; virtual reality 227–228
neutral monism 149
Nietzsche, Friedrich 88
nothingness: as fullness 202; in Hua-Yen School of Buddhism 207; metaphysical principle of 206

objective psyche 5
"On Psychic Energy" (Jung) 95
"On Synchronicity" (Jung) 137–138
"On the Nature of Psyche" (Jung) 36
"On the Nature of Qualitative Evidence" (Lincoln) 78–79
opposition, mechanism of 210
Origins and History of Consciousness (Neumann) 43
orthodoxy, issues of 42

paradigm shifts 262–263
paradise on earth, myth of Brazil as 245–246
parallel external events 136
parapsychology and synchronicity 138–139, 142
Pauli, Wolfgang 5, 35–37, 92, 138, 159; *see also* dual-aspect monism
Pauli–Jung conjecture 145, 159
peptide theory 101
personal equation 114–116
personal unconscious 96
philosophical alchemy 95–96
"The Philosophical Tree" (Jung) 165
physics, complex systems in 54–56
Pleroma 204, 205
postmodern culture and psychotherapy 13–14
postmodern thought: discourse, social production of knowledge, and 25–26; importance of language in 23–25; overview 19–23, 30–32; potential for AP to contribute to 7–8; researcher self-reflexivity and 26–28; theoretical pluralism and 28–30
power and authority 216–217
power law distribution 184, *185*
probability and synchronicity 141
process philosophy, relation of synchronicity to 144
projection, layers of 126–127
psyche: as abstract level of functioning 123; as complex system 6, 10–12, 54, 56–58, 157; conscious, unconscious, and 96–97;

criticism of concept of 49; dissociative 189–190; emotion and 98–100, 107; essence and task of 93; forms of 22; Jungian perspective on 116–117; language of 30–32, 123–124; layers of 242, 261; meditation as attention to 10, 124–125, 129–130; reality and 201; scale-free model of 160; symbolic aspects of 8–9; *see also* cultural complexes
psychiatry and emotion 90
psychic energy 51–52
psychic state 136
psychoid: adoption of concept of 50; archetypes as 137; emotional experience and 92; as level in ecological networks 161, 162–163; as logical concept 53, 62
"Psychological Commentary on *The Tibetan Book of the Great Liberation*" (Jung) 173
psychological infrastructure, loss of: experience of *232–233*, 232–236, *234–235*; ubiquitous self-consciousness in 228–232
psychological stance 116–118
"Psychological Types" (Jung) 201
psychological type theory 43–44
psychology, birth of 224, 225
Psychology and Alchemy (Jung) 5, 36–37
psycho-psychic energy 101
psychosis 59–60
psychotherapy: cultural complexes in 251–252; development of 224; elements for effective 13; emotion in 96–98; postmodern culture and 13–14; subjectivity in 64; synchronicity and 139, 145; transcendence and 208–209
psychotherapy research: in context of transformation process 210–212; in Lithuania 212–216; as multidimensional process 220–221; overview 210; on psychotherapy process 216–220

qualitative evidence, nature of 77–80
qualitative research 7–8
quaternity and quaternary structure 188–189

racial persona in Brazil 250
reality: Four Domains of 204–206; psyche and 201; virtual reality and neurosis 227–228
rebirth, release from cycle of 173–174
The Red Book (Jung): eco-orientation of 164; images in 177–178, *179*, 180–181, *182*; *Liber Primus* 199; *Liber Secundus* 199–201; overview 5, 6, 7, 58–60; reviews of 59; "Scrutinies" 202, 205; Spirit of the Depths in 19; subjectivity and 60–62

"*The Red Book:* Entrances and Exits" (Cambray) 177–178
re-integration 189–190
"Relations between the Ego and the Unconscious" (Jung) 206
religion: Communion, Jung experience of 197–198; emotion in 86–87; James and 89; meditation and 120; psychology of 37–39; split between science and 69–70, 76–77; synchronicity and 139
religious syncretism in Brazil 239
repressed cultural complexes in Brazil 248–249
research: Jungian approach to 69–70; possible trajectories for 259–263; qualitative 7–8; subjectivity in 26–27
researcher self-reflexivity 26–28
rhizomatic networks 160–165
robustness of complex systems 56
Rogers, Eric M. 72–73
Rosenbaum, Erna 36

Santa Fe Institute 159, 183, 185, 259
scale-free networks 160
scaling phenomena in structure and behavior of systems 183, 185
schizophrenia 59, 204
Schmid-Guisan, Hans, Jung correspondence with 35, 43–44
science: split between religion and 69–70, 76–77; status of synchronicity in relation to 138
scientific method, development of 75–80
"The Self, The Symbolic and Synchronicity" (Hogenson) 184–185
self-consciousness: features of 225; in Japan 228–230; as subject and methodology of psychology 130, 224
self-observation, as central tenet 223
self-organizing, complex systems as 55, 158
self-reflexivity 26–28
Seminar on Analytical Psychology, lecture 16 (Jung) 242
sensitivity of complex systems 55
"Septem Sermones ad Morteos" (Jung) 202, 203–204
sexuality and rebirth 173–174
sickness of dissociation 225
slavery cultural complex in Brazil 248–249
social production of knowledge 25–26
Soul and Earth (Jung) 244
Spinoza, Baruch 87, 159; *see also* dual-aspect monism

"The Spirit Mercurius" (Jung) 162–163, 164
Spring Journal Books Cultural Complex Series 75–76
"The State of Psychotherapy Today" (Jung) 40
strange attractors 56–57
subjectivity: in clinical situations 64; Jung on 60–62; in research 26–27
surprise, experience of 215
"Symbol and Transformation of Libido" (Jung) 198
symbolic density 12, 183–186
symbolic understanding and ecological networks 165–168
symbols: archetypes and 137; defined 4–5, 157; fractal dimensions of 181; natural and traditional 128–129; process of understanding 116–117; research on 5–6
Symbols of Transformation (Jung) 198
symmetry and complex systems 55
synchronicity: as acausal principle 62–63, 136, 141; approaches to research on 138–139, 146–148; clinical research on 145; conceptual research on 140–142; cultural research on 145–146; definitions and theoretical framing of 135–138; eliciting wider interest in 148–150; empirical research on 142; future research on 139–140, 150; historical research on 142–143; holistic perspectives and 148–149; overview 10–11, 135; Pauli and 37, 92; theoretical research on 143–145
"Synchronicity" (Jung) 138, 148
synesthesia 119

teleology 62–63
texts, word frequency in 184, *184*
theoretical pluralism 28–30
The Tibetan Book of the Dead: backward reading of, by Jung 174, 189–190; meditation and 129; as needing work 172; overview 11, 172–173; peaceful deities *175*; wrathful deities *176*
time, relationship of synchronicity to 140–141
transcendence: defined 197; experience of 199–201; in Hua-Yen School of Buddhism 204–206; loss and recovery of 12, 208–209; loss of 197–199
"The Transcendent Function" (Jung) 185
transferential chimera 64
transformation process, psychotherapy research in context of 210–212, 216–220
Trickster figure 219, 240–241
trophic cascade effect 166
Two Kinds of Thinking (Jung) 23

ubiquitous computing 226–227, 231–232
unconscious 128–129, 210; *see also* collective unconscious
unconsciousness 20–21
union 206–207
unknowing, as starting point for research 24–25
unus mundus 102, 144

vectors in emotion studies 101–103
Vilnius University, Lithuania 212–216
virtual reality and neurosis 227–228
"The Vision of Zosimos" (Jung) 164
vitalist movement 50

ways of knowing 76–77
Western esotericism and synchronicity 142, 147
White, Victor, Jung correspondence with 35, 37–39
whitening of race in Brazil 250
wind, as personified and associated with spirits 245
Wolff, Toni 6, 39
wolves, symbolism of 166–167
word association experiments 90, 94
Word Association Test (Bleuler) 50
working hypotheses 73, 74
Wotan (Jung) 242

Yellowstone National Park 166
yoga practice, traditional 120, 121, 123–124

Zipf-Mandelbrot law 184–185
Zipf's law 183–184

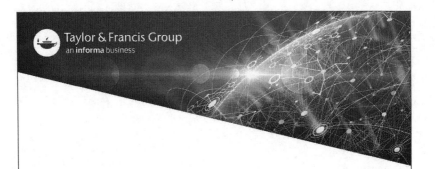